IS JOHN'S GOSPEL TRUE?

IS JOHN'S GOSPEL TRUE?

Maurice Casey

London and New York

First published 1996
by Routledge
11 New Fetter Lane, London EC4P 4EE

Simultaneously published in the USA and Canada
by Routledge
29 West 35th Street, New York, NY 10001

Routledge is an International Thomson Publishing company

© 1996 Maurice Casey

Typeset in Garamond by LaserScript, Mitcham, Surrey
Printed and bound in Great Britain by
Mackays of Chatham PLC, Chatham, Kent

British Library Cataloguing in Publication Data
A catalogue record for this book is available from the British Library

Library of Congress Cataloguing in Publication Data
A catalogue record for this book has been requested

ISBN 0–415–14630–5

In Memoriam
Florence Casey

CONTENTS

CONTENTS

PREFACE

This book was mostly written between 1987 and 1993. It was revised and seen through the press while I held a British Academy Research Readership (1994–6). I am extremely grateful to the Academy for this award, which enabled me to complete a major piece of research on the Aramaic sources of Mark and of Q, and to see this book through the press without serious disruption to that research.

I am also grateful to all those colleagues who have discussed Johannine problems with me while I have been writing it, especially Dr J. Ashton, Prof. J.D.G. Dunn, Dr J.M. Lieu, Dr J. Painter, Mrs W.E. Sproston and Dr Mark Stibbe, who wrote a very helpful reader's report under his own name for Routledge. I alone am responsible for what I have said.

I have reused some material from my previous book, *From Jewish Prophet to Gentile God* (1991). This is done with the permission of the publisher, James Clarke.

This book is dedicated to my late mother, who died suddenly in her own home when it was almost complete. To her I owe life itself. Without her practical assistance I could never have begun academic research, and she took a keen interest in this work until the end of her days. She was a marvellous grandmother to Sian and Jonathan.

ABBREVIATIONS

Most abbreviations are standard. Those for biblical books follow the RSV: those for periodicals and series of monographs follow S. Schwertner, *International Glossary of Abbreviations for Theology and Related Subjects* (Berlin: De Gruyter, 1974). Others are as follows:

AB   Anchor Bible
ABRL   Anchor Bible Reference Library
AJBI   Annual of the Japanese Biblical Institute
ANRW   *Aufstieg und Niedergang der Romischen Welt*, ed. H. Temporini
            and W. Haase (Berlin: De Gruyter, 1972–)
BJRLM   Bulletin of the John Rylands Library of Manchester
CBQ.MS   Catholic Biblical Quarterly, Monograph Series
ET   English translation
IJSL   International Journal of the Sociology of Language
JSNT   Journal for the Study of the New Testament
JSNT.SS   Journal for the Study of the New Testament, Supplement Series
JSOT   Journal for the Study of the Old Testament
JSOT.SS   Journal for the Study of the Old Testament, Supplement Series
JSP.SS   Journal for the Study of the Pseudepigrapha, Supplement Series
SBL.DS   Society of Biblical Literature, Dissertation Series
SNTU   Studien zum Neuen Testament und seiner Umwelt
TDNT   *The Theological Dictionary of the New Testament* (1933–73: ET
            Grand Rapids: Eerdmans, 1964–76, 10 vols)

1

INTRODUCTION

The Gospel attributed to St John has for centuries been part of Christian scripture. It has played a major role in the average Christian's picture of Jesus. As scripture, it has usually been thought to be completely true. Christians normally suppose that Jesus walked this earth making statements such as 'I am the way and the truth and the life' (Jn 14.6), calling himself 'the Son' and expounding his relationship with the Father. The distinctive picture of Jesus in this Gospel has been generally ascribed to its authorship by 'the beloved disciple', John son of Zebedee, who reclined on Jesus' breast at the Last Supper (cf. Jn 13.23, 25; 21.20).

Critical scholarship has called this picture into question. Whatever the person in the pew believes, most Christian scholars believe that much of the material in this Gospel is not historically accurate. Jesus did not say 'I am the way and the truth and the life' (Jn 14.6): but some early Christians believed that he was, so they attributed this saying to him. The discourses in which he expounds his Sonship are products of 'the Johannine community'. Christian scholars have however drawn a distinction between the historicity of John's Gospel and its spiritual insight. Though they do not believe that it is literally true, they have continued to take the early church's view that it is the most spiritual of the Gospels, valuable for its theological truth (e.g. Barrett 1978: 141–2). Commentators coming in from this perspective have not needed to spend too much time arguing that John's Gospel is not historically true, and this has had an unfortunate consequence for scholarship – there is no recent book which gives the reasons for such a view in detail with satisfactory arguments.

Evangelical Christians have rejected the critical view. Scholars such as Morris and Carson have continued to maintain that John's Gospel is literally and historically true in every detail (Morris 1969, 1971; Carson 1991). This view has been enthusiastically championed by evangelists and by some of the faithful. A somewhat less extreme defence of the essential historicity of John's Gospel has also continued on the scholarly wing of the churches. In recent years, the most extensive defence from this perspective has been the posthumous work of J.A.T. Robinson (Robinson 1985; cf. Higgins 1960;

1

Hunter 1968). Though its effect on serious scholarship has been limited, it has many admirers.

One purpose of this book is to contribute to this debate. I shall argue that conservative and fundamentalist views are demonstrably false. Moreover, I shall not merely repeat this. I propose to prove it beyond all reasonable doubt. I do not of course mean that I hope to convert all conservative evangelicals to an accurate view of the fourth Gospel. We are all dependent on our social groups for our existence and identity, and the myth of scriptural truth is too functional to be removed overnight by evidence and argument, however true, and however clearly presented. I do mean that I propose a proof, not merely a plausible hypothesis.

I also put forward some new suggestions to explain how and why this Gospel originated, how and why the 'Johannine community' attributed so much of their own theology to Jesus. The outstanding problem with the critical view has been its failure to explain how and why so much secondary material has been attributed to Jesus, particularly when this Gospel has been regarded as the work of one or more eyewitnesses of his ministry. It is however clear that the practice of secondarily attributing material to major figures was widespread, and this is much clearer now than it was a few years ago. Thus the attribution of sayings and theology to both John the Baptist and to Jesus himself was part of a widespread cultural pattern. This particular instance was due to a particular social situation, which arose when the Johannine community were banned from Jewish meetings, and took on Gentile self-identification.[1] It is this which led to this Gospel's hostile use of the term 'the Jews', and to the stunning allegations that 'the Jews' are children of the devil and do not believe Moses (cf. Jn 5.45–7; 8.39–44). Hence also the well-known declaration 'I am the way and the truth and the life' is immediately followed by 'No-one comes to the Father except through me' (Jn 14.6). This excludes 'the Jews' from approaching their own God.

It was during this conflict that the Johannine community took the fatal step of hailing Jesus as fully divine. This Gospel reflects real historical events when it presents Jewish allegations of blasphemy in the same context as the presentation of the divinity of Jesus (cf. Jn 5.17ff.; 8.58–9; 10.30–3). In these circumstances, the need for legitimation of specifically Christian rather than Jewish theology was especially important. The Old Testament had played a significant role in the Johannine community, and it continued to be used, but it could not legitimate the violation of Jewish monotheism. The need for secondary attribution of the new developments of the tradition to its fountainhead was therefore unusually acute.

This raises sharply the question of the truth of this Gospel, and this is the subject of the final chapter. Historical inaccuracies may be explained on cultural grounds, so they do not necessarily entail that this Gospel is devoid of spiritual insight, or unfit to be sacred scripture. Two related points are more serious. Firstly, the fourth Gospel is vigorously anti-Jewish. This is understandable, but it is nonetheless a basic fact which makes it unsuitable for too much veneration. What is worse, this Gospel has fostered Christian anti-Semitism. Its anti-Jewish polemic is moreover closely associated with the deity of Jesus. This breaches Jewish monotheism, monotheism which was part of the identity of Jesus of Nazareth and of all the first apostles. The answer to the title of this book is therefore: 'No.' The Gospel attributed to John does not give a truthful account of Jesus of Nazareth, nor of his ministry, nor of the Jewish people.

2

FROM BEGINNING TO END

INTRODUCTION

It has long been established that the earliest Gospel to be written was that of Mark. It was extensively used by Matthew and Luke. The fourth Gospel is formally independent of them, whether because the Johannine community did not know them, or because they chose to produce a very different kind of work. There are some overlaps, all of which may be due to direct use of synoptic Gospels by vigorous Johannine editors, or to independent use of old traditions. When we compare the outline of the ministry as portrayed in Mark and John, three major differences are evident, differences so serious that both Gospels cannot be right. These are the position of the Cleansing of the Temple, the date of the Last Supper, and the apparent length of the ministry. I argue that the position of the Cleansing of the Temple is one of those points at which the fourth Gospel is verifiably wrong: that it dates the Last Supper on the wrong day: and that the length of Jesus' ministry was, and still is, unknown.

THE CLEANSING OF THE TEMPLE: MARK'S ACCOUNT IS TRUE

Mark tells us that, during his last visit to Jerusalem, Jesus stayed with the twelve in Bethany (Mark 11.11, cf. 11.12, 15, 19, 27; 14.3). This is reasonable, since at Passover Jerusalem was too crowded to accommodate all the pilgrims. The account of the Cleansing is straightforward in itself.[1]

> And (they) came to Jerusalem, and (he) went to the Temple, and began to throw out those who sold and those who bought in the Temple. And he overturned the tables of the moneychangers and the seats of those who sold the doves. And he did not allow a man to carry a vessel through the Temple. And he was teaching, and he said, 'Is it not written "My house shall be called a house of prayer for all the nations"? [Is 56.7]. But you have made it "a robbers' cave"' [Jer 7.11].

This was a vigorous and intelligible prophetic act. Jesus evidently felt that the Temple was not being kept as holy as it should have been. Two halakhic judgements are recorded. One is a prohibition of buying, selling and changing money: the other is a prohibition of carrying objects through the sacred space. The buying, selling and changing of money was done in what we often call the Court of the Gentiles, the outermost court, 'which everyone, even foreigners, were allowed to enter' (Jos. c. Ap. II, 103). Jesus' action in throwing people out of this Court was vigorous, and may have been somewhat violent. In its cultural context, however, it might have been perceived as a violation of the central sanctuary, an attack on the cultus rather than a defence of God's house. This is because changing money and buying doves were essential for the divinely ordained conduct of the Temple cultus, and the disruption caused at a major pilgrim feast might be felt to be especially serious. The same applies to Jesus' prohibition of carrying through. This will have prevented people from carrying birds in any kind of cage or container through the Temple courts to be sacrificed. Equally, it prevented the use of 'vessels' to carry joints of larger animals which had been sacrificed back from the edge of the Court of the Priests through and out of the Temple, and it perhaps agrees with M. Ber. IX, 5 in preventing people from carrying moneybelts. More directly, it would stop merchants and moneychangers from having any sort of container for carrying money, without which they could not do business. It would also prevent priests from having containers for taking money out of the Court of the Women, where the trumpets for the shekel offerings were placed. In that case, they would have to collect the offerings outside the Temple, which was significant because the offerings were made in Tyrian shekels, each of which bore the image of another God, Melkart.

Jesus must have had a reason for such action, and he would have had to explain what that reason was. Mark follows immediately with his explanatory teaching: 'My house shall be called a house of prayer for all the nations' (Is 56.7). This provides the reason and the legitimation that were necessary. Jesus argued that the Court of the Gentiles should be part of the sacred space and he legitimated this view from scriptural tradition. The context in Isaiah is that of foreigners who join the covenant. A need to worship God, attested in Scripture, forms the strongest kind of reason that a Jewish prophet could have had and given. The reference to the 'robbers' cave' (Jer. 7.11) should also be seen in the light of its scriptural context. It does not necessarily mean that the people changing money and selling doves were charging higher prices than the chief priests said they should. In the first place, they should not have been doing these things in the Temple at all. The scriptural context is part of a speech delivered by Jeremiah in the gate of the Temple, criticising Jews who worshipped in the Temple but did not do the will of the Lord. It includes a conditional threat to them. They would be allowed to dwell in the land if they repented, a process which would have to include not oppressing the alien and the widow, and not shedding innocent blood. The thrust of 'robbers' should therefore be seen in quite broad terms.

Jesus' ministry includes many attacks on the rich over against the poor. We know from Jewish sources of the immense wealth of the Temple. This was greatly augmented by the Temple tax being collected from individuals each year, rather than once a lifetime. This was a burden only on the poor. Some of the chief priests were also rich. T. Men. 13.21 records woes against important families, concluding 'For they are high priests, and their sons treasurers, and their sons-in-laws supervisors, and their servants come and beat us with staves'. This can only refer to extortion by rich priests, and its *Sitz im Leben* is certainly before the destruction of the Temple (cf. T. Zeb. 11.16; bT Pes. 57a). The passage goes on to suggest that the Second Temple could not have been destroyed like the first, because they laboured over the Torah and were careful about tithes, a priestly perquisite whose handling was also criticised by Jesus (Mt 23.23–6//Lk 11.42, 39–41). The problem was that they loved money and hated one another (T. Men. 13.22). M. Ker. I, 7 records that the price of a brace of doves was reduced by a ruling of Jesus' younger contemporary, Simeon son of Gamaliel, a ruling apparently sparked off by their excessive price.

The scriptural term 'robbers', or 'bandits', 'brigands', will also have been dependent on the trouble experienced from such people in Israel. The Royal Portico, in which the trading took place, was built by Herod the Great, whose first major achievement as governor of Galilee was the defeat of brigands (Jos. B.J. I, 203–7//A.J. XIV, 158–62). His son Archelaus prevented Passover from continuing in 4BCE by sending his troops into the Temple, and shedding a lot of innocent blood (B.J. II, 8–13, 30; A.J. XVII, 208–18, 230–1, 237). Another son, Herod Antipas, the tetrarch, had recently shed the innocent blood of John the Baptist (Mk 6.16–29; Jos. A.J. XVIII, 116–19), and sought to kill Jesus (cf. Lk 13.31; Mk 11.27–33). The biblical metaphor would be memorable for these reasons too.

All our evidence is coherent. We must infer that the observance of the Law in the Temple was making the rich richer at the expense of the poor and observant. Jesus attacked this system from the prophetic perspective which he so vigorously recreated. He used the expression 'robbers' cave' from Jeremiah 7.11 to call up the whole tradition of criticism of worship in the Temple by people who should have been devoted to God and their neighbours, and who should accordingly have been more careful of the poor and observant and should have refrained from amassing riches.

It is not only Mark's account of the incident which is coherent. His account of the sequel is equally coherent, and this marks him off all the more clearly from the fourth Gospel. The Temple was run by the chief priests. An attack on the basic running of it was an attack on the centre of their lives. Temple halakhah was also the concern of observant Jews in

general, and the halakhah was studied and discussed by scribes. Jesus'
action would therefore outrage chief priests and similarly-minded scribes.
He had moreover already incurred the opposition of scribes and Pharisees,
some of whom had come from Jerusalem to Galilee to observe him, and he
had been in vigorous conflict with them (Casey 1991a: 61–4). This conflict
would therefore be renewed by his attack on the running of the Temple.
There was however a problem for them, when they considered what action
to take. Jerusalem was crowded out for Passover. Any attempt to arrest Jesus
could therefore cause a riot, resulting in defilement of the holy places and
numerous deaths. The fact that he had a significant number of supporters
would intensify the risk. Immediate action would therefore have been most
unwise (cf. Mk 11.18; 14.1–2).

The temporary hesitation of the authorities did not prevent them from
asking an obvious question. Mark's account is again sound, though his use
of the definite articles gives an impression of hordes of chief priests, scribes
and elders, when a manageable group is not only more likely, but will also
have been the intention of his source.[2]

> And they came again to Jerusalem. And he was walking in the Temple,
> and (the) chief priests and (the) scribes and (the) elders came to him,
> and they said to him, 'By what authority do you do these things? Or
> who gave you this authority to do these things?'
>
> (Mk 11.27–8)

Jesus' reply is revealing. It implies both his known support for John the
Baptist, and an indirect claim that his own ministry was divinely inspired,
like that of John. 'I will ask you one thing, and answer me and I will tell you
by what authority I do these things. The baptism of John, (was) it from
heaven or of men? Answer me!' (Mk 11.29–30).

There is no way that such a response would have been produced by the
early church! This is the true tradition of Jesus' words, in which he defended
his prophetic action by direct reference to the divine authority of the
prophet who baptised him. Mark's account also informs us that John still
had considerable popular support, and had been opposed by these same
authorities (Mk 11.31–3, cf. Mt 21.31–2). This means that the cultural nexus
of severe opposition between these authorities and the prophetic stream of
Judaism was already in place, and had already led to the death of a much
revered prophet. At this stage, Jesus' powerful opponents were sensible
enough to bide their time and ask awkward questions, as Mark portrays
them. The important point for our purposes is that their opposition is
predictable, given the Cleansing of the Temple, coming after a ministry in
which Jesus had already incurred the opposition of scribes and Pharisees, in
a social context of known opposition of the authorities to John the Baptist.
After inserting a collection of Jesus' teaching, some of which is due to the
early church, Mark again makes the main point with clarity: 'And (the) chief

priests and (the) scribes were looking for ways to arrest him by trickery and kill him, for they said, "Not in the festival (crowd), in case there is a riot of the people"' (Mk 14.1–2). It is this dilemma which Judah of Kerioth solved for them by betraying him in the garden of Gethsemane, where there was no crowd to riot, and little enough opposition to his arrest (Mk 14.41–52).

One problem remained. What could they kill him *for*? They were not arbitrary murderers, and it was in their interests that they were not held responsible for the death which they brought about. Some of them may have felt that Jesus' action in the Temple was blasphemous, but it was not contrary to any law of blasphemy, and neither that nor anything else that Jesus had done was contrary to a law that carried the death penalty. The Roman governor was however in Jerusalem, with a force of troops. He always came at Passover, in case of any breach of the peace. This gave the authorities their chance. They handed Jesus over to Pilate. Since he was crucified as 'king of the Jews', we must infer a charge of sedition, and Jesus' preaching of the kingdom must have been employed to make the charge stick. At this point, Mark fails us. His account of the meeting of the sanhedrin is so unsatisfactory that we must infer that he did not know what had happened there. Up to that point, however, he is coherent.[3] The incident of the Cleansing of the Temple is comprehensible in itself, and all its consequences are understandable.

THE CLEANSING OF THE TEMPLE: JOHN'S MAIN ALTERATIONS ARE WRONG

When we turn to the Johannine account, we find two basic changes. The incident is placed at the beginning of Jesus' public ministry, and its function as the trigger of the Passion is taken by the raising of Lazarus. It is here that the fourth Gospel is verifiably wrong. We also find that its account of the Cleansing itself has omitted some points which make sense of Jesus' action against the background of his own Jewish culture. The Johannine account starts on the wrong foot with the description 'the Passover of the Jews' (Jn 2.13), an external use of the term 'the Jews' absent from the synoptics. This becomes much more serious at 2.17ff., where 'the Jews' and 'the disciples' are treated as two separate groups. Yet all the disciples were Jewish! This is straightforward evidence that this account has been worked over by people remote from the original environment, so remote that their own Gentile self-identification has overridden the description of the main parties involved. Mark told us who asked the awkward question – chief priests, scribes and elders (Mk 11.27–8): the description of them as 'the Jews' as opposed to 'the disciples' comes from an environment where followers of Jesus were in conflict with the Jewish community.[4]

The detailed description of the scene in the Temple has people selling sheep and oxen. This is not probable. No Jewish source mentions the sale in the Temple of animals so big that they would have caused serious problems in polluting the sacred space with dung. Jesus then makes a whip, which he would need for driving out sheep and oxen. These details are not quite impossible, but, given the other problems of this narrative, they are much more likely to be secondary attempts to explain aspects of the original narrative which puzzled people fifty years after the event. What were people buying and selling, given doves are mentioned separately? Animals for sacrifice, so sheep and oxen. Why drive out people who bought, for they surely had no choice where to buy animals for sacrifice? Leave them out. How did he drive out? Dove-sellers with words, but for big animals he needed a whip made of cords (not a stick, which some thought was not allowed in the Temple).

The order to the dove-sellers replaces the coherent rationale of the original account with the authority of Johannine Christology. The term 'my Father' is rare in the synoptic Gospels, except in the editorial work of Matthew, and it never occurs in authentic sayings of Jesus.[5] Had this been part of Jesus' public preaching, both it and the disputes consequent upon it would have featured in the synoptic Gospels.[6] This is another point at which the fourth Gospel is certainly wrong. Without it, however, Jesus' words to the dove-sellers are not very sensible. If he is not the authoritative Son of God *telling* them the will of his Father, no one could know that it *was* the will of God that they should not sell doves in the Court of the Gentiles. A possible reference to Zechariah 14.21 is not enough. This describes a situation after an eschatological battle which had clearly not taken place at the time of Jesus, and merely predicts that in that time there will no longer be a trader in the house of the Lord: it says nothing to justify banning them sooner. Accordingly, Jesus' action in John, deprived of the scriptural reasoning given at Mark 11.17, lacks proper motivation. This illuminates further the introduction of sheep and oxen: they look obviously out of place and they are, so out of place that their removal seems mundanely reasonable.

By this stage, the whole of Mark 11.16–17 has become irrelevant. The destroyed Temple had not become a house of prayer for all nations, indeed it was no longer a house of prayer at all, so the whole quotation is dropped, where Matthew and Luke dropped only part of it: 'robbers' cave' appears equally out of place because the Zealots had been conspicuous in the Temple during the Roman war, and had not arrived at the time of Jesus: and a prohibition of carrying through was as irrelevant to the Johannine community as to Matthew and Luke. In place of what was once a coherent rationale for Jesus' action, the fourth evangelist has *the disciples remember* a quite different text, Psalm 69.9. But 'the zeal of your house will consume me' does not explain Jesus' actions. Zeal for God's house could as easily have led to vigorous support for arrangements which made it easier for Jewish pilgrims to buy sacrificial animals. In the New Testament, however, Psalm

69 is elsewhere used to look forward to Jesus' death (Jn 15.25; Rom 11.9–10; 15.3; cf. also Mk 15.36; Mt 27.34, 48; Lk 23.36; Jn 19.28–9; Acts 1.20). Here it leads not to Jesus' death in the practical sense required by the original historical narrative, but to theological reinterpretation of the destruction of the Temple in terms of Jesus' death and resurrection. Thus the historically accurate narrative which was originally transmitted has been quite rewritten for theological purposes.

The rest of the discussion has little to do with the Jesus of history and has a very clear *Sitz im Leben* in the Johannine community. A discussion is initiated by 'the Jews', a group differentiated from 'the disciples', as we have seen. They request 'a sign', as a lead-in to a rewritten saying of Jesus, who now declares, 'Destroy this Temple and in three days I will raise it up' (2.19). This may be based on a genuine saying, the form of which however we are no longer in any position to recover (cf. Mk 13.2; 14.56–9//Mt 26.60–1; Acts 6.14). The Johannine interpretation is more obviously secondary: 'But he spoke of the Temple of his body' (Jn 2.21). There is nothing like this in the authentic teaching of Jesus, whose predictions of his death, though indirect, were *about* death and resurrection (cf. Casey 1991a: 51–2, 64–7). The saying has been clarified and allegorised to declare the replacement theology of this Gospel. This is almost stated openly at 2.22, where the disciples 'remembered' the saying after Jesus' resurrection (cf. 12.16; 14.26).[7] The development has been fundamental. Not only is sin taken away by the Lamb of God (1.29) instead of by means of the Temple cultus, but now the Temple itself is replaced by the body of Jesus. God dwells especially in Jesus' body while he is on earth, rather than in the Temple, and by the death and resurrection of his body the forgiveness of sins becomes possible. Thus Jesus has replaced the Temple. This, surely, is the reason for moving the Cleansing of the Temple to the beginning of this Gospel. Here the Temple is not merely cleansed, it is made redundant, to the point where its actual destruction is not even worthy of mention (save for the ironical prophecy of 11.48f.).

One of the most devastating faults of putting the Cleansing of the Temple at the beginning of the Gospel follows at once, if nothing can properly be said to follow anything. For there are no more consequences. This when Jesus has interrupted the arrangements for the sacrifices at a major pilgrim feast, driven animals and probably people out of the Temple with a whip, and answered a question from 'the Jews' in terms incomprehensible until after his death and resurrection. As a response from the chief priests, this inaction is historically ludicrous.

What is more, Mark's coherent and accurate account has the Cleansing of the Temple as the trigger of the Passion. But if the Cleansing of the Temple is placed at the beginning of the ministry, what then was the trigger of the Passion? The Johannine answer is the raising of Lazarus! We shall discuss the position and function of the raising of Lazarus in Chapter 10. We shall see that, in presenting it as the immediate cause of the Passion, the Johannine narrative is, from an historical point of view, chaotic and unconvincing. Like the Cleansing of the Temple, it is theologically controlled from beginning to end.

It follows that much of the Johannine narrative is historically inaccurate. At this point, we should be able to stop. We might spare a thought for church Fathers, committed to the truth of holy scripture before the advent of critical scholarship. Misled by the combination of ignorance and commitment, some of them supposed that Jesus cleansed the Temple twice! What an extraordinary notion, not supported by the text of any Gospel, produced by harmonising different accounts on the assumption that all of them must be true. Surely no one familiar with modern scholarship could continue to propound this view? Some do. As recently as 1991, Carson has done it again, in a hefty commentary which amply displays familiarity with the critical scholarship which he has rejected. A vigorous defence has also been offered recently by C.L. Blomberg, in the context of a defence of the historical reliability of the Gospels as a whole (Blomberg 1987: 170–3).

Blomberg offers six points, of which the first is: 'Except for the bare minimum of content required to narrate a temple cleansing, all the details differ from the one account to the other.' This argument is circular, meaningless and omits a main point. It is circular because it depends on the Gospels to find out 'the bare minimum of content required to narrate a temple cleansing'. Otherwise, there is no need for the main character to be Jesus of Nazareth, the Temple to be in Jerusalem, the occasion to be Passover, the people thrown out to include moneychangers or the immediate consequence to be an awkward question about his authority put to Jesus by his opponents. It is meaningless, because it fails to put forward criteria for distinguishing between two separate narratives of Temple cleansing on the one hand, and a substantially rewritten account alongside the original version on the other. It omits the main point that the accounts of the supposedly second occasion give no hint of there having been a previous occasion of a basically similar kind. Blomberg's second argument follows: 'If Jesus felt strongly enough about the temple corruption to purify it once at the outset of his ministry, it would be only natural for him to do it again at the end.' What an 'if'! This *presupposes* the Johannine account, and fails to explain both its inadequate consequences and the synoptic Gospels' failure to mention the first occasion. Blomberg's third argument is that Jesus 'could probably have done the deed once with impunity'. Carson pushes this further. 'If there were two cleansings', the main point 'if' again, 'they were separated by two years, possibly three. During that interval Jesus visited Jerusalem several times for other appointed festivals, without attempting another temple-cleansing' (Carson 1991: 178). Carson's stronger form of this argument, like Blomberg's second argument, presupposes his result. If John's narrative is not literally true, the evidence of

Jesus visiting Jerusalem with impunity after cleansing the Temple is not to be found. Blomberg's weaker form of the argument continues, 'since it was an overtly Messianic act which at least some of the Jews would have approved'. It is not overtly messianic, but if it were, Roman opposition would have been quicker. Some Jews did indeed approve, disciples of Jesus and the wider group who agreed to prohibit carrying through. We have seen that this is not enough to prevent vigorous opposition from those who were in charge of the Temple.

Blomberg's fourth argument depends on an accusation reported at Jesus' trial in Mark 14.58–9, where he is accused of threatening to destroy the Temple. Blomberg suggests that Mark's narrative 'makes more sense as a confused recollection of something said two or three years earlier, not just a few days ago' (likewise Morris 1971: 191). Several things are wrong with this. In the first place, Mark's whole narrative of the meeting of the sanhedrin is seriously at fault, to the point where it cannot possibly depend on the account of eyewitnesses.[8] Accordingly, we cannot rely on the report of Mark 14.58–9. Secondly, Joseph Caiaphas gathered a sanhedrin to try to find a way to kill Jesus: the malice of false witnesses can garble anything in a few minutes, let alone days; it need not take years. Thirdly, Jesus preached on Jeremiah 7, which contains a conditional threat to the Temple: exposition of it might lead even sympathetic eyewitnesses to disagree about the nature of Jesus' threat. Fourthly, we have seen that the Johannine form of Jesus' saying has its *Sitz im Leben* in Johannine theology, where it refers to Jesus' death and resurrection: whatever may have been garbled at any trial, it was not John 2.19.

Blomberg's fifth argument belongs to the anti-Jewish tradition which has characterised Christianity since the days of the Johannine community.

> The difference in the severity of Jesus' remarks is appropriate to each of the two contexts; only at the end of his ministry does he call the Jews thieves and incite racist outrage by referring to the Gentiles' need to pray in the temple court originally reserved for them.
>
> (Mk 11.17)

Differences of this kind cannot make any stories true. We have moreover seen that the Johannine account fails to explain why Jesus cleansed the Temple. Mark's account does not call 'the Jews' thieves. All Jesus' disciples and supporters were Jewish: the term 'robbers' was applied, in a scriptural context, to those whom he criticised. There is no evidence in any Gospel that Jesus' action incited 'racist outrage'. The outer court was not 'reserved' for Gentiles, it was the only one they were allowed to enter. If Jesus found their need to worship in that part of the Temple a significant point at the end of the ministry, he is likely to have thought it significant earlier.

Blomberg's final argument depends on chronology and is desperately uncertain. He takes the forty-six years of John 2.20 to refer to Herod's

Temple,[9] and calculates from Jos. A.J. XV, 380 that this puts the event in AD 27 or 28. 'But Jesus was probably not crucified until at least AD 30, and John would not have invented such an incidental confirmation of chronology if he were freely reshaping the Synoptic version with little concern for keeping the facts straight.' John 2.20 however implies that the Temple was finished in forty-six years, which it was not: or perhaps that the inner part was completed, which had happened long ago. The date of Jesus' crucifixion is uncertain, between 27 and 34 CE: 27–8 is by no means out of the question. More profoundly, Blomberg's argument is quite remote from a culture in which history was so often rewritten.[10] The fourth evangelist was writing a highly theological reinterpretation of a saying about the destruction of the Temple. Many of his debates move by means of not very bright questions, a narrative technique very rare in the synoptic Gospels. Getting the date right makes his narrative plausible, and putting speeches in the mouths of main characters was a feature of secondary rewriting in the Jewish and Greek worlds alike. Blomberg has too limited a view of what was possible. He can envisage only literal accuracy on the one hand, and careless fiction on the other. Deliberate rewrites are in between these extremes.

Recent conservative scholarship has produced two more arguments which must be noted. Morris argues that apart from the work of the Baptist, nothing else in Chapters 1–5 is in the synoptic Gospels. He comments, 'Of course, it is not impossible that John took one lone Synoptic episode and bound it firmly into his own framework as far from its correct historical setting as he could make it' (Morris 1971: 190). Morris, however, does not consider such a view reasonable. Carson puts it more strongly: 'Why or how an ancient editor managed to secure this pericope alone and insert it into his material is hard to fathom' (Carson 1991: 177). The first thing wrong with this is its major exception. This Gospel does incorporate very old material about John the Baptist: the authentic saying rewritten at John 1.26–7 still has its original Aramaism in it! As we shall see, John the Baptist has been drastically rewritten (see Chapter 4), like the Cleansing of the Temple. Moreover, Chapter 5 begins with a sabbath healing. This is also a significant overlap with synoptic controversies. More fundamentally, however, Morris has invented a standard of judgement. If John's aims had been best achieved by putting all his synoptic material in the latter part of his Gospel, with one solitary exception, he might have done this.

Carson homes in on the different explanations offered for John moving the narrative to the beginning of his Gospel. At one level, this attacks a genuine problem for critical scholarship, from which Carson takes a quite illegitimate advantage. Our basic evidence consists of the four Gospels, with the fourth substantially different from the other three. No Gospel writer ever tells us why he has moved anything. Our reasons have to be inferences from our texts, and consequently there are cases where we can see *what* an author has done a great deal more clearly than *why*. This is never a satisfactory argument for supposing that he hasn't really done so. Carson continues,

> any argument that provides a reason why John 2:13ff. 'fits' into the thematic development of the Fourth Gospel could equally well serve to explain why, on the assumption there were two cleansings, John chose to report *this* cleansing instead of the *later* one.
>
> (Carson 1991: 178)

I hope this does not apply to the argument offered above. If there had been two cleansings, this Gospel's replacement theology would have been well served by reporting them both, together with comments on the increasing blindness of 'the Jews' (cf. Jn 2.18–22; 12.9–11, 37–43). Carson's argument underlines the fact that no Gospel reports two cleansings.

As the most recent author of a large commentary which rejects critical scholarship, Carson deserves to have the last conservative word. He summarises, 'In short, it is not possible to resolve with certainty whether only one cleansing of the temple took place, or two; but the arguments for one are weak and subjective, while the most natural reading of the texts favours two' (Carson 1991: 178). Surely, then, at least one Gospel text reports two? As we all know, no text does. Carson's summary underlines the extraordinary nature of the conservative arguments which we have examined. Some are circular: several assume the result which they are supposed to achieve: all of them, supposedly in obedience to scripture, achieve a result related by no scriptural text whatever. This is neither critical scholarship, nor Obedience to the Word: it is the shibboleths of a social subgroup which rejects modernity, and critical scholarship with it. For those who can face evidence and argument, only one result is plausible. The Temple was 'cleansed' once, when our oldest source says it was, towards the end of Jesus' ministry, and that event led directly to his death.

THE LAST SUPPER: MARK'S ACCOUNT OF A PASSOVER MEAL IS TRUE

Mark portrays the Last Supper as a Passover meal, held on Thursday evening after dark, when the 15th day of the Jewish month Nisan began. Jesus was crucified on Friday, still 15 Nisan. The fourth Gospel, however, has Jesus slaughtered at the same time as the Passover victims, on Friday, 14 Nisan. Consequently, the two Gospels imply a different year for Jesus' death, though neither author was enough of an annalist to give us a date. Jeremias did enough to show that Mark's dating is right, and his work was carried further by Pesch (Jeremias 1966; Pesch 1978). I shall go through the Marcan narrative, building on the work of Jeremias and Pesch, but taking it much further. In particular, I shall point out how the Jewish assumptions of Mark's Aramaic source alone make sense of his narrative.[11]

Mark's account of the preparations for the meal begins, 'And on the first day of Unleavened Bread, when they were sacrificing the Passover' (Mk 14.12). It was therefore Thursday afternoon, 14 Nisan. Mark has described as 'the first day of Unleavened Bread' the day when leavened bread had to be removed from the house (so Jos. B.J. V, 99; cf. A.J. II, 317; IX, 271). The content of the second phrase is of primary importance. These few words, 'when they were sacrificing the Passover', tell us where Jesus and his disciples were, and what they were doing. With that information, all Jewish Christians, that is, all the earliest Christians, will have known at once that Jesus and his disciples were in the Temple. There Jesus slit the throat of a 1-year-old lamb or goat, known as *pascha*, an Aramaic word found in Mark's Greek text and generally translated 'Passover'. Jesus drained the blood from this animal into a bowl held by a priest. Many other victims were being slaughtered at the same time, to the accompaniment of the Hallel psalms (Pss 113–18).

After being slaughtered, the animals were taken to somewhere else in Jerusalem to be roasted and so on. Mark's narrative continues in the most natural way possible. 'His disciples said to him, "Where do you want us to go to, and prepare for you that you may eat the Passover?"' The word 'Passover' refers again to the actual victim. We should picture them standing beside Jesus in a packed and noisy crowd of people, all with dead lambs or goats. They assumed that he had made arrangements which they would carry out. He sent two of them, enough to carry the dead animal comfortably, and to split up if anything went wrong. Their ignorance of the arrangements, their intention to prepare for 'you' rather than 'us' to eat the Passover, the fact that they went away and prepared the Passover while Jesus came in the evening 'with the twelve' (14.17), all these points combine to show that these two disciples were not two of the twelve. They recognised the prearranged signal of a man carrying a waterpot. The man will have been recognisable because waterpots were normally carried by women, one of the assumptions which our author took for granted. The nature of these arrangements surely implies that they were a mode of escaping detection. This also applies to the description 'teacher', translating the conventional 'rabbi', rather than any clear identification of Jesus. Their password is also significant because it again mentions the Passover: 'the rabbi says, "Where is my guest-room, where I will eat the Passover with my disciples?"' (Mk 14.14).

At verse 15, the large upper room makes good sense only if there were to be lots of people there. At verse 17, Jesus comes with the twelve, making fifteen people mentioned, and there is further confirmation of a sizeable group of disciples at verse 20. The women are not mentioned because the presence of the women at Jesus' final Passover was too obvious to be worthy of mention. Women were generally present at Passover. Jesus was not likely to have excluded some of his most faithful followers from his final

Passover, and had he really determined to celebrate his final Passover with only the twelve, he would have had a remarkable reason, and our source would surely have remarked upon his remarkable behaviour. It follows that we do not know how big the company was. If we imagine thirty, we have a margin of error, but the conventional thirteen is simply wrong.

Verse 16 records the success of the arrangements, ending with the preparation of the Passover. By this stage, it should be blindingly obvious to any reader of Mark that Jesus and the disciples are going to eat a Passover meal. The narrative also contains a number of pieces of circumstantial evidence that this was a Passover meal, and it begins with two of them. At verse 17, Jesus comes with the twelve 'when it was evening'. The Passover meal had to be eaten after dark, when 15 Nisan began. Secondly, the company reclined to eat, as Jews did at Passover, to symbolise that they were free people, no longer enslaved in Egypt. Jesus then announced his forthcoming betrayal, seeing it foretold in Psalm 41. The disciples were naturally sorrowful, wondering who would betray him, and Jesus revealed the shocking truth: 'One of the twelve, who dips with me into a dish.' If the twelve were the only people with him, that would have been a very odd thing to say. In fact, it narrowed down the group from whom the traitor was taken.

We should infer that Jesus expected to be betrayed by Judah of Kerioth. Though Judah will not have forewarned Jesus deliberately, he will not have been able to keep his profound hostility a secret. It follows that Jesus could have escaped, if he had felt it right to do so. We can also see why the meeting of the two disciples with the man carrying the waterpot was memorable: it was part of Jesus' arrangements for avoiding arrest before he ate the Passover.

In typically Jewish fashion, Jesus believed both that his death was in accordance with the will of God, and that the traitor was profoundly wicked. He commented, 'A/the[12] son of man goes as it is written of him, but woe to that man by whom a/the son of man is betrayed! (It would be) good for him if that man had not been born!' (Mk 14.21). Further scriptural passages are not enumerated, but they were easy to find. We can see some in the Hallel psalms (Pss 113–18), those set for singing at Passover. For example, Jesus can hardly have helped seeing himself referred to at Psalm 116.15, 'Glorious in the eyes of the Lord is the death of his pious ones'. Mark refers only to those psalms sung at the end of the meal (14.26), not to those sung at an earlier stage (Pss 113–14, or perhaps only 113). It is not likely to be coincidental that references to Jesus' fate can be found only in the group to which Mark refers. The earlier tradition must have known this, and will have assumed that we know it too.

As leader of the group, Jesus was obliged to comment on the major elements of the Passover meal. His contemporary Gamaliel I specified the Passover offering, the unleavened bread and the bitter herbs (M. Pes. X, 5), three biblical elements (Ex 12.8), and Gamaliel would not have made this pronouncement if customs were already fixed and universal. The interpretation of a cup of wine was natural because drinking wine was obligatory, and because of the similarity of blood to red wine, 'the blood of the grape' (e.g. Deut 32.14; Sir 50.15). We should infer that Jesus interpreted the bread, the wine, the bitter herbs and the lamb, or kid. Why does Mark not mention the animal and the bitter herbs? Because his source intended to explain how and why Jesus died, and left out straightforward information about Passover meals, which it expected us to know. We must infer that Jesus' interpretation of the animal and the bitter herbs was traditional.

A traditional interpretation of some of the major elements was essential for the success of the new references to Jesus' forthcoming death. All the disciples were profoundly religious Jews, who had come on pilgrimage to Jerusalem to celebrate this major feast, when all Israel looked back to their deliverance from Egypt, and some at least looked forward to deliverance in the future. Jesus was therefore bound to make reference back to their deliverance from Egypt by the mighty hand of God, on whom alone they could rely for their deliverance in the future. The establishment of this cultural context was a matter of activity as well as words. The animal had been slaughtered in distinctively Jewish fashion in the central cultic sanctuary; they had gathered for the meal after dark and begun with the first course in the traditional way, before the unleavened bread was broken and eaten. The words amplified the tradition, and Jesus' interpretation of the bread as his body is likely to have come after a traditional interpretation of the bitter herbs, and perhaps the meat. This is also the necessary hermeneutical context of the explicitly sacrificial interpretation of a cup of wine as his blood.

Mark records one more saying from the Passover meal. 'Amen I say to you, I will not drink again of the fruit of the vine until that day when I drink it new in the kingdom of God' (14.25). Jesus knew that this was to be his last meal with his disciples. At one level, the sentence merely says that they will not drink together again until the kingdom comes. At another, however, it presupposes that God will establish his kingdom soon, having been enabled to do so by Jesus' redemptive death.

Mark's account of the Last Supper concludes with a brief reference to the singing of the second group of Hallel psalms, those in which Jesus' death was foretold. Jesus then went with his disciples to the Mount of Olives, and to Gethsemane. Although they were staying at Bethany, they remained in the greater Jerusalem area that night, to fulfil their Passover obligation.

When we look back over Mark's account as a whole, the combination of explicit and circumstantial evidence is overwhelming. Mark tells us several times that this was a Passover meal, and he records both Jesus and his disciples mentioning it explicitly. Mark's account shows signs of use of an Aramaic source which made a number of Jewish assumptions. This source included both explicit reference to the Passover victim, and circumstantial points such as the beginning of the meal after dark. All this cannot be secondary generation. If Mark were trying to *convince* us that the meal was a Passover meal, he would have supplied the traditional interpretation of the victim and the bitter herbs. If his Aramaic source were wrong, it would not have included so indirect a reference to those Hallel psalms that could be interpreted as predictions of Jesus' death. Moreover, the early Christians had no motivation for portraying this as a Passover meal if it was not one. Paul used it as the foundational meal for the Lord's Supper at an early date (1 Cor 11.23–5): he did not mention that it originated at an annual Jewish feast, and it was not useful for the first Christians to invent this idea. We should therefore not doubt Mark's account: the Last Supper was a Passover meal.

THE LAST SUPPER: JOHN'S DATE IS WRONG

If there is such clear evidence that the Last Supper was a Passover meal, it follows that the Johannine date is wrong. It should not be in doubt: the meal is dated 'Before the feast of Passover' (Jn 13.1). Jesus was arrested after the Last Supper, as in Mark. When he was taken from Caiaphas to Pilate, 'they did not enter the praetorium, so they should not become unclean but should eat the Passover' (18.28). It follows that the Passover meal had not yet been eaten. When Pilate sat to give judgement, 'It was the preparation of the Passover, at about the sixth hour' (19.14). The meaning of the term 'preparation of the Passover' ought to be beyond doubt. It is the equivalent of a Jewish term which invariably means the eve of Passover, i.e. 14 Nisan. The fourth Gospel's date is therefore unambiguous. Jesus' last meal with his disciples took place on 14 Nisan, and it was accordingly not a Passover meal.

The Johannine narrative has many other faults. Since, however, these are not caused by its dating, they are discussed elsewhere in this book, and call for only the briefest survey here. Firstly, the final discourses at the meal, and the prayer of Chapter 17 are full of Johannine theology, which was not produced by the Jesus of history. They include the high Christology, with the description of Jesus as 'the Son' (14.13; 17.1), his pre-existence (17.5), his indwelling with the Father (14.9–11), his centrality in an 'I am' saying (14.6), his ability to answer prayer (14.13–14) and his sending of the Paraclete (15.26). The lack of cause and effect in the aftermath of the raising of Lazarus is important here too, for it shows that, from an historical perspective, the whole structure of the final events has been thrown into chaos.[13] The trial before Pilate, reported by Mark with such brevity that we must infer the absence of reliable tradition (Mk 15.1–5),[14] has ever more unlikely features in the fourth Gospel.[15] Jesus distinguishes between his followers and 'the Jews' (18.36). 'The Jews' tell Pilate that according to their Law he deserves to die 'because he made himself the Son of God' (19.7), a view which requires the replacement of the Sonship of the faithful Jew with specifically Johannine Christology. Pilate is so determined to find Jesus innocent that, were the Johannine narrative correct, the historical Pilate would have released him.

The function of the meal not being a Passover meal is to remove a large quantity of specifically Jewish material from the narrative. Some things happen which Jews might do, but they are not specifically Jewish things, they might be done by Gentiles too. So, for example, Jesus washes the disciples' feet (13.4–17), prefiguring the baptism by which Gentiles entered the Christian community, and instituting the custom of footwashing which the community practiced (cf. Weiss 1979; Manns 1991: 321–37; Thomas 1991, with bibliography; R.B. Edwards 1994). They are not said to recline for the meal. At 13.23, it emerges that they must be reclining, because one of them is reclining in Jesus' bosom. With the Passover context gone, this is no more than a Gentile custom. The meal is not said to have taken place after dark. Only when Judas Iscariot has left after the meal are we told, 'Now it was night' (13.30). This symbolises the darkness in which Judas walks, and leads to Jesus' arrest at night, but neither the late end to the meal nor the symbolism is particularly Jewish. There is no indication that anyone except Jesus and the twelve is present, but with the Passover context gone, there is no reason for anyone else to be there. The scriptural prophecy of Jesus' betrayal is cited explicitly, complete with the bread (Ps 41.9 at Jn 13.18), which is given by Jesus to Judas after Jesus has dipped it. There is nothing distinctively Jewish about giving someone dipped bread. It replaces the common dipping of the twelve with Jesus, with the bread conspicuously absent at the beginning of a Passover meal (Mk 14.20). There is no interpretation of any of the elements of the Passover meal: the significance of Jesus' death is explained in purely Christian terms. There is no mention of singing, so the Hallel psalms have gone too. Jesus spends the night in greater Jerusalem, but with the Passover context gone, the fourth evangelist explains that Jesus often went there with his disciples (18.2), so the peculiarly Jewish rationale for being there has been removed.

The removal of Jewish custom is accompanied by some indications of Gentile self-identification.[16] At 13.33, Jesus refers to 'the Jews' in a typically Johannine way, as a group to whom the disciples evidently do not belong. At 15.25, he refers to something written in *their* Law, again treating it as a characteristic of an alien group. This is paralleled theologically by 15.23, 'He who hates me, hates my Father too'. Although this is formally in a context of criticism of 'the world' rather than 'the Jews', it is Jews who are effectively damaged by it, for it was non-Christian Jews, not Gentiles, who rejected Jesus yet believed at the same time that they loved God. Similarly at 14.6, Jesus declares, 'No-one comes to the Father except through me'. This excludes non-Christian Jews from salvation. This complex of secondary rejection is completed by the prophecy that the disciples will be banned from Jewish meetings (16.2): this too belongs to the situation of the Johannine community, not to that of the historical Jesus and the twelve.[17]

We can now see the cause of the fourth evangelist's change of date: it is part of the replacement theology of this Gospel.[18] Jesus does not eat a Passover meal because Passover was a feast 'of the Jews' (2.13; 6.4): he replaces it. He is crucified at the same time as the Passover victims were slaughtered, on the afternoon of 14 Nisan. Consequently, a scripture which refers directly to the Passover victim is fulfilled in him: 'A bone of it shall not be broken' (Ex 12.46//Num 9.12 at Jn 19.36). Thus he became more than the Passover victim, for unlike it he took away sin, the sin not of 'the Jews' but of 'the world' (Jn 1.29, 36). The dating of the Last Supper is therefore all of a piece with the change of position of the Cleansing of the Temple and the attempt to turn the raising of Lazarus into the trigger of the Passion. All these changes are due to people whose theological convictions were so strong that their symbolism caused them to alter the historical outline of the narrative.

Here again, we have reached the point where we should be able to stop, for evidence and argument are clear. Once more, however, trouble has been caused by scholarship. Most, though not all, is due to fundamentalists, whose absolute convictions in the truth of the whole of scripture would be infringed if John were wrong. From their perspective, John must be right, and since Mark is clear, they have generally argued that John really meant what Mark says.

At 13.1 the fourth Gospel gives us a clear date, 'before the feast of Passover'. Bultmann accepted this as the date of the Last Supper, but refused it as a date for the end of 13.1, apparently because it does not give a reason for Jesus loving his own, and it would be absurd to date this love: in typical Bultmann fashion, he decided that most of verse 1 is secondary (Bultmann 1941: 463–4). Bultmann's frame of reference should not be accepted. The text makes excellent sense as it stands. The date does apply to the meal, but also to the attendant circumstances of Jesus' knowledge of his approaching death and his demonstration of his love for his own by going obediently to his death. It was of central importance to the Johannine community that these events took place before Passover, and that Jesus' final act of love in dying took place at the same time as the slaughter of the Passover victims. Hence, after the end of the public ministry in the previous chapter, the final events begin with this clear date. Jeremias took up Bultmann's contention that, in the present state of the text, the phrase 'before the feast of Passover' must apply only to the word *eidōs*, 'knowing', thereby removing the fourth Gospel's contradiction of the synoptic date (Jeremias 1966: 80). This is no improvement on Bultmann's view, because of the extraordinary way in which it carves the text into pieces, and ignores the Johannine community's central concern to date these final events before Passover.

It is this unhappy separation of this account into pieces which is taken up by fundamentalist scholars, who then argue that the date does not refer to the meal. Thus Geldenhuys takes 'Before the feast of Passover' purely with 'knowing', and then supposes that 13.2 makes a fresh beginning and describes the Passover meal (Geldenhuys 1951: 657–60). This effectively contradicts the text, which has the single time indication at 13.1, and does not refer to the meal as a Passover at all. Carson, on the other hand, takes these words as an introduction to the footwashing only, and not to the following discourses (Carson 1991: 460). This makes the meal a Passover meal, so that the footwashing alone takes place before it. It also makes fair nonsense of the fourth Gospel's phraseology, 'before the feast of Passover'. As a description of a time after the sacrifices, after dark, with the meal available in front of them and to be eaten in a few minutes' time, this is extremely odd. Story gives part of the rationale: 'Inner connections between John and the Synoptics indicate that the supper ($\delta\varepsilon\tilde{\imath}\pi\nu\text{o}\nu$) of John 13:2 is none other than the Passover meal climaxed by the institution of the holy eucharist (cf. $\delta\varepsilon\tilde{\imath}\pi\nu\text{o}\nu$ in 1 Cor. 11:20)' (Story 1989: 317). As a description of narratives most of which do not mention 'the institution of the holy eucharist' (Matthew, Mark, John and the shorter text of Luke), this evinces commitment rather than evidence. Story's list of common items begs the question. They consist entirely of things such as the presence of Judas and Jesus, and the prediction of Peter's denial, which are not inherently specific to Passover. This underlines the fact that the meal is a Passover in the synoptics, and not in the fourth Gospel. Story's view that such points show that John's meal is the Passover depends on his conviction that all four Gospels must say the same thing really: the evidence contradicts him.

There have effectively been two attempts to deal with 18.28. Either this is late in Passover night, but not too late for 'the Jews', including 'the chief priest and their servants' (19.6), to eat the meal already eaten by most people earlier during that night: or the word 'Passover' does not refer to the Passover eaten on 15 Nisan, but to another meal eaten later that week. The first view is that of Story (Story 1989). It is quite beyond reasonable belief. The Passover was eaten after dark, not just before daylight. Story knows the tradition of M. Zeb. V, 8 (cf. M. Pes. X, 9) that the Passover had to be eaten by midnight. He suggests that Exodus 12.10, read with bT Ber. 9a, shows that midnight to 6 a.m. was viewed as a 'grace period'. This is not the case. Exodus 12.10 is about not having leftovers for the next day, not about when the victim is eaten. BT Ber. 9a is a Talmudic debate arising out of the fact that M. Ber. I, 1 does not mention the Passover. It cites named rabbis from after the fall of Jerusalem, none of whom mentions a 'grace period'. This has nothing to do with the behaviour of chief priests meeting Pilate 'early'. They could not expect the meeting to be over in a few minutes, nor was it. By John 19.14 it was 'about the sixth hour', in an apparently unbroken narrative, as was liable to happen if they went to meet the Roman governor on a matter of importance which could take a long time. This was more than too late in the night, it was after it was over. Story suggests that the terminology of 18.28 favours the identification of John 13.2 with the Last Supper in the synoptic Gospels, because the word 'eat' (18.28) presupposes that the lamb has already been slaughtered, prepared and roasted. This is based on passages such as Exodus 12 and Mark 14.12ff., where the preparations are mentioned before the eating, and passages such as 2 Chronicles 35, where the preparations are mentioned and the eating, though not mentioned, is obvious. This argument is quite unsatisfactory, since descriptions of the preparations and eating of the Passover cannot control the meaning of the word 'eat' in passages which are concerned about the central point of the celebrations, not about the preparations. Story's view presupposes a belief in inspiration so literal that the associations of a word can be read off selected occurrences in the Bible, irrespective of its normal usage.

Most harmonisers have preferred to argue that the words 'the Passover' at 18.28 do not mean the actual Passover meal. Carson wants the reference to be to the 'continuing Feast of Unleavened Bread, which continued for seven days. In particular, attention may be focused on the *ḥagigah*, the feast-offering offered on the morning of the first full paschal day (cf. Nu. 28:18–19)' (Carson 1991: 589). This is clean contrary to ancient usage, as scholars knew long before Carson wrote (e.g. Jeremias 1966: 20–1; Morris 1971: 778–9). What harmonisers like Carson fasten on is the perfectly true fact that the whole eight-day feast, including offerings every day, might be referred to as 'the Passover'. What is not found, because it would be so confusing, is 'eating the Passover' as a reference to the sacrifices on 16 Nisan *rather than* the main meal on 15 Nisan. If the fourth evangelist meant what Carson says, he could easily have said it. We must infer that he meant what he wrote: they had not yet eaten the Passover meal.

The discussion of John 19.14 has focused on the word 'preparation' (*paraskeuē*), in the crucial statement 'It was the preparation of the Passover . . .'. Noting that it is often used, even on its own, with reference to Friday, some scholars have argued that the phrase 'preparation of the Passover' means the Friday in Passover week, not the day before Passover. Torrey argued the same for the equivalent Aramaic *'rūbhtā di pisḥā*, literally 'the eve(ning) of Passover'. Jeremias allowed this, adding that *'rūbhtā*, 'eve(ning)', is used with reference to Friday, and suggested that *paraskeuē*, 'preparation', means 'Friday' at John 19.31 (Torrey 1931, 1951–2; Jeremias 1966: 80–1; cf. Zeitlin 1932, 1951–2). Carson, repeating this after demonstration to the contrary, adds that the equivalence of the Greek *paraskeuē tou paschā*, 'preparation of the Passover', to the Hebrew *'erebh hapesaḥ*, 'eve(ning) of the Passover', is the point which has to be demonstrated (Carson 1991: 603–4).

As can be seen from the varied collection of scholars involved here, the underlying problem is one of language as much as theology. The basic mistake stems from an assumption that words have meanings in themselves, regardless of context, so that the reference of a word in any text may be posited as its meaning in any other text. So *rūbhtā*, 'eve(ning)', and *paraskeuē*, 'preparation', may *mean* 'Friday', because each is used with reference to that day. This is not satisfactory: *rūbhtā* and *ha'erebh* are approximately equivalent to the English word 'eve(ning)', so may conveniently be said to mean 'eve(ning)'; likewise, the Greek *paraskeuē* is approximately equivalent to the English word 'preparation', so may conveniently be said to mean 'preparation'. In Judaism, however, the period before dark on Friday was very important, because it was the evening during which people stopped work before the sabbath and prepared to celebrate it. Moreover, this eve(ning), the preparation for the sabbath, took place every week. Consequently, these terms are used without the word 'sabbath', when it is clear which eve(ning)/preparation is being referred to. So, for example, at Didache 8.1 *paraskeuē* is used with reference to Friday because the term 'sabbath' has already been clearly set up in the context. It does not constitute evidence that the Greek word *paraskeuē means* Friday.

On the other hand, a word may develop a more specialised meaning, and there is later evidence that the Greek term *paraskeuē*, 'preparation', came to be used so frequently for Friday that it became the equivalent of the English 'Friday'. This is a significant shift in meaning, however, so it is important that there is no early evidence of it. Moreover, the expression 'preparation of the Passover', meaning Friday in Passover week, and not the day before Passover, has not been recorded from any Jewish Greek document. The meaning 'preparation for Passover' is such a natural reading of these words that the only place where they could reasonably be used to mean 'Friday in Passover week' would be one in which *paraskeuē* had meant 'Friday' for a very long time, and had ceased to mean 'preparation'.

How do our texts describe the day before Passover? Hebrew and Aramaic texts add the term 'Passover', so that we find expressions such as *'arbhē psāḥim*, 'the eves of Passovers' (M. Pes. IV, 1), or *rūbhtā dpisḥā* (Ruth. R. III, 4), 'the eve of Passover', just as we get 'eve of the New Year' (e.g. pT Meg. I, 70d, 10), and 'eve of the Great Fast' (e.g. pT AZ II, 41a, 63). Hence the word for 'sabbath' must be used to form a clear sentence in a context such as bT Pes. 50b: 'Why is the topic "eves of Passovers", even if this is true of eves of sabbaths and eves of festivals too?' It is unfortunate that equivalent Jewish Greek texts do not survive, but there should be no doubt about how to proceed. Since *paraskeuē*, 'preparation', is the word used for the preparation of the sabbath, the equivalent of the Hebrew/Aramaic 'evening of the sabbath', a reasonable Greek expression would be *hē paraskeuē tou paschā*, literally 'the preparation of the Passover', the term we have at John 19.14. The equivalence of these expressions is further shown by the Palestinian Syriac lectionary at John 19.14, *rūbhtā dpsḥā*, 'the eve(ning) of Passover', with a similar expression in the peshitta. In other circumstances, the semantic area of the Aramaic *'rūbhtā*, 'eve(ning)', is so different from the Greek *paraskeuē*, 'preparation', that this translation can only be explained by the cultural fact that these words were known equivalents for the eves of sabbaths and festivals. If therefore the fourth evangelist wanted to indicate the Friday in Passover week, he would have said something else here, and dated the final events more clearly in complete sentences elsewhere. We must infer that the Johannine phrase means about midday on Friday, 14 Nisan. Jesus is sentenced to die, and is crucified on Golgotha, so that the whole process coincides approximately with the slaughter of the Passover victims in the Temple.

The evangelist's motivation has also been denied. The point has been put with most force by Robinson (Robinson 1985: 152–3; cf. Dodd 1953: 233–5; Carson 1991: 456–7). His first point concerns the 'slaughter of the lambs' at the same time as Jesus' death:

> it is hard to believe that readers of the Gospel in Asia Minor could be expected to know these details or to guess that the synchronicity was the significant point, when no attempt is made by the evangelist to explain it or to draw attention to it.

This objection is remote from the culture of the Johannine community. Asia Minor contained significant Jewish centres. Ephesus had already enough Jews who maintained their identity for Paul to teach his Christians away from the synagogue (Acts 19.8–10): Sardis had an ancient and flourishing Jewish community, later renowned for its magnificent synagogue: Smyrna and Philadelphia both had vigorous Jewish communities which produced opposition to Christianity (Rev 2.9; 3.9).[19] The Johannine community included people who had to be kept out of Jewish meetings because they would otherwise have attended them, and those who left the Jewish community took with them a profound knowledge of the scriptures. Passover was the main pilgrim feast in the Jewish world: it celebrated the Exodus, the story of which was in the Torah, and there were old stories of it celebrated later (e.g. 2 Chron 30; 35.1–20). Each year before the Roman war, some Jews in Ephesus will have gone on pilgrimage to Jerusalem for Passover. Accordingly, the Johannine community must have known that the Passover victims were slaughtered on the afternoon of 14 Nisan. And that is sufficient – more detailed 'synchronicity' is neither mentioned nor required, the main point being replacement theology for which death at the same time is helpful. Consequently, this Gospel did not need to spell out these details, any more than it needed to say that light and water were the major symbolic features of Tabernacles, which Jesus also replaced (cf. Jn 7.37; 8.12).

In theological terms, the replacement of the Passover victim with Jesus is explained with the quotation of Exodus 12.46//Numbers 9.12 at John 19.36, where Jesus is pierced instead of his legs being broken, so he fulfils

Zechariah 12.10 (Jn 19.37) as well as the Passover scripture 'a bone of him/it shall not be broken'. Robinson suggests the reference is more probably to Psalm 34.20,[20] and argues that there is 'no compelling evidence that he [sc. John] sees the death of Christ in terms of the sacrifice of the Passover lamb' (1985: 152–3). This is also remote from the culture of the Johannine community. They may well have intended a reference to Psalm 34.20 as well as to the Passover scripture, but theirs was not a culture which could leave this major festival out. As so often with Old Testament quotations in this Gospel, the wording is not identical to any text.[21] What is culturally quite impossible is that the Johannine community could read of Jesus' death on the afternoon of 14 Nisan, believe that it fulfilled the scriptures, and leave out of account the death of the Passover victims, of which the Torah says, clearly and twice, that a bone is not to be broken. It follows that the Johannine community did see Jesus' death as a major event in which he replaced the Passover victims.

In conclusion, therefore, none of these objections to the most natural reading of our text is convincing. The Johannine community dated Jesus' death on 14 Nisan, and they were wrong. They did so because they had a profound theological conviction that Jesus replaced the Passover victims, a conviction which was part of a much broader theological conviction that Jesus replaced many aspects of Judaism. How long the tradition on which they depended may have been, we do not know. In the second century, Asian fathers who celebrated Jesus' death on 14 Nisan appealed to the ancient traditions of their churches (cf. Dodd 1963: 110–11). It is possible that this tradition is significantly older than the final composition of the fourth Gospel, for the conviction that 'Christ our Passover was sacrificed' was already expressed by a missionary, who preached for years in Ephesus, thirty or more years before this Gospel was written (1 Cor 5.7; cf. Acts 18.19–21; 19; 20.17–38). Be that as it may, the present text of the Gospel is clear: Jesus' death has been incorrectly dated, owing to the authors' theological symbolism.

THE LENGTH OF JESUS' MINISTRY

The fourth Gospel also disagrees with the synoptics in its apparent assumptions about the length of Jesus' historic ministry. It has often been argued that it is right. I shall argue that its view seems plausible, but is not at all probable. Mark has often been held to presuppose a ministry of less than one year in length, and to be followed in this by Matthew and Luke. The fourth Gospel, however, is said to presuppose a longer period, because the number of annual festivals makes this imperative. This is then said to be inherently more probable. Moreover, the Johannine view that Jesus kept going to Jerusalem for the major festivals is held to be plausible. It is to be noted, however, that not one of the Gospels says how long Jesus' ministry was. We should therefore treat the evidence of all four of them with great circumspection.[22]

We may begin with Mark. The arrangement of Mark's Gospel has been significantly illuminated by form-critical analysis. While some of its outline is likely to be historically accurate, it has to a significant degree been affected by the thematic arrangement of material which may not have had any chronological context at all. An undue proportion of the parables are all together in Chapter 4. A majority of the miracle stories are in the central section. A high proportion of eschatological teaching (much of it secondary) has been collected into Chapter 13. A lot of the conflict stories are placed in sequence at 2.1–3.6. Short sayings at both 4.21–32 and 9.42–50 have been collected together on the catchword principle. Since Mark gives no length for the ministry, we should infer that the tradition did not tell him how long Jesus' ministry was. The absence of repeated mention of Jewish festivals merely means that his sources assumed that Jesus went to festivals, and neither they nor Mark thought the matter worthy of mention.

Matthew and Luke followed suit, inserting their other material into the Marcan outline. Luke's behaviour is especially illuminating. He is most careful to date the beginning of the ministry (Lk 3.1–3, 21), so he would surely have been interested in its length and outline. Yet he never mentions its length, and he incorporates a massive amount of Jesus' teaching into a single journey, surely one of the most static accounts of a journey ever written (Lk 9.51–19.45, rejoining the Marcan source at Lk 18.15//Mk 10.13). We must infer that Luke was in the same position as Mark. He did not know the length of the ministry because the tradition did not tell him. He therefore arranged the material as best he could, following the Marcan outline where he had it, and inserting material from his other sources where it seemed suitable, and in one almighty chunk. He was not interested enough in Jesus' observance of Jewish festivals to insert them (except when he was taken, as a child, 2.27ff., 41ff.).

Scholars have searched the synoptic Gospels for positive indications that the ministry lasted more than a year. Perhaps the most striking is Matthew 23.37–39//Luke 13.34–5, where Jesus says to Jerusalem, 'How often I wanted to gather your children, as a bird gathers her nestlings under her wings, and you were not willing.' In its context, referring to Jerusalem's record of killing prophets, and threatening destruction, this must surely refer to unsuccessful efforts by Jesus, preaching in Jerusalem, to bring its inhabitants over to his version of Judaism. That mission cannot have taken place during his last visit. Both the plucking of the grain (Mk 2.23–8) and the green grass on which the 5,000 sat (Mk 6.39) imply that it was spring or rather early in the summer when the ministry had not just begun. Both the narratives of the entry into Jerusalem, where a colt had probably been previously arranged for (cf. Mk 11.1–6), and the preparations for Jesus' final Passover, where an upper room had been arranged,[23] imply that Jesus had connections in Jerusalem. While most of these points are not decisive on their own, Matthew 23.37–9//Luke 13.34–5 is a weighty piece of evidence, and all add cumulative weight to the other points.

The Johannine account is different. Like the synoptics, the fourth Gospel does not tell us the length of the ministry. Moreover, one of its crucial dates is secondary and external: 'And the Passover of the Jews was near' (2.13). We know the origin of this date – it is the true and correct date of the Cleansing of the Temple! We have already seen that its presence so early in the ministry is secondary.[24] It follows that this festival dating is secondary too. The same applies to the Passover of 6.4. This is the occasion of a discourse which reaches its climax in an exposition of the Christian eucharist (6.51ff.).[25] This was connected with the Last Supper as early as Paul (1 Cor 11.23ff.), but the fourth Gospel could not take up this tradition directly because it has Jesus crucified on the day before the Passover meal. Accordingly, this discourse has been moved to a separate Passover. We now have the whole chronological structure of this Gospel, and it is derived from Jesus' final Passover split into three! It follows that the length of the ministry inferred from Johannine festival datings is not a reliable piece of evidence.

With this, we must consider the function of the fourth Gospel's repeated mention of festivals which are omitted by the synoptics. They are part of its replacement symbolism. We have noted already that in the narrative of the Cleansing of the Temple, Jesus effectively replaces the Temple, and that in the witness of John the Baptist and the account of the passion, he replaces the Passover victim: we shall see that he replaces the other festivals too.[26] This theology cannot be expounded unless the festivals are mentioned and attended. For example, light and water were the central symbols of Tabernacles. Jesus replaces Tabernacles, declaring, 'If anyone is thirsty, let him come to me and drink' (7.37), and 'I am the light of the world' (8.12). In thus offering salvation to Gentiles, Jesus replaces 'the feast of the Jews, Tabernacles' (7.2). This is the reason why the fourth evangelist has Jesus go to Tabernacles, it is the reason for the external description of it as the feast of 'the Jews', and it is the reason for the extension of the light from 'the Jews' to 'the world'.

We must infer that the fourth Gospel's reports of Jesus' attendance at the festivals are secondary. Though it is right to assume that Jesus' ministry lasted more than one year, its narrative is based on the needs of secondary theology, not on primary tradition. The length of the ministry is not directly mentioned because it was not considered important and was not known.

The most conservative wing of the churches was bound to defend the Johannine chronology. Blomberg offers three arguments (Blomberg 1987: 169–70). Firstly, he suggests that purely symbolic interpretation of chronological indicators such as 'on the third day' is inadequate. So it is, but this is not a powerful argument. As I have noted above,[27] Blomberg has too limited a view of what is possible. No narrative is true merely because its indicators of chronological sequence are intended to be taken literally. Secondly, Blomberg notes the plausibility of Jesus making several trips to Jerusalem to attend major feasts. Once again, he is right, but his true comments are not sufficient to defend the Johannine narrative which we have got, in the light of the above comments. Rather, in constructing a narrative round symbolic use of feasts, the fourth evangelist has relied on the plausibility which Blomberg has noted. Thirdly, Blomberg argues that the synoptic Gospels also 'contain specific hints' of trips to Jerusalem before this one. We have seen that this is true, but like Blomberg's first two arguments, what this demonstrates is not the truth of the Johannine narrative, but only that Jesus' ministry lasted for more than one year.

Robinson is more thorough, but no more convincing (Robinson 1985: 123ff.). His basic argument is that the Johannine framework should be accepted as historically accurate, and that the synoptic material should be fitted into it. This argument is faulty in method. The Johannine chronological outline is self-consistent, the synoptic one barely exists before the final events, and most of the overlaps are in the same order, either because the Johannine community knew the synoptic Gospels, or because they used similar old traditions. Accordingly, the fact that the synoptic material can be incorporated into the Johannine outline demonstrates nothing. Robinson has not got far before he meets the Cleansing of the Temple, and we have already seen that this is in quite the wrong place. Robinson then places the ministry of John the Baptist before that first Passover, but this merely reflects the relative coherence of the Johannine narrative, it does nothing to make all of it true. All Robinson has really done is to put synoptic material into the Johannine framework as he pleases.[28]

We must therefore conclude that we do not know the length of Jesus' ministry. The synoptic Gospels only appear to imply that it was less than a year. In fact, none of them had an outline of the ministry, so they arranged their material partly by topic and did not tell us how long the ministry was. The Johannine community did not know how long it was either. Their Gospel correctly reports that Jesus went up to Jerusalem for festivals, and this gives the impression of a more plausible length of between two and three years. This outline is however quite secondary.

CONCLUSIONS

The following conclusions should therefore be drawn. The chronology of the fourth Gospel is verifiably wrong at two significant points. It wrongly places the Cleansing of the Temple at the beginning of the ministry, thereby removing its historical function as the trigger of the Passion. Secondly, the date of the Last Supper has been altered, and with it significant evidence of Jesus' Jewishness has been removed. It was a Passover meal, but this Gospel has altered its date so as to replace Passover with Jesus as the Lamb of God. Both these mistakes are dependent on the anti-Jewish life-stance of the Johannine community. Thirdly, the Johannine community were right to assume that Jesus' ministry lasted more than a year, but their presentation of this is also the result of secondary theologising. Jesus attends several festivals so that he can be presented as a replacement of them.

The first two of these points are the most important, because they show that a conservative evangelical view of scripture is verifiably false, and that the fourth Gospel contains significantly secondary material. The third point is also significant for this reason, that it illuminates the secondary nature of Johannine material even at a point where it looks plausible.

3

CHRISTOLOGY

INTRODUCTION

The Christology of the fourth Gospel[1] is one of its most remarkable features, and one which distinguishes it sharply from the synoptics. Here Jesus is clearly God, pre-existent and incarnate, walking this earth expounding the relationship between himself, the Son, and the Father. Moreover, salvation is dependent on acceptance of himself as the Son – acceptance of the Father is not enough. This is one of the strongest arguments against the historicity of the fourth Gospel. One important point is that all this material is absent from the synoptics. This cannot be because it was private teaching – much of the Christology is expounded in open debate with 'the Jews'. Nor can the synoptics have known it and rejected it all, for much of it confirms Christian identity, and some of it, especially the use of the term 'the Son', occurs in synoptic editing even when it was absent from the teaching of the historical Jesus. This cannot be explained if the historical Jesus really was the figure whom the fourth Gospel portrays. It is however perfectly comprehensible if Johannine Christology is secondary development, the deposit of the theology of the early church.

Some of the Christology, however, goes too far to be attractive to the synoptic writers as we have them. Such, for example, is Jesus' demand that people should drink his blood (6.53–6). This is as un-Jewish as possible, and it would be unfair to the synoptic writers to suggest that they would have reproduced such material if it were available to them. This, however, doubles the strength of the argument rather than diminishing it. Firstly, it is a further reason why we should not believe in the historicity of this material. Its *Sitz im Leben* is too far removed from the ministry of Jesus. Secondly, had Jesus really made such demands and claims, disputes more serious than indicated at John 6.66 would have been inevitable, and some traces would surely survive in documents which retail as much controversy as do our synoptic writers. The same applies to the fourth Gospel's presentation of Jesus' deity. Jewish people have perceived this as a breach of Jewish

30

monotheism, and the controversies in this Gospel show that this perception was already found when it was written (e.g. Jn 5.18). We must infer that this would be too much for Matthew, as it stands. Yet again, this intensifies the argument, for it shows how far this Gospel has come away from the historical Jesus. If the impossible had occurred, if God had been so self-contradictory as to send his Son to breach the monotheism previously revealed to the chosen people, the ructions caused would have been at least as serious as the fourth Gospel says. Whatever resulted, it would surely not have been the synoptic Gospels as they stand, without any trace of the Johannine discourses nor of the disputes which they inevitably produced.

We must consider these points in greater detail. It is clearest to begin as far as possible from the historical Jesus, with his deity and incarnation.

DEITY AND INCARNATION

The Gospel begins with a prologue in which Jesus' deity is openly declared: 'In the beginning was the Word, and the Word was with God, and the Word was God' (Jn 1.1). At the prologue's climax, 'the Word was made flesh and dwelt among us', and his name and title are given as 'Jesus Christ' (Jn 1.14, 17). This is an explicit declaration of the incarnation in the strong sense in which I use that term, that is, of the process by means of which a fully divine being is born as a person (Casey 1991a: 166–8). The prologue ends with a brief summary of Jesus' nature and mission on earth: 'No-one has seen God. Only-begotten God,[2] who is in the bosom of the Father, he revealed him' (Jn 1.18). This also makes the deity of Jesus quite explicit, straight after describing the incarnation and naming him 'Jesus Christ'. It follows already that we are justified in describing this document's presentation as that of the deity of Jesus, not merely the deity of the pre-existent Word. This is made more obvious by the other equally explicit declaration of Jesus' deity, towards the end of the original Gospel. Here, doubting Thomas declares on behalf of those who had not seen the historical Jesus but who had faith in him, 'My Lord and my God' (Jn 20.28).

This makes the fourth Gospel's view clear enough, but it gives us only one actual saying which is striking for its lack of synoptic parallel. It is therefore particularly important that, throughout this Gospel, Jesus is portrayed as conscious of his position as the incarnate Son of God who is co-equal with the Father. The classic declaration is 'I and the Father are one' (10.30), a declaration so provocative that 'the Jews' immediately take up stones to throw at Jesus. At 10.33, they give their reasons – 'for blasphemy, and because, although you're a man, you make yourself God'. This reaction is as important as the sayings. Not only must we explain the absence of Jesus' declaration from the synoptics – we must also explain why there is no trace of such vigorous Jewish reaction to it, a reaction which takes place in public during open debate. At 17.5, Jesus refers in a prayer to his position with God the Father before the incarnation: 'And now you glorify me, Father, with yourself, with the glory which I had beside you before the world was.' Throughout this Gospel, Jesus refers to himself as 'the Son' (*huios*) and to God as his Father. God is the Father of others as well, but this Gospel calls other people God's children (*tekna*), never his 'sons', reserving the term 'son' for Jesus alone. This is another indication that the Johannine community saw an ontological rather than merely functional difference between Jesus and other people, and its significance is brought out particularly well at 5.17ff.

Chapter 5 begins with a healing on the sabbath, at which Jesus orders a man to carry his pallet. In the debate with 'the Jews' which follows, Jesus justifies his apparent breach of sabbath law by identifying himself closely with God his Father: 'My Father works until now, and I work' (5.17). Many Jews believed that God was continuously active, on the seventh day as on others (cf. e.g. Philo Leg. All. I, 5; Gen. R. XI, 10). Jesus associates himself so closely with the divine activity that he effectively lays claim to divinity, claiming God as his own Father as well. We are told that 'the Jews' understood his words in this way: 'For this reason, therefore, the Jews sought all the more to kill Jesus, because he not only abrogated the sabbath, but also called God his own Father, making himself equal with God' (Jn 5.18). It is striking that, whereas Jesus justifies his action in appearing to break the sabbath, he does not attempt to answer any charge that he called God his own Father, or made himself equal with God. Similarly at 10.33ff., when 'the Jews' threaten to stone Jesus for blasphemy, and on the ground that he makes himself God, Jesus does not deny the charge but justifies his position, asserting as he does so 'I am the Son of God', and 'the Father is in me and I am in the Father'. Thus the deity of Jesus, including his position as the unique Son of God, was known to him and publicly set forth by him not only to his disciples but also in public debate with hostile contemporaries.

Jesus' exalted position is expounded throughout this Gospel. At 8.58 he declares his pre-existence in open debate with 'the Jews': 'before Abraham was, I am'. The Jewish reaction of taking up stones to throw at him shows that they have interpreted his words as a claim to divinity. There are passing reference to his pre-existence elsewhere in the Gospel, and lengthy exposition of him as the bread which came down from heaven in Chapter 6, which is also delivered in open debate with 'the Jews'.

> For the bread of God is he who comes down from heaven and gives life to the world. . . . I am the bread of life. . . . I have come down from heaven not to do my own will but the will of him who sent me . . . what then if you see the Son of man going up where he was before?
>
> (Jn 6.33, 35, 38, 62)

His unity with the Father, and his position as the revealer of the Godhead, are expounded in his reply to Philip's request, 'Show us the Father' (Jn 14.8).

Jesus said to him, 'Have I been with you for such a long time and you do not know me, Philip? He who has seen me has seen the Father. What do you mean, "Show us the Father"? Do you not believe that I am in the Father, and the Father is in me? The words which I speak to you I do not say of my own accord, but the Father remains in me and does his works. Believe me that I am in the Father and the Father in me.'

Given the exposition of Jesus' divinity already noted, we must interpret passages like this of the mutual indwelling of two persons of the Godhead. Jesus' divine position is further indicated by a passage in the same discourse where he can answer prayer, in a context which evidently refers to the period after his return to the Father: 'And I will do whatever you ask in my name, so that the Father may be glorified in the Son. If you ask me anything in my name, I will do it' (Jn 14.13–14). Another function which Jesus claims after his resurrection is that of sending the Paraclete, the distinctive Johannine description of the Holy Spirit: 'For if I do not go away, the Paraclete will not come to you, but if I go away, I will send him to you' (Jn 16.7).

All this material is coherent, and quite unlike anything in the synoptic Gospels. The measured and open declaration of the deity of the Word in the first verse of the Gospel demonstrates that the author was determined to declare the full divinity of Christ. It sets up the unique interpretation of Jesus' pre-existence as evidence of deity, an interpretation attributed both to 'the Jews' and to Jesus himself, yet absent from other literature of this period. The absence of such material from the synoptics, and the absence of the associated conflicts, shows that all this material is historically secondary, and was formed in conflict with the Jewish community. This evidence also shows that in this document, unlike others, the description of Jesus as 'the Son' is an expression of his deity. We must look at the use of this term in more detail.

SON OF GOD

The term 'the Son' or 'the Son of God' is used by Jesus as a description of himself no less than twenty-three times in the fourth Gospel. Moreover, Jesus uses it in public debate as well as in private teaching. This is in striking contrast with the synoptic tradition. Mark attributes such a term to Jesus no more than once (Mk 13.32), and the whole of Q contains just one such saying, in which 'the Son' occurs three times (Mt 11.27//Lk 10.22). We can alter these figures slightly by including the purely parabolic Mark 12.6, or Jesus' acceptance of the term 'Son of the Blessed' from the high priest at Mark 14.62, but we cannot remove the massive difference between synoptic and Johannine usage. If the historical Jesus had used this key term as extensively as this evangelist says he did, the faithful Christians who transmitted the synoptic tradition would have transmitted it extensively. In that case, the Gospel writers would not have failed to record Jesus' extensive use of this term, for all of them have further examples of it in their own editorial work, as well as in comments attributed to other beings (Casey 1991a: 44–6, 148–9).

This point is quite decisive. Mark's seven occurrences include the climactic points of the heavenly voices at Jesus' baptism and Transfiguration, as well as the high priest's question at his trial (Mk 1.11; 9.7; 14.61–2). If such an author knew the twenty-three Johannine occurrences, he could hardly have left them all out. If the Jesus of history said all twenty-three occurrences, an author who wrote as accurate an account of his ministry as did Mark could not have been ignorant of them all. Hence the particular importance of those passages where Jesus uses the term in open debate with 'the Jews', and especially those passages where the Jewish reaction is hostile. These passages reveal both the secondary nature of these occurrences, and the conflict with the Jewish community in which debates about Jesus must have played an important role. Luke's twelve occurrences show his acceptance of the secondary traditions of its use by heavenly voices, and by Jesus himself in the saying which gives him a unique revelatory role (Mt 11.27//Lk 10.22). He too would have included some Johannine material about 'the Son' if it had been available to him. Matthew's usage is even more striking. The number of occurrences goes up to seventeen, no less than ten of which are propositional. Moreover, Matthew can be seen adding the term in. For example, Peter's confession in Mark is 'You are the Christ' (Mk 8.29): Matthew expands this to 'You are the Christ, the Son of the living God' (Mt 16.16). This is then legitimated by Jesus' declaration that it was revealed to Peter by God himself. An author who thought that Jesus' Sonship was so important could not have omitted all the Johannine occurrences, if he knew them.

The synoptic evidence is confirmed by the absence of such terms from the early speeches of Acts (Casey 1991a: 105–9, 134–5). If 'the Son' had been the main term which the historical Jesus used to express his divinity, the earliest apostles were bound to have used it too, and it would have been transmitted to Luke. Luke produced and used the secondary summary of Paul's earliest preaching of 'Jesus, that he is the Son of God' (Acts 9.20). If the term was significant enough to be used in such a summary, Luke could hardly have omitted its use by the first apostles, if such usage had been transmitted to him.

Some of the associations of the term 'the Son' are also significant. An outstanding example is John 3.16–18.

For God so loved the world that he gave his only-begotten Son, so that everyone who believes in him should not perish but should have eternal life. For God did not send the Son into the world to judge the world, but so that the world might be saved through him. He who believes in him is not judged, but he who does not believe has already been judged, because he has not believed in the name of the only-begotten Son of God.

The first thing to strike us is the terminology. We have had 'only-begotten God' (1.18): now we have 'the only-begotten Son', and given that believers have been given the power to become 'children' (1.12) rather than 'sons', this also expresses the full deity of Jesus expounded in the prologue. The second piece of remarkable terminology is 'the world', and it indicates a more fundamental development away from the Jesus of history. The word itself is relatively rare in Jesus' teaching in the synoptics,[3] and it is never used in this typically Johannine way to indicate the field of Jesus' eternal mission. That leads us to the more fundamental point. The function of this passage is to permit salvation to Gentiles who have faith, and to deny it to Jews who do not. John 3 opens with the necessity of rebirth, fired at an uncomprehending 'leader of the Jews' (Jn 3.1), who naturally expects salvation by being born into the covenant community. We then move midrashically through Jesus' death, the purpose of which was effectively the salvation of Gentiles (3.14–15). This takes us to the present passage, where the Sonship of Jesus is central to the declaration that salvation is through faith in him. This is the central shift in covenantal nomism consequent upon the Gentile mission: it is not to be found in the teaching of the historical Jesus. If it had been, the controversies engendered would have been transmitted to us, and it would have been seized on by the synoptic writers, all three of whom believed that Jesus was the Son of God and that the Gentile mission was central to salvation. Sonship has profoundly similar connotations at John 6.40, in a context of the eucharist and the final resurrection. We should also note the centrality of the assertions that God 'gave' and 'sent' the Son (3.16–17). These supposedly subordinationist declarations are part of the warp and woof of the highest Johannine Christology, because they assert that the Jewish God is responsible for Jesus' ministry and status: 'the Jews' should therefore have accepted him.

Another significant set of associations is found at John 5.19–27. This follows a dispute in which Jesus is accused of blasphemy both for abrogating the sabbath and because 'he called God his own Father, making himself equal to God' (5.18). Jesus' discourse therefore begins with the subordinationist statement, 'The Son cannot do anything of himself, except what he sees the Father doing' (5.19). This is essential, to associate Jesus directly with the God acknowledged by 'the Jews'. Once this is clear, he is given a number of elevated functions: revelation, giving life, judgement. The purpose of these elevated functions is made clear: 'so that everyone may honour the Son as they honour the Father' (5.23). Some of these items have some parallel in the synoptics: Jesus is the revealer at Matthew 11.27//Luke 10.22, and he has the function of judgement in the present form of Matthew 25.31–46. The complex of items in this public debate with 'the Jews' has no such parallel. There is sufficient for us to be certain that if the synoptic writers knew the material of this public debate, they would have used it. We must infer that they did not know it, and that can only be because it did not take place.

A few passages associate Jesus' Sonship with his glory. This is straightforward at 17.1. At 11.4 it is associated with the raising of Lazarus, a remarkable story, absent from the synoptics, and one which causes historical chaos in the subsequent Johannine narrative.[4] At 14.13, it is associated with the normally divine function of answering prayer. This time the problem is not just the absence of the material from the synoptics: one occurrence is associated with chaos, and one is more clearly a late development. This takes us to the most classically inaccurate use of the term. At 19.7, 'the Jews' explain to Pilate, 'We have a Law, and according to the Law he must die, because he made himself the Son of God' (19.7). All faithful Jews were sons of God, and entitled to call themselves so without blasphemy. The comment makes sense only if the term 'Son of God' is understood in a perfectly Johannine sense, indicating Jesus' full deity. It leads to Pilate's extraordinary fear, and his no less extraordinary question, 'Where are you from?' (19.9). Only a pre-existent deity can be known to be from somewhere else, on the ground that he is 'Son of God'.

All these points form a coherent whole. The term 'the Son (of God)' was welcome to the synoptic writers, but they rarely use it in the teaching of Jesus because he did not use it himself. The fourth Gospel uses it frequently, as its main Christological title, to express the deity of Jesus, a belief which the Jesus of history did not hold. In the Johannine conversations, this term has associations rare in or absent from the synoptics. Only one conclusion is possible. The Johannine use of this term is secondary. Jesus did not walk this earth calling himself 'the Son' and expounding his relationship with 'the Father'. The unhistorical presentation of Jesus emerged in conflict with the Jewish community. The Johannine presentation of debates with 'the Jews' is culturally accurate even as it is unconvincing as an account of the historical Jesus: conflict with the Jewish community was the cultural context of the presentation of Jesus as fully God.

This is so contrary to the convictions of conservative scholars that a recent defence of the literal accuracy of the Johannine account might reasonably be expected. In fact, there is very little such work. Conservative commentators generally content themselves with simply expounding passages as if they were a literal account of historical fact. The most serious defence of John in recent years is that of Robinson. His attempt to downplay the evidence is extraordinary:

> Equally, 'Son of God' as a title occurs but once on the lips of Jesus during the ministry, in 11.4, where the purpose of Lazarus' illness is

seen as being not death but the glorification, i.e. the manifest vindication, of the Son of God.[12]

> 12. 3.18 must be regarded as evangelist's comment and 5.25 refers to the Son of God's activity at the last day. In 1.49; 10.36; 11.27; and 19.7 the title is addressed or attributed to Jesus by others; and in 1.34; 6.69; and 9.35 other readings are to be preferred on textual grounds.
>
> (Robinson 1985: 348)

This is a stunning effort to remove one of the main pieces of evidence. The opening statement results partly from Robinson's decision to refer only to the full form 'Son of God'. If we include references to 'the Son', the correct figure is twenty-three. We must include them, because 'the Son' is consistently used by the fourth Gospel to denote Jesus as Son of God, sometimes in contexts which imply his deity (cf. 5.18–26; 10.30–39). The decision to regard 3.18 as evangelist's comment is arbitrary, and if 5.25 referred only to the last day, it would still refer to Jesus as the Son of God. At 10.36 Jesus is quoting himself, and 19.7 represents the Johannine Christ perfectly accurately. Robinson has not laid out the evidence, but removed it. He continues,

> Father–Son language is of course constantly on the lips of Jesus in John, but this again is an elaboration of the intimacy of the *abba* relationship familiar to us from the Synoptists. We have seen that it is originally parabolic language, and the process of its allegorization into 'the Father' and 'the Son' already occurs both in the material common to Matthew and Luke (Matt. 11.27 = Luke 10.22) and in Mark (13.32).

Here, John's use of his major Christological title has been written down to 'Father–Son language', as if this were something ordinary. This is combined with the assertion that it is an elaboration of something else, 'the intimacy of the *abba* relationship', and this functions to conceal massive development. Passages like John 5.18–26 do not occur in the synoptics: calling God *abba* is not the same as calling oneself 'the Son'. Moreover, 'abba' occurs but once in the synoptic Gospels (Mk 14.36): it is not obvious that it underlies most references to God as Father, and its 'intimacy' has been much exaggerated (Barr 1988; D'Angelo 1992). Robinson has also described our sources misleadingly. He gives the impression that we have Mark + Q, when we have only two sayings (Mk 13.32 and Mt 11.27//Lk 10.22), and there are good reasons for regarding them as secondary.[5]

This methodological fault runs right through Robinson's book. He often argues as if demonstrating that something occurs in a synoptic Gospel removes evidence that it is secondary in John. For this purpose, he uses *anything* in a synoptic Gospel. These items are however frequently secondary tradition. This is a particularly bad example, because Sonship is demonstrably edited into Mark by Matthew (cf. Mt 14.33; 16.16; 27.43), and both Mark and Luke have editorial examples of it (cf. Mk 3.11; Lk 4.41).[6] That there is one example attributed to Jesus in Mark, and one saying in Q, shows the term entering the Jesus tradition before the fourth Gospel: it does nothing to make Johannine tradition sound.

Robinson completes his argument as follows:

> A high christology of sonship is, as we know from Paul, extremely early (cf. Gal. 1.16; Acts 9.20, tracing it back to his conversion). What John affords is more insight into the process by which the points became stars in the church's usage. For the parabolic base lies close beneath the surface in 1.14; 5.19f; and 8.35, as does the functional rather than the titular understanding of sonship in 10.31–38.

The first sentence is not clear enough: 'high christology of sonship' and 'extremely early' should be defined. Galatians 1.16 was written long after Jesus' death. Jesus is clearly God's son in a special sense, but this is not defined, and other people are God's sons in Paul, as in Judaism (e.g. Rom 8.14; Gal 3.26). Acts 9.20 is neither early nor Pauline. Its proposition that Jesus 'is the Son of God' does not occur in Paul's epistles. Jesus is referred to as the Son (of God) no more than fifteen times in the whole Pauline corpus. Every occurrence is functional, in contexts where Jesus is so important that a term was needed which both indicates a close relationship to God and yet allows for the prime initiative, uniqueness and superiority of God himself. We must infer that the term was just coming into use in Paul's epistles, and that Luke has summarised Pauline teaching with his own formula (cf. e.g. Lk 4.41; Acts 13.33; and the propositional use of 'Christ' at, e.g., Acts 9.22, 17.2–3) (Casey 1991a: 111–12, 134–5).

Robinson concludes with analogy and assertion. What is meant by 'the process by which the points became stars'? Nothing, unless it be a confession that significant development did take place. The descent into allegory is not however new: it comes from a poem by Browning quoted by Westcott and Brooke (Westcott 1908: I, 1, n. 1; Brooke 1909: 299). That the Sonship of Jesus, like the Fatherhood of God, may reasonably be described as 'parabolic' or the like, does not remove the difference between synoptic and Johannine usage. Of course Sonship at 10.31–8 is functional: it is associated with the deity of Jesus, a charge of blasphemy and an attempt to stone him. This does not fit the environment of the historical Jesus, in which all faithful Jews were sons of their heavenly Father, nor is it found in Paul or Acts. It is specific to the Johannine community, for here Jesus' Sonship implied his deity (cf. 10.33, 36), a development which became possible only when the Christian community ceased to be identified as Jewish (Casey 1991a: Chapter 3; 1994a). Hence there is nothing like it in Matthew, Mark or Luke. In the fourth Gospel, the term 'the Son' is as titular as could be: it is no help to Robinson that it is also functional.

We must conclude that Robinson's defence of Johannine tradition is a total failure.

PRE-EXISTENCE

I have noted Jesus' pre-existence in the Johannine prologue, where his deity is so clearly stated. We have seen also the extraordinary interpretation of 'Son of God' in these terms at 19.7. The fourth Gospel's treatment of this belief is more extensive, and again one main problem is the absence of any such belief from the synoptic writers. One of the clearest declarations attributed to Jesus is in the so-called high-priestly prayer: 'And now you glorify me, Father, as well as yourself, with the glory which I had beside you before the world was' (17.5). Here Jesus' existence is placed before the beginning of the world, the same kind of thinking that we know from the presentation of him in the prologue as the divine word involved in the creation of the world. We find him pre-existent and descending from heaven also in debate with Nicodemus (3.13), but that debate fizzles out, and it is the more public debates in which the reaction is more dramatic. The first of these is in Chapter 6, where Jesus speaks of 'the bread of God' as 'he who comes down from heaven', and then announces 'I am the bread of life' (6.33, 35). In the subsequent discourse, Jesus repeats that he has come down from heaven, and this forms an actual point of dispute with 'the Jews' (6.41–2). In this discourse, Jesus' pre-existence is closely bound up with the Christian eucharist, and we shall see that this too is important material absent from the synoptics.[7]

The most dramatic presentation of Jesus' pre-existence is in Chapter 8, where it concludes a very acrimonious debate with 'the Jews'. At 8.23, Jesus declares that he is 'of the above', not 'of this world'. As the discourse proceeds, he claims divine origin as well as divine inspiration, accusing the Jews of having the devil rather than Abraham as their father. At the climax of the discourse, he declares, 'Amen, amen I tell you, before Abraham was, I am' (8.58). The reaction to this is as important as the declaration itself: 'The Jews therefore picked up stones to throw at him' (8.59). Stoning was the traditional penalty for blasphemy. The fourth Gospel's Jews, in open debate, have espoused the peculiarly Johannine interpretation of Jesus' pre-existence as an indication of his deity, thereby indicating the *Sitz im Leben* of this interpretation of Jesus' pre-existence in the conflict between the Johannine community and the Jewish community.

It is not only Jesus and this Gospel's authors who declare Jesus' pre-existence: this declaration is put in the mouth of John the Baptist as well! The first occurrence is without historical context in the prologue (1.15); the second is part of a speech to an undefined audience: 'This is him of whom I said, "After me comes a man who has become before me, because he was before me"' (1.30). Jesus comes after John because his ministry began later:

he has become before him in status because he was before him in time as the pre-existent Word. That association is especially obvious in the context of 1.15. As a word of John the Baptist it is quite incredible, and we shall see that it is only part of the Johannine community's massive rewriting of this historical figure to legitimate their belief.[8]

In the light of all this evidence of Jesus' pre-existence in this Gospel, we must interpret in a similar way its language about the sending, giving and coming of Jesus. This is most obvious in passages where these descriptions form an associative complex with a clear declaration of pre-existence. The description of Jesus as 'the one who came down from heaven' at 3.13 is at once followed both by the description of him as 'the only-begotten Son' (3.16, 18), and by the statements that God 'gave' and 'sent' him (3.16–17). The same passage also offers the description 'the light has come into the world' (3.19, cf. 1.9ff.). The eucharistic discourse of Chapter 6 has at its centre the exposition of Jesus as the bread which came down from heaven. In the course of this exposition, Jesus declares 'my Father gives you the true bread from heaven' (6.32), and 'I came down from heaven' (6.38): he also describes God as 'the Father who sent me' (6.44). The clear declaration of Jesus' pre-existence at 17.5 is preceded by his description of himself, in prayer to God, as 'Jesus Christ whom you sent' (17.3). This is the cultural context for discussion of Jesus' origin, and part of the reason for the steam generated by him saying that, for example, 'I have not come of myself, but he who sent me is true' (7.28). It follows that much of the 'subordinationist' language of Johannine Christology, so functional in debates with 'the Jews', implies the very high Johannine Christology even in passages which do not formally state it.

The fourth Gospel means all this when it has Jesus refer to 'him who sent me' (e.g. 5.24), or declare 'I have come in the name of my Father' (5.43). It follows that Jesus' pre-existence is effectively pervasive in this Gospel. It is absent from all the synoptics. Had it been part of the preaching of the historical Jesus, they would not have failed to record it. It leads to several disputes important enough also to have been recorded if they had taken place. Our conclusion is once more clear. Jesus' pre-existence, fundamental to Johannine Christology, was not part of the preaching of the Jesus of history. The evangelist has put Johannine Christology into Jesus' mouth: he has not recorded his teaching. Moreover, the development of belief in Jesus' pre-existence into an aspect of his deity took place in a situation of severe conflict with the Jewish community, among whom the historical Jesus exercised his ministry. This should be regarded as a fundamental reason for considering it untrue, rather than a possible insight into Jesus' real significance.

I AM

Unlike the synoptic Jesus, the Johannine Christ repeatedly declares his status. Nowhere is this more striking than in a series of 'I am' sayings. The most central is near the beginning of the final discourses to the disciples: 'I am the Way and the Truth and the Life' (14.6). We might expect this symbolism to mean that Jesus is central for salvation, and this is stated explicitly in the rest of the verse: 'No-one comes to the Father except through me.' The term 'Way' is strongly reminiscent of 'halakhah', the Hebrew term for observable Law, from the word meaning 'to walk'. For the Johannine community, Christianity has replaced Judaism, and this is implicit at 14.6, for it was the whole Jewish community who thought that they came to the Father, but not through Jesus. As Morris put it, oblivious of his remoteness from the Jesus of history,

> John is insisting that Jesus is the one way to the Father. He will not allow for one moment that the way of the Jewish priestly leaders with their insistence on the place of the law and the significance of circumcision is another possible way to God.
>
> (Morris 1989: 118)

John 8.12 is equally central for Gentiles: 'I am the light of the world.' The occasion of this declaration was 'the feast of the Jews, Tabernacles' (7.2). Light was central to the symbolism of Tabernacles. Jesus has effectively replaced this feast, and become the light for everyone: 'he who follows me will not walk in darkness, but will have the light of life' (8.12). The discourse ends with his rejection by 'the Jews'. These two sayings are thus central symbols, and they are absent from the synoptics, as are the disputes inevitably produced by their exposition. They are present in this Gospel in the midst of their real *Sitz im Leben*, a vicious confrontation with 'the Jews'.

It is equally remarkable that all the rest of these sayings are absent from the synoptics, together with their powerful symbolic associations. The first is at 4.26, where Jesus identifies himself to the Samaritan woman as the messiah, a title not in use during the historic ministry.[9] The next occurrence comes from tradition (6.20, cf. Mk 6.50//Mt 14.27), but it is placed after Jesus' ascent of a mountain (6.15). This is reminiscent of Moses receiving the revelation of 'I am' (Ex 3.14), and Jesus using it rather than receiving it should probably be taken as a hint of his deity. In the eucharistic discourse which follows, Jesus twice declares, 'I am the bread of life' (6.35, 48), and then 'I am the bread of life who comes down from heaven' (6.51). This reference to his pre-existence further indicates his deity. The discourse as a whole makes it clear that Jesus is the centre of the Christian eucharist, which is in itself essential for the salvation which is denied to 'the Jews'.[10] At a more symbolic level, 'I am the good shepherd' (10.11, 14), and 'I am the true vine' (15.1, cf. 15.5). The vine was a standard symbol of Israel, and Jesus' replacement of Israel is well symbolised by 'I am the vine, you (are) the branches' (15.5). The shepherd was also a standard symbol of the leaders of Israel, and this is taken up by Jesus being the good shepherd as opposed to a hireling. It is preceded by a more metaphorical description, 'I am the door' (10.7, 9), an image of him as the way into salvation. This is also the connotation of the vigorous description of Jesus, 'I am the resurrection and the life' (11.25). This is in the context of the raising of Lazarus, a remarkable miracle which is also absent from the synoptics, and which has caused chaos in the narrative of the fourth Gospel.[11] Here Jesus deliberately shifts beyond the concept of resurrection at the last day (11.24), and explains the meaning of himself as the resurrection and the life: 'He who believes in me will live even if he dies, and everyone who lives and believes in me will never die for ever' (11.24–5). Life is thus membership of the Christian community.

The final 'I am' saying is remarkable for the reaction to it. When the cohort who come to arrest Jesus say that they seek Jesus of Nazareth, Jesus identifies himself with the words 'I am'. 'When therefore he said to them "I am", they retreated backwards and fell to the ground' (Jn 18.6). This dramatic reaction further suggests that the 'I am' statements are intended to recall Old Testament passages such as Exodus 3.14 and Isaiah 52.6, and to hint thereby at Jesus' deity. We shall see that this is not the only reason for regarding the Johannine account of Jesus' arrest as the product of secondary rewriting.[12]

We must conclude that the group of 'I am' sayings are fundamental to the picture of Jesus as this Gospel expounds him. At least the majority of them, and many of their associations, would surely have been congenial to the synoptic writers, if they had known of them. It is not that *one* of these sayings is not found elsewhere – that could happen by accident, and the eucharistic ones might have been too much for the synoptic writers because of their associations. It is that *none* of them, nor most of their associations, are found in the synoptics. Nor are the disputes which they were bound to cause. This cannot be explained on the assumption that they are genuine, but they are not difficult to understand as products of the Johannine community. We must infer that that is what they are. Jesus did not walk this earth explaining who he was in Johannine terms: he was so described half a century later. Moreover, like other aspects of Johannine Christology, most of these sayings were associated with the conflict with the Jewish community.

THE EUCHARIST

In John 6, Jesus is presented as pre-existent, twice declares 'I am the bread of life' (6.35, 48) and expounds the eucharist as essential for salvation (6.53–8). The narrative sets off from the feeding of the 5,000, an old story found also in the synoptics (Mk 6.31–44//Mt 14.13–21//Lk 9.10–17). It is followed by the story of Jesus walking on the water, another story with synoptic parallels (Mk 6.45–52//Mt 14.22–33). John 6.1–2 appears dependent on information from a similar source, and other mundane aspects of the discourse have parallels in Mark, whose tradition had already doubled the feeding story (4,000 at Mk 8.1–10). The tradition inherited by the Johannine community, whether Mark or something very like it,[13] already included Jesus blessing[14] the bread and feeding the multitude, sufficient symbolism to encourage a Johannine author to expound the eucharist (cf. 6.23). It could also bring to mind the feeding of Israel with manna in the wilderness. The tradition also had Jesus identify himself with the words 'I am' (Jn 6.20//Mk 6.50//Mt 14.27). The fourth Gospel has inserted a passage in which people recognise Jesus as the prophet like Moses, fulfilling Deuteronomy 18.15 and 18.18; but to stop them (wrongly) hailing him as king he goes alone to a mountain, as Moses had done (Jn 6.14–15). Where Moses had God's self-revelatory expression 'I am' revealed to him (Ex 3.14), Jesus reappears using it (Jn 6.20), and this leads to a series of 'I am' sayings (6.35, 48, 51). All this underlines the absence of anything remotely like the main contents of the eucharistic discourse from the synoptic Gospels.

Serious exposition begins with allusions to the Pentateuchal narrative of Israel being fed with the manna in the wilderness, including the quotation 'He gave them bread from heaven to eat' (Jn 6.31, cf. Ex 16.4, 15; Neh 9.15; Ps 78.24).[15] In the next two verses, Jesus effectively announces the superiority of Christianity to Judaism:

> Moses has not given you the bread from heaven, but my Father gives you the true bread from heaven, for the bread of God is he who comes down from heaven and gives life to the world. . . . I am the bread of life.
>
> (6.32–3, 35)

Several of the main points are thus made at once. Jesus is pre-existent, the bread of God who comes down from heaven. As the 'true' bread, he is more important than Moses. The Father himself has given him, a central point in debate with Jews who believed that God had made them the real covenant community. Hence also the Father sealed him, and God sent him (6.27–9). Jesus thus gives life not to 'the Jews', but to 'the world', that is, the Johannine community with its Gentile self-identification. Hence the discourse moves straight to faith, and to Jewish rejection of it (6.35–6). The exposition of these points gradually becomes clearer, concluding, 'For this is the will of my Father, that everyone who sees the Son and believes in him should have eternal life, and I will raise him up at the last day' (6.40). This makes faith in the Son crucial for salvation, and asserts that this is the will of God himself, so that the Jews ought to accept it.

This was the ideal moment to introduce an objection from 'the Jews' (6.41). They are now called 'the Jews', not because they are a different group from 'the crowd' (Jn 6.22, 24), but because Johannine theology has now got to the point where faithful Jews were bound to reject it. For this purpose, the description 'the crowd', which was taken from old tradition (Jn 6.22, 24, cf. Mk 6.34//Mt 14.14, Mk 6.45, Mk 8.1–2//Mt 15.32, Mk 8.6//Mt 15.35), was no longer adequate. The first objection concentrates on the very idea that Jesus could be the bread which came down from heaven (6.41–2). The underlying rejection of 'the Jews' is so strong that the largely repetitive discussion refers back to the wilderness generation as '*your* fathers' (6.49, my italics). Jesus' superiority to Moses is quietly stressed with the assertion that (unlike Moses) he has seen God (6.46, contrast Ex 33.18–23). The discourse then moves to more careful definition of the bread, and the question of eating it: 'If anyone eats of this bread he will live for ever, and the bread which I will give is my flesh, for the life of the world' (6.51). That has the eating of the bread as crucially necessary, and 'the world' is again the field of salvation. The second Jewish objection follows at once, concentrating this time on how Jesus could give his flesh to eat. This leads directly to a clear eucharistic statement, including the rejection of those who do not participate: 'Amen, amen I tell you, unless you eat the flesh of the Son of man and drink his blood, you do not have life in yourselves' (6.53). This is stunningly anti-Jewish. Jewish people drain blood from meat in obedience to the biblical injunctions not to eat blood. The requirement that they should drink blood, even symbolically, shows that the eucharist has been rewritten to be as offensive as possible to 'the Jews'.

At the most literal level, the question as to how Jesus could give his flesh to eat is not answered, because everyone in the Johannine environment would understand that 6.53 referred to the Christian eucharist. Consequently, it does function as an answer to the question put by 'the Jews': Jesus gives his flesh to eat in the Christian eucharist. Symbolic identity statements equating bread and wine with Jesus' body and blood are found in much older sources (Mk 14.22–4//Mt 26.26–8//Lk 22.19; 1 Cor 11.24). Long before the fourth Gospel was written, Paul sought to control Corinthian meals by arguing that this identification was normative for the Christian eucharist. His account of Jesus' words at this last supper with his disciples includes the repeated command 'Do this in memory of me' (1 Cor 11.24–5). We must infer that the Johannine community did so. The synoptic accounts have the context of Passover, and of Jesus' forthcoming death. The latter point is vigorously developed by Paul. He has the function of the eucharist being to show forth the Lord's death until he comes (1 Cor 11.26), and abuse of the meal serious enough to cause sickness and death. The Johannine account results from further development of a cultural nexus which was very old tradition to the Johannine community when the fourth Gospel was written. It is also another point at which the Johannine narrative cannot be historically accurate. If one imagines the situation in the ministry of Jesus, the question of 6.52 is never answered for people who were supposed to understand it before the eucharist had even been heard of. The twelve were in no better position than 'the Jews' to do so.

The discussion excludes from salvation anyone who does not participate in the Christian eucharist, that is, all non-Christian Jews. Describing Jesus' flesh and blood as 'true' food and drink, the discourse concludes with another statement of the superiority of Christianity to Judaism: 'This is the bread who came down from heaven, not like the fathers ate and died: he who eats this bread will live for ever' (6.58). Many of the disciples leave after this discourse. They had good reason to do so. With Jesus' pre-existence taken as an indication of deity, the Christian eucharist necessary for salvation and faith in Jesus as an equally fundamental criterion, the normal form of covenantal nomism has been rejected in favour of a different community, Christians as opposed to Jews. That left the Johannine community with a problem. Those who left had already taken part in the eucharist, which should have resulted in eternal life, mutual indwelling in the Son of man and resurrection at the last day. The fourth Gospel's response is at 6.63: 'It is the Spirit which gives life, the flesh is of no value. The words which I have spoken to you are spirit and life.' To obtain the benefits of the eucharist, it was necessary to believe what the Johannine Jesus says of it. 'The Jews' who left did not believe that they had drunk Jesus' blood, nor that fellow Jews could not have eternal life.[16] They had therefore abandoned salvation, and John 6.64 equates them with Judas. Peter ends with a Christological confession which a faithful Jew could have made, immediately preceded by the main point which no faithful Jew could accept: 'You have the words of eternal life, and we have believed and know that you are the Holy One of God' (6.68–9). The 'words of eternal life' include pre-existence, Sonship, deity and the validity of a highly developed theology of the eucharist.

This discourse as a whole does not have a feasible *Sitz im Leben* in the life of Jesus. In this case, it is not that the material is absent from the synoptics. A eucharistic discourse before the institution of the eucharist is a problem in itself. If the Jesus of history had really been in a debate with Jewish people, he would have had to give a literal, not only a theological answer to the question, 'How can this man give us his flesh to eat?' (6.52). The un-Jewish language of 'drinking his blood' would have caused a Jewish audience to say something more precise and critical than 6.60. In a sense, this discourse is the one which the synoptic writers most obviously could not have inherited, since it requires an assumption of later Christianity to have taken place at all.

A further problem lies in the breach of covenantal nomism. This discourse makes it clear that Jewish people who do not take part in the Christian eucharist will not be saved. That is not a feasible view for Jesus of Nazareth to have taken, not least because he had not instituted the Christian eucharist. More fundamentally, he did not seek to exclude faithful Jews from salvation. His criticisms of his fellow Jews were basically aimed at scribes and Pharisees whose attachment to the minutiae of the Law overrode love of God and one's neighbour. Nothing in his teaching is comparable to the exclusion from salvation that we find in the fourth Gospel.

We must therefore conclude that the discourse and debate of John 6 belongs to Johannine theology, not to the situation of Jesus' ministry. Scholarly treatment of it has been grievously distorted by Protestant rejection of the Catholic sacraments.[17] In a very influential discussion, Bultmann excised 6.51b–58 as the work of an ecclesiastical redactor (Bultmann 1941: 218–20). He argued that it contradicts the earlier part of the discourse. He noted, for example, that at 6.32ff. the bread of life which the Father gives by sending the Son from heaven is the Son himself, and that those who come to him are those who believe in him. He concluded, 'In all this there is no need for a sacramental act . . .'. This argument is methodologically unsound, because it precludes any possibility of a coherent theology including Christology, sacraments and faith, and it does so fundamentally because Bultmann believed in Jesus the Revealer, and not in sacraments. For the Johannine community, the bread of life in the eucharist was the Son whom the Father had sent, and the sacrament of the eucharist was effective only for those who had faith in him. This is expounded in stages, beginning from a miraculous feeding in the wilderness and leading to a *climax* in the eucharist. The treatment of the discourse as self-contradictory, because the early part can be read quite wrongly without the later part, and because the climax comes towards the end, is most unsatisfactory. Bultmann further argued that the terminology of 6.51b–58 is taken from a quite different circle of ideas from that of 6.27–51a. This argument has partly the same problem, since it presupposes that different ideas *cannot* be welded into a coherent whole. It also suffers from misinterpretation of a text from its supposed origins rather than its real *Sitz im Leben*. It is not probable that Johannine Christians formed their view of the eucharist from Hellenistic mysteries: if they did, they had long since abandoned Hellenistic mysteries. If the notion of the bread of life owes anything to Iranian tradition, that tradition was long ago and far behind. The present text of the fourth Gospel should not be judged inconsistent because of these remote conjectures, when it makes such excellent sense as it stands.

Bultmann further argued that the eschatology of John 6.39, 40, 44 and 54 is 'quite different from the Johannine view (3.18f.; 5.24f.; 11.25f. etc)', and proposed that the refrain 'and I will raise him up at the last day' was added by the editor at 6.39, 40 and 44 (Bultmann 1941: 219, 236). This is because Bultmann failed to understand Johannine eschatology. The Johannine community inherited and firmly believed in resurrection at the last day, and this uncontroversial belief is stated in the fourth Gospel when necessary (cf. 5.28–9; 11.24; 12.48, etc.). They also lived in serious dispute with 'the Jews'. They were banned from Jewish meetings which some of them would otherwise have attended, and some of 'the Jews' had previously belonged to their community. In this situation, salvation depended on whether people were in or out of the new covenant community, the Johannine community, so Jesus is presented as arguing that, for example, 'he who hears my word and believes in him who sent me has eternal life and does not come into judgement, but has passed from death to life' (5.24). It is precisely such a person whom Jesus will raise up at the last day. This may be somewhat paradoxical, but it is entirely coherent as a theological interpretation of the world in which the Johannine community lived, and should not be used to slice this document into ribbons. This Bultmann finally did when he confessed that the text is in a state of disorder, and proceeded to rewrite it as 6.27, 34, 35, 30–3, 47–51a, 41–6 and 36–40 (Bultmann 1941: 220–1). His detailed reasons are extraordinarily uncomprehending. For example, 'v. 41 is quite unmotivated as a direct continuation of vv. 37–40'. This is not the case. John 6.35, an integral part of the exposition which leads to 6.41, identifies Jesus as the bread of life. Verses 6.37–40 forcefully make the point that Jesus' descent from heaven and mission on earth were the will of the Father, in whom 'the Jews' also believed. John 6.40 expresses this with the term 'the Son', which in this Gospel is an indication of the deity of Jesus. It follows that 6.41 is a very suitable moment to introduce an objection by 'the Jews', who grumble like the wilderness generation and do so on the ground of his identification as the bread which came down from heaven, an objection founded both in the Exodus tradition of the descent of the manna, and in the specifically Johannine interpretation of Jesus' pre-existence as indicating his deity. We must therefore reject Bultmann's methods, and leave this discourse intact.

Bornkamm followed Bultmann in excising 6.51c–58, adding another influential argument, that 6.60–5 refer back to 6.35–50, not to 6.51c–58 (Bornkamm 1956). He firstly argues that the 'hard word' of 6.60 refers to Jesus' ascent (6.62), which correlates with his 'descent' at 6.33, 38, 50–1, but not with 6.51c–58. Secondly, he argues that the pair of concepts spirit/flesh at 6.63 are different from flesh/blood at 6.53f., and are to be associated rather with the Johannine spirit/flesh contrast at 3.6. Both arguments are remote from the Johannine environment. The development of the discourse has the description 'harsh word' after the most anti-Jewish exposition, which includes the need for drinking blood in its presentation of eucharistic theology, as well as Jesus' pre-existence, which in this document indicates his deity. We are not justified in removing verses merely because the next point, Jesus' ascent, i.e. resurrection, does indeed correlate with the earlier part of the discourse, as well as referring again to Jesus' pre-existence, which is in the earlier part of the discourse and at 6.58. From a Johannine perspective, it is also decisive vindication of Jesus, and it shows that 'the Jews' were wrong. The term 'flesh' refers especially clearly to 6.53–6, and does not even occur in 6.35–50. Finally, the departure of many disciples is especially well motivated by the quite un-Jewish theology of 6.53–8. Bornkamm's methods are hardly any improvement on those of Bultmann.

Dunn argues that even 6.51–8 does not expound the Christian eucharist (Dunn 1970–1). His argument is methodologically unsatisfactory. In considering the discourse as a whole, he argues for example that the word 'bless' at 6.11 need not be eucharistic, and that 'eating' and 'drinking' at 6.35 are comprehensible as a vivid metaphor for 'coming to and believing in Jesus' (Dunn 1970–1: 332–3). At first sight, such comments look plausible, for the word 'bless' is used in other contexts, and it is not difficult to assemble an array of Jewish texts in which eating and drinking are used metaphorically, and to note such passages as John 7.37, where coming to Jesus to drink is metaphorical, and faith in Christ who has replaced Tabernacles may reasonably be regarded as the reality symbolised. But Dunn's argument ignores the cultural context of these terms. Both John 6.11 and 6.35 are part of a complete passage which leads up to 6.51–8, and John 6 was written when the eucharist had been celebrated for years. We should therefore not interpret the earlier part of the discourse in isolation from the end of it, nor in isolation from known aspects of ancient Christian culture. It follows that 6.51–8 is crucial, as Dunn knows. He does not offer a detailed exegesis of these verses, which would surely be necessary if his view were to be maintained. He starts with 6.63, which he interprets literally, and takes to exercise a controlling influence over the previous exposition, so that 6.51–8 cannot be eucharistic because this is excluded by 6.63. He comments, '*vv*. 53–8 can hardly be taken to indicate that eternal life comes through eating the bread (σάρξ) and drinking the wine (αἷμα) of the Lord's Supper; for *v*. 63 explicitly rebukes any such false literalism' (Dunn 1970–1: 334). This again ignores the background culture, in which 6.63 deals with the problem of people who have taken the eucharist and left the Johannine community. Moreover, having missed the eucharistic significance of John's language, Dunn has to find another reason for it. 'The anti-docetic polemic of this latter passage is surely the principal reason for its inclusion . . . the situation addressed in Jn vi seems to be one where the Christology of docetism has made a strong challenge' (Dunn 1970–1: 335, 337). But the text of the fourth Gospel has made absolutely clear who the opponents are – 'the Jews'! At 6.41, faced with the pre-existent Son who descended from heaven, 'the Jews were grumbling', by 6.52 'the Jews were disputing vigorously with each other', and after the anti-Jewish material which follows, even disciples leave. There is no mention of docetists. Dunn's view should therefore be rejected.

Carson and Morris argue that the discourse is not primarily eucharistic, on account of the chaos which this would cause for their conviction that it is historically accurate. Morris argues that sacramental references could not have been discerned by Jesus' audience (Morris 1971: 352). This is true. It shows that the discourse could not have been delivered by the historical

Jesus, and the contrary assumption leads Morris into some very forced exegesis. An example follows immediately, with his view that John 6.53 is too unequivocal for the sacramental interpretation:

> But it is impossible to think that Jesus (or for that matter the Evangelist) should have taught that the one thing necessary for eternal life is to receive the sacrament . . . it excludes from salvation infants, and whole communions, like the Quakers and the Salvation Army.
>
> (Morris 1971: 352–3, with n. 50)

John 6.53 teaches that the eucharist is essential, not 'the one thing necessary', and this made membership of the Johannine community essential. The salvation of infants had not yet become an issue, and neither Quakers nor the Salvation Army existed. Morris has been led by his situation in the modern world to distort the exegesis of his sacred text.

Carson argues from what John does *not* say:

> if the Evangelist's intent is to provide sacramentarian theology, the language of John 6 misses several fine opportunities to echo the institution of the Lord's supper . . . he fails to record the institution of the eucharist at the appropriate place in John 13.
>
> (Carson 1991: 278)

This objection is remote from the environment of the Johannine community. They were in open and severe conflict with 'the Jews', and would gain little from reminding everyone that Jesus originally celebrated the Passover, a fact which 'the Jews' will have known and interpreted within a normal Jewish framework. The question at issue was how Jesus' words should be interpreted. They have been rewritten to be as anti-Jewish as possible, the main point of John 6.53. Morris and Carson both argue that John's use of 'flesh' (*sarx*) rather than 'body' (*sōma*), attributed to Jesus at Mark 14.22// Matthew 26.26//Luke 22.19 and 1 Corinthians 11.24, shows that he was not referring to the eucharist (Morris 1971: 374–6; Carson 1991: 278, cf. 275). This misses the point as comprehensively as possible. Jesus' recorded words could be seen within a normal Jewish framework as an interpretation of some of the elements of the Passover meal with reference to his forthcoming death. These words have been rewritten to exclude 'the Jews' from salvation, thereby providing an interpretation of the eucharist which Jewish people could not accept. The use of the word 'flesh' is part of this deliberate rewriting. The date of the crucifixion has also been changed so that Jesus did not *celebrate* the Passover but replaced it. He replaces it in John 1, where he is 'the lamb of God who takes away the sin of the world' (1.29); in John 19, where he is crucified when the Passover lambs and goats were being slaughtered; and in John 6, where the true bread who came down from heaven replaces the manna, and the eucharist, essential for salvation, is expounded when the obsolete 'Passover, the feast of the Jews, was at hand'

(6.4). It would not be at all appropriate for Jesus to institute the eucharist in John 13.

Carson then objects to the view, which distinguishes critical from conservative scholarship, that the discourse represents Johannine theology:

> to argue that he created so much out of so little assumes he is such a dullard that he does not mind introducing blatant anachronisms, when in fact he is constantly drawing attention to what was understood in Jesus' day over against what was understood only later (*e.g.* 2:19–22; 20:9).
>
> (Carson 1991: 278)

The introduction of anachronisms into the narrative of sacred history was a normal part of Jewish culture, paralleled elsewhere.[18] It was done by normal people, not by 'a dullard'. The two passages cited by Carson apply to reinterpretation of the direst kind. One reinterprets a supposed prophecy of the restoration of the Temple as a prophecy of Jesus' resurrection. It portrays 'the Jews' as uncomprehending, and by legitimating the Johannine community's reinterpretation of a prophecy, it both legitimates secondary reinterpretation and solves any problems arising from a troublesome prophecy. Carson's second example comes from the rewritten and rewritten narratives of the resurrection itself. It presents faith in the resurrection in story mode, with one character who was not even there at the time, and its assertion that Peter did not know the scriptures predicting Jesus' resurrection is most improbable. These comments do nothing to convert the narrative rewriting of other traditions, done in line with the rewriting normative in the culture from which he emerged, into historical fact.

Carson further argues that the discourse would contradict itself if a primarily sacramental interpretation were adopted. He suggests that there is a close parallel between 6.40 and 6.54.

> The only substantial difference is that one speaks of eating Jesus' flesh and drinking Jesus' blood, while the other, in precisely the same conceptual location, speaks of looking to the Son and believing in him. The conclusion is obvious: the former is the metaphorical way of referring to the latter.
>
> (Carson 1991: 297)

There are two things wrong with this. One is that drinking blood is so alien to Judaism that to regard 'looking to' and 'believing' as metaphors for it is culturally ludicrous. 'Drinking blood' is a deliberate eucharistic rewrite. The second problem is more profound. Like Bultmann before him, Carson has not entered into John's thought-world. In it, the eucharist was taken by those who believed in the Son, for they alone could realise that they were eating his flesh and drinking his blood. To announce that one is a metaphor for the other is to deprive Johannine language of all its content.

A different kind of attempt to defend the historicity of John 6 was made by Robinson (Robinson 1985: 190–211). Most of his discussion is devoted to arguing that the Johannine account is independent of its partial synoptic parallels. He further argues that the Johannine account is in certain respects more explanatory, and therefore superior. This discussion is marked by subjective and improbable judgements. For example, Robinson would have us believe that Jesus withdrew because he knew that people were coming to seize him to make him king (Jn 6.15). He argues that this explains the 'manic excitement of the mob' at Mark 6.32–44. He suggests that their being 'like sheep without a shepherd' has a political background in the Old Testament, that the companies of hundreds and fifties may perhaps have quasi-military overtones, and even uses the fact that they are numbered as 'males' as evidence of a nationalist setting in the desert (Robinson 1985: 203–4).

There are two faults of method here. If information in an independent Johannine account appears to explain a Marcan setting, there are always two possible reasons for this: the fourth Gospel may be right, or the Marcan problem may have been solved secondarily. There is good reason to prefer the second view here: if a whole crowd wanted to make Jesus king, if this was a plausible reaction to his ministry, if Jesus did nothing more drastic than send the disciples away and follow, the problem would have recurred, and we would have other reports of it. The supporting arguments for a political background are exceptionally feeble: Robinson pushes small points because there are no big ones. His discussion is most remarkable for its omission of main points. Neither the highly developed theology of the eucharist, nor its anti-Jewish nature, is ever confronted.[19]

We must therefore conclude that attempts to defend the historicity of John 6 have not been successful. Nor have the efforts of Protestant scholars to show that the eucharist is not central to it. This discourse does not belong to the Jesus of history. Its *Sitz im Leben* is entirely in the Johannine community, which produced its theology of the eucharist. It did so in vigorous opposition to the Jewish community, a fact responsible for the anti-Jewish rewrite of Jesus' words at 6.53, and the presentation of Jews who left the Johannine community as the equivalent of Judas Iscariot (6.64).

SIGNS

All four Gospels report that Jesus performed miracles. The fourth Gospel has two major differences from the synoptics. Some of its miracles have been written up to be quite clearly a presentation of something, in some cases an event which is known not to occur in other circumstances. Secondly, the Johannine miracles are for the most part deliberately presented as 'signs', through which Jesus reveals his glory. They should therefore lead to faith, but actually divide people into believers and unbelievers.[20]

The first sign takes place at Cana of Galilee (Jn 2.1–11).[21] To provide wine for the wedding, Jesus changes water into wine. This event is, in normal circumstances, impossible. Jesus does it quite abundantly, producing no less than 120 gallons. There are reports of somewhat analogous incidents in stories to do with Dionysus. For example, it was reported that at Elis, three empty jars were sealed at the festival of Dionysus, and later the jars were opened and found to be full of wine (Athenaeus, *Deipnosophistae* I, 34a, citing Theopompus of Chios). The centre of the symbolism in our story is at John 2.6 and 2.11. At 2.6, the stone waterpots were for the purification of 'the Jews', which is culturally accurate, stone being used because it is not subject to uncleanness. The narrator tells us that in the first of his signs Jesus 'revealed his glory', and as a result 'his disciples believed in him' (2.11). We already have the division of people into 'the Jews' and 'the disciples'. We have seen this division in the Cleansing of the Temple, and we shall see that it arises from the Gentile self-identification of the Johannine community in conflict with 'the Jews'.[22] We must therefore interpret the running out of the wine (Jn 2.3) and the excellence of the new wine (2.10) symbolically, indicating the inadequacy of Judaism and the excellence of the new revelation through Jesus. The fact that the chief steward is known only from sources concerned with Gentile weddings rather than Jewish ones probably also indicates the Gentile origin of the story. All these points, taken together, form a devastating argument of cumulative weight against the historicity of the story.

The next sign referred to is Jesus' resurrection. This is in debate between 'the disciples' and 'the Jews', the same nexus of conflict. In response to the demand of 'the Jews' for a 'sign' to justify his action in the Temple, Jesus repeats a version of a prediction of the destruction of the Temple, in which he undertakes to build it in three days, and the reference to the resurrection is explained through 'the disciples'.[23] Two more references to 'signs' follow. The first has many people in Jerusalem believe in his name because they saw the signs which he did (Jn 2.23). Nonetheless, we find that Jesus did not entrust himself to them (2.24). This is another indication that signs may have different effects: they may lead to permanent faith, temporary faith or hostility. This will reflect the effects of telling these stories in Ephesus. We must infer that the signs had been important in bringing members of the Johannine community to faith; that this had also happened to people who had left the community; and that hostile Jews did not believe the stories. The next reference is of the same kind. Nicodemus tells Jesus, 'Rabbi, we know that you have come from God, a teacher, for no-one can do these signs which you are doing, unless God be with him' (Jn 3.2). This is a quintessentially Jewish reaction to such signs. It puts Nicodemus on the way to faith, which he never quite reaches, and this will reflect the reaction of real people in Ephesus.

The next sign is a traditional healing story (Jn 4.46–54; cf. Mt 8.5–13//Lk

7.1–10). The official whose son is cured is probably Gentile: there is certainly no mention of Jews. The sign leads him and his household to faith.

The next miracle is a healing of a man who was apparently paralytic, so it is similar to some stories in the synoptics. It has two unsynoptic features. One is the information that the man had been ill for thirty-eight years, which intensifies the miracle. More central to this Gospel's purpose is Jesus' action in telling the healed man to carry his pallet, when it was the sabbath. This is precisely what the synoptic Jesus does not do, for it is contrary to the written Law (Jer 17.20–1). As we have seen, Jesus' defence of himself as working like his Father implies his deity.[24] This also sets the scene for the description of his 'works', a broader term than 'signs', one which includes but is not confined to miracles. At once, 'the Jews' seek to kill him, both for sabbath-breaking and because he called God his own Father. At the beginning of the discourse which follows, Jesus tells them that the Son does what he sees the Father doing, and that the Father will show him greater works than these: resurrection and judgement follow. Further on in the debate, he declares that 'the works which the Father has given me so that I may do them, the works themselves which I do bear witness concerning me that the Father sent me' (5.36). This is the same complex of material as in the changing of the water into wine, but in partly different language. A major similarity is the opposition of 'the Jews'. Jesus revealing his glory at 2.11 is functionally equivalent to the emergence of his deity from the miracle in Chapter 5, and 'works' here are evidently supposed to have the same effect as a 'sign' elsewhere. From an historical point of view, the whole complex is unconvincing. Jesus did not operate in opposition to 'the Jews', and he did not declare anything so un-Jewish as his deity. Thus the miracles, as the fourth Gospel has rewritten them, are quite secondary and profoundly involved in its anti-Jewish outlook, regardless of whether they are based on old traditions.

The next two miracles, the feeding of the 5,000 and the walking on the water, are preceded by a reference to 'signs' which are evidently healing miracles (6.2). We have seen that the two stories themselves are found also in the synoptic tradition, and that they lead to a Johannine discourse whose *Sitz im Leben* is in the Johannine community.[25] In the discourse at Tabernacles, 'many of the crowd' believe in Jesus, commenting, 'The Christ, when he comes, will he do more signs than this man has done?' (7.31). We shall see that this use of 'Christ' is anachronistic.[26] The chief priests and Pharisees respond to this debate by seeking to arrest Jesus. Once again, the tradition has been secondarily written up. In the historic ministry, scribes and Pharisees, confronted with an eminently successful exorcist, someone who did what was possible exceptionally well, accused him of casting out demons by Beelzebub. Equally, Jesus' healing on the sabbath, another possible event, led Pharisees to take counsel with Herodians against him (Mk 3.6). Serious opposition from chief priests followed the Cleansing of the

Temple. If the Johannine account were true, the synoptics would surely have reported it: conflict over Jesus' significance has again led to the rewriting of the tradition.

This is more serious with the healing of John 9.[27] Like that of Chapter 5, it is of a generally synoptic type, but it has been written up in three ways. Firstly, the man is blind from birth, so the healing is an impossible event. Secondly, Jesus is said to have spit on the ground and made a paste, with which he anointed the man's eyes, all on the sabbath. Though this is not as clearly against the written Law as carrying a pallet on the sabbath, it is obviously reasonable to regard kneading clay (cf. M. Shabb. VII, 2) and anointing someone (cf. pT Shabb. XIV, 14d, 17f.) as work. This is presaged by Jesus' declaration that 'the works of God' will be revealed in the man (9.4), and indicated by the judgement of 'some of the Pharisees' that Jesus 'does not keep the sabbath' (9.16). That judgement was answered at one level in Chapter 5, and is answered at a symbolic level in the following dispute: it is not however suggested that Jesus' actions might not really be work.

This symbolism is the third way in which the miracle story has been written up. John 9 begins with the question of whether the blind man or his parents sinned, that he should be born blind: it ends with the Pharisees saying that they are surely not blind, only to be told that their sin remains because they claim to see. Before carrying out the actual healing, Jesus repeats his declaration 'I am the light of the world' (9.5, cf. 8.12), taking up the imagery with which he replaces the Jewish feast of Tabernacles. The man washes in the pool of Siloam, from which the water was drawn at Tabernacles, and Siloam means 'Sent' (9.7), which is Christologically significant. All this is specifically Johannine, and we have seen that both the 'I am' sayings and the replacement theology of this Gospel are secondary.[28] We shall see that the centre of the controversy in this chapter, the agreement of 'the Jews' to ban people from Jewish meetings if they confess Jesus as Christ, is completely anachronistic, its *Sitz im Leben* in the quarrel between the Johannine community and the Jewish community in Ephesus.[29] The unsynoptic write-up of this miracle is completely intertwined in this late *Sitz im Leben*. When investigated by the Pharisees, the man recalls 'He put paste on my eyes . . .' (9.15), which immediately causes some of the Pharisees to say, 'This man is not from God, because he does not keep the sabbath': and others to say, 'How can a man who is a sinner do such signs?' (9.16). When 'the Jews' question the healed man's parents, they testify that 'he was born blind' (9.19). When further interrogated, the man makes this a decisive point: 'It was never heard of that anyone opened the eyes of a man born blind. If this man were not from God, he could not do anything' (9.32–3). All Johannine material of this kind cannot be historically accurate, else we would find it in the synoptics too. We must rather infer that the miraculous element in the earlier tradition has been deliberately written up to reflect the sharp controversy with the Jewish community. This healing is presented as an impossible miracle to give the appearance of rectitude to the condemnation of 'the Jews', and particularly 'the Pharisees', which the Johannine community needed so much.

We can now see how inadequate it is to approach the historicity of a miracle like this as if the main point were simply whether miracles happen. We know that communities produce stories of events which never really happen: the details of John 9, when compared with the evidence of the synoptic Gospels, show that this miracle has been deliberately written up to be an event which does not occur, as part of a whole programme of rejecting the Jewish community. The subsequent debate between Jesus and 'the Jews' at Hanukkah has further controversial material relating to Jesus' deity and his 'works', which, as we have seen, include his 'signs'. Jesus declares 'the works which I do in the name of my Father, these bear witness concerning me' (Jn 10.25). This is illuminated by the central declaration, 'I and the Father are one' (10.30). Having raised Jesus to full deity, the Johannine community had a logical option of believing in two Gods. In that case, however, they would have breached monotheism in their own eyes, because this is expressed in the sacred text and elsewhere with formulations such as 'the LORD is one' (Deut 6.4). John 10.30 shows them opting for what became a standard Christian paradox, that Jesus is God, he is not the Father, but, nonetheless, God is one. 'The Jews', however, do not accept this, which is culturally accurate, even as the whole incident is historically unconvincing. Jesus' declaration that he and the Father are one has no *Sitz im Leben* in the teaching of Jesus because Jesus was a faithful Jew, and if Jesus had breached Jewish monotheism from a Jewish perspective, we would read of the resulting controversies in the synoptic Gospels. In his response to the accusation of blasphemy, Jesus again uses the term Son of God, the standard Johannine term for his deity (10.36). It is in this context that he says to 'the Jews', 'But if I do [sc. the works of my Father], even if you do not believe me, believe the works, so that you may realize and know that the Father is in me and I am in the Father' (10.38). This again shows the 'works' as revealing Jesus' deity, and it is for this reason that they sought to seize him (10.39).

The last story explicitly designated a 'sign' is the raising of Lazarus. This is problematical from beginning to end. Lazarus is not mentioned until the story of his death and resurrection. His resurrection is a remarkable miracle. People who are thought to be dead occasionally revive (Derrett 1982: Chapter 5), which led to the ruling that the bereaved could visit the grave for up to three days (bT Sem. 8, 1). Lazarus is deliberately portrayed as dead for four days (Jn 11.39), so that, here too, Jesus is deliberately portrayed as achieving the impossible. If this story were true, then even in itself it surely would not have dropped out from the synoptic tradition, and this would be doubly so if the fourth evangelist's account of its effects were true.[30] Moreover, the story is shot through with secondary Johannine features. At

11.4, Jesus refers to himself as 'the Son of God', the term used by Martha in the full propositional confession of 11.27. We have seen that this is secondary. So is the title 'Christ', which she uses in the confessional manner typical of this Gospel.[31] 'The Jews' are mentioned five times in 11.1–44, and at 11.45, 54 and 55. John 11.8 is as external and hostile as possible: 'The disciples said to him, "Rabbi, the Jews were now seeking to stone you . . . ".' This has the drastic division between 'the disciples' and 'the Jews' which we have already noted in the first 'sign', and which has its *Sitz im Leben* in Ephesus after 70CE.[32] At 11.25, we have one of Jesus' 'I am' sayings, a quite secondary group.[33] Johannine concepts of 'light' (11.9–10) and 'the world' (11.9, 27) are here too. 'To believe' occurs seven times in 11.1–44, and at 11.45 and 11.48.[34] John 11.25–6 offers a classic summary of Johannine features, with faith in Jesus bringing salvation and the eschatology somewhat transmuted: 'I am the Resurrection and the Life. He who believes in me will live even if he dies, and everyone who lives and believes in me will not die for ever.'

The concept of glory is even more fundamental. We have seen that in the first sign Jesus 'revealed his glory' and 'his disciples believed in him' (2.11), and we have seen the same basic notion elsewhere, summarised as 'we beheld his glory' (1.14). At 11.4 Jesus declares Lazarus' sickness not fatal, 'but for the glory of God, that the Son of God may be glorified through it'. This is the constant and historically secondary presentation of Jesus as divine, and revealing the deity. Just at the point where Martha declares that Lazarus has been dead four days (and therefore cannot be resuscitated), Jesus declares 'Did I not tell you that if you believe you will see the glory of God?' (11.40). The chief priests and Pharisees, however, do not see his glory, because they do not believe. Even when they know that he is performing many signs (11.47), therefore, they take measures to bring about his death. This is theologically coherent even as it is historically secondary.

It follows that this narrative is a Johannine composition.[35] Some features have no possible *Sitz im Leben* in the ministry of Jesus: others cannot come from there, because the synoptic tradition could not have failed to pass on such clear and good news, if it had been part of the original message. And this is the *main* point. Like the healing of the blind man, this story has been deliberately written up so as to *make* Jesus' opponents turn down life and be responsible for death. This sign divides people, as the signs do as a whole. Its immediate effect is stated at once: 'Many therefore of the Jews who came to Mary and saw what he did believed, but some of them went away to the Pharisees and told them what Jesus had done' (11.45–6). This leads the high priest to prophesy the significance of Jesus' death, and the chief priests and Pharisees to take counsel to kill him. Consequently, 'Jesus no longer walked openly among the Jews', but stayed in a city called Ephraim 'with the disciples' (11.54). His death would lead to what might be regarded as the greatest sign of all, his resurrection (cf. 2.18–22). We shall see that the accounts of his death and resurrection have been quite rewritten.[36]

Two summaries put the function of Johannine signs in a nutshell. At the end of the public ministry, 'Though he had done such great signs before them, they did not believe in him . . .' (12.37). This is followed by scriptures from Isaiah with which the community could understand this lack of faith (Is 53.1; 6.10), and the quite anachronistic declaration that 'many of the rulers' believed, but did not confess so as to avoid being banned from Jewish meetings (12.42).[37] This is followed by a short and characteristically Johannine speech in which Jesus attributes his words to the Father. This whole complex is secondary. The signs should have led people to believe in him. Historically, however, Jesus' healing ministry was not so unambiguous: it is the Johannine rewriting which has made some events impossible and others contrary to Jewish Law. The other summary is at the end of the original Gospel, where Jesus is said to have done many other signs before his disciples, 'but these have been written so that you may believe that Jesus is the Christ the Son of God, and that, as you believe, you may have life in his name' (20.31). This has two secondary Christological titles, and puts the function of the signs very neatly. What it does not say is that they have been rewritten or even created for this purpose.

We must therefore conclude that the whole of the Johannine handling of Jesus' 'signs' is historically spurious from beginning to end. These stories have been deliberately written up in a secondary manner to make the Johannine community satisfied that it was right in its vitriolic quarrel with 'the Jews'. The deity of Jesus is presupposed, so that in the signs Jesus reveals his glory.

CHRIST

The term 'Christ' occurs nineteen times in the fourth Gospel. These occurrences include the first definition of the incarnate Word as 'Jesus Christ' (1.17), and a propositional use intended to put the purpose of the Gospel in a nutshell: 'so that you may believe that Jesus is the Christ, the Son of God, and so that, as you believe, you may have life in his name' (20.31). We must infer that the term was important to the Johannine community, and this makes its virtual absence from the teaching of Jesus rather surprising.

Jesus uses the term himself just once, in prayer to God in the presence of the inner circle of disciples (17.3). This is in a context of people's knowledge of him, Jesus Christ, alongside their knowledge of God himself. Thus it has in common with the other examples that it is used in a fundamentally confessional context. Jesus also identifies himself as the messiah to the Samaritan woman. It is she who actually uses both the Aramaic/ Hebrew term 'messiah' and the Greek 'Christ' (4.25–6), and Jesus' response 'I am' (4.26) is probably intended as a hint of his deity.[38] Jesus' acceptance of the term 'Christ' must also be inferred from the fact that he does not criticise or modify the confession of Martha (11.27). Nonetheless, he does not respond with this term when he replies to a request of 'the Jews', 'If you are the Christ, tell us openly' (10.24). In the surrounding discourses, he tells them a great deal plainly and openly, but without using the term. Other people are thus responsible for fifteen occurrences of the term, a much higher number than in any of the synoptics. 'Some of the people of Jerusalem' and 'the crowd' are responsible for five occurrences in their debates about whether he is the Christ (7.26, 27, 31, 41, 42). This is sufficient to cause the chief priests and the Pharisees to try to arrest him. John the Baptist declares that he is not himself the Christ, and clearly implies that Jesus is (1.20, cf. 3.28ff.). The messengers sent to him from Jerusalem use it in the same propositional way (1.25). Andrew uses the term to describe Jesus to Peter (1.41).

These uses cannot be historically accurate. The term was congenial to all the synoptic writers, and if people had used it on this scale, these authors were bound to have recorded such usage. Moreover, the term was not a fixed title which could be used in the way that people use it in the fourth Gospel (De Jonge 1966, 1986; Casey 1991a: 42–4). It translates the Aramaic and Hebrew term 'messiah', which means 'anointed', and which the fourth evangelist uses, with the translation 'Christ', twice (1.41; 4.25). This term was not a title in Second Temple Judaism, and the term 'messiah' or 'anointed' on its own was not specific enough to refer to the messianic son of David, nor to any single individual at all. Anointing was not confined to Davidic kings; priests and prophets could be anointed as well. For example, at 1 Kings 19.16 Elijah is instructed by God to anoint Elisha as a prophet instead of himself: at Leviticus 4.3 the high priest is called 'the anointed priest': and at Isaiah 45.1, the Persian king Cyrus is referred to as 'his anointed', that is, God's anointed. The War scroll from Qumran refers to the prophets as 'anointed ones' (1 QM XI, 7, cf. CD VI, 1), while, in 11QMelchizedek, a figure subordinate to Melchizedek is referred to as 'anointed'. In the Christian church, however, 'Christ' became a title for Jesus, and one which was central to the church's identity. Propositional uses of it occur in all the Gospels, and are uniformly secondary (Casey 1991a: 149). It is this Christian usage of the term 'Christ' in Greek which appears in the fourth Gospel, where it reflects real debates between Johannine Christians and 'the Jews'. Its position as a confessional term is reflected in the Johannine epistles (1 Jn 2.22; 4.2; 5.1; 2 Jn 7).

This also explains the most anachronistic use of the term, at John 9.22: 'the Jews had already agreed that if anyone confessed him [sc. Jesus] as Christ, he would be made *aposunagōgos*'. We shall see that this agreement to ban people from Jewish meetings cannot date from the period of the historic ministry.[39] It is not mentioned by the synoptics, it is not a feasible reaction to the confession and the disciples are never threatened with being banned from Jewish meetings, not even in this Gospel. As an historical account, therefore, the Johannine narrative is internally incoherent. The origin of this account lies in the experience of the Johannine community, some of whose members had been banned from Jewish meetings. The term 'Christ' is used at 9.22 because, at the time when this Gospel was written, the specifically Christian use of 'Christ' had developed to the point where it formed a boundary marker between the Jewish and Christian communities.

We must therefore conclude that the fourth Gospel's use of the term 'Christ' is altogether unhistorical. It originated from the confessional use of this term in the early church. Consequently, it was also involved in the conflict with the Jewish community. This was so serious that use of this term in confessing Jesus could be given as a reason for keeping people away from Jewish meetings, so that in effect confessing Jesus as Christ entailed leaving the Jewish community. This is also the *Sitz im Leben* of the historically false reports that the chief priests and Pharisees sought to arrest Jesus because of debates about his messiahship. Once again, historically inaccurate material has resulted from the Johannine community's conflict with 'the Jews', not only from their veneration of Jesus.

SON OF MAN

The use of the term 'son of man' has proved to be very difficult for scholars to unravel. That debate is too complex to be entered into here. I propose rather to make use of the solution which I have proposed elsewhere.[40] The term 'son of man' itself is not normal Greek. It is a literal translation of the Aramaic term *bar nash(ā)*, which was a normal term for 'man'. It entered the synoptic tradition from the teaching of Jesus, who used it as a normal term for 'man', because this is what the Aramaic term *bar nash(ā)* meant. In particular, he used it in an idiomatic way, according to which Aramaic speakers used general statements to refer particularly to themselves, or themselves and a group of associates. They did so in order to avoid sounding either boastful or humiliated. So, for example, the original Aramaic of Mark 14.21a might be translated, 'A/the son of man goes as it is written of him.' This has two levels of meaning. At one level, Jesus had in mind scriptures referring to many people, such as 'Glorious in the eyes of the Lord is the death of his pious ones' (Ps 116.15). The point of the saying, however, was in the reference to his own forthcoming death, and that of any disciples who might die with him. Jesus used this indirect way of speaking about his forthcoming death because death is humiliating, and because he believed that his own death was an atoning sacrifice for the deliverance of Israel (Casey 1987: 40–1; 1991a: 64–5).

In the fourth Gospel, there are no examples of the term 'son of man' being used in this idiomatic way, a fact which measures the distance between the Johannine discourses and the speech patterns of the Jesus of history. Instead of this, the term 'Son of man' is a Christological title which refers to Jesus alone, as it is in secondary synoptic sayings.[41] The Johannine sayings show other points of contact with synoptic material, but much of this synoptic material is also secondary. Some sayings refer to scripture. A group of synoptic sayings use Daniel 7.13, in midrashic combination with other texts (Casey 1980: Chapter 8). This may also be suspected at John 1.51, where the angels ascending and descending on the Son of man reflects exegesis of Genesis 28.12, where some Jewish exegetes saw the angels going up and down Jacob's ladder on Jacob/Israel. It is plausible to suppose that the Son of man = Israel has come from Daniel 7.13, cf. 7.18, 22 and 27, and that 'you shall see' is from Zechariah 12.10. In any case, the exegetical replacement of Jacob/Israel with Jesus reflects the replacement theology of the Gospel as a whole. Scripture is also used at John 3.14, where 'Moses lifted up the serpent in the desert' refers to Numbers 21.9. It is tempting to suppose that 'Son of man' is again from Daniel 7.13, and that this has been combined with Isaiah 52.13 for the lifting up of the Son of man. The lifting up of the Son of man is referred to again at John 8.28, where Jesus tells the Jews that 'When you lift up the Son of man, then you will know that I am he', probably to be regarded as his use of the divine revelatory formula from Exodus 3.14.[42] The glorification of the Son of man at John 12.23 and 13.31 could also be from Isaiah 52.13 (cf. 49.3). Some of this is very conjectural. The central points are that scripture has certainly been used in the formation of secondary Son of man sayings, and this is the same process as is found in secondary sayings in the synoptic Gospels.

John 3.14 and 8.28, with the reference back at 12.34 (cf. 12.23 also), show another point of contact with the synoptic tradition, the further development of Passion predictions. Some of the synoptic predictions are already developed from original general statements in which Jesus indirectly predicted his death (Casey 1987: 40–9). The Johannine versions cannot be authentic in their present form, because complete Aramaic sentences cannot be satisfactorily reconstructed from them. The word 'must' at 3.14 is an indication of secondary development already found in a synoptic prediction (Mk 8.31//Mt 16.21//Lk 9.22), while the expression 'I am' at John 8.28 is specifically Johannine. These sayings make perfect sense as further developments carried out after study of the scriptures, a process already lying behind the authentic prediction of Mark 14.21 and normative throughout the early church.

All the Johannine Son of man sayings have an excellent *Sitz im Leben* in Johannine theology. The Passion predictions illustrate Jesus' total control over his destiny, as he heads towards his atoning death in obedience to the Father's will. The double sense of 'lifting up' is amplified in the prediction of his glorification at 12.23 and 13.31, expressed without the term 'Son of man' at 17.1. His pre-existence is indicated at 3.13 and 6.62, both of which also declare his return to the Father after his earthly ministry. Specifically eucharistic theology is adumbrated at 6.27, and carried to its Johannine heights at 6.53. We have seen that this has been deliberately written up to exclude 'the Jews' from salvation, so this shows the term 'Son of man' being used creatively at the final stage of the redaction of the Gospel material. It is also profoundly involved in the vitriolic controversy with the Jewish community.

It is entirely probable that this material is heading for the later patristic interpretation of the term 'Son of man' as a reference to Jesus' human nature, his divine nature being indicated by the term 'Son (of God)'. Perhaps the clearest example is at 5.27. The power of judgement is given to Jesus, as stated at 5.22–3, where Jesus is referred to as 'the Son'. At 5.27, we are told again that God has given him power to exercise judgement, 'because he is (a) son of man'. It is difficult to interpret this except as at T. Abr. XIII, where Abel is given the power of judgement so that people should be judged by a man (Casey 1980: 198–9). The eucharistic saying of 6.53 is immediately preceded by the uncomprehending question of 'the Jews', 'How can this [sc. man/person] give us his flesh to eat?' The immediately succeeding reference to eating the flesh, and drinking the blood, of 'the Son of man' incorporates a reference to his human nature, on account of which he could die the atoning death which would make possible the life-giving nature of the eucharist. Finally, the Passion predictions themselves, in the importance which they attribute to Jesus' death, predict what is characteristic of man rather than God. The Word could not die unless it became flesh (cf. 1.14), the realm in which 'the Son of man' could be lifted up and consequently give his flesh to eat.

All this is quite remote from the Jesus of history. The way the term 'Son of man' itself is used indicates this, and it is supported by the content of some of the sayings. Some of them are also involved in the anti-Jewish life-stance of the Johannine community, which reaches one of its climaxes at John 6.53 (cf. 6.62).

CONCLUSIONS

The study of Johannine Christology gives us a quite clear result. Many of its most significant points are derived from the Johannine community, not from the Jesus of history. Jesus did not walk this earth presenting himself as the pre-existent Son of God, expounding his relationship with his Father, declaring that he is the Way and the Truth and the Life. People did not confess him as messiah, and he was not accused of blasphemy on the ground that he made himself equal with God, for he did not do so. He did not change water into wine, nor raise Lazarus from the dead. Johannine Christology reveals that this Gospel is a late work, which incorporates a large amount of secondary material. It has been deliberately worked over from a perspective of conflict with the Jewish community. Its Christology has gone higher and higher because this is what the Jewish community could not accept, and it has retained subordinationist elements to tell everyone that the God of 'the Jews' was responsible for the whole of Jesus' ministry, his exposition of its high Christology included.

It follows that this Gospel's presentation of Jesus is seriously false. His deity, the presentation of the eucharist as drinking his blood, the notion that 'the Jews' rejected him because of his messiahship or signs when all the disciples were Jewish, all these points are a contradiction of the Jewish identity of the Jesus of history. Whatever case can be made for the Christology of the early speeches of Acts, or the Gospel of Mark, as deeper Christian insight into what Jesus really was, no such case can be made for the Gospel attributed to John. It gives us an un-Jewish presentation of Jesus, one which was formed in conflict with the Jewish community, to which Jesus and all the first apostles belonged.

4

JOHN THE BAPTIST

INTRODUCTION

The picture of John the Baptist in the fourth Gospel differs sharply from that of the synoptics. All four Gospels portray a person who exercised a ministry which involved baptism, and who predicted the coming of someone else. But the historical John the Baptist was a Jewish prophet of judgement who was not sure whether Jesus was the one who was coming, whereas the main function of the Johannine John is to give clear and unambiguous witness to Jesus. Here too the fourth Gospel is wrong at a crucial point.[1]

HISTORICAL FACT

Some basic points of the fourth Gospel's account agree with the synoptics and with Josephus (A.J. XVIII, 116–19). John exercised a successful baptising ministry, and he said something on the lines of 'I baptise in water: among you there stands one whom you do not know, the one who comes after me, of whom I am not worthy to unloose the strap of the sandal of him' (Jn 1.26–7). This retains the redundant 'of him', necessary in John the Baptist's native Aramaic, but not in Greek or English. John baptised in the wilderness (cf. 1.23), and he had disciples (1.35; 3.25). But that is virtually the limit of the historical John the Baptist in the fourth Gospel. What is missing is a Jewish prophet of judgement.

Mark's Gospel begins with a brief account of John's ministry in the wilderness. Crowds flocked to him there, and were baptised in the river Jordan, confessing their sins. Mark portrays John as an ascetic figure, clothed in camel's hair and eating locusts and wild honey. His disciples fasted when disciples of the Pharisees fasted, and Jesus' disciples did not fast (Mk 2.18). Mark says later that 'everyone', that is, people in general as opposed to chief priests, scribes and elders, believed that John was truly a prophet (Mk 11.32). Josephus notes that John's highly effective preaching required people to exercise 'righteousness towards each other' (A.J. XVIII,

117), and Luke transmits some detailed ethical instructions (Lk 3.11–14). Mark notes his condemnation of Herod's marriage to Herodias (Mk 6.18), and attributes even to Herod the opinion that John was a 'righteous and holy man' (6.20). Matthew and Luke have his warning to those baptised by him that they should 'do fruit worthy of repentance'. This is accompanied by prophetic undermining of the conventional form of covenantal nomism, a warning not to rely on being children of Abraham, and by a prophecy of 'the coming wrath' (Mt 3.7–10//Lk 3.7–9).

This vigorous and successful prophetic ministry was the cultural context of a prediction which the synoptic writers believed that Jesus fulfilled. Part of it is in Mark, but there was evidently a Q version as well. To recover what we can, we must follow Mark's version with the additional material from Q:

> My strong one follows me,[2] the strap of whose sandals I am not fit to bend down to unloose. I baptise you with water, and he will baptise you with holy spirit and with fire: whose winnowing-fork is in his hand, and he will cleanse his threshing floor, and he will gather the wheat into the barn, and he will burn the chaff with unquenchable fire.
>
> (cf. Mk 1.7–8; Mt 3.11–12; Lk 3.16–17)

This picks up on many Jewish pictures of judgement (cf. e.g. Jer 4.11–14; Ps 50.3–4; 66.10–12; 1QS IV, 20–2). The gathering of the wheat into the barn implies the salvation of many of the crowds who flocked to John's baptism. Equally, the threat to the wicked is clear: the winnowing-fork and burning of the chaff mean perdition for them. It is clear from Mark 6.18 and 11.31–2, and Matthew 21.32, that conventional Jewish leaders were among the wicked, and the implication of John's preaching as a whole is that they would not be alone.

We can now see what attracted Jesus to John. He exercised a prophetic ministry of repentance to Israel. He called upon the whole of Israel to return to the Lord, and backed this up with ethical teaching. He offered salvation and predicted judgement in terms which recreated the Judaism of the prophetic tradition. This explains why Jesus underwent John's baptism (Mk 1.9–11//Mt 3.13–17//Lk 3.21–2). He thereby joined this vigorous renewal of prophetic Judaism. Our earliest source shows no concern that this implied repentance (cf. Mk 10.18). Mark also records that Jesus saw the Spirit descend on him. It follows that Jesus had a personal vision not seen by others. That has its *Sitz im Leben* at his baptism, not in the theology of the early church. While this may have been written up with the words of the heavenly voice, the immediate sequel is equally probable: the Spirit drove him out into the wilderness (Mk 1.12).

None of the synoptics offer any account of Jesus' existence as a disciple of John the Baptist. Mark starts his account of Jesus' ministry after John's arrest (Mk 1.14–15, amplified at Mt 4.12–17, replaced by Lk 4.14–15). This may be true, and there may have been a period in which Jesus was subordinate to John the Baptist, but we have no way of confirming such an interpretation of the meagre synoptic accounts. We do have some information about Jesus' view of John the Baptist, from later in the ministry. The clearer passages include a vigorous speech to the crowds, asking what they had gone out into the wilderness to see. 'But why did you go out? To see a prophet? Yes, I tell you, and more than a prophet!' (Mt 11.9//Lk 7.26). Jesus then identifies John as God's messenger (Mal 3.1, cf. Ex 23.20). Elsewhere, he has him fulfil the prophecies of Elijah's return (Mk 9.11–13, cf. Mt 11.14; 17.13; Mal 3.23–4; Sir 48.10). Jesus was so confident of John's position in the estimation of most Jews that he used him in an image of how much better it will be in the kingdom of God: 'Amen I tell you, there has not arisen among those born of women anyone greater than John, and a/the little one[3] in the kingdom of God is greater than he' (Mt 11.11//Lk 7.28). His comparison of his own ministry with that of John the Baptist presupposes that each of them brought the word of God to Israel (Mt 11.16–19//Lk 7.31–5). He used him in his own defence against chief priests, scribes and elders, asking, 'The baptism of John, was it from heaven or of men?' (Mk 11.30). He even declared that tax collectors and prostitutes would precede them into the kingdom of God, because they believed John when he came to them 'in the way of righteousness' (Mt 21.31–2).

John's uncertain view of Jesus is also recorded. He sent a message through his disciples, 'Are you the one who is coming, or do we expect another?' (Mt 11.2–3//Lk 7.18–19). This uncertain reaction was entirely reasonable. On the one hand, Jesus had been baptised by John, and was exercising a dramatic ministry of preaching, teaching, exorcism and healing, including severe criticism of Jews who were not sufficiently faithful: like John himself, he recreated and embodied Jewish identity from a prophetic perspective. On the other hand, he did not follow John's ascetic example, and John may well have felt that he did not fit his expectation of powerful judgement. We should have no doubts about the authenticity of John's question: the church would not have produced it.

Finally, both Mark and Josephus record John's death at the hands of Herod Antipas. Josephus records a Jewish view that the later destruction of an army of Herod was divine vengeance for his mistreatment of John (A.J. XVIII, 116, 119). This illustrates John's massive influence among Jews at the time. Mark records the view of Herod and perhaps others that Jesus was John the Baptist raised from the dead (Mk 6.14, 16; cf. 8.28). This reflects not only a positive view of John the Baptist, but also the perceived similarity between John and Jesus. Like Jesus, John the Baptist embodied Jewish identity from a prophetic perspective, and did so over against the temporal, legal and cultic authorities of his time.

We must conclude that, meagre though they are, the synoptic accounts provide us with accurate information about John the Baptist. There are also signs of serious rewriting. For example, Luke has everyone wondering whether John the Baptist was the Christ (Lk 3.15), a redactional addition dependent on the use of the title Christ characteristic of Christian sources. He also has an entertaining birth story (Lk 1.5–25, 39–45, 57–80). Matthew removed 'forgiveness of sins' from his account of John's baptism (cf. Mk 1.4), and inserted it into Jesus' interpretation of his death (Mt 26.28). He added a conversation in which John the Baptist was reluctant to baptise, and did so when Jesus told him to (Mt 3.14–15). It is also difficult to be sure how much truth there is in the rather gossipy story of John's death (Mk 6.17–29, contrast Jos. A.J. XVIII, 118–19). It is the editorial rewriting which the fourth evangelist was to take so much further.

There have been attempts to understand the synoptic accounts in the light of the fourth Gospel. Dodd argues that Matthew 11.16–19//Luke 7.31–5 implies that the ministries of John the Baptist and Jesus were contemporaneous (Dodd 1963: 290–2). His method is not satisfactory. He knows that these sayings occur in documents which do not present these ministries as contemporaneous, and that the synoptic Gospels also have sayings which imply that John the Baptist's ministry was over (he cites Mk 11.29–30, Mt 11.12 and perhaps 7–11). His method is to remove these sayings from their contexts, label this taking 'the parable, with its application, at face value', and infer from the straight comparison of the reactions of people to John the Baptist and Jesus that their ministries were contemporaneous. No saying was said or transmitted without some kind of context. There is no doubt that John the Baptist and Jesus were contemporaries, and that Jesus thought very highly of John. This is sufficient reason for the comparison. Dodd goes on to say that the placing of the saying in the Galilean ministry of Jesus 'seems clearly wrong' (Dodd 1963: 292). However, Dodd offers no justification for this. We must conclude that his whole argument consists of decontextualising the saying, and reading it in the light of a source, the fourth Gospel, which does not contain it.

Dodd infers from John 1.26 that John the Baptist's prophecy was in terms of 'the idea of the Unknown Messiah', and finds this 'necessarily presupposed' by his question at Matthew 11.2 (sic)//Luke 7.19 (Dodd 1963: 289–90). There is however no evidence that 'the idea of the Unknown Messiah' was known to anyone as early as this. John 1.26–7 does not mention the messiah. It prepares for the revelation that Jesus is the Lamb of God who takes away the sin of the world (1.29), and it is not tied closely to the subsequent mention of the messiah (cf. 1.41). John the Baptist's question at Matthew 11.3//Luke 7.19 does not mention the messiah either, for the title had not yet crystallised into usable form. It asks whether Jesus fulfils John the Baptist's expectation of a mighty disciple. Robinson also seeks to understand John the Baptist's question in the light of the fourth Gospel. He suggests that it presupposes disillusionment: 'The question, I believe, assumes rather than rules out that John had once seen in Jesus the fulfiller of his hopes' (Robinson 1985: 169). The question, however, merely presupposes uncertainty. If John the Baptist had previously seen Jesus as 'the fulfiller of his hopes', the synoptic writers would surely have said so.

THE REWRITING OF JOHN

The narrative of the fourth Gospel misses out most of the historical John the Baptist altogether, together with most of the evidence of the nature of the relationship between him and the historical Jesus. There is no threat of judgement, no baptism of Jesus by John, and no uncertain question as to whether or not Jesus is the one who is coming. The fourth Gospel has removed this, in order to present a quite misleading picture of John as an unambiguously positive witness to the Johannine Christ. It does not call John 'the Baptist' (cf. Mk 1.4; 6.14, 24, 25; 8.28; Mt 3.1, etc.; Lk 7.20, etc.; Jos. A.J. XVIII, 116); rather, it has Jesus baptise with greater success than John did (Jn 3.22–4.3). Nor is there any mention of the forgiveness of sins (Mk 1.4//Lk 3.3; cf. Mk 1.5//Mt 3.6; Jos. A.J. XVIII, 117); this is replaced by John's witness that Jesus is 'the Lamb of God who takes away the sin of the world' (Jn 1.29).

The purpose of John the Baptist's ministry is set forth in the prologue: 'He came for witness, to bear witness about the light, so that everyone might believe through him' (1.7). This function is repeated in the following verse, with the first of a number of emphatic denials: 'He was not the light, but (he came) to bear witness about the light' (1.8). Immediately after the incarnation of the Word, John's witness is given in a vigorously distorted version of his original prophecy. 'John bears witness concerning him and has cried saying, "This was he of whom I said, 'He who comes after me has become before me, because he was before me'"' (Jn 1.15). The tenses are of crucial importance here, especially 'This *was*', not 'is', 'the one of whom I said . . .'. It follows that we are looking back on the historical John the Baptist from the perspective of the church, and that we must take the tenses of the introduction quite literally – John is still bearing witness, he has cried and still does (the classical force of a Greek perfect). The explanation of this is given in verse 16: 'for we all received of his fullness, and grace instead of grace'. If we had not all received of his fullness, and the grace of the new covenant in place of the old (cf. Edwards 1988), we could not perceive John's witness carried by the church, we could perceive only mundane past events fit for disinterested report by Josephus. When we do perceive John's witness carried by the church, we can see that 1.15 is looking back on 1.30. Of John the Baptist's original historical prediction, precious little remains. Even the words 'come after me', all that does remain, have been rewritten as 'The one who comes after me', to make clear a reference to Jesus absent from the original. The words 'has become before me' are quite new and quite wrong. John the Baptist did not confess the superior status of Jesus, he was uncertain as to whether he was the fulfilment of his prophecy or not. The end of the sentence, 'because he was before me', is quite specifically Johannine, for it refers to Jesus' pre-existence. In the historic ministry, neither John the Baptist nor anyone else believed this of Jesus. Thus the prologue has fully prepared the thorough rewriting of John the Baptist which follows in the subsequent narrative.

Like the synoptics, the fourth Gospel begins its narrative of the ministry of Jesus with a piece on John, before Jesus comes on scene. Unlike the synoptic accounts, this begins with a series of denials, to a delegation of priests and Levites sent from Jerusalem by 'the Jews' (1.19), who turn out somewhat belatedly to be Pharisees (1.24). The term 'the Jews' indicates the work of the final redactor(s), who took on Gentile self-identification when members of the Johannine community were banned from Jewish meetings.[4] A delegation of priests and Levites sent from the Pharisees is not probable: the *Sitz im Leben* of the denials is in the Johannine community, not in the life of the historical John the Baptist. The first is a response to an open question, 'Who are you?' John's response is vigorously stressed with the introduction, 'And he confessed and did not deny, and confessed . . .' (1.20). Its content is simple: 'I am not the Christ' (1.20). That is not historically plausible. In Aramaic, it could equally mean, 'I am not anointed', an unlikely view of a man sent from God and too feeble to be useful. This denial presupposes later Christian development of the title Christ.[5] We have seen that, in this Gospel, Christ is a definably confessional term for Jesus. This is sufficient explanation of John's denial, whether or not there were already people who thought that John the Baptist was the messiah, as there were later (Scobie 1964: 87–95; Wink 1968: 99–105).

Dodd argued on the basis of Luke 3.15f. and Acts 13.24–5 that the fourth evangelist was using earlier tradition (Dodd 1963: 256–9). This is possible, but Dodd's discussion misses the main point. We know that the Johannine community rewrote traditions which they received, and we know that they created new material. This denial is certainly secondary. It is no less secondary for the plausible hypothesis that the final redactor was following earlier tradition. Dodd concludes that there is 'no difficulty in finding an early *Sitz im Leben* for such a tradition as I have inferred'. Neither Luke 3.15 nor Acts 13.24–5 is early. Nothing in Dodd's argument implies an origin before 70CE, and the dogmatic structure of the Johannine account gives it an excellent *Sitz im Leben* where it is. We must beware of this shift from 'the fourth evangelist' through 'earlier tradition' to 'early'.

The next denial is equally remarkable. 'And they asked him, "What then? Are you Elijah?" And he said, "I am not"' (1.21). This explicitly disagrees with Jesus' estimate of him, implied both in Mark (9.13, cf. Mt 11.14; 17.12–13) and in Q (Mt 11.10//Lk 7.27). It is not probable that Jesus and John differed so radically in their estimates of him. When the fourth Gospel was written, however, John the Baptist could not be seen fulfilling the prophecy of Elijah coming before the day of the Lord (Mal 3.23–4), for the day of the Lord had obviously not come. The *Sitz im Leben* of this denial is therefore in the Johannine community, and coherent with its rejection of Jesus' preaching of the imminent coming of the kingdom.[6] The third denial is not very convincing as an historical statement either: 'Are you the prophet? And he said, "No."' This must be a reference to the prophet predicted at Deuteronomy 18.15, 18 (cf. Jn 6.14; 7.40; Acts 3.22; 7.37; 1QS IX, 11). But it is not made with clarity, and Aramaic has no separate definite article, so that the question אנת הוא נביא does not clearly mean more than 'Are you a prophet?' John the Baptist is not likely to have answered this question with such a clear denial.

John is next presented as putting himself in his real place, identifying himself as the voice of Isaiah 40.3. This text is applied to him in the synoptic Gospels (Mk 1.3//Mt 3.3//Lk 3.4): the function of attributing the use of it to John himself is to ensure that he personally defines and limits his role to that of being a forerunner of Jesus. Dodd argued that 'the Fourth Evangelist may have followed a good tradition in representing him as citing Isa. xl.3 to define his own mission, and in this he may be closer to the facts than the Synoptics' (Dodd 1963: 252–3). Dodd gave two reasons for this judgement. Firstly, the fourth Gospel is not dependent on the other Gospels for its other Old Testament quotations. This is true, but not enough. This quotation is not identical with any of the synoptic versions. It differs from LXX only in using the word 'make straight' (*euthunate*), which is attributed to Aquila's translation of this verse. This may well have been preferred to 'prepare' (LXX *hetoimasate*), because it is easier to reconcile with his presentation of the ministries of John and Jesus as contemporaneous (cf. Menken 1985; Schuchard 1992: 1–15). We must infer that, if the fourth Gospel used Mark or something very like it, he used his own version of the quotation. This may have come from a testimonium, but that does nothing to make the attribution to John himself correct, especially since the exact form fits the fourth evangelist's needs so well.

Dodd's second point is that the attribution to John himself is culturally plausible, especially in the light of the use of Isaiah 40.3 at 1QS VIII, 13–16. That is true, but not sufficient, not least because such use of scripture was just as natural to the Johannine community as to John the Baptist. But what is completely wrong about Dodd's argument is the lack of any sense of proportion in its conclusion: 'may be closer to the facts than the Synoptics'. We have seen that the setting and most of the contents of this scene are secondary. Even if the Johannine community had had access to a separate tradition, and had picked up a true fact about John the Baptist's application of scripture to himself, its presentation of this little fact would still be quite misleading because of its secondary context.

In response to the question as to why he baptises, John has another version of the original prophecy of Mark 1.7–8//Matthew 3.11–12//Luke

3.16–17. This has been rewritten down to the last detail. Two changes are especially important. 'Among you stands one whom you do not know' implies that there is a defined figure who is already known to John the Baptist. The reference to him, 'the one who comes after me', likewise indicates a definite figure. These two changes prepare the way for John's revelation that Jesus is that person, as God himself had revealed. They are further evidence that the Johannine account is secondary, for we can easily explain why these changes should be made to an account something like that of Mark. The synoptics, however, faced with the Johannine version, would not have had reason to change it. This applies also to Mark's aorist *ebaptisa*, literally 'I baptised', a literal rendering of a generalising Aramaic perfect tense, properly changed to the decent Greek present *baptizō*, 'I baptise', by Matthew and Luke, possibly both transmitting Q, and by the fourth evangelist, who also removes 'you' from a saying now addressed to a delegation of priests and Levites rather than to the people.

Dodd argued that the fourth evangelist was following a special line of tradition (Dodd 1963: 253–6). He constructed a very strong argument of cumulative weight, and it is important to note how little he proved. For example, like Q, but not verbally identical to either Matthew 3.11 or Luke 3.16, John 1.26 has 'I baptise in water' before the prophecy of the coming one: it does follow that what the fourth evangelist rewrote was not, or not only, Mark. But the central point is that the Johannine community rewrote their traditions for theological reasons, and thereby produced a wholly misleading picture of John the Baptist, as of much else. This is important, whereas to conjecture exactly what the final redactor rewrote is merely entertaining. Like John 1.27, Matthew 3.11 has the words 'he who comes after me' as if they refer to a definite person who will be coming next: like Acts 13.25, John 1.26–7 does not use the word 'stronger'. It is possible that the fourth evangelist inherited a version of these sayings in which these two changes had already taken place, and it makes no difference to any of the main points.

The passage ends by locating the incident at Bethany beyond the Jordan, a place which we cannot locate. Origen was already unable to find it, though it was the name read by Heracleon and nearly all the manuscripts which Origen knew (*On the Gospel According to John* VI, XL, 204–7). Carson takes up the suggestion that John meant Batanea, which is hardly what the text says, though it may be considered a possible source of confusion (Carson 1991: 146–7). Morris regards this verse as evidence of the evangelist's topographical knowledge (Morris 1969: 228), but we cannot verify the notion that he was knowledgeable rather than mistaken when we do not know the place. We must conclude that the fourth Gospel is probably mistaken. The arguments of both Morris and Carson depend on their conviction that holy scripture is literally true, whether it is to be believed (Morris) or altered without noticing (Carson).

There follows the main exposition of the witness of John the Baptist to Jesus, a passage which is almost entirely secondary. When John the Baptist sees Jesus, he declares, 'Behold! the Lamb of God who takes away the sin of the world' (Jn 1.29). This is not just atonement theology which is absent from the preaching of the historical John the Baptist: it also has the shift in covenantal nomism characteristic of the fourth Gospel, in that salvation is achieved for 'the world', not for faithful Jews. This is a central matter, far more important than the considerations advanced by Dodd in arguing that it comes from early tradition (Dodd 1963: 269–71).

Dodd's argument begins with an error of method. He describes the title 'Lamb' as 'strange to the Fourth Gospel', and concludes at once that there is 'no *prima facie* probability that we are dealing with a pure piece of Johannine theology'. The function of John the Baptist's witness is however important to the fourth Gospel, which has rewritten him to make him witness to Jesus, and for which the salvation of 'the world' is quite central. For this purpose, the fourth evangelist has replacement theology running through his Gospel from beginning to end.[7] For example, he replaces Tabernacles. The water symbolism leads Jesus to call the thirsty to *him* to drink (7.37), and the light symbolism has him set off a discourse 'I am the light of the world' (8.12). Moreover, we are supposed to *know* that water and light were central to Tabernacles, without being told. We are also supposed to know that the sacrificial system was central to Judaism. The community sacrifices were paid for by the Temple tax, which was contributed by adult male Jews, both in Israel and throughout the diaspora, and the purpose of the whole could be described as to make atonement (Ex 30.15–16). The selection of a lamb to symbolise the replacement of the sacrificial system will be due primarily to the Tamid, the continual offering of a lamb every morning and evening, the symbol of God's presence with Israel (Ex 29.38–46, cf. Dan 8.11–14). At least 50 per cent of the Passover victims were also lambs, and we have seen that their replacement by Jesus was so important to the Johannine community that it caused the chronology of the Passion to be changed.[8] Isaiah 53.4 and 53.7 may also have been influential, as well as the ram sacrificed by Abraham in place of Isaac. Many sacrifices were held to bring about atonement for sin. The fourth Gospel's word for 'lamb', *amnos*, is that of the basic regulations for the Tamid at LXX Exodus 29.38–41. It is therefore a very suitable word to symbolise the replacement of the sacrificial system by Jesus. Dodd's description has missed the wood for the trees.

Dodd proceeds to declare 'with certainty' that the fourth evangelist 'regarded it as a messianic title', quoting 1.41. This is not the case. The messiahship of Jesus was an identity factor of the Johannine community, and this is what is presented at 1.41. The preceding declarations of 1.29 and 1.36 establish 'Lamb (of God)' as a title of Jesus in the fourth Gospel, but they do nothing to establish it as a messianic title which was inherited. On the contrary, it first appears in this creative production of replacement theology. Dodd further argues that 'who takes away the sin of the world' (1.29) 'does not readily derive from the general theology of the Fourth Gospel, which offers no parallel'. Yet he knows and mentions 1 John 3.5, where 'you know that he was revealed, to take away sins'. Dodd may declare that this is 'not the same thing', but it establishes the removal of sin viewed as a main point of Jesus' ministry in the Johannine community. There are further indications of this in the Gospel. In Chapter 8, people who do not believe in Jesus will die in their sins (8.24), whereas the Son will set them free (8.36). He can hardly not take away their sins. A similar view of sin permeates the discourse of Chapter 9, and at 20.22–3 Jesus passes on the power to forgive or retain sins to the disciples. We should infer that 1.29 is programmatic, and does not need to be literally repeated. Dodd's method is horrendous. He knows we are dealing with a creative theologian, yet his criteria of judgement are such that, if the fourth evangelist does not repeat himself rather exactly, Dodd will infer that his comments come from earlier tradition.

Finally, Dodd invokes an apocalyptic lamb (Dodd 1953: 230–8; 1963: 270; Sandy 1991). Apocalyptic is not the most obvious *Sitz im Leben* for Johannine theology, and an apocalyptic lamb cannot be shown to have existed outside the creative symbolism of the book of Revelation, which uses a different word for 'lamb' (*arnion*), and is surely not a source for the fourth Gospel's symbolism. Dodd appeals to 1 Enoch 89–90 and T. Jos. 19.8. But 1 Enoch 89–90 is part of a massive animal apocalypse in which sheep symbolise various people, including the people of Israel, Moses, Aaron and Elijah. David becomes a ram and Judas Maccabaeus is represented as one of umpteen lambs, one which grows a big horn, but it is not clear that the messiah becomes a lamb at all. This is not sufficient to give rise to the independent symbolism of 'lamb' = Messiah. T. Jos. 19.8 really does refer to the messiah, indeed it refers to Jesus, for it belongs to a Christian recension, and its 'spotless lamb' who was born of a virgin was not part of a tradition which either John the Baptist or the fourth evangelist could use. If there had been an apocalyptic tradition, however, it would have been altogether more plausible if it were the work of John the Baptist himself, and that is how Dodd ends his argument. This is not convincing either, not least because the apocalyptic tradition has not been shown to exist. It has been taken up by Beasley-Murray, whose argument is heavily dependent on the book of Revelation.[9] The book of Revelation is however too apocalyptic to serve as a source for the fourth Gospel, which uses a different word for 'lamb', and it is too late in date to have served as a source for John the Baptist. None of John the Baptist's work shows signs of the imagery of the animal apocalypses, and 'the world' is used in the sense particular to the fourth Gospel and following from the successful Gentile mission. It does not have a satisfactory *Sitz im Leben* in the mission of John the Baptist at all.

We must reject Dodd's methods, as well as his conclusions. No creative theologian should be judged dependent on an unknown source merely because he does not repeat himself. A clear declaration like that of John 1.29 must lead us to seek its *Sitz im Leben* in the universe of the fourth Gospel, not to search Judaism for one which did not exist and does not fit. Apocalyptic symbolism must be seen as such: single items cannot be isolated from complex apocalypses as if they must have enjoyed an independent existence. Such methods cannot be used to attribute a Johannine concept such as 'the world' to John the Baptist, whose preaching as extant in the synoptic Gospels and Josephus shows no concern with the salvation of Gentiles.[10]

The identification of Jesus as 'the Lamb of God' is followed by a third rewriting of John the Baptist's original prediction. 'This is he of whom I said, "After me comes a man who has become before me, because he was before me"'(1.30). All that is left of the original prediction is 'After me comes', to be followed by 'baptize in water' (1.31, 33) and 'baptize in holy spirit' (1.33). Compared with the rewriting of John 1.15, we have 'This *is*', rather than 'This *was*', appropriately for the moment of identification. The words 'I said' point back to 'the one who comes after me' of 1.27. Otherwise, the saying has again been rewritten in terms of Johannine Christology. Jesus is presented as pre-existent, and this is given as the reason for his being superior in status to John the Baptist.

The rewritten John the Baptist goes on to declare that the very purpose of his baptising ministry was 'so that he [sc. Jesus, the Lamb of God] might be revealed to Israel' (1.31). Then we have the replacement of John's baptism of Jesus with John's witness to Jesus. He explains that he has seen the Spirit descend on Jesus, and he claims divine authority for his identification:

> I have seen the Spirit descending like a dove from heaven, and it remained on him. And I used not to know him, but he who sent me to baptise in water said to me, 'The one on whom you see the Spirit descending and remaining on him, he is the one who baptises with holy spirit'.
>
> (1.32–3)

This not only omits Jesus' baptism by John and the vigorous prediction of baptism 'with holy spirit and fire' found in Q (Mt 3.11–12//Lk 3.16–17). It makes John the Baptist have no doubts because he has been personally informed of the identification by God himself.

To explain the omission of Jesus' baptism we must recall that the Johannine community was in severe dispute with 'the Jews'.[11] What might 'the Jews' make of, say, Mark's account? Firstly, it was a 'baptism of repentance' (Mk 1.4), so Jesus repented because he was a sinner (cf. e.g. Mk 3.22; Jn 9.24; 10.20). Secondly, John the Baptist was superior to Jesus. Thirdly, they could argue that Jesus was not the stronger one whose sandals

John the Baptist was unworthy to unloose, for he had not baptised anyone with holy spirit. If the argument were conducted on these terms, the Johannine community could hardly win it. Hence the omission of the event in the fourth Gospel's rewriting. We have noted also that Mark's account does not indicate that John the Baptist saw anything.[12] 'The Jews' would surely notice this, and deny that Jesus really received the holy spirit. This is met by the assertion that John the Baptist saw the Spirit not only descend on Jesus, but also remain on him. Finally, John the Baptist claims a direct revelation from God, who told him that he could identify 'he who baptises in holy spirit' (1.33, cf. Mk 1.8//Mt 3.11//Lk 3.16) by the fact that he saw the Spirit descend and remain on him.

John's witness concludes for the time being, 'And I myself have seen and have born witness that this is the chosen one of God' (Jn 1.34). That is a category which any Jew could accept. It probably indicates fulfilment of Isaiah 42.1, where God puts his spirit on his chosen (cf. also Mk 1.11//Mt 3.17//Lk 3.22).[13] There is also a mass of Old Testament references to the place chosen by God for the people to go to sacrifice (e.g. Deut 12.5–7, 11, 13–14). Jesus replaces the sacrificial system (Jn 1.29) and the Temple (Jn 2.13–22), and Jerusalem is becoming redundant (Jn 4.20–4). The evangelist had therefore good reason to regard 'the chosen one of God' as a suitable term to close this stage of the revelation to Israel (cf. 1.31), before moving on to 'messiah' (1.41) and 'Son of God' (1.49). Once revealed as 'the chosen one of God', Jesus accepts the disciples whom he has chosen (1.35ff., in the light of 6.70; 13.18; 15.16, 19).

The day after his first clear witness to Jesus, John repeats one of his comments in front of two of his disciples, declaring 'Look! The Lamb of God' (1.36). This leads them to follow Jesus at once. One of them is identified as Andrew, and he is already sufficiently convinced to go and tell his brother, 'We have found the Messiah', which is interpreted as 'Christ' (1.41). The title is again implausible as an historically accurate comment. It has its *Sitz im Leben* in the fourth Gospel, where 'Christ' is a major confessional term.[14] Andrew takes Simon his brother to Jesus, who at once names him Cephas, which is rendered into Greek as Peter. The close involvement of John the Baptist in the call of some of the twelve, including no less than Peter, was unknown to the synoptic writers. It is therefore unlikely to be historical. The Johannine form of it is certainly unhistorical because of the witness expressed both by John and by Andrew. We should infer that the stories of the calling of these disciples have been rewritten to ensure that John again makes it clear that it is Jesus, not he, who is now to be followed.

The inconsistency between the Johannine and synoptic narratives has often been noticed. Conservative scholars propose to believe both. Morris argues that 'The Fourth Gospel tells of a call to be disciples; the Synoptists of a call to be Apostles' (Morris 1971: 155). This is not true. Mark records the call 'Come after me' (1.17, cf. 1.20), a literal translation of Jesus' Aramaic call to Simon and Andrew to be his disciples (Mk 2.14 has the more idiomatic Greek 'follow'). Only at Mark 3.14 does Jesus call the twelve 'so that he might send them out', the act which made them apostles, and caused both Matthew and Luke to use this term (Mt 10.2; Lk 6.13). Nor does this take account of the other arguments for regarding the Johannine version as secondary. Morris correctly records that, in the Johannine account, the first four are not strictly called, but this is because the incident has been rewritten to make John the Baptist's witness the first important point. At no point does Morris's harmonising argument explain why Mark and Matthew have one story, and John has the other. Carson argues that the synoptic call 'is psychologically and historically more plausible if that was not their first exposure to him or their first demonstration of fealty toward him' (Carson 1991: 154). This is true, but it does not follow that the later Johannine account accurately relates an earlier occasion.

Dodd put forward decisive arguments for supposing that Jesus' naming Simon 'Cephas' is an old tradition 'either in Aramaic or very closely related to the Aramaic tradition of the Church's earliest days' (Dodd 1963: 306–9). It is important to recognise the limited significance of this finding. At one level Mark 3.16 supports it; its tradition that Jesus called Simon 'Peter' is merely the Greek translation of him being called *Kepha*, the Aramaic for 'rock', generally Anglicised via Greek as 'Cephas'. However, the evidence of Paul shows that 'Cephas' was in use among Greek-speaking Christians who knew him and so referred to him (1 Cor 1.12; 3.22; 9.5; 15.5; Gal 1.18; 2.9, 11, 14). It is therefore entirely plausible that the tradition of Jesus naming him 'Cephas' was handed down separately from other Gospel traditions. Moreover, the truth of this tradition must be considered in the light of other arguments for the secondary nature of most of this passage. Dodd has merely isolated one of the old traditions which the Johannine community rewrote, and his work should not be used as if it implied the general accuracy of Johannine traditions.

There has also been vigorous rewriting in the passage which finally puts John's witness in its place (3.22–36). This has Jesus baptising (3.22, 26), which is quite remarkable in itself, and is omitted both from the synoptics and from the subsequent Johannine narrative (cf. 4.1–2, which highlights the muddle by first having Jesus baptise more people than John, and then declaring that it was really Jesus' disciples who did the baptising, not Jesus at all). The notion that Jesus baptised should have been attractive to the authors of all four Gospels and of Acts, since it could so obviously be the foundation of Christian baptism. We should infer that this is not a piece of historically correct information, but a setting invented for the witness of John, that Jesus was greater than himself.

Murphy O'Connor is notable among scholars who have recently sought to defend the historicity of Jesus baptising (Murphy O'Connor 1990: 363–6; likewise Hollenbach 1982: 204–7; France 1994: 105–7). His account is marked by colourfully definite descriptions: we should not generally accept his view of what is 'obvious', 'blatant' or 'facile', let alone 'fact'. He begins with the blunt assertion that 'After this' (3.22) is an 'obvious redactional seam', arguing that Jesus has come from Peraea, and giving this as the reason for his coming 'into Judaean territory'. He labels the interpretation of *eis tēn Ioudaian gēn* as meaning 'into the Judaean countryside', from Jerusalem, 'blatant harmonization'. Most of this is altogether uncertain, and 'blatant harmonization' is a quite inaccurate description of scholarly efforts to interpret a document in terms of its author's intentions. The author has had Jesus expound to a 'ruler of the Jews' (Jn 3.1) the need for rebirth 'by water and spirit': he is quite capable of having Jesus come 'into the Judaean countryside' so that he can baptise successfully and put John the Baptist in his place, ready for Jesus' rejection by his own (cf. 1.11; 3.32, 36; 4.44–5). This is not sufficient to show that he used a source, still less that the supposed source was right. Murphy O'Connor supports his view that the source saw Jesus coming from Peraea with the reference to Peraea in 3.26, but this surely refers to the unhistorical scene of John the Baptist and Jesus at John 1.19–42.

Murphy O'Connor proceeds to declare that the words 'he remained there with them' (3.22) 'counteract the opinion (cf. John 4.2) that the visit was brief, and the personal involvement of Jesus insignificant', and that 3.24 confirms this 'concern for the accuracy of the historical record'. The first of these points overinterprets the setting, and the second is circular. John 3.24 does deliberately contradict the synoptic tradition, but that does not ensure that 'accuracy' is the centre of the concern of an author so much of whose work is historically inaccurate. Murphy O'Connor also has 3.24 make it clear that the 'baptising ministry of Jesus . . . was both prior to, and distinct from, that carried out by Jesus in Galilee at a later date' (Murphy O'Connor 1990: 363). It is here that Murphy O'Connor's creative writing leaves the ground, for no such ministry is reported in any Gospel. He has Jesus return to Galilee (Jn 4.1–3), and since this move was inspired by the news of John's arrest (Mk 1.14; Mt 4.12), surely a piece of blatant harmonising, he infers that Jesus was carrying on John the Baptist's ministry (Murphy O'Connor 1990: 371). This is not however in accord with our primary evidence at all. Murphy O'Connor has this confirmed by Herod's verdict that Jesus was John the Baptist *redivivus* (Mk 6.14; Mt 14.2). Dismissing the reasons given by Mark, Murphy O'Connor then supposes that this was because Jesus was baptising. Murphy O'Connor's method, which combines hypercritical rejection of primary source material with creative invention, could never obtain correct historical results.

Dodd offers a vigorous defence of the historicity of the dispute between the disciples of John and a Jew reported at John 3.25 (Dodd 1963: 280–1). Its basis is however merely that Dodd cannot see any connection with the following dialogue, so that it looks like 'the remnant of an introduction to a dialogue which has not been preserved'. Dodd's argument is remote from the concerns of the fourth Gospel. All it needs is a plausible setting for the following dialogue. A dispute with a Jew is enough to send John's disciples to him with the vital information that Jesus is baptising and everyone is going to him. 'Cleansing' is a reasonable thing to argue about, in the first place because it was known to be a major concern of Jews (cf. Jn 2.6). It is moreover obvious that baptism in water cleanses in one sense or another. Jesus made his disciples clean by washing their feet, except for Judas Iscariot (Jn 13.10–11), and by his word (Jn 15.3). In the similar world of 1 John, Jesus' death cleanses Christians from all sin (1 Jn 1.7–9). In Johannine terms, therefore, a dispute about cleansing is an excellent start to the shift from a Jew to disciples of John to John to Jesus himself.

John's disciples inform him that Jesus 'is baptising, and everyone is going to him' (3.26). John implies the heavenly origin of Jesus' ministry (3.27), and then recalls his earlier witness: 'You yourselves bear me witness that I said I am not the Christ, but that I have been sent before him' (3.28). This looks back to the denial of 1.20, which we have seen is not historically accurate in the first place,[15] and summarises the role which John is said to have taken up for himself in 1.23ff. He proceeds to summarise the whole point of his ministry being presented as overlapping with that of Jesus: 'He must increase, but I must decrease' (3.30). We are in a different world from the uncertain question of Matthew 11.2–3//Luke 7.18–19!

Several scholars have defended the antiquity of 3.29. It is indeed possible that this is an old parable which has been rewritten, though this is less obvious than is sometimes thought. It can be set out in parallel lines, but anyone half as familiar with the Old Testament as the fourth evangelist could write in parallel lines if they wanted to. Plays on words in Aramaic have been suggested (cf. Black 1967: 147; Manns 1991: 59–60), but these do not exceed those which an Aramaist can produce from many texts in other languages. Dodd notes the Johannine nature of the end of the verse (Dodd 1963: 282). All we actually know is that this discourse is secondary. It may have been formed by rewriting some older material in the same way that we know that some synoptic material was rewritten, possibly even by cogitating on something like Mark 2.18–20 (Brodie 1993b: 77–8). This is not however as important as the demonstrable fact that the result is a secondary discourse.

John 3.31–6 has more typically Johannine theology, so much so that many commentators have wanted to move it, while others consider it a comment by the evangelist. The main points have now been seen by Rensberger, who comments,

> The closing verses of John 3 make excellent sense in their present context as a summons to the disciples of John the Baptist to accept Jesus as the Son of God into whose hands the Father has given all things, so that in this faith in him they too may have eternal life.
>
> (Rensberger 1988: 58–9; cf. Wilson 1981; Van Tilborg 1993: 70–7)

This is the reason why John sounds as if he could be Jesus speaking elsewhere in the Gospel. He is intended to, and the lack of stage directions at 3.31 should be taken literally – the rest of the chapter continues John's speech. The chapter has begun with the concept of rebirth which distinguishes Christianity from Judaism, and which is presented in the wholly secondary debate which begins with Nicodemus.[16] At 3.16–21, it has moved to its central point, a presentation of salvation as found in Christianity. The reintroduction of John the Baptist puts in its place his baptism in water only, now to be replaced by Christian baptism by water and the spirit. When John's baptism has been put in its place, he confesses to more and more Johannine theology. The end of the chapter is accordingly as secure in its Johannine place as it is historically secondary. So far from being any kind of rival to Jesus, John the Baptist concludes with the central point of his witness to the light: 'He who believes in the Son has eternal life, but he who does not believe in the Son will not see life, but the wrath of God remains on him' (3.36). What a tiny, distorted, fragment of the prophet of judgement remains at the end!

There are two further passages in which the fourth Gospel puts John the Baptist in his place. At 5.33–6, Jesus himself comments on him. He first of all recalls the unhistorical report of the mission of 'the Jews' to him, at 1.20–8, and his comment 'and he bore witness to the truth' is a Johannine summary of John's function. At 5.34, Jesus says that he does not need the witness of a man, but he recalls it for their salvation. This again underlines John's function, as 5.35 does metaphorically. Finally, 5.36 declares that Jesus' works are a greater witness than that of John. We have seen that the presentation of Jesus' works as reflecting his deity has resulted from secondary rewriting of the tradition.[17] As with the picture of John the Baptist as a whole, this brief report of Jesus' verdict on him has two significant features. It is not historically accurate, and Jesus' actual verdict on John the Baptist has been omitted. We do not read here of 'a prophet . . . and more than a prophet' (Mt 11.9//Lk 7.26). John the Baptist's function is wholly centred on Jesus, and it is secondary. The verdict of 'many' at 10.40–2 also shows the function of John the Baptist's witness as for the salvation of others. They declare, 'John did no sign, but everything which John said about this man [sc. Jesus] was true'. So 'many believed in him [sc. Jesus] there'. Yet the theology of the signs is secondary, and John the Baptist said virtually nothing that the fourth Gospel has attributed to him. What a complex of secondary material this is, so directly dependent on what was not said! Moreover, with 5.34 showing John's witness as not really necessary, and 10.41 declaring that he did no sign, both passages dismiss John as a figure not remotely comparable to Jesus.

CONCLUSIONS

The following conclusions must therefore be drawn. The Johannine community inherited some correct tradition about John the Baptist. In the fourth Gospel, however, this figure has been completely rewritten. The purpose of this rewriting was to make John witness with clarity that Jesus was chosen by God to be the central salvation figure. For this purpose, words are put into his mouth which John the Baptist did not say, and Jesus is portrayed as baptising. Most of the historical John the Baptist has been omitted, including his doubts about whether Jesus was the figure whose coming he had prophesied. Here again, therefore, this Gospel is quite centrally misleading. It is not just that new features have been added to the picture of John the Baptist: he has been rewritten to make him a different kind of figure. This rewriting has been done in accordance with the needs of the Johannine community. It is for their sake that John is portrayed as bearing unambiguous witness to Jesus, pre-existent, the messiah, the Son, the Lamb of God who takes away the sin of the world. Though not as prominent as in this Gospel's Christology and chronology, the dispute with 'the Jews' also lies behind this development. It is probably responsible for the omission of Jesus being baptised by John: John's rewritten witness certainly contains Christological elements which faithful members of the Jewish community could not accept. Hence this historically inaccurate picture is theologically coherent.

5

WORDS: CONTENT
AND STYLE

INTRODUCTION

The traditional view of the authorship of the fourth Gospel has it written by the same person as the Johannine epistles. This view may reasonably be excluded on stylistic grounds,[1] but the connections are important for us in a different way. Given that much of the information in the fourth Gospel is historically inaccurate, we must ask where it came from. The Johannine epistles are a significant piece of evidence. They show that some people believed in Johannine theology, and wrote it down in a way generally similar to some of the fourth Gospel's discourses. This is partly how we know that secondary material in the Gospel is the theology of the Johannine community, secondarily attributed to Jesus.

The style of the Gospel is of more direct historical significance, because Jesus' style is different from that of the words attributed to him in the synoptic Gospels. These differences are so extreme that both cannot be right. Moreover, the actual words which the fourth Gospel uses show more fundamental differences than those of authorship. They show that concepts and even activities have been altered to provide the Johannine portrait. On the other hand, there is some evidence of the influence of Aramaic, the language which Jesus spoke. We must assess this, to see whether the language of the fourth Gospel provides evidence that its traditions are older than we might otherwise imagine.

THE FOURTH GOSPEL AND THE SYNOPTICS

One purely stylistic point is of direct historical significance. In the fourth Gospel, Jesus expounds most of his teaching in connected theological discourses. These may be interrupted by other people. Their interruptions are largely functional – however unintelligent the questions, they enable the discourse to proceed, often asking about the next point to be expounded. For example, John 3 begins with a vigorous statement of the necessity for rebirth. Nicodemus' first two questions express incredulity, not least by taking the idea of rebirth so literally as to suggest going back into the womb (3.4). The function of this is to lead to a lengthier exposition by Jesus, mentioning water and stressing the role of the spirit. Nicodemus' next question is more general, 'How can this be?' (3.9). This leads Jesus to a more complex theological exposition, explaining the central role of his death in the salvation of the world.

In these respects, John 3 is representative of Johannine style as a whole. There are no genuinely similar discourses in the synoptics. The longest expositions are Mark 13//Matthew 24//Luke 21, and the Sermon on the Mount (Mt 5–7). Both are complexes of small pieces of material. Mark 13 does have a question from four of the twelve (13.3–4), but that directly gets the discourse going, and they take no further part. Neither discourse is comparable to Johannine exposition. As so often, it is the absence of Johannine material from the synoptics that makes its historicity so unlikely. When we recall how much of the contents are likewise not found in the synoptics, a very strong argument of cumulative weight has been formed. Nor is this all. Some of the Johannine narrative is also expository. John the Baptist has similar theological exposition attributed to him at John 1.29–34 and John 3.27–30. When considering John 3.31–6, scholars have found it difficult to be sure whether he continues, or whether the author himself has taken over with his own comments. This is because the comments attributed to John the Baptist are also quite Johannine.[2] When we turn to 1 John, we find more theological exposition of the same kind. This concludes another decisive argument of cumulative weight. The Johannine discourses were written by one or more theologians: they are not correct reports of the Jesus of history.

Style may be further classified by means of vocabulary. This is the point at which it overlaps with content. It is not that Jesus' authentic speeches have been rewritten, as Tacitus rewrote a speech of Claudius, altering the style and reorganising the piece, but keeping the main arguments.[3] The vocabulary measures significant differences of content too, and the complete picture adds up to a significant distortion of the life and teaching of Jesus. We may begin with some words which are common in the synoptics, but rare in, or absent from, the fourth Gospel.[4] (See Table 1)

Some of these figures measure style, but for the most part they measure content too, and in many cases this means that the fourth Gospel has omitted something which was important in Jesus' ministry. The kingdom of God was the central concept of his teaching. It has been virtually removed, and of the five remaining instances, two are associated with the Hellenistic concept of rebirth and the change in covenantal nomism (Jn 3.3, 5), and in the others Jesus discusses 'my kingdom' in terms equally absent from the synoptics (18.36). There were two strong reasons for removing the central concept of Jesus' teaching. Firstly, Jesus predicted that the kingdom would come very shortly, and his prediction was false (Casey 1991a: 58–9, 168, 170–4).

Table 1 Synoptic words

	English translation	Matthew	Mark	Luke	John	1 John
ἁμαρτωλοί	sinners	5	5	10	1	0
ἄρχομαι	begin	13	24	31	1	0
βασιλεία	kingdom	57	20	46	5	0
γραμματεύς	scribe	23	21	14	0	0
δαιμόνιον	demon	10	10	23	6	0
δύναμις	power	12	10	15	0	0
καλέω	call	26	4	43	2	1
κηρύσσω	preach	9	12	9	0	0
λαός	people	14	3	36	2	0
μετανοέω	repent	5	2	9	0	0
μετάνοια	repentance	2	1	5	0	0
παραβολή	parable	17	13	18	0	0
πρεσβύτερος	elder	12	7	5	0	0
προσεύχομαι	pray	15	11	19	0	0
τελώνης	tax collector	8	3	10	0	0
ὑπό + genitive	by	23	8	24	1	0

We can see this causing trouble for Luke. Mark correctly reported that Jesus went into Galilee, preaching that 'the time has been fulfilled and the kingdom of God is at hand' (Mk 1.14–15). Luke has him return to Galilee, 'and he taught in their synagogues, being glorified by all' (Lk 4.14–15). Jesus' prediction has thus been removed. Mark reports Jesus' prediction, 'there are some of those standing here who shall not taste death until they see the kingdom of God come in power' (Mk 9.1). Luke drops the words 'in power', and edits the beginning of the following narrative of the Transfiguration, 'Now it came to pass about eight days after these words' (Lk 9.27–8). Hence we can imagine the kingship of God displayed in the Transfiguration, instead of its final establishment. Acts begins with a story in which the apostles ask the risen Jesus whether he will restore the kingdom to Israel 'at this time'. He tells them it is not for them to know the times or seasons set by the Father, and they are to go on mission instead (Acts 1.6–8). The Johannine community had the same problem, and they had 'the Jews' to make capital out of it! The Jewish community could hardly help reading past the prophet predicted at Deuteronomy 18.15 and 18.18, a prediction supposedly fulfilled by Jesus (Jn 6.14; 7.40; Acts 3.22; 7.37), not by John the Baptist (Jn 1.21). There they found that

> the prophet who presumes to speak a word in my name which I have not commanded him to speak . . . that prophet shall die. . . . When the prophet speaks in the name of the Lord and the word does not happen and come to pass, that is the word which the Lord did not speak.
>
> (Deut 18.20–2)

The authentic teaching of the Jesus of history will surely have led to a charge of false prophecy. It was not generally suitable for Johannine exposition. Hence its omission, and the drastic transmutation of John 3.3 and 3.5.

A second problem lay in Jesus' crucifixion. This was the most severe punishment meted out by the Roman state. Bandits were always liable to be crucified, if they could be captured (cf. Horsley and Hanson 1985; Horsley 1987; Crossan 1991: Chapter 9). Jesus was crucified as a bandit, between two other bandits. His offence, written on his cross, was to have been 'king of the Jews' (Mk 15.26–7). By this, Pilate will have meant that he was a guerrilla leader, like Athronges and others (Jos. B.J. II, 60–5; A.J. XVII, 278–84). One possible interpretation of Jesus' preaching that the kingdom of God was at hand was that the Jews would shortly revolt and throw off the Roman yoke. Hostile Jews in Ephesus could interpret Jesus' ministry in this way. This was a second reason to drop Jesus' genuine preaching of the kingdom of God, and offer the drastic transmutation of John 18.36, 'my kingdom is not of this world'.

Jesus preached the coming of the kingdom, and with it the need for repentance. The words 'preach', 'repent' and 'repentance' have all gone from the fourth Gospel. The removal of the word 'parable' is also drastic, for parables were a characteristic feature of Jesus' teaching. The disappearance of the word illustrates the virtual disappearance of the reality. Jesus no longer teaches in the same way as in the synoptics. Many parables were about the kingdom of God, and others had proved difficult to understand when separated from their original environment (cf. Mk 4.10–20). Others, again, are quite long stories. A perceived need for concentrated theological exposition has controlled their general replacement. A few short parable-like sayings have been integrated into the expositions (e.g. Jn 3.29; 12.24). The method, however, and associated content, have gone.

Exorcisms were central to Jesus' ministry. By this means, he offered salvation from the devil (Lk 13.10–17). This was the real source of his view that healing is right on the sabbath (Mk 3.1–6). It was so important that the twelve were sent out to do it too (Mk 3.14–15). When they were unable to carry out a particularly difficult exorcism, Jesus did so (Mk 9.14–29). He was so effective that exorcism in his name could be done by people who did not belong to the Jesus movement (Mk 9.38–9). Here again, the Johannine community had 'the Jews' to contend with. Mark tells us that scribes who came down from Jerusalem accused Jesus of casting out demons by Beelzebub, the ruler of the demons (Mk 3.22). Authentic sayings from this dispute are recorded in both Mark and Q (Mk 3.22–30; Mt 12.24–32; Lk 11.15–23). The same dispute is reflected in later sources (Justin, *Trypho* 69; bT San. 43a). We must infer that 'the Jews' made a meal of this accusation too. The fourth Gospel has transmuted it into little more than an accusation of madness (cf. Jn 7.20; 8.48–52; 10.20–1, which account for all six Johannine occurrences of *daimonion*, 'demon'). The final example is part of a passage in which Jesus replaces the feast of Hanukkah, and this takes up the tradition that Antiochus IV Epiphanes was mad.[5] The accusation has been downgraded to the point where it could be coped with theologically. We must infer that 'the Jews' effectively won the arguments about exorcism, and caused it to be expunged from the historical record.

Similar reasons will have caused the removal of *telōnēs*, 'tax collector', and the almost complete removal of *hamartōloi*, 'sinners'. Criticism of Jesus for his association with tax collectors and sinners is found in Mark and Q (cf. Mk 2.16//Mt 9.11//Lk 5.30; Mt 11.18–9//Lk 7.33). We must infer that it was taken up vigorously by 'the Jews', and that the fourth Gospel preferred to drop the matter rather than defend Jesus' practice (cf. 1 Jn 3.4–10). Likewise, the detailed descriptions of Jesus' opponents as 'scribes' and 'elders' have been removed, leaving the still central 'chief priests' and 'Pharisees', as well as adding 'the Jews'. The removal of *proseuchomai*, 'pray', will have been related to this. The associated noun, *proseuchē*, 'prayer', was distinctively the term for a place where Jews went to pray, what we might call a synagogue if there was a building (cf. Acts 16.13, 16).[6] This presumably gave the verb 'to pray' unfavourable connotations in the Johannine community, so that Jesus 'speaks' when he prays (Jn 12.27; 17.1), while the disciples may 'ask' (14.13).

The cumulative effect of the changes indicated by these differences in vocabulary is devastating. Despite retailing some true facts about the Jesus of history, the Johannine community have rewritten their account of his ministry so extensively that most of the main points about his life and teaching are no longer to be found.

THE FOURTH GOSPEL AND 1 JOHN

A second group of words appear frequently in the fourth Gospel, but much less frequently in the synoptics, and a high proportion of them are found also in 1 John.[7] (See Table 2)

Like the first group of words, the second measures both style and significant theological content. The major theological concepts of 'life', 'light', 'love', 'truth', 'witness' and 'world' are not to be found on any considerable scale in the teaching of Jesus in the synoptics. Given how short 1 John is, all are used in it on a comparatively large scale as well. We have once more a massive argument of cumulative weight for the standard critical view that this material represents the discourse of the Johannine community, not that of the historical Jesus. At the same time, the contact with 1 John is not absolute, indicating separate authorship.[8] It is also to be noted that most of this group of words are associated with the shift in covenantal nomism characteristic of the Johannine community when compared with the synoptics. The main 'truth' is that Jesus, the 'light', was 'sent' by 'the Father' to save the 'world', rather than 'the Jews': to this John

Table 2 Johannine words

	English translation	Matthew	Mark	Luke	John	1 John
ἀγαπάω	(to) love	7	5	11	36	28
ἀγάπη	love (n)	1	0	1	7	18
ἀλήθεια	truth	1	3	3	25	9
ἀληθής	true	1	1	0	14	2
ἀληθινός	true	0	0	1	9	4
γραφή	scripture	4	3	4	12	0
ἐντολή	commandment	6	6	4	10	14
ἔργον	work (n)	6	2	2	27	3
ζωή	life	7	4	5	36	13
Ἰουδαῖοι	Jews	5	6	5	67	0
κόσμος	world	8	2	3	78	22
μαρτυρέω	(to) witness	1	0	1	33	6
μαρτυρία	witness (n)	0	3	1	14	6
μένω	remain	3	2	7	40	22
πατήρ	Father (God)	45	4	17	118	12
πέμπω	send	4	1	10	32	0
πιστεύω	believe	11	10	9	93	9
τηρέω	keep	6	0	0	18	7
υἱός	Son (of God)	17	7	12	28	22
φανερόω	reveal	0	1	0	9	9
φιλέω	(to) love	5	1	2	13	0
φῶς	light	7	1	7	23	6
χριστός	Christ	17	7	12	19	8

the Baptist, the 'scripture', his 'works' and others bear 'witness', and those who 'believe', mostly Gentiles, have 'life'. They 'love' Jesus and 'keep' his 'commandments', so they 'love' each other (and do not keep the Law). This whole complex of theological concepts is not merely profound. It is alien to the Jesus of history, and it functions to legitimate the salvation of the Gentiles and the rejection of 'the Jews'.

This simple measurement of words indicates some of the close contacts between the fourth Gospel and 1 John. I have also noted the basically similar expository style. The First Epistle of John neither begins nor ends as a letter. Most of it could belong to discourses like those in the fourth Gospel. Despite its brevity, it contains most of the Gospel's main theological concepts, and a similar, though not identical, version of covenantal nomism. As in the Gospel, the central Christological term is the 'Son', used no less than twenty-two times in this short epistle. The fourth Gospel and 1 John are the only New Testament documents to call him 'only-begotten' Son (Jn 3.16, 18; 1 Jn 4.9; cf. Jn 1.14, 18). This has become so exalted a term that believers are termed 'children', rather than 'sons' (e.g. Jn 11.52; 1 Jn 3.1–2). As in the Gospel, God himself is frequently referred to as 'the Father', and sometimes this correlates strongly with the description of Jesus as 'the Son' (e.g. 1 Jn

4.14, where we read that the Father sent the Son, a thought characteristic of the Gospel).[9]

The term 'Christ', used secondarily by several characters in the Gospel,[10] is also important (eight occurrences) in 1 John. The prologue refers to Jesus as the 'Word of life', associating this with his pre-existence and Sonship, a complex of ideas notable in the prologue to the Gospel. The term 'Paraclete' is also distinctive of this literature.[11] It is usually used in the Gospel of the Holy Spirit, who will be sent to the community after Jesus' death (Jn 14.16–17; 15.26; 16.7–15). John 14.16, however, calls the Holy Spirit 'another paraclete', and 1 Jn 2.1 explains this by saying that 'we have a paraclete with the Father, Jesus Christ the righteous'. A declaration of Jesus' deity should probably be found in 1 John as well as in the Gospel. This is the most natural interpretation of 1 John 5.20: 'and we are in the true one, in his Son Jesus Christ. He is the true God and eternal life.' The Greek word *houtos*, rendered 'He', normally refers to what has just been mentioned, in this case 'Jesus Christ'. This is the same interpretation of Jesus as the pre-existent only-begotten Son as we found in the Gospel.

I noted also in the Gospel the exposition of the atoning death of Jesus.[12] This takes away the sin of 'the world', thereby being associated with the shift in covenantal nomism characteristic of the Gospel. The first epistle likewise comments that Jesus 'is a propitiation for our sins, yet not for ours alone but also for those of the whole world' (1 Jn 2.2, cf. 1.7; 3.5; 4.10). We shall see that, in John 3, covenantal nomism is quite undermined by the concept of rebirth, the mode of entry into the Johannine community which replaces being born into the Jewish community.[13] It is evidently associated with baptism. The First Epistle of John puts these things in a slightly different way, but it has the same basic concepts. For example, at 1 John 5.1 we read that 'everyone who believes that Jesus is the Christ has been born of God'. Here the propositional use of 'Christ' functions as an identity marker of the Christian community, and it is their members who are 'born of God'. At 5.6, we learn that Jesus Christ is 'he who comes through water and blood'. It follows that underlying the language of 1 John is the same basic idea, that baptised members of the Johannine community are those who are 'born of God'.[14]

The concept of faith in Jesus as necessary for salvation performs the same function. For example, at 5.13, 'those who believe in the name of the Son of God' are not only the recipients of the letter, they are evidently the saved community. The actual word 'believe' does not have to be used to express this. The First Epistle of John 5.12 puts it even more bluntly: 'He who has the Son has life. He who does not have the Son of God does not have life.' As in the Gospel, this is expressed with the imagery of light and darkness. For example, 'God is light and there is no darkness in him. If we say that we have fellowship with him and we walk in the darkness, we lie and do not do the truth' (1 Jn 1.5–6).

This brings us to the one major difference in both language and covenantal nomism between the Gospel and the epistles attributed to John. The use of the term 'the Jews' is a very striking feature of the Gospel, and one which is absent from the epistles. The Gospel uses it no less than sixty-seven times, almost always in narrative. 'The Jews' are a group evidently opposed to 'the disciples', despite the fact that at this stage all Jesus' disciples were Jewish. We shall see that this usage cannot be explained except as evidence of the Gentile self-identification of the final redactor and his community.[15]

The situation behind the Johannine epistles is more difficult to unravel. The word 'Jew' is not used, but some of the author's opponents look very Jewish. For example, at 1 John 2.22 the 'deceiver' is 'he who denies that Jesus is the Christ'. The author adds, 'everyone who denies the Son does not have the Father either. He who confesses the Son has the Father too' (1 Jn 2.23). This sort of comment was necessary in conflict with Jewish people who did not accept Johannine Christianity. Why then are these opponents not identified as Jews? We must infer that some Christians continued to call themselves 'Jews' because they were ethnically Jewish. The varied perceptions of identity among Johannine Christians are thus quite complex, and we shall examine them in a subsequent chapter.[16]

Finally, we must note that Johannine style is relatively homogeneous. Schweizer, Ruckstuhl and Dschulnigg have shown how far characteristic features of Johannine style permeate the Gospel, a result which militates against a number of traditional source-critical theories.[17] This homogeneity may however be due to the sociolect of the Johannine community, rather than the idiolect of a single author.[18]

THE ARAMAIC QUESTION

The Gospels are written in Greek: Jesus spoke Aramaic. The degree of Aramaic influence on Johannine Greek is therefore a factor to be taken into account in considering the age of the traditions which this Gospel transmits. Burney and Torrey argued that the whole of the fourth Gospel was translated from an Aramaic document: Burney went so far as to claim that it was written in Antioch by an eyewitness of the events which it describes (Burney 1922; Torrey 1923, 1937). Black, though not persuaded by several of Burney's arguments, found enough evidence to convince him that there was an Aramaic sayings-source behind the fourth Gospel, and that 'the evidence points to a similar Aramaic tradition forming the basis of the Prologue and the sayings of the Baptist in the third chapter' (Black 1967: 274, cf. Schuyler Brown 1964; Zimmermann 1979). Research into the remains of ordinary Hellenistic Greek has however cast doubt on such claims. Phenomena which are similar to Aramaic do not demonstrate Aramaic sources merely because they are absent from the New Testament and/or classical Greek: the whole of ancient Greek must be taken into account. Many of Burney's examples were thereby shown to be spurious by E.C. Colwell (1931). Another problem is that we do not know exactly how Jews in, say, Ephesus, spoke to each other. For all we know, Jews could have communicated with each other in Greek which was more Semitic than normal, owing to the presence and influence of bilingual people, reinforced by the LXX.[19] More recently, R.A. Martin has suggested a new approach to such problems (Martin 1989). He believes that the difference between original and translation Greek can be measured by the frequency of use of particular words. However, none of these major studies has concerned itself with the possible impact of indigenous languages on the Greek spoken in Asia Minor. We must review typical features of the evidence.

Firstly, there is a handful of Aramaic words written in Greek letters, and correctly interpreted. Some of these, such as 'rabbi' (1.38, 49, etc.) and 'Cephas' (1.42),[20] were well known to the general tradition: others, such as Siloam (9.7) and Thomas (11.16; 21.2), are less obvious. These words show that the Johannine community's traditions included a few Aramaic words and their meanings, and that the fourth Gospel was written for audiences which included people who did not understand Aramaic. One word is transliterated, declined and not interpreted: *pistikēs* (12.3) is the Aramaic *pīstāqā*, meaning that the ointment was made from the pistachio nut (Black 1967: 223–5). This is already found at Mark 14.3, so this tells us no more than that the fourth evangelist repeated the old and correct tradition of the anointing narrative. The same applies to calling the lake of Galilee a 'sea' (*thalassa*, Jn 6.1, 16–19, 22, 25; 21.1, 7; but also Mk 1.16//Mt 4.18; Mk 4.1// Mt 13.1, etc.), rather than a 'lake' (*limnē*, Lk 5.1–2; 8.22–3; Jos. B.J. III, 506ff., etc.). More promising is a construction, 'believe' (*pisteuō*) followed by 'in' (*eis*), thirty-three times in the fourth Gospel. This is a genuine Semitism, a literal translation of a construction found in both Hebrew and Aramaic and not generally in natural Greek. It is however found elsewhere in the New Testament (e.g. Mt 18.6; Acts 10.43; Gal 2.16; 1 Pet 1.8), including 1 John (5.10, 13). We must infer that Christians did use this expression in natural Greek.

Some other features of Johannine style also look promising. Parataxis, the joining together of verbs with 'and', is much commoner in Aramaic than in Greek, and frequent in the fourth Gospel. It is however also found in Greek papyri, so it can hardly function on its own as evidence of translation Greek. Another characteristic of Johannine style is asyndeton, the placing together of sentences with no connecting particle. This is characteristic of Aramaic documents too. Again, however, asyndeton is found in some Greek documents. Denniston notes the deliberate use of asyndeton by good classical writers, and comments on the mundane nature of it on many occasions in Andocides and Xenophon (Denniston 1954: xlv). The *Shepherd of Hermas* has been prominent in the discussion, because it is written in

Greek which has been influenced by Semitic idiom, and has more asyndeton than a normal Greek document.[21]

The relative pronoun has caused considerable debate. The Aramaic relative particle d^e, or *di*, is indeclinable, and is therefore frequently taken up by another word later in the sentence. This is not supposed to be done in decent Greek. We have seen an example at John 1.27, 'of whom I am not worthy to unloose the strap of the sandal of him'.[22] There is another example at 1.33, 'On whom you see the Spirit descending and remaining on him': though this harks back to the traditions which the author has rewritten, it is certainly not an authentic statement by John the Baptist.[23] Once again, examples have been found in Greek authors, most frequently those who stand nearest to popular speech (Moulton and Howard 1920: 435). The Aramaic relative particle d^e also introduces the Aramaic equivalent of purpose clauses. Burney argued that the frequency in John of the Greek particle *hina* was due to Aramaic influence, and that some examples were due to mistranslation of the relative particle. His examples include John 6.50: 'This is the bread which comes down from heaven, so that one may eat of it and not die' (Burney 1922: 76). Burney supposed that this originally meant '*which* a man shall eat thereof and shall not die'. There are two things wrong with this. In the first place it is quite arbitrary. The evangelist's purpose clause makes excellent sense. Jesus did become incarnate in order to bring salvation, and as the metaphor of bread is carried through, it becomes clear that the Christian eucharist is essential for salvation.[24] Secondly, Burney's judgement, that John uses *hina* so frequently that his usage requires this kind of explanation, is based on comparing the fourth Gospel with three other documents, the Gospels of Matthew, Mark and Luke. Some Greek documents use the particle *hina* more frequently than they do, so that a more thorough comparison would be needed before we could regard John's usage as non-Greek (Colwell 1931: 92–3).

This example takes us into the murky world of supposed mistranslations. At first sight, they look like a very good criterion, but a vast number of proposed examples should be excluded by simple application of two criteria correctly laid down by Black: 'the mistranslation must at least be credible; and the conjectured Aramaic must be possible' (Black 1967: 8). These criteria are not enough, however. At John 12.23, Burney suggested that the Greek particle *hina* was a mistranslation of the Aramaic db^eh, 'in which'. The Greek text, however, makes excellent sense as it stands: 'The hour has come for the Son of man to be glorified.' Burney found John's use of *hina* to be unsatisfactory because it is in accordance with ordinary Hellenistic Greek, not with classical excellence (Burney 1922: 78).

With methods like this, we can read all sorts of things into an imagined Aramaic substratum. Burney and Torrey found the virgin birth behind John 1.13 (Burney 1922: 34–5; Torrey 1937: 151–3). The Aramaic relative particle, d^e, like the English 'who', could be singular as well as plural. Burney notes that the plural of the verb 'were born', *'īthīlīdhū*, is the same as the singular, *'īthīlīdh*, 'was born', with the addition of the one letter *ū* or *w*, which on its own is the word for 'and', the first word of John 1.14. So Burney suggests an accidental doubling of this letter, *ū* or *w*, which mistakenly caused the verb to be taken as a plural, 'were born'. He then proposes the sense 'inasmuch as', rather than 'who', for the relative particle *d^e* and translates his hypothetical Aramaic source, 'inasmuch as He was born, not of blood, nor of the will of the flesh, nor of the will of man, but of God'. Thus he ends up with the author 'drawing out the mystical import of the Virgin-Birth for believers'. The driving force of this interpretation has nothing to do with Aramaic! The mechanism proposed by Burney is not only quite without positive evidence in its favour, it also involves having the Aramaic verb 'was/were born' in its natural Greek position as the last word of the sentence. The result is to produce a belief important to Burney, but without clear attestation in the fourth Gospel (cf. 8.41). We should not play ideological tricks like this.

Great play has also been made with 'poetic structure'. Again this looks hopeful at first sight. If a work written in Greek prose shows clear signs of Semitic poetry, an earlier version in Aramaic or Hebrew is indicated. This approach appears to get off to a good start with parallelism. Burney sets out John 3.18: 'He that believeth on Him is not condemned He that believeth not is already condemned' (Burney 1925: 72). There are two things wrong already. Anyone who is as steeped in the Old Testament as the author(s) of the fourth Gospel could write parallel lines in Greek if they wanted to: and Burney has omitted the rest of 3.18, which does not fit his schema quite as beautifully: 'for he has not believed in the name of the only-begotten Son of God'. It has been characteristic of attempts to parallelise longer passages that 'interpolations' have had to be removed. The argument could however be strengthened if more features of Aramaic verse emerged. Burney translated John 10.1ff. into what he called 'rhymed quatrains, with the exception of the second stanza, which on account of its weight stands as a distich' (Burney 1925: 174–5). But the arrangement of the structure is quite seriously arbitrary, hardly Semitic verse: the 'rhyme' depends heavily on arranging symmetrically in the arbitrary structure Aramaic words which have more homogeneous endings than Greek or English words: Aramaic poetry does not rhyme like this: and several details depend on the selection of particular words. For example, at the end of 10.1, Burney writes *ūlīstā'ā* for 'robber', using the Greek word used by the fourth evangelist, *lēstēs*, as an Aramaic loanword and putting it in the definite state. It is true that the Greek word *lēstēs* was eventually borrowed into Aramaic, but it is not probable that this development had already taken place. We are at least as entitled to write *gzl*, the participle of a native Aramaic word for 'rob', and this would not fit Burney's schema.

We should also note that the opening section of John 3 has a Graecism, the double meaning of *anōthen*, 'again' and 'from above', which cannot be reproduced in Aramaic. Nicodemus is instructed about being born again/ from above. Rebirth is itself a Greek concept, and the presentation of it shows a vigorous shift in covenantal nomism, so that believers are saved and non-Christian Jews are not saved.[25] It follows that this discourse was written in Greek. We have an author who put the traditional 'rabbi' (Jn 3.2), 'Amen' (3.3, 5) and Jesus' term 'kingdom of God' (3.3, 5) into a discourse composed in Greek, using elements from older tradition. His use of the neuter 'his own' (place/culture, *ta idia*), and the masculine 'his own' (people, *hoi idioi*) at 1.11, is also impossible in Aramaic, and there is an apparent play on Greek words at John 15.1–3. It is also difficult to understand the use of *dei* (ten times) and *opheilō* (Jn 13.14; 19.7), both words for 'must', as the work of someone translating from Aramaic, as these involve such distinctively Greek modes of expression (cf. Bonsirven 1949: 411ff.).

At first sight, the argument for an Aramaic underlay to John's Gospel looks like a massive argument of cumulative weight. On being critically examined, however, all the work prior to that of R.A. Martin turns out to consist of 10,000 leaky buckets, which, in the long run, hold no more water than one. All that has been shown is that some of the traditions used by the fourth evangelist go back ultimately to Aramaic sources. From them come 'rabbi' and 'pistic', from them come John the Baptist's authentic prediction which was rewritten to form John 1.27. Yet every single piece may be at several removes from the original sources, and most pieces of genuine tradition have been rewritten. The term 'Son of man' says it all. It would not be used in this Gospel if Jesus had not used it in Aramaic: yet not one of the Son of man sayings in this Gospel was spoken by him.[26] This faint relationship to the original Aramaic of Jesus, John the Baptist and their disciples guarantees the correctness of not one fact, and the authenticity of not a single saying.

Such was the situation in 1989, when R.A. Martin proposed a new approach. Martin's contribution has been to measure the *frequency* of linguistic phenomena. All of them are phenomena which occur in natural Greek, but Martin argues that they occur more frequently in translation Greek than in original Greek. This is a different world from alleging that a document must be translated from Aramaic because it contains Semitisms, or mistranslations. Martin developed this method in a series of publications, culminating with a treatment including the Gospel and Epistles of John (Martin 1989). Martin concludes that this Gospel 'in its present form goes back to a written Aramaic Gospel' (Martin 1989: 80, accepting the view of Burney 1922). This result would evidently be important, if it could be shown to be true. Martin goes further, suggesting that 'this Gospel's earliest milieu is to be sought in Palestine (or Southern Syria)', and that the phenomena indicating translation Greek in 1 and 2 John 'certainly imply a Palestinian Aramaic-speaking milieu' (Martin 1989: 34, 99).

To obtain these results, Martin measured the frequency of seventeen linguistic phenomena. The first is the frequency of the Greek preposition *en*, 'in'. The next eight items are the occurrences of eight other Greek prepositions, each seen as a function of the frequency of *en*. So for example, in measuring John 1, Martin notes thirteen occurrences of *en*. He next measures *dia* + genitive, 'through'. His figure for this preposition is not however five, for its five occurrences, but 0.38, its frequency when compared to that of *en*. Another feature measured is the use of the dative case not with *en*, compared with its frequency with *en*. It follows that the frequency of *en* is of exceptional importance, because it controls the measurement of ten features, not just of itself. Another feature measured is the frequency of *kai*, 'and', compared with *de*, a connecting particle approximately equivalent to a rather weak English 'but'. We have already noted that parataxis, the joining together of clauses with 'and', is a feature of the fourth Gospel also found in papyri.[27]

Using these criteria, Martin measured the Gospel as a whole, each of the epistles, and a variety of subunits, including those of 31–50 lines in length, and those of 16–30 lines in length. These different measurements are useful. Each document should be measured, because each might be uniformly original or translation Greek, and because the method is more reliable with larger pieces. Equally, however, Martin claims a high degree of reliability with passages of 31–50 lines in length, and this Gospel might be a combination of passages translated from Aramaic with redactional work done in Greek. All measurements are necessarily dependent on criteria for telling the difference between original and translation Greek. In this respect, Martin's work on the Johannine literature depends on his earlier work. His criteria for translation Greek are dependent on a selection of passages from the LXX, including both Hebrew and Aramaic parts. His criteria for original Greek are dependent on a selection of Greek writers, including for example 138 lines of Epictetus and 630 lines of papyri. The consistency with which these criteria differentiate between the two types of literature is striking, and indicates that genuine differences are being measured.

It follows that Martin's work is to be welcomed. Above all, its use of the frequency of the occurrence of linguistic phenomena offers us verifiable tests, a strong contrast with the frequently unverifiable and often wrong suggestions in the earlier secondary literature. For these reasons, I shall suggest that in certain respects this work should be further developed. However, it also has serious problems, which make all Martin's most important deductions from it dubious. Firstly, it is doubtful whether this method can always differentiate between translation Greek and Greek written by someone whose first language was Aramaic. Equally, the Johannine literature could have come from a community whose normal spoken Greek was influenced by Hebrew and Aramaic. In other words, we may be dealing with the idiolect of one or more bilingual people, or with the sociolect of a particular group. This might have been influenced first of all by bilingual people, and certain linguistic habits might then have been reinforced by Martin's sole source for translation Greek, the LXX.

This is particularly obvious in the case of the dominant feature, the preposition *en*. This is not only a feature of written translation Greek. Since it is a feature of normal Greek which is more common in translation Greek because it is a feasible equivalent of Hebrew and Aramaic expressions, it could also have occurred more commonly in the speech of bilinguals than in the speech of monoglot Greeks. Since it is a feature of the sacred text, the LXX, the influence of bilingual people constantly reinforced by the sacred text could have led to increased frequency of *en* in the sociolect of a community. This could have been true of the Johannine community. This should also be obvious for the frequency of *kai*, 'and', and the relative lack of other Greek connecting particles. If some people used *kai* far more than monoglot Greeks, the habit could have spread, and would certainly receive constant reinforcement from readings of the sacred text, the LXX. Now what is obvious for *en* and *kai* is also true of all the other linguistic features which Martin has measured.

At this point we must note a serious weakness which Martin shares with other New Testament scholars. He shows no awareness of the massive amount of work on bilingualism and translation studies done by scholars in those fields.[28] This is vital, because the features which he attributes to 'translation Greek' might be due to bilingualism. It is very difficult to test for the possibility that the frequency of *en* is due to the influence of people whose first language was Aramaic, but if we cannot test for this, we cannot exclude it. Accordingly, it is difficult to see how Martin's data could demonstrate that we have translation Greek in front of us, rather than the work of a bilingual person. Another major known fact is the emergence of whole language forms when speakers of one language are affected by the speakers of another. Pidgin and creole languages are caused in this way. Equally, where bilingual societies have existed for a long period, monoglot speakers may be influenced by features of another language which they cannot speak. Accordingly, we might have a sub-dialect of Greek which had more Semitic features than normal Greek.

Another major omission is the study of other Jewish languages. These may be fruitfully studied together, because problems in one are often similar to problems in others (cf. Fishman 1981, 1985, 1987; Wexler 1981a). A significant feature of Jewish languages is a continuous process of enrichment from Aramaic and Hebrew. This can always take place through the knowledge and use of sacred texts in these languages, and in our period there may have been a significant number of people in Ephesus who were bilingual in Aramaic and Greek, and fluent readers of Hebrew. It follows that Martin's traditional inferences that this Gospel was written in Aramaic, and that a Palestinian or Southern Syrian milieu is to be sought, are completely insecure. The phenomena to which he has drawn attention are susceptible to a much wider range of possible explanations.

Another complicating factor is the existence of indigenous languages in Asia Minor (Neumann 1980; Bubenik 1989; Brixhe forthcoming). Ephesus was a massive metropolis, gateway to a hinterland where several indigenous languages were spoken. Johannine Greek, with its relatively restricted vocabulary, repetitive mode of expression and lack of distinctively Greek particles, is very well adapted for communication between people who had several different first languages, and Greek as their second language. We need to know how far the actual influence of Carian and other languages could account for features of Johannine Greek. We already know, for example, that the Lycian *se*, 'and', was equivalent to the Greek *kai* (Bubenik 1989: 278). This might have been just as important as Hebrew and Aramaic in the emergence of Johannine Greek, if this really functioned as a sociolect, possibly that of a larger and more diverse group of language speakers than the Johannine community.[29]

All this illustrates the omission of important points characteristic of traditional scholarship. Martin's work has one other worrying problem. Some of his results are difficult to fit with other evidence. It is, for example, difficult to believe that someone wrote 2 John in Aramaic for translation, and yet wrote 3 John in original Greek (Martin 1989: 95–9). We shall see, moreover, that some passages of the fourth Gospel will not function properly in Aramaic, though Martin's theory requires them to be rather literal translations. Any theory of his kind ought to be complemented by reconstruction of the proposed Aramaic sources, to see that they are in fact viable.

All this does not mean that Martin's work is too faulty to be used. Rather, it requires further refinement, and greater caution about the limitations of its significance. Three developments may be suggested. Firstly, additional tests can be run, such as verb–subject word order (cf. Martin 1989: 171–2, 177–81). Secondly, the extent and accuracy of the data could be improved by a properly funded computer-assisted research project (Wright 1985). Thirdly, the scope of the results must be carefully defined. In particular, we need to know how far translation Greek can be differentiated from the work of bilingual authors, and how far the influence of Aramaic can be differentiated from the influence of Hebrew and the LXX, and from multilingual communication involving people who spoke other first languages.

One further point must be considered, another one which has not received proper discussion in the secondary literature. Some of the sentences in the fourth Gospel cannot be literal translations from Aramaic sources, because no feasible Aramaic underlay can be reconstructed for them. A full treatment of this would require a major research project, and the results could not be presented here. I propose accordingly to exemplify the main points. Two are outstanding. There was no definite article in

Aramaic, and some of the Christological titles are so different in Aramaic and Greek that sentences very like the fourth Gospel's Greek sentences could not function properly in Aramaic.

We may begin with John the Baptist's denial at John 1.20, 'I am not the Christ'. This might be reconstructed, אנה לא הוא משיחא, and this could equally mean 'I am not a/the anointed'. This is an unlikely thing for the tradition to say, even when writing John the Baptist down to the level found in the fourth Gospel, for he is still a significant witness to Jesus. The passage makes sense only if John the Baptist clearly denies that he has Jesus' role in fulfilling the messianic prophecies of the Old Testament. That can easily be done in Aramaic: to try to do it with the above sentence is not very sensible. The same applies to John 3.28. Similar remarks apply to John 1.21, '"Are you the prophet?" And he answered, "No".' We can reconstruct this: אנת נביא לא ועננ,. Again, the question means 'Are you a/the prophet?' The fourth Gospel is sufficiently scripturally centred to use 'the prophet' to mean the prophet predicted by Moses, a prophecy fulfilled in Jesus.[30] Were it written in Aramaic, however, it would surely have made that reference clearer, rather than let John the Baptist make such a sweeping denial of being a prophet.

Some of the references to Jesus as messiah are also very dubious. By the time the fourth Gospel was written, the Greek word 'Christ' had become an identity marker of the Christian community. The Aramaic M[e]shiḥa, however, still meant 'messiah' or 'anointed', and consequently had a much wider range. Moreover, after 70CE it was still in the process of crystallising in Jewish circles into a term for the future Davidic king.[31] While it was later used in Christian Aramaic as a fixed term for Jesus, meaning 'messiah' or 'Christ', it must be very doubtful whether it could be used during the first century CE as it is used at John 1.41, 7.26, 27, 31, 41, 42 and 10.24. The use of Messias, the Aramaic M[e]shiḥa transliterated into Greek, intended to mean 'messiah' and glossed by the fourth evangelist as 'Christ' (Jn 4.25), is equally improbable, for Samaritans are not known to have used the term 'messiah'. The Samaritan woman's comment 'I know that (the) Messiah is coming' betrays a Christian perspective.

Some uses of the term 'Son of man' are equally implausible.[32] Some of the problems are indicated at John 12.23, 'The hour has come for the Son of man to be glorified'. This makes excellent sense in Johannine Greek, as a reference to Jesus' forthcoming death. Trying to reconstruct an Aramaic original, however, is to enter a world of chaos. Let us try: שעתא אתת בר ריתהדר אנשא. Here we must suppose that the Aramaic hdr, 'glorify', underwent a change of semantic field identical to that of the Greek doxazō, 'glorify', so that it could refer to Jesus' death. That is not impossible, but we should be aware that postulating too many developments in Aramaic to account for Johannine Greek would become more and more dicey if we had to increase the number of examples. That all such developments took place in Greek, once, is the more economical hypothesis. The major problem with this verse is the term *bar nash(ā)*, 'son of man', itself. This is an ordinary term for 'man'. Where the fourth evangelist, writing in Greek, chose an unusual term which had become a Christological title, we have to suppose that his Aramaic source used an ordinary term for 'man'. The term itself does not have enough referring power to mean Jesus himself with any clarity. Nor is it an example of the traditional idiom which the historical Jesus in fact used to refer to himself. It would accordingly have been a very unsatisfactory choice as a means of predicting Jesus' death.

John 6.53 is the most extreme case of these problems. As we have seen, its *Sitz im Leben* is in the Johannine community, far removed from the Jesus of history.[33] In Greek, in its present context, it makes excellent sense: 'Amen, amen, I say to you, unless you eat the flesh of the Son of man and drink his blood, you do not have life in you.' This makes the Johannine eucharist essential for salvation, and with the expression 'drink his blood' it has been written to be anti-Jewish, thereby legitimating the rejection of 'the Jews' which is one of the main points of the chapter. If we reconstruct any possible Aramaic, however, a major fault appears: כשרא רכר אנשא ותשתון רמה, לא להון חיין כנם שונאמן אמן אמר אנה לכון, הן לא תאכלון. Here there is a problem at the end of the verse, where it is mundanely difficult to reconstruct anything convincing. The major problem is again the term 'son of man', which means simply 'man'. This saying needs to play the key role which it does play in the Greek text of the fourth Gospel if the passage is to hang together properly. It cannot do so with a mundane word for 'man', which makes it sound cannibalistic. There were several other ways of making the point, including the use of the first person as in the following verses. We must infer that this verse was written in Greek.

Two other problems may be briefly noted. Some of the fourth Gospel's particular terms are not just used in a particularly Johannine way; it is genuinely difficult to see what Aramaic word might have been used in their place. Such are *aposunagōgos*, 'out of the synagogue', and *paraklētos*, 'Paraclete'.[34] Against an hypothesis of large-scale translation, there are other passages which are difficult to fit, because one cannot see an Aramaic expression which could have been translated to produce what we have got. Such passages include John 13.1ff., with 'having loved' (*agapēsas*) at 13.1 difficult to fit into a reasonable structure, and 19.7, where the Johannine and un-Jewish use of 'Son of God' must not only be reproduced in Aramaic, but accompanied by something which gave rise to 'he made himself'.[35]

Finally, we must bear in mind one of the main points which is often omitted. Aramaisms are no guarantee of historicity. In a sense, John 6.53 says it all: 'Amen, amen I say to you, unless you eat the flesh of the Son of man and drink his blood, you do not have life in you.' 'Amen' is a Hebrew word. The use of it at the beginning of sentences is a characteristic of sayings of Jesus. 'Son of man' is an Aramaic expression, which Jesus used to refer to himself. Yet the saying as a whole is as remote from the Jesus of history as possible, and does not even permit the reconstruction of a satisfactory Aramaic sentence. It presupposes the Christian eucharist, it excludes non-Christian Jews from salvation, and to this end it is expressed in as anti-Jewish a way as possible.[36] If a saying which contains two characteristics of Jesus' idiolect can be so far removed from him, we can see what sort of tradition we are dealing with. It has rewritten him so effectively that not one characteristic of his speech, not even specifically Aramaic or Hebrew characteristics, gives us sufficient evidence that a given tradition is old, let alone authentic. Further study of Johannine language will be worthwhile for the increased precision that it may bring to our understanding of its *Sitz im Leben*. We may not, however, expect any evidence of historicity to emerge from it.

CONCLUSIONS

Some aspects of the style and wording of the fourth Gospel are of fundamental importance in assessing its historicity. Its Aramaic background does not support the conservative conclusions which have been based on it. A handful of Aramaic words, and one or two constructions, have survived the process in which the Jesus of history has been completely rewritten. Though we cannot exclude use of Aramaic sources, the Gospel as we have it was written in Greek. It includes sayings which do not permit proper Aramaic reconstructions. The evidence of the Johannine epistles is fundamental, for it enables us to see in their proper cultural context the major differences in style and content between the synoptic Gospels and the Gospel attributed to John. The comparison between the different Gospels is enough to show us that the Jesus of history has been drastically rewritten for the fourth Gospel. No longer an exorcist, hardly mentioning the kingdom of God, he sets forth his divine nature as the Son of God, together with a revised version of covenantal nomism. He sets forth the 'truth', that he, 'the Son', was sent by 'the Father' as 'the light' to save 'the world', so that those who 'believe in' him 'love' each other and have 'life'. All these positive points are found also in the Johannine epistles. We must infer that there was a Johannine community, which had reasons for rewriting its central figure. To find out more about this community, we must turn to the most anachronistic piece of evidence in the fourth Gospel, the agreement to keep people out of Jewish meetings.

6

BANNED FROM JEWISH MEETINGS

INTRODUCTION

The fourth Gospel, unlike the synoptics, contains two dramatic threats that people who confess Jesus will 'become *aposunagōgoi*', a unique expression universally held to mean that they would be thrown out of the synagogue. At 9.22, we are told that the parents of a man healed by Jesus were afraid because 'the Jews' had already agreed that if anyone confessed Jesus as Christ, he would 'become *aposunagōgos*'. After examining the man, 'the Pharisees' (9.13, 15, 16, 40) or 'the Jews' (9.18, 22) 'threw him out' (9.34, 35). At 12.42–3, the condemnation of 'the Jews' for rejecting Jesus is followed by the even more surprising information, 'however many even of the rulers believed in him, but they used not to confess him because of the Pharisees so that they might not become *aposunagōgoi*, for they loved the glory of men rather than the glory of God'. The seriousness of these measures is intensified by the prediction of 16.2: 'they will make you *aposunagōgoi*, but the hour is coming that everyone who kills you will suppose he is performing a service for God'.

APOSUNAGŌGOS

The Greek word *aposunagōgos* does not occur in Jewish sources written in Greek, nor in earlier Greek sources of any kind, nor does it have any obvious Aramaic or Hebrew equivalent. We must therefore proceed by its etymology and the usage of its parts. It is formed from two Greek words. The first is *apo*, which is basically equivalent to the English 'away from', and in compound words has a semantic field which stretches as far as the English 'without'. The second Greek word is *sunagōge*, which is generally translated 'synagogue'. This translation can however be misleading, because it is sometimes assumed that this word, and this word only, means a building for worship. Greek usage was however much more complex than this, so we must examine aspects of Greek usage, and of synagogue buildings, in the ancient world.[1]

98

There is no doubt that many communities had buildings. One of the most splendid, somewhat later than our period, was at Sardis.[2] This was a large gymnasium complex, quite rebuilt, and it had at least three functions: religious services, education and community meetings. A building like this might be known as a *sunagōge*. Other terms were however possible.[3] Josephus quotes a decree of Lucius Antonius which says that the Jews of Sardis had had from the beginning 'their own place', in which they decided their affairs and their disputes with each other (A.J. XIV, 235). It follows that there was already in our period a place for meetings in general. The commonest alternative term in extant sources from the Second Temple period is *proseuchē*, the normal term for 'prayer'. This indicates a major function of such a place.[4] Josephus uses this term of a 'very big building' in Tiberias which could hold a 'large crowd'. The subsequent narrative shows prayers being said, but also a large Jewish meeting for other purposes (Jos. *Life* 277–303). It follows that people kept away from it would miss more than community prayers.

Such a building could be referred to with the Greek word *sunagōge*. For example, one of the fourth evangelist's contemporaries, Luke, portrays 'elders of the Jews' praising a centurion, saying 'he built the synagogue (*sunagōge*) for us' (Lk 7.5). Another contemporary, Josephus, records that young men from the city of Dora caused trouble by bringing an image of the Roman emperor 'into the synagogue of the Jews' and setting it up (A.J. XIX, 300). The term *sunagōge* did not originally refer to a building, however. The centre of its semantic area in Greek was approximately equivalent to the English 'gathering together', whether of people or things. Used of people, it could mean an 'assembly', and in early examples of its use with reference to Jews, it means a gathering of Jews, rather than a building. For example, an Egyptian inscription of the first century BCE refers to 'the assembly (*sunagōge*) held in the prayer-house (*proseuchē*)' (Tcherikover and Fuks 1957: 252–4, no. 138).

These meanings of *sunagōge* should not be kept separate. By the time the fourth Gospel was written, the semantic area of *sunagōge* covered both an assembly and a building in which an assembly might be held. This is especially clear in passages in which it has both references. The effect of the men of Dora bringing the emperor's image 'into the *sunagōge* of the Jews' and setting it up was said by the governor of Syria to have been to 'prevent there being a *sunagōge* of the Jews' (A.J. XIX, 300, 305). They evidently prevented a meeting (*sunagōge*, 305) by setting up the statue in a place (*sunagōge*, 300). The same usage is found in an inscription from North Africa, dated 56CE: 'It seemed good to the *sunagōge* of the Jews in Berenice to inscribe on a stele of Parian stone (the names of) those who contributed to the repair of the *sunagōge*' (Oster 1993: 187). The first occurrence refers to the assembly which took a decision, the second to the building which was repaired. This semantic area is entirely natural, if an assembly normally met in a building.

The Jewish community at Ephesus[5] was so old and well-established that we would expect it to have a building in which to hold its meetings. Dolabella renewed their right to assemble (*sunagomenois*) for sacred and holy purposes, in accordance with their native customs, in 44–3BCE (Jos. A.J. XIV, 225–7). The narrative of Acts implies that they had a building, referring to it as a *sunagōge* (Acts 18.19, 26; 19.8–9). An imperial inscription (I. Eph. IV, 1251) refers to *archisunagōgoi*, 'synagogue rulers' and *presb(uteroi)*, 'elders'. The Acts account has Apollos and Paul expounding the scriptures, one of the activities abundantly attested in our sources as taking place in the synagogues, especially on the sabbath. Eventually, Paul ran into opposition, so he separated the disciples and taught them elsewhere. The general picture of what happened in such a place can be filled out from other sources. We must infer meetings every sabbath. As well as prayers, the scriptures would be read, and expounded. There would also be meetings at the major festivals. Other activities are recorded in diaspora synagogues, including the ritual slaughter of animals (Jos. A.J. XIV, 260, at Sardis) and the eating of communal meals. Community meetings are also known to have discussed a variety of topics (e.g. military leadership and loyalty in Tiberias, Jos. *Life* 277ff.).

We can now see what happened when people 'became', or 'were made', *aposunagōgos*: they were prevented from attending meetings of the Jewish community, necessarily including those at which Christian claims might be discussed. Scholarly attempts to align this situation with disciplinary measures inside the Jewish community have never quite succeeded because it was not a disciplinary measure inside the Jewish community. It was a way of keeping Christians out, whether they were regarded as Jews or Gentiles, or whether their identity was variable and differently perceived by different people. The means of keeping them out are not specified, because the community would use any means at their disposal. John 9 portrays the excommunication of a single individual by 'the Pharisees'. It concludes that 'they threw him out' (Jn 9.34, 35), which so powerful a group could easily do to a single individual. Acts has a number of narratives in which Paul and other missionaries split Jewish communities, and those who rejected their message got together with Gentiles to take violent action against them, but apparently not against those whom they converted. This includes being 'thrown out' again, but the term is used of being thrown out of whole areas, not just of meetings (Acts 13.50; 16.37). Josephus records that Jesus, the 'leader' at the synagogue in Tiberias (*archōn*, the term used for Nicodemus at Jn 3.1), kept most of Josephus' followers out of a meeting by keeping watch at the door, a procedure which could evidently be carried through by force of arms (Jos. *Life* 294).

We must infer that people who were made *aposunagōgoi* would be kept out of Jewish meetings by all necessary means. The narrative of John 9.13ff. shows that these means included investigations of individuals by prominent

Pharisees, but not that this was the only option. John 16.2 shows that people were at least afraid of being put to death.

We must now return to the historical question. Do these measures make any sense as an accurate account of procedures during the historic ministry of Jesus?

HISTORICITY

The *Sitz im Leben* of these measures should not be in doubt: threats to keep people out of Jewish meetings do not belong to the environment of Jesus' ministry. There are four obvious difficulties with the historicity of the threats of 9.22 and 12.42–3. In the first place, confession of a person, whether as messiah (9.22) or more vaguely (12.42–3), is not a feasible cause of preventing people from attending meetings of the community. Judaism at the time of Jesus allowed massive latitude in belief. Some people expected deliverance by means of a Davidic king, but the observant authors of the book of Daniel did not think him worthy of mention, declaring instead that the archangel Michael would stand up for the people of Israel (Dan 12.1). Some people believed in survival after death, others did not. There was also considerable variation in the practice of Judaism. The halakhah of the Dead Sea Sect was not the same as that of the Pharisees, and in many respects neither was observed by the 'people of the land', the average Jew. Neither these variations in belief nor these variations in practice led to people being kept out of Jewish meetings. If Jesus healed at a meeting on the sabbath, some Pharisees might want to do something about him (Mk 3.1–6). Keeping possible followers out of all Jewish meetings was not however a live option.

The second objection arises from the terms of 9.22, where the supposed offence is described as confessing him 'Christ'. This makes excellent sense in Ephesus after 70CE, for confessing Jesus as Christ had become an effective identity marker of the Christian community. Hence it is largely a confessional term in the fourth Gospel.[6] At the time of Jesus, however, it was not so. The Aramaic term 'messiah', the equivalent of the Greek 'Christ', was not characteristic of Jesus' preaching, nor of 'confessions' by his 'followers'.[7] Accordingly, the proposed confession is as anachronistic as the threat of 'the Jews'. The same applies to Jesus' question to the blind man when he was supposedly thrown out: 'Do you believe in the Son of man?' (9.35).[8] The Aramaic term for 'Son of man' was *bar nash(ā)*, an ordinary term for 'man'. Isolating it for use in a significant confession would therefore have been a quite unrealistic ploy.[9] The Greek term for 'Son of man', *ho huios tou anthrōpou*, was however a significant Christological term. Accordingly, the terms of the confessions in Chapter 9 belong to the environment of the Johannine community, not to the time of the ministry of Jesus.

The third objection arises from the terms of 12.42, where we find that 'many even of the rulers believed in him, but they did not confess (him)

101

because of the Pharisees, so that they might not become *aposunagōgoi*'. The trouble with this is that 'many of the rulers' would form too powerful a group to be kept out of Jewish meetings. They are not defined with any precision, but they cannot be the Pharisees of whom they were afraid, and it is difficult to see who they would be other than chief priests. In Jerusalem, they would meet to a considerable degree in the Temple complex anyway. Indeed, any attempt to imagine in a practical way the supposed situation in Jerusalem must envisage the most absolute chaos. The Gospels agree that Caiaphas and his sanhedrin were responsible for handing Jesus over to Pilate. Who, then, can the rulers be? They cannot have been those who wielded most power, and if they were a little lower down (Nicodemus?), why are they not afraid of the central group of chief priests, who alone had power to keep people out of the most important Jewish meetings in Jerusalem? On the other hand, if they were senior enough, they could block any attempt to kill Jesus, especially if there were any truth in the story that Pilate also tried to have him released (Jn 19.12). This underlines the main point: they cannot be both 'many of the rulers', and insufficiently powerful. We must conclude that John 12.42 is remote from historical reality. This is because it belongs to the reality of late first century Ephesus, where 'many of the rulers' of the local Jewish community were favourably disposed towards Jesus, but afraid of central Jewish authorities, and too attached to their Jewish identity to want to leave the Jewish community.

A fourth objection is equally devastating. If confessing Jesus had resulted in people being kept out of Jewish meetings, the disciples would have been kept out of Jewish meetings. Of this, however, there is no trace, not even in the fourth Gospel, let alone in the synoptics. There is no lack of disputes, but measures against the disciples are not suggested in any of them. The Johannine material is the most striking, because there is so much confessing of him. Why was John the Baptist not kept out of Jewish meetings? When the crowds dispute about him, why is the threat never repeated? By the time we get to the end of the ministry, why has only one man been examined and thrown out? Why are these threats neither repeated, nor carried out, in the early chapters of Acts?

These points form an overwhelming argument of cumulative weight. The agreement belongs to a later period. The terms of 9.22 enable us to analyse it further. Here the confession is explicitly that of Jesus as Christ: at the time of Jesus, the Aramaic term 'messiah' was not used in this way.[10] By the time of Paul and Acts, however, the Greek term 'Christ' had become a central identity factor of the Christian community (Casey 1991a: 105–6, 129–31, 133–4, 141, 143, 147, 149). Christians were people who confessed Jesus, or even confessed him as 'the Christ'. Further, the agreement at 9.22 is that of 'the Jews', not of 'the Pharisees' or 'the chief priests' or 'the rulers', despite the fact that all Jesus' disciples and sympathisers were Jewish. This is the particularly Johannine use of 'the Jews', the usage which reflects Gentile self-identification.[11] We have reached the point of a split between Christianity and Judaism. What happened in Ephesus was that Christians were kept out of Jewish meetings. They were kept out of them because they were regarded as an alien group. This is indicated by their Gentile self-identification. The social background may be further illuminated by study of the Benediction of the Heretics.

Our Jewish sources give us a rough date of c. 90CE for the formulation of this benediction.[12] The Palestinian redaction of the twelfth of the Eighteen Benedictions is extant only in later sources. A text found in the Cairo Genizah runs as follows:

> For apostates may there be no hope, and may the insolent kingdom be quickly uprooted. And may the Nazarenes and the heretics perish in a moment, may they be erased from the book of Life, and may they not be written with the righteous. Blessed art thou, Lord, who humbles the insolent.

The 'Nazarenes' can hardly be anyone other than Christians. It follows that Christians cannot have been normal, acceptable members of the Jewish community in any environment where this text of this benediction was used. Jewish Christians, and other Christians associated with them, could also be subsumed under the more general description 'heretics' (*minim*). The story of the origin of this benediction is given in tractate *Blessings* of the Babylonian Talmud.

> Simeon the cotton merchant arranged eighteen blessings/benedictions in order before Rabban Gamaliel at Yabneh. Rabban Gamaliel said to the sages, 'Is there anyone who knows how to formulate the blessing concerning heretics?' Samuel the Small rose and formulated it.
>
> (bT Ber. 28b)

Gamaliel II was one of the small group of sages who worked for the survival and renewal of Judaism after the sack of Jerusalem in 70CE (Neusner 1970: Chapters 6–8; Cohen 1984). Their work was centred at Yabneh, at first under the leadership of Johanan ben Zakkai. It was partly Pharisaic halakhah which they expanded and enabled to serve as the public identity of Judaism. Gamaliel II himself was son of Simeon, son of Gamaliel I. Since Gamaliel I and Simeon his son are two of only ten people from this period identified by our sources as Pharisees (Acts 5.34; Jos. *Life* 190–1), we may reasonably infer that Gamaliel II was a Pharisee. Moreover, the many judgements ascribed to him (cf. Kanter 1980) include careful expansions of the Law to apply it to the whole of life. For example, he decided that three blessings should be said after eating figs, grapes and pomegranates (M. Ber. 6.8): that pulse could be rinsed and separated on a festival (M. Bets. 1.8): and his judgement that a menstruating woman imparts uncleanness to anything she has touched, since she last examined herself, is shown in the behaviour of his servant-girl Tabitha, who is reported to have inspected herself after every wine jug that she corked and the like (pT Nid. II, 1, 49d, 29–32; bT Nid. 6b). Personally, he is also recorded to have eaten ordinary food in a state of purity (T. Hag. 3.2).

Equally, neither Gamaliel nor other sages are reported in our sources as Pharisees, for they were concerned to take charge of and reconstitute Judaism for all Jews, and our sources do not wish to believe that they separated themselves. So, when New Year fell on a sabbath, Johanan ben Zakkai had the *shofar* sounded at Yabneh, thereby putting the sages in control of what the priests had done in the Temple (M.R.H. 4.1). Gamaliel's rulings included laying down that the delegate of the congregation fulfilled the obligation of the whole congregation on Rosh Hashanah by saying the prayers on their behalf (M.R.H. 4.9): and that a mourner does not behave as a mourner on the sabbath (Sem. 10.3). These measures are concerned with the behaviour of Jewish communities as a whole, regardless of differences in the extent and strictness of observance.

This is the cultural context in which we must see the arrangement of the Eighteen Benedictions before Rabban Gamaliel in Yabneh. Simeon the cotton merchant arranged all eighteen benedictions, not just the twelfth (bT Ber. 28b; bT Meg. 17b). The tenth benediction blesses God in the hope that he will gather in the exiles; the eleventh asks for the restoration of judges and counsellors; the thirteenth asks for God's compassion on true proselytes; and the fourteenth asks God's mercy on Jerusalem, the Temple and the kingdom of the house of David. Thus the twelfth benediction fits very logically in its place. It blesses God for removing serious threats to Judaism, apostates, heretics, Christians and the occupying Roman power. Christians, whether singled out as Nazarenes or subsumed under *minim*, heretics, were an obvious threat to the Jewish community, because they claimed to *be* the covenant community and were not observant. Thus the twelfth benediction gives us evidence that, at about the time when the fourth Gospel was written, central Jewish authorities were taking the kind of measures that would be associated with keeping Christian Jews and Judaisers out of Jewish meetings.

We should not exaggerate. The effects of this benediction in itself were not universal nor were they yet permanent, and the surviving texts vary in who exactly was condemned. We should not imagine that Gamaliel II could forcibly compel the Ephesian Jews to keep people away from their meetings: he could have had no effect unless Jewish communities were willing to listen to him. The secondary narratives of the fourth Gospel show that the twelfth benediction was not an important means of keeping people out of Jewish meetings in Ephesus, for they do not mention it. Nonetheless, all our evidence from this period is coherent. Authoritative declarations from leading Pharisees could be vigorously interpreted and acted upon by Jewish communities who needed to interpret them vigorously and act on them. Our Jewish sources show such a declaration being made before a leading Pharisee at approximately the time when we must deduce from John 9.22 and 12.42–3 that Johannine Jews were prevented from attending Jewish meetings.

By this time social conditions were such that many Jews might well perceive a sufficient threat to their identity for them to act on the views of leading Pharisees. Gentiles had sacked the cultic centre in Jerusalem with much slaughter, defiling and destroying the holy places. Many Gentiles had entered the Christian churches, and in doing so had remained Gentiles rather than becoming Jews. Jews who joined the Christian community were liable to assimilate into the Gentile world, believing that salvation meant membership of the largely Gentile Christian community which did not observe the Law, rather than membership of the Jewish community which did. If it was to survive, Judaism had to reconstitute itself round its basic identity. It did so, with Pharisees like Gamaliel II at the centre because they encapsulated visible and measurable Jewish identity. This is the situation in which local rulers of the Jews might well fear the Pharisees, and decide that activity within the covenant community was more important than continued adherence to Jesus. We must infer that this was the situation in Ephesus.

SOME RECENT SCHOLARSHIP

These main points have been somewhat obscured in the most recent scholarship, much of which has been written by people defending their own ideological community.[13] In a sense, the immediate source of trouble was the work of J.L. Martyn, who drew too tight a link between the Benediction of the Heretics and the expulsion of Johannine Jews from the synagogue (Martyn 1968: esp. 50–62). The most important attack on this view is that of Kimelman, who argues that there was no such connection. Most of his arguments are not however new, but consist of points previously made by Jewish scholars in perceptible defence of their community.

Kimelman argues that the word *nōṣerim*, generally translated 'Nazarenes', was absent from the earliest text of the Blessing of the Heretics. This was not directed against Gentile Christians, but against Jewish sectarians. He suggests that the 'context of the mention of "Pharisees" (12.42) indicates that it is a derogatory reference to local leadership': indeed, the whole charge that the Jews excluded people from the synagogue may have been 'concocted to persuade Christians to stay away from the synagogue'. He thinks there is 'abundant evidence that Christians were welcome in the synagogue'. Consequently, the Blessing of the Heretics did not cause irreparable separation between Judaism and Christianity. This separation was the result of a long process dependent ultimately 'upon the political power of the church' (Kimelman 1981: 234–5, 244).

Some of Kimelman's points are perfectly reasonable. For example, we do

105

not have early manuscripts of the twelfth benediction, and consequently we cannot demonstrate that Samuel the Small included the term 'Nazarenes' in his version of it. Kimelman is also right to doubt whether rabbinic enactments were immediately enforceable everywhere. More centrally, Kimelman is right to point out that 'John makes no reference to the prayers of the Jews nor to any curse' (Kimelman 1981: 235). This does show that the twelfth benediction was not central or universal as a means of keeping members of the Johannine community out of Jewish meetings. Nonetheless, Kimelman's argument suffers from three profound defects. Firstly, he has not taken the Christian evidence of the fourth Gospel seriously enough; secondly, he shares the oversimplified concept of identity characteristic of scholars in the fields of ancient Judaism and early Christianity; and thirdly, his hidden agenda has caused him to underplay, and indeed omit, evidence that Jews persecuted Christians.

In the first place, it is not plausible to restrict the reference to Pharisees at John 12.42 to 'local leadership'. This primary source says that 'many of the rulers' believed on Jesus. They would hardly have been deterred by fear of such Pharisees as are likely to have been in the sort of place where the fourth Gospel was written, unless these were acting in accordance with a powerful group of Pharisees, such as were involved in reconstituting Judaism in Israel at the time. Further, Kimelman's notion that exclusion from the synagogue might have been 'concocted to persuade Christians to stay away from the synagogue' is clean contrary to the *Sitz im Leben* of this whole document. On the one hand, it is ferociously hostile to 'the Jews'. On the other hand, it includes a massive amount of Jewish tradition. This presupposes scriptural exegesis extant in later Jewish sources, such as that the angels at Genesis 28.12 went up and down 'on him', i.e. on Jacob/Israel, not on the ladder (Jn 1.51). It includes the halakhic decision that circumcision overrides the sabbath, which is creatively used to justify Jesus' Jewish decision that healing is right on the sabbath (Jn 7.22–3). It presupposes knowledge of the central place of water and light in the symbolism of the Feast of Tabernacles (Jn 7–8). Moreover, the document is associated with the Johannine epistles, which do not have the Gospel's hostile use of 'the Jews', and do have an external use of the term 'Gentiles' (3 Jn 7). We must infer the existence of people so Jewish that they would have to be kept out of Jewish meetings, because otherwise they would have attended them. We must therefore accept the clear implications of our primary source that people were kept out of Jewish meetings. Moreover, the terms of John 12.42 are not probable in a concocted charge. If someone were concocting a charge, they would need the agreement of 'the Jews' reported at 9.22. Having ended the ministry with the blindness of those who did not accept Jesus, they would surely not be motivated to produce the faith of 'many of the rulers' followed by fear of the Pharisees. For if the Pharisees were not the powerful men of Yabneh really supporting the

106

rejection of Christians, or a group of Ephesian Pharisees dependent on their power, attributing this action to a group of people who could not normally have had such power in Ephesus would be hopelessly unconvincing.

Moreover, Kimelman does not discuss John 16.2. Here exclusion from Jewish meetings is not only predicted but amplified: 'They will make you *aposunagōgous*, but the hour is coming that everyone who kills you will think he is offering a service to God.' The terms 'offer' and 'service' are especially appropriate to offerings made by priests in the Temple. Before this Gospel was written, the high priest Ananus conspicuously fulfilled this pseudoprophecy. In 62CE, he gathered a sanhedrin and accused Jacob, Jesus' own brother, and some others of transgressing the Law, and had them stoned (Jos. A.J. XX, 200). Ananus and his sanhedrin will surely have thought they were offering a service to God. When most of the verse has been written in the light of such an event, the notion that the first part might be a concocted charge is the more peculiar. We must surely conclude that members of the Johannine community were kept out of Jewish meetings, as a result of measures associated with very powerful Pharisees. The terms of 16.2 imply that more Christians had died at Jewish hands.

The effects of Kimelman's oversimplified assumptions about identity are more subtle and more complicated to trace out. The basic problem is that he contemplates only two sorts of people, Jews and Gentiles. Consequently, when discussing the people at whom the Benediction was aimed, he considers 'Jewish sectarians' and 'Gentile Christians' as simple alternatives. He does not envisage people with doubtful or shifting identities at all. This is particularly clear in his discussion of Origen (Kimelman 1981: 230). This is part of his argument that *minim*, generally translated 'heretics', in Palestinian Amoraic literature refers to Jews. He comments, 'If there ever were a Gentile who would be referred to as a *min* it would be Origen.' His grounds for this judgement are that Origen was a biblical scholar, resided in Palestine, knew some Hebrew, studied under 'Hebrew' teachers and maintained contact with some rabbinic authorities. But suppose such a person also observed the sabbath and the major Jewish festivals? What if he undertook circumcision? At that point, some people would consider him Jewish. Or consider a person with two Jewish parents who observed none of these things. Would he be an apostate Jew or a Gentile? Once again, perceptions vary.

These shifting identities and varied perceptions were central to the situation faced by Asian Jews and, for the same reasons, by the rabbis at Yabneh. Hence the terms of their respective measures. The twelfth benediction curses *minim* with or without Nazarenes, or Nazoreans. It could therefore be used by local communities to mark out Jewish Christians, if local Jewish communities proposed to make their lives uncomfortable and/or exclude them from Jewish meetings. If Jewish Christians went, Gentile Christians and Christians whose identity on a Jewish/Gentile scale was variable and variably perceived, could hardly stay. The rabbis at Yabneh were concerned with the preservation, maintenance and fostering of Jewish identity. Their interests were well served by a curse which excoriated people who could be defined in accordance with the needs of Jewish communities. The term 'Nazoreans', or 'Nazarenes', could be inserted, changed and omitted as required. Jews who had visions of Metatron, or who said that fish should have the blood drained from them before they were eaten, could be accepted or condemned as *minim* or not, as the Jewish community needed at the time.

The Johannine community was concerned with the formation, maintenance and fostering of Christian identity. This involved conflict with the Jewish community. In the Gospel, this was such that the Johannine community had taken on Gentile self-identification.[14] Thus the Gospel records a massive conflict with 'the Jews'. However, some members of the community were so Jewish that this terminology is absent from the Johannine epistles. Moreover, some members of the community behind the Gospel were so Jewish that they had to be kept out of Jewish meetings: otherwise they would have attended them. Some people very favourable to Jesus, including local Jewish rulers, stayed in the Jewish community when the crisis came. Hence this Gospel's selection of information. Making people *aposunagōgos* is a repeated threat, and a man is portrayed as being questioned and thrown out, because such events had been dramatic and damaging. The opponents are usually called 'the Jews' because the members of the community had Gentile self-identification. The opponents are sometimes Pharisees, certainly because of the leading role of Pharisees at Yabneh, possibly also because such Pharisees came to Ephesus. Confessing Jesus as Christ is isolated as crucial because Christ was the central identity factor by which Christians were identified for removal. Whether a prayer and/or curse was involved in this process is not relevant to this Gospel. It follows that it was not the main point. It does not follow that the split between Christians and Jews in the Johannine situation was unrelated to the preservation and reinforcement of Jewish identity by the rabbis at Yabneh.

Finally, Jewish persecution of the followers of Jesus began as soon as it became clear that his crucifixion had not put an end to the movement. At this stage, disciplinary flogging of Jews by Jews is recorded (Acts 5.40). Persecution continued with vigorous action by Paul of Tarsus. He records this with clear description of his reason: 'zeal' (Phil 3.6). He records the sufferings of the churches of God in Judaea at the hands of Jews (1 Thess 2.14–16). He records his own sufferings, after his conversion, at the hands of Jews (e.g 2 Cor 11.24–5), and Acts gives a longer narrative account of this. Paul, his opponents and Acts all agree about the basic reason for this: 'zeal'. At Thessalonica and Beroea, Paul and Silas fled from 'zealous' Jews. At Ephesus, non-violent opposition was so serious that Paul separated his disciples from the synagogue and taught them elsewhere (Acts 19.9). When he was arrested in Jerusalem, more than forty Jews vowed not to eat or drink until they had killed him. They reported this to the chief priests and elders (Acts 23.14): they surely were trying to offer a service to God. We have seen that the high priest and his sanhedrin will have taken the same view when they killed Jesus' brother Jacob, and other Christians. All this led up to the Johannine situation: all this Kimelman omitted. Jewish opposition to Christianity has continued ever since. In the second century, keen Jewish participation in the martyrdom of Polycarp was noted, not far away in Smyrna (Mart. Pol. 13.1). Justin and other Fathers note the cursing of Christians in synagogues (e.g. Justin *Dial*, 16, set in a port identified by Eusebius as Ephesus). Kimelman's view that this does not all refer to use of the twelfth benediction is plausible: it must not lead us to omit the main point.

Kimelman's presentation of evidence that 'Christians were welcome in the synagogue' also suffers from his oversimplified view of identity. The evidence is real, and important. It shows that the normal processes of acculturation between Christians and Jews did not come to an end when official church measures against Jews began. However, the earlier split between Christianity and Judaism, of which the fourth Gospel provides much clear evidence, has proved irreparable. The Blessing of the Heretics is a symptom of it, not a single cause. Throughout the centuries, it has not been unmitigated, nor is it now. But the fourth Gospel shows the split into separate identities which has been normative ever since. Kimelman's presentation is faulty because it fails to take seriously the severity of Jewish opposition to Christianity in the earliest phases of Christian existence.

Kimelman's work was a necessary foundation of that of Robinson (1985: 72ff.). Robinson starts from Martyn's presentation of the Johannine situation as directly caused by the twelfth benediction. Treating this as the position to refute, he takes up and agrees with Kimelman, thereby radically separating the Johannine situation from that benediction. He proceeds to argue that the situation reflected in the fourth Gospel is prior to 70CE (Robinson 1985: esp. 80–1). He refers to Paul persecuting the churches, but at this early stage there was no agreement among the Pharisees to keep Christians out of Jewish meetings. That would have been highly dysfunctional, because almost all Christians were Jews. Putting them out of any synagogue would not have reduced their influence, and would have tended to split the community. Trying to keep them out of the Temple in Jerusalem, where they continued to worship and to preach, would have required security measures far in excess of the measures recorded in the earliest period. Moreover, some Pharisees were impressed by the recreation of Jewish identity in the Jesus movement. Some warned Jesus that Herod was after him (Lk 13.31, cf. Mk 3.6). The Pharisees were not sufficiently prominent in moves against him to be mentioned in the accounts of the Passion. In the earliest days of the church, Gamaliel I opposed severe measures against the movement (Acts 5.33–40), which was under attack from the high priest and his associates, not particularly from Pharisees. Some Pharisees joined it (Acts 15.5, cf. Jos. A.J. XX, 200–3). An agreement among the Pharisees to keep people out of Jewish meetings does not fit in this period.

Robinson moves to the situation faced by Paul and his fellow-Christians after his conversion, but the same considerations apply to this. Paul was literally thrown out of a number of places, but this was due to immediate outrage caused by the first preaching of the Gospel, and it involved physical attacks by Gentiles as well as by Jews (cf. e.g. Acts 13.45–14.7). We have no sign in our sources at this stage of a general agreement emanating from the Pharisees. As time went on, the increasing influx of Gentiles made such an agreement more probable, as violent measures against Christians became increasingly impractical and liable to backfire. If Gentile Christians in the diaspora were beaten in synagogues, thrown into prisons and so on, Gentile authorities were liable to take counter-measures. Jewish communities might also be wary in case the persecution of assimilating Jewish Christians had the same effect. The crisis following the Roman war intensified the effects of the gradual change in the identity of the movement originally begun by Jesus. At this stage, if Christians could be kept out of the Jewish community, it would retain everyone who opted to maintain their Jewish identity, and Gentile authorities would not be motivated to defend people whom they perceived as Judaising, a generally unpopular life-stance. Christians would thus be isolated from 'the world' as well as from 'the Jews'. At this stage also, Pharisees, heavily involved in recreating Judaism, would be prominent, rather than chief priests who had controlled the Temple. An agreement to keep Christians away from Jewish meetings is accordingly found just at the point when it was functional, and Pharisees are mentioned prominently just at the time when this becomes feasible.

CONCLUSIONS

There is only one feasible interpretation of our primary sources. The threat to make people *aposunagōgoi* on the ground of confessing Jesus is quite anachronistic. It is out of place in the historic ministry of Jesus, and has a perfectly good setting at a later period. The Johannine community contained people who were banned from Jewish meetings after 70CE, when Jewish identity was being recreated and renewed under Pharisees like Gamaliel II. They were kept out in circumstances which were originally related to the formulation of the twelfth benediction. Once again, the people responsible for the fourth Gospel have told us their central concerns in the guise of narrative about the ministry of Jesus. We have therefore been able to deduce a little more information about the Johannine community. We must see how much more we can find out about this community, so that we can go on to see why they rewrote history in such a drastic way.

7

THE JOHANNINE
COMMUNITY

INTRODUCTION

We have seen that this Gospel emanates from a community whose members were not allowed to attend meetings of the Jewish community. We must now see how much further we can carry our analysis of the identity and situation of the Johannine community. A central point is its 'Gentile self-identification', a term which I introduced into scholarly discussion of the New Testament because it clarifies situations of this kind (Casey 1991a: esp. 12, 14–16, 27–38, 154–6, 158–9, 169–70). We can establish the 'identity' of a person, or of a social group, when we all agree as to what that identity is. When their identity changes, however, and when their identity may be differently perceived by different people, we need the term 'self-identification' to isolate and describe their own view of themselves. By 'Gentile self-identification', I mean that the community identified itself as not 'the Jews'. If follows that the central piece of evidence of the Gentile self-identification of the Johannine community is its hostile use of this term, 'the Jews'.

GENTILE SELF-IDENTIFICATION

The fourth Gospel uses the term 'the Jews' more than sixty times, and in the majority of cases it denotes opponents of Jesus, despite the fact that, during the historic ministry, all Jesus' disciples were Jewish. The Johannine version of the Cleansing of the Temple begins, 'And the passover of the Jews was near' (Jn 2.13). This indicates Gentile self-identification, and it typifies many uses of the term in narrative. Immediately after the Cleansing, 'his disciples remembered that it is written, "Zeal for your house will consume me". The Jews therefore answered and said to him, "What sign do you show us, that you do this?"' (2.17–18). This contrast is reinforced with further mention of these two groups, 'the Jews' and 'his disciples', in the immediate sequel.

At John 13.33, Jesus himself speaks of 'the Jews' as if they were an outside group: 'Children, yet a little while I am with you: you will seek me, and as I told the Jews "Where I am going, you cannot come", now I am telling you too.' Similarly, on two occasions Jesus refers to the Law as 'your Law' (8.17; 10.34), and at 15.25 he explains to the disciples the hatred of the world by quoting scripture: 'but so that the word may be fulfilled which is written in their Law, "they hated me without cause"'. The description *their* Law' indicates a Gentile perspective.

With this also goes the perception of the Jews as a group rejecting the Gospel. At the time of Jesus, some Jews did reject him, but other people who were quite obviously Jewish became his disciples, accepted his message and formed the nucleus of the early church after the resurrection. The fourth Gospel's description is quite blunt. In the prologue, 'his own (people) did not receive him' (1.11). In Chapter 5, it is 'the Jews' who sought to kill him (5.18), and to them he says, 'Your accuser is Moses, on whom you have set your hope. For if you had believed Moses, you would have believed me, for he wrote about me' (5.45–6). The implication is quite clear – 'the Jews' do not believe Moses, on the ground that they do not accept Christological exegesis of the Old Testament. In Chapter 8, it is 'the Jews' who, having been told that their Father is the devil (8.44), respond to Jesus, 'Aren't we right to say that you are a Samaritan and have a demon!' (8.48), and the same group take up stones to throw at him when he declares his pre-existence (8.58–9). In Chapter 9, it is 'the Jews' who have agreed that if anyone confesses Jesus as Christ, they will be prevented from attending Jewish meetings. In Chapter 10, it is 'the Jews' who seek to stone Jesus for blasphemy (10.31–3). In the Passion narrative, it is 'the Jews' who insist that Pilate must have Jesus crucified.[1] After the resurrection, 'the disciples' meet behind closed doors for fear of 'the Jews' (20.19).

In addition to this direct evidence of Gentile self-identification, there is indirect evidence of the presence of Gentiles in the Johannine community. In Chapter 10, Jesus expounds and interprets the parable of the good shepherd, commenting,

> And I have other sheep who are not of this fold: these too I must lead, and they will hear my voice, and they shall become one flock with one shepherd. Because of this, the Father loves me because I lay down my life to take it up again.

> (Jn 10.16–17)

The 'other sheep' are surely Gentiles, and this is a prediction of the entry of Gentiles into the community, a process which did not begin until after Jesus' death. The suggestion that the 'other sheep' are diaspora Jews (Robinson 1959a, 1985: 60ff.) is remote from this Gospel's environment (Casey 1991a: 28–9). There are no criteria on which Judaean Jews are more likely than diaspora Jews to have belonged to the sheep mentioned earlier in the passage. Any feasible dating of the fourth Gospel, even before 70CE, puts it after a successful large-scale mission to the Gentiles, so the Gentiles are not likely to be omitted from consideration: they should therefore not be removed from descriptions of this kind. Jesus' death and resurrection were essential to enable the Gospel to be spread to the Gentiles, because only vigorous interpretation of his death enabled them to be admitted to the covenant community without doing the Law, whereas the good news could be taken to diaspora Jews at any time. Barring information to the contrary, the natural assumption would be that Jesus himself preached to diaspora Jews, because this Gospel sets some of Jesus' discourses and debates with 'the Jews' at major festivals when everyone knew that Jerusalem was invaded by pilgrims, from the diaspora as well as from Israel. The Gentile mission is also necessary to explain the very strong statement of 10.17.

Again, the high priest's declaration that one man should die for the people is interpreted at 11.51–2:

> He did not say this of his own accord, but since he was high priest that year he prophesied that Jesus would die for the nation, and not for the nation only, but so that he might gather together the scattered children of God into one.

Here the reference to Gentiles is especially clear, since diaspora Jews belonged to 'the nation' and 'the people' just as much as Judaean Jews. The reference to 'the scattered children of God' cannot be confined to diaspora Jews because the power to become children of God has been given to 'as many as received him', 'those who believe in his name' (Jn 1.12), and after a successful Gentile mission these necessarily included Gentiles. Thus when 'some Greeks' came to see Jesus (12.20–1), they did not succeed in doing so. We should not imagine that the fourth evangelist was so confused as to refer to diaspora Jews as 'Greeks' in a context where he could so easily be thought to be referring to Gentiles. Moreover, Jesus' reply is entirely in terms of his death (12.23f.), for which Gentile Christians were profoundly grateful because it brought them salvation without 'their Law' (15.25). The Gentiles could not see Jesus because the Gentile mission could not begin until after his death: 'now the ruler of this world will be cast out and I, when I am lifted up from the earth, will draw everyone to myself' (12.31–2).

All our evidence is thus consistent. Direct evidence of the Gentile self-identification of the Johannine community is supported by indirect evidence of Gentiles in the community. This kind of evidence is further supported by the Greek background to the theology of this Gospel. The Hellenistic concept of rebirth employed in Chapter 3 is outstanding because it is purely Hellenistic.[2] It is also difficult to understand such things as the choice of the Greek term *logos* in the prologue, if the author was not deliberately seeking to appeal to Gentiles as well as to Jews. The procedure of the discourses, with questions, often none too intelligent, which do no more than move the exposition forward, is also suggestive of Greek influence. Further evidence of Gentiles in the community is provided by the author's habit of explaining Jewish terms and customs. For example, the first occurrence of the term 'rabbi' is accompanied by the explanation that it means 'teacher' (1.38), and at 2.6 the six stone waterpots are 'for the purification (ceremonies) of the Jews', an accurate description of a Jewish custom from a Gentile perspective, necessary only if the prospective audience included a significant proportion of Gentiles.

We can describe this Gentile self-identification more incisively with the eight-point scale which I devised for such purposes (Casey 1991a: 12–17, 29; 1994a: 701, 707–8). The eight identity factors in this scale are the following: ethnicity, scripture, monotheism, circumcision, sabbath observance, dietary laws, purity laws and major festivals. These eight factors were isolated because our primary sources treat them as serious indices of Jewish identity and of acculturation. From an ethnic perspective, a community which was Jewish enough to mind being prevented from attending meetings of the Jewish community, but which also included Gentiles, must have contained Jews, Gentiles and people who might be considered to be of mixed ethnicity. We cannot measure the proportions accurately, so I symbolise mixture with a half. Scripture gets another half: the community accepted the authority of scripture as a witness of Jesus, but did not accept its commands to follow its halakhah. Monotheism gets another half: the deity of Jesus means that the community was not monotheistic from a Jewish perspective, though it remained monotheistic from a Gentile perspective. This does not give us a symbolic 1½ out of 3, where the halves might be thought too symbolic to be accurate: it is 1½ out of 7 or 8, a difference which is big enough to be real and decisive.

Circumcision is presented as an alien custom: 'Moses has given *you* circumcision . . . and on the sabbath *you* circumcise a man' (7.22, my italics). The sabbath is explicitly removed: Jesus 'abrogated the sabbath' (5.18). Dietary laws are never mentioned: it may be argued that we should not count them (so 1½ out of 7, not 8), for the community may well have contained people who could not stomach pork or prawns because they had never been part of their diet, not because they still believed that eating them was wrong. Purity, like circumcision, is identified as belonging to an alien group: the stone waterpots at Cana of Galilee were 'for the purification of the Jews' (2.6, cf. 11.55). The figurative use of purity as resulting from washing by Jesus (13.10, implying baptism), and from the word of Jesus (15.3), should thus be interpreted as the replacement of Jewish purity laws by Christian purity. Major festivals are repeatedly identified as belonging to an alien group. For example, 'Now the feast of the Jews, Tabernacles, was near' (7.2), and again, 'Now the Passover of the Jews was near' (11.55). In this instance, the measurement of 1½ out of 7 or 8 is not precise in numerical terms, but the message is clear. When we look at the basic identity factors of Judaism, the community is overwhelmingly identified as Gentile. Hence the predominant use of 'the Jews', and the occasional description of 'your Law' (8.17; 10.34) and 'their Law' (15.25).

The evidence is therefore unambiguous. However deeply we may think this document is imbued with Jewish culture, the self-identification of the community which produced it was Gentile. It was written after the successful Gentile mission, and some members of the community were Greeks. The Gentile self-identification of the community is to be closely associated with its exclusion from Jewish meetings. The community which rejected them was universally known as 'the Jews', and this explains Johannine terminology. It may have been the final straw in the self-identification of assimilating Jews, who came at that point to the certainty that they were not Jews, whatever they were.[3]

We can now see what is wrong with the classic arguments of Westcott and Morris, that the author of the fourth Gospel was a Jew (Westcott 1908: I, x–xx; Morris 1969: 219–27). Westcott argued this on the basis that he was familiar with Jewish customs, such as 'the law of the sabbath which is shown to be overruled by the requirements of circumcision (vii.22f.)'. In the ancient world, that would merely have shown that he was a person familiar with Jewish customs, just as Westcott was, not that he had Jewish identity, any more than Westcott had. Mere knowledge of Jewish culture tells us little about a person's identity, nor should we apply our own view of Jewish identity to ancient sources. We must rather utilise a scale constructed in accordance with the perceptions of our primary sources as to what constituted identity and how it could change.

It is illuminating to compare the self-identification of the authors of the Johannine epistles, which have so much in common with the theology of the fourth Gospel. The term 'Jew' is not used, but some of the author's opponents look very Jewish. For example, at 1 John 2.22 the 'liar' is 'he who denies that Jesus is the Christ'. The author adds, 'Everyone who denies the Son does not have the Father either. He who confesses the Son has the Father too' (1 Jn 2.23). This sort of comment was necessary in conflict with Jewish people who did not accept Johannine Christianity. They believed that they had the Father, and they did not accept that Jesus is the Christ and the Son. It was therefore necessary to state explicitly that they were excluded from salvation, even though they continued in the covenant community which was partly defined by its allegiance to God the Father. Hence 'everyone who denies the Son does not have the Father either', a statement clean contrary to the life-stance of the Jewish community.

Why are these opponents not identified as Jews? We must infer that the author knew Christians who continued to call themselves 'Jews' because they were ethnically Jewish. This is not only an abstract inference. The elder who wrote 2 and 3 John uses the description 'Gentiles' as a reference to an outside group (3 Jn 7): however assimilated he was, he must have retained his Jewish self-identification. What the elder thought of the deity of Jesus we are not told – it is not mentioned in two documents too short for the absence of anything to be regarded as significant. We can however see him

115

embracing the Sonship of Jesus, and the second occurrence is in a context which entails the rejection of anyone who does not do so, and which consequently entails the rejection of most Jewish people (2 Jn 9–11). We must infer that the elder and his followers no longer belonged to the Jewish community, even though the Jewish background of some of them caused them to retain Jewish self-identification. As for 1 John, we cannot deduce the self-identification of the author(s) with certainty. It is however a very probable hypothesis that they belonged to a community which had effectively Gentile identity in that it did not observe the Law, but that, as in 2 and 3 John, there were enough assimilated Jews who retained Jewish self-identification for them not to use 'the Jews' in a hostile sense.

This makes the Gentile self-identification of the author of the fourth Gospel all the more significant. Basic Johannine theology was expounded by some people who retained their Jewish self-identification. The author of the fourth Gospel clearly did not belong to such a group. Whatever his origins, he and his fellow Christians, Jewish enough to need keeping out of Jewish meetings because otherwise they would have attended them, identified very strongly against 'the Jews' who had rejected them. This necessitated a change in covenantal nomism, so that salvation depends on faith in Jesus, not on membership of the Jewish community.

It follows that the fourth Gospel is very anti-Jewish. For centuries, it suited some Christians very well to have so anti-Jewish a work in the Word of God. It could be used to support persecution of the Jews. In the wake of the Holocaust, however, good Christian people have somewhat belatedly come to feel that anti-Semitism is wrong. Moreover, the Jewish community has a few people who study early Christianity, and who need to defend the Jewish community. There are thus two profound ulterior motives for supposing that Johannine *Ioudaioi* are not really 'Jews', for in that case the fourth Gospel would not really be anti-Jewish. The two main suggestions have been that the *Ioudaioi* are Judaeans, or the Jewish authorities.

THE JEWS[4]

We may consider first the view that this Gospel's *Ioudaioi* are not 'Jews' but 'Judaeans'. This view should be rejected for two reasons. Firstly, the Greek word *Ioudaioi* does not generally mean 'Judaeans': it means 'Jews', as we know from thousands of examples. There is a very small number of texts where it may reasonably be translated 'Judaeans'. Some of these are texts which discuss the administration of Judaea. For example, at the beginning of A.J. XVIII, Josephus reports the appointment of Quirinius as governor of Syria, and of the equestrian Coponius 'to rule over the Judaeans with authority over all' (XVIII, 2). Here the term *Ioudaioi*, which we normally translate 'Jews', may be properly translated 'Judaeans', because Coponius did not have authority over Jews outside Judaea, and did have authority over any Gentiles who lived there. The term could be used like this because everyone knew that Judaea was the ethnic homeland of Jews, a place populated almost entirely by Jews, from which Jews who lived elsewhere ultimately originated. There are also texts where an author feels a need to contrast Judaeans with Samaritans, Galileans and the like. For example, at the beginning of his account of Pentecost in Jerusalem in 4BCE, Josephus wants to make the point that Jews from elsewhere came in great numbers to the city. After words for large numbers, therefore, he continues 'of Galileans and of Idumaeans, and there was a multitude of Jerichoites and those who live across the river Jordan, and there was a multitude of Judaeans themselves (*autōn te Ioudaiōn*) . . . .' (A.J. XVII, 254). The term *Ioudaioi* can function in such contexts because Judaeans were Jews who lived in the ethnic homeland of Judaea, so the literary context can show that these are the Jews who are being contrasted with Galileans, Idumaeans and so on. Josephus had little choice in the matter, because there was no other word for 'Judaeans', for a separate word was not normally needed. Later in the same account, he refers to all these people as 'Jews' (*Ioudaioi*, A.J. XVII, 257, 258, 261, 265, 267), for they were all Jews as opposed to Romans. Consequently, this small number of passages do not show that the Greek word *Ioudaioi* normally means anything other than 'Jews'.

Secondly, the view that the fourth Gospel's *Ioudaioi* are really 'Judaeans' is not consistent with several examples of Johannine usage. The majority of examples are typified by John 2.13, which should not be translated 'And the Passover of the Judaeans was near'. The reason for this is a straightforward cultural one. Passover was, and is, a major feast for all Jews. It was not particularly a feast for Judaeans. It follows, therefore, that the *Ioudaioi* are 'Jews' (likewise 5.1; 6.4; 7.2; 11.55). In three further passages, the *Ioudaioi* are not Judaeans but Galileans. The two clearest examples are 6.41 and 6.52. John 6 is set in Galilee (Jn 6.1, 17, 23, 24, 59). These Galileans are properly called 'Jews', from just that point where the Johannine theology of the discourse becomes unpalatable for faithful Jews.[5] John 2.1–11 is set in Cana of Galilee, where the large stone waterpots are surely 'for the purification of the Jews' (2.6), not of the Judaeans.

All our evidence is therefore coherent. The fourth Gospel uses the Greek word *Ioudaioi* in a lexically normal manner, to mean 'Jews', not 'Judaeans'. In recent years, there has been one thorough attempt to argue that it does mean 'Judaeans', that of Lowe (1976). Lowe comes in from a Jewish perspective, and ends by associating his results with a vigorous rejection of anti-Semitism. The conventional rendering of *hoi Ioudaioi* as 'the Jews' 'is not only incorrect . . . but also pernicious. . . . Thus this philological error . . . has provided, in practically all modern translations of the gospels, a constant excuse for antisemitism whose further existence cannot be permitted' (Lowe 1976: 130). Lowe's central life concerns have led him to be quite confused over the relationships between religion, ethnicity and

117

homeland. This is evident in the definitions with which he begins his work.

Lowe's first definition is that 'to-day its only meaning is "members of the Jewish religion"' (Lowe 1976: 102). Unfortunately, 'its' is not very clear, but he seems to mean the word for 'Jews' in any language, so *Ioudaioi*, יהודים, Jews, juifs, Jüden, etc. The selection of religion is quite biassed. Many Jews do not perceive themselves as religious, but the perception that they are still Jewish is widespread, and nowhere more so than in Israel, where it is especially difficult to confuse irreligious Jews with Gentiles, because their Jewish descent, self-identification and language are obvious, and they maintain many Jewish customs. This bias runs through the whole of Lowe's article. He goes on to 'presuppose three basic meanings of the word'. This approach is not satisfactory. We should not 'presuppose' meanings, but infer them from usage, nor should we separate out three 'meanings' unless we have empirical justification for so doing. Lowe's three meanings are:

(a) 'members of the tribe of Judah' *as opposed* to members of other tribes;
(b) 'Judeans' *as opposed* to people living in (or originating from) other areas (notably both Galileans and Samaritans, if Judea is understood in the strict sense) of the area west of the Jordan between Samaria and Idumea);
(c) 'Jews' *as opposed* to members of other religions (notably Samaritans, Romans, Greeks).

(Lowe 1976: 102–3)

In meaning (c), the specification of 'religions' is misleading. The Greek word *Ioudaioi* generally means 'Jews', rather than members of other religions and/or ethnic groups.[6] These Jews had Judaea as their ethnic homeland, and were perceived to be the same people as those who lived there. Lowe's profound mistake misstates the common meaning of this term, and helps to separate out *distinct* meanings in a manner not generally found in the primary source material. Naturally, the connection between what Lowe has described as separate meanings is not often explicitly stated, because most passages are about either Jewish people in Judaea, or Jewish people somewhere in the diaspora. It is accordingly significant that when what Lowe has categorised as two 'meanings' occur in the same passages, an author may pass from one to the other without comment. I have noted A.J. XVII, 254ff., where Josephus first uses *Ioudaioi* of Jewish people in Judaea, mentioning also Galileans, Jerichoites and others; subsequently, he calls all these people *Ioudaioi*, 'Jews' as opposed to Romans. He did not expect to be misunderstood, because everyone knew that Judaea was the ethnic homeland of Jewish people. Equally striking are passages such as the decree of Dolabella to the people of Ephesus in 43BCE, for transmission to other Asian cities (Jos. A.J. XIV, 225–7). This notes a plea from Hyrcanus, 'high priest and ethnarch of the Jews (*Ioudaiōn*)', on behalf of 'his citizens'. This tells the Ephesians to allow these people to follow their own customs, being for example exempted from military service because they cannot carry arms or journey on the days of the sabbath. Thus it deals with Jews in Ephesus, and secondarily with Jews in other Asian cities. It is an assumption of such passages that Jews in Ephesus and elsewhere have their homeland in Judaea, where their fellow Jews live, and are therefore properly pleaded for by the high priest.

This illuminates the meaning of *Ioudaioi* in descriptions like that of Hyrcanus. It does not *mean* 'Judaeans', merely because it is used with reference to Jews who lived in Judaea, any more than it *means* 'Jerichoites' or 'Ephesians' when it is used with reference to Jews who lived in Jericho or Ephesus. The Greek word *Ioudaioi* has to be translated 'Judaeans' occasionally because English is *different* from Greek. The semantic area of *Ioudaioi* permits it to be used somewhat differently from the relevant English words, because English has separate words 'Jews' and 'Judaeans', and Greek did not. The Greek word *Ioudaioi* could be so used because everyone knew that Judaea was the ethnic homeland of Jews.

As a result of these errors of method, many of Lowe's examples are unconvincing. John 2.13 typifies several examples. As we have seen, this begins, 'And the Passover of the Jews was near', for Passover was a major pilgrim feast for all Jews. Lowe seeks to override this main point by arguing that such phrases 'occur only in reference to feasts requiring a pilgrimage to Judea' (Lowe 1976: 116). There are two profound things wrong with this. One is that the central argument carries no weight. The fact that the ethnic homeland is journeyed to cannot possibly mean that only its inhabitants were there. Hence the force of the second main point, the known fact that Passover was a major pilgrim feast when Jews came from all over the Roman empire, and from outside it. There is also an empirical fault. At John 6.4, Passover is described as 'the feast of the Jews', as Lowe notes, but 'no journey to Judea ensues'. Lowe therefore questions the authority of the verse, observing that it 'did not exist in versions of John's Gospel known to some early authorities' (Lowe 1976: 117). This is quite misleading. The verse is found in all early manuscripts and versions. It is moreover essential to the argument of the chapter. At Passover, Jews celebrated the redemption of Israel from Egypt at the Exodus. In John 6, Jesus, as the bread who came down from heaven, replaces the manna which came down from heaven, in a midrash on part of the Exodus narrative. This develops into an exposition of the eucharist, which brought life permanently to Christians, not temporarily to Jews in the wilderness. Moreover, John 6 contains two further examples of 'the Jews' (6.41, 52), who cannot be Judaeans because John 6 is set in Galilee.[7] Nor can this approach cope with John 2.6, set in Cana of Galilee, where the waterpots can hardly be for the purification of Judaeans only.[8]

119

We must therefore conclude that, owing to serious errors of method which derive from his ideological motivation, Lowe has offered impossible interpretations of several passages. His hypothesis should therefore be rejected.

The other major scholarly theory about the meaning of *Ioudaioi* is that it really means 'Jewish authorities' or the like. There are several versions of this theory, with many differences of detail. The most recent complete presentation of this view is by Von Wahlde, and the most recent variation is that of Dunn (Von Wahlde 1982; Dunn 1991: Chapter 8; more briefly Von Wahlde 1989: 31–5; Dunn 1992: 195–203; 1994). I therefore concentrate on these two presentations. There are three reasons for rejecting this view. Firstly, the Greek word *Ioudaioi* means 'Jews', not 'Jewish leaders', 'Jewish authorities' or the like. There are thousands of examples of this: they do not differ in major ways from the use of words such as 'juifs' and 'Jüden': and for the most part they are not contested. Since, however, various Jewish leaders and authorities at various times speak and/or act on behalf of the Jewish people, the word *Ioudaioi* may *refer* to leaders or authorities. We must not confuse meaning with reference. There are naturally examples of this usage in John. At 1.19, for example, 'the Jews' who sent priests and Levites to question John the Baptist must have been in some kind of position of authority. It does not however follow that the word *Ioudaioi means* 'Jewish authorities'.

Secondly, and consequently, the fourth Gospel has perfectly good words for Jewish authorities. Nicodemus is described as 'a ruler of the Jews' (Jn 3.1), and 'the rulers' (*tōn archontōn*) are referred to as a group (7.48). The author could have referred to 'rulers', or 'the rulers of the Jews' repeatedly, if he had meant this. On many occasions, he specifies Pharisees, as for example at 12.42, where even 'many of the rulers' are afraid that the Pharisees will ensure that they are kept away from Jewish meetings if they confess Jesus. The evangelist could have referred to 'the Pharisees' instead of 'the Jews', if he meant Pharisees. Again, there are several references to the chief priests (*archiereis*): in some passages, 'the chief priests and the Pharisees' have servants (e.g. 7.32, 45), and it is they who gather a sanhedrin (11.47), and give orders for Jesus' arrest (7.32; 11.57; 18.3). The author could have referred to 'the chief priests' or 'the chief priests and the Pharisees' repeatedly, if they were the Jewish leaders whom he meant. It follows from all this that this Gospel does not mean the Jewish authorities when it says 'the Jews'.

Thirdly, there are passages in which 'the Jews' cannot mean the authorities. References to Jewish customs are of this kind. For example, 'And the Passover of the Jews was near' (2.13). Passover was no more confined to Jewish authorities than it was especially for Judaeans: it was a major pilgrim feast for Jews in general. So *Ioudaioi* in this passage means 'Jews' (cf. 2.6; 4.9; 5.1; 6.4; 7.2; 11.55; 19.42). There are other passages where the interpretation in terms of Jewish authorities is especially inappropriate. Nicodemus was 'a ruler of the Jews' (3.1), he was hardly a ruler of the Jewish authorities (cf. 7.45–52). This Gospel's grasp of God's revelation of himself is so firm that it says 'salvation is of the Jews' (4.22, cf. 1.11, 16–17; 5.45–7; 8.56; 10.34–5; 12.41): this does not mean that salvation is from the chief priests and Pharisees. In the eucharistic discourse of Chapter 6, 'the crowd' become 'the Jews' just when the theology becomes impossible for faithful Jews (6.41, 52), not especially for Jewish authorities. The expression of this at 6.53, where eternal life depends on eating the Son of man's flesh and drinking his blood, is especially offensive to Jewish sensibility, not particularly for authoritative Jews.[9] It is not probable that 'the Jews' who went to Mary and Martha (11.19, 45) were chief priests or Pharisees. The 'large crowd of the Jews' who went to see not only Jesus, but also Lazarus whom he had raised from the dead (12.9), are surely not authorities either. Once again, all our evidence is coherent. When the evangelist says *Ioudaioi*, he means 'Jews', not Jewish authorities. Since however there are cases where Jewish authorities may speak and/or act on behalf of the Jewish people as a whole, there are examples which can be fitted into that mould (e.g. 1.19; 2.18; 5.16, 18).

We must now consider the detailed arguments of Von Wahlde. After noting that the use of 'the Jews' has implications for the question of anti-Semitism in the fourth Gospel, Von Wahlde begins with a survey of previous scholarship. This ensures that any bias traditional among the Gentile Christian men who dominate scholarship will perpetuate itself, and this is evinced in Von Wahlde's organising category. While he notes several different positions, such as 'Jews as contrasted with Samaritans', and 'an explanation of feasts and customs of the Jews', he tabulates them all under the headings 'Authorities and people' and 'Authorities only' (Von Wahlde 1982: 37–40). The pass has already been sold. As we have seen, *Ioudaioi* cannot mean 'authorities only' because the word means 'Jews', and the fourth Gospel uses 'rulers', 'Pharisees' and 'chief priests' when appropriate. Even 'authorities and people' isolates aspects of a word which refers to a whole ethnic and religious group, and this isolation is quite arbitrary.

Having perpetuated the traditional distinctions of scholarship, Von Wahlde offers reasons 'for seeing at least some of the uses of "Jews" as referring to religious authorities' (Von Wahlde 1982: 41–2). This is quite slippery, because many examples of 'Jews' (*Ioudaioi*) *referring* to religious authorities could be quite consistent with the term *meaning* 'the Jews', and the slipperiness becomes clear when, after further discussion, Von Wahlde concludes that the original author probably saw the Jews 'as the religious authorities exclusively' (Von Wahlde 1982: 45). Von Wahlde's examples include John 9, where he sees the term 'Pharisees' (9.13, 15, 16) 'replaced' by 'Jews' (9.18, 22), and 'Pharisees' used again at 9.40 (Von Wahlde 1982: 42). There is some truth in this, but Von Wahlde misses the function of some passages altogether. The Pharisees conduct this investigation because they were an authoritative group already in the tradition (e.g. Mk 2.24; 3.6), at Yabneh and probably in Ephesus. 'The Jews' is appropriate at 9.22 because the Johannine community were prevented from attending Jewish meetings, not Pharisaic cabals. At 9.18, it reflects the unbelief of Jews in general, and prepares for 9.22. The blindness of the Pharisees is especially important at 9.40 because they were prominent in Jewish leadership at the time, and it completes the symbolism of the chapter as a whole.[10] Variation of this kind was possible because all Pharisees were Jews: it does not imply that all 'the Jews' were Pharisees, authorities, chief priests or anything of the kind.

Von Wahlde's discussion is quite defective in failing to allow for authors to vary their usage. Nor does he allow for the author to have a perspective which would cause him to use the term 'the Jews' when we would not use it. This is clear in another argument according to which ethnically Jewish people are said to 'fear the Jews' (citing 7.13; 9.22; 20.19). 'These "Jews" then are clearly not the common people but some authoritative group' (Von Wahlde 1982: 42). Comments of this kind fail to explain *why* the authoritative group are called 'the Jews', and the fearful people are not. I have noted that this term is used at 9.22 because it was of central importance that the Johannine community were kept out of Jewish meetings. At 20.19, the opposing groups are clearly labelled 'the Jews' and 'the disciples', as at 2.17–22 and 11.8, 54. An alternative possibility is accordingly available, one that works in terms of perspective rather than reality, and sees 'the Jews' as an alien group, whether authoritative or not. We have seen that this can give us a complete explanation of Johannine usage. Accordingly, we must not shift the meaning of the term *Ioudaioi* away from 'Jews' to 'authorities' on the basis of evidence like this.

Another major mistake runs through Von Wahlde's discussion. He classifies Johannine examples into two groups, the 'neutral' use and the 'Johannine' use. This classification is as wrong as possible. The fourth evangelist has many examples of the so-called 'neutral' use, and they should not be put on one side when we try to understand the others. Von Wahlde proceeds, 'In order to provide an objective standard for determining the Johannine usage, we would make explicit the following criteria which are used in determining that usage' (Von Wahlde 1982: 47). The proposed criteria are not objective, because so many examples have already been excluded. Two serious mistakes follow. Von Wahlde's first characteristic is that the term in these instances 'does not have its nationalistic meaning', by which he evidently means to exclude references like 2.13, 'the Passover of the Jews'. But this is only because Von Wahlde has classified the 'neutral' use separately. The fourth Gospel actually has abundant references to 'the Jews' as an ethnic group with their own customs. Von Wahlde's third characteristic of these texts 'is that they represent a single undifferentiated reaction'. This completely misrepresents the fourth Gospel's usage, which includes both the hostility of 'the Jews were seeking to kill him' (sc. Jesus, Jn 5.18; 7.1), and the more neutral 'the Passover of the Jews was near' (2.13). With mistakes like this, Von Wahlde could not possibly reach a correct solution.

Von Wahlde's discussion has two further errors of method. He notes from Fuller 'the similarity between the sequence of 6.1–71 in John and that of Mark 6.30–54 and 8.11–33'. Fuller used this to argue that the Jews in the Johannine discourse play the same role as the authorities in the Marcan account, and thus that 'the Jews' means 'authorities' even at John 6.41 and 6.52. Again, Von Wahlde notes Leistner's argument that the appearance of authorities outside Judaea is like the situation at Mark 3.20–2. Von Wahlde finds these arguments difficult to assess (Von Wahlde 1982: 43). They are not difficult to assess, they are wrong. The outstanding feature of the evidence is that the fourth Gospel's account is *different* from that of Mark. To interpret it as if it somehow must be really the same is therefore quite inaccurate (though a necessary ploy, if one is committed to believe in the literal truth of the whole of scripture).

Von Wahlde's remaining error of method is to resort to a redactor when irretrievably stuck. It is a measure of the weakness of his position that he must do this even after most examples of 'the Jews' not meaning 'authorities' have been removed by biassed classification. He resorts to a redactor because he finds the usage at 6.41 and 6.52 'idiosyncratic'. We have seen, however, that it is quintessentially Johannine. The 'crowd' turn into 'the Jews' just at the point where the theology becomes impossible for faithful Jews, and the description is repeated just before 6.53, which has been written up to be as anti-Jewish as possible.[11] Von Wahlde tentatively suggests that 10.19 is the work of a redactor, noting 'a peculiar mixture of features associated with both the hostile and the non-hostile use of *Ioudaioi*' (Von Wahlde 1982: 51). The mixture is not peculiar. The apparent peculiarity has been produced by Von Wahlde's arbitrary classification of 'neutral' usage separate from Johannine usage.

We must therefore conclude that Von Wahlde is quite wrong. Nonetheless, Dunn has put forward a new version of this view. Confronted with my previous work on this Gospel, he suggests that the many hostile references to 'the Jews'

> surely indicate a breach with those so designated; but most scholars identify 'the Jews' in these passages with the Jewish authorities in the area where the Johannine congregations were meeting. And it still leaves a similar range of references where 'the Jews' in question are the common people, the crowd.
>
> (Dunn 1994: 442)

This illustrates how scholarship feeds on itself. I offered a new analysis of the identity of the Johannine community and its opponents. Rather than look for the identity of 'the Jews' only in who they were, I looked also at the perspective from which they were being observed, and inferred that the author(s) of the fourth Gospel had Gentile self-identification. I also produced the first analysis of this in terms of the identity factors which made it up. For example, I noted the removal of sabbath observance, and Jesus' replacement of the major feast of Tabernacles (Casey 1991a: 27ff., esp. 29–30). This new analysis is not properly met by repeating the work of Von Wahlde and others.

Dunn further comments that

> the concepts of 'Jewish identity' and 'Gentile identity' can simply not be drawn as sharply as he [sc. Casey] strives to do. And, in particular, the arguments that there was in effect a shift in identity between the earlier and other Christian (diaspora) communities and the Johannine community, and that the Johannine community had Gentile, that is, non-Jewish identity, are altogether too casually drawn.
>
> (Dunn 1994: 443)

Dunn's comments presuppose his earlier work, in which he sought to extend the nature of Jewish identity to include nascent Christianity within it (Dunn 1991: 143ff.). To this we must therefore turn. Dunn relies on the discussion of K.G. Kuhn to suppose that 'in the post-biblical ("intertestamental") period, *Israel* was the people's preferred name for itself (cf. e.g. Sir 17.17; *Jub.* 33.20; *Pss. Sol.* 14.5), whereas *Ioudaios* was the name by which they were known to others' (Dunn 1991: 145, citing Kuhn 1938: 359–65). This comment shows no awareness of the extent of the evidence which would be required to establish so general a proposition. Only a massive social survey could settle it: the next best thing would be clear statements to this effect in our primary sources. There is no such statement. All Dunn has cited is three texts which show that Jewish authors could refer to Israel as Israel. They could, and did, and other cases could be cited. In other texts, however, Jewish authors refer to their own people as 'Jews': so, for example, the Elephantine papyri in Aramaic, and 2 Maccabees in Greek. Second Maccabees, written by Jews to and for Jews, begins: 'The Jews (*Ioudaioi*) in Jerusalem and those in the land of Judaea to the brethren the Jews (*Ioudaioi*) in Egypt, good peace.' This is as intra-Jewish as possible, and falsifies Dunn's claim that the term 'Jew' 'always had something of an outsider's perspective' (Dunn 1991: 145). The author naturally used the term 'Israel' as well (e.g. 2 Macc 1.25–6).

Dunn goes on to find 'striking' the usage of the Damascus Document where he regards 'Israel' as 'clearly the preferred self-designation' (citing CD III, 19), while 'the sect sees itself as those who "have gone out from the land of Judah" and who will "no more consort with the house of Judah" (4, 2–3, 11)'. From this stunningly small amount of evidence, Dunn concludes, 'It would be possible, then, for an early Jewish believer in Jesus Messiah to cede the use of the name "Jew" to others within the broad spectrum of late second Temple Judaism, while clinging to the title "Israel(ite)" – as did the Qumran covenanters.' Dunn's comments contradict Jewish identity, from a perspective of Christian commitment. The Qumran community, though wholly untypical of Jews in cutting themselves off from the mainstream of Judaism and living in the wilderness, did not cede the use of the name 'Jew' to others. They recorded that they had left the land of Judah because their predecessors had done so. At the same time, they recorded that 'all Israel went astray' (CD III, 14); 'Belial shall be sent against Israel' (IV, 13–14); and they referred to 'the books of the prophets whose words Israel despised' (VII, 17–18). Thus they used 'Israel', as well as designations such as 'the house of Judah', when they criticised most of the Jewish people. Equally, in the last days, this same document predicts, 'and all those who entered the covenant and breached the bound of the Torah, when the glory of God is displayed to Israel, they shall be cut off from the midst of the camp and with them all those who did evil to Judah in the days of her trials' (XX, 25–7). Here, where 'Israel' is used for the triumphant people, 'Judah' is used in the same sentence for those who held fast to the Law in the Hellenising crisis. There was a real crisis in Israel at this time, one which is important for understanding Christian origins. When they wrote about it, faithful Jews did use the term 'Israel' of their own group. They did not deny the term 'Jew' and cede it to others. Their purpose in life was to maintain Jewish identity, not to reject it, and their religious criticism of other Jews is quite centrally misstated by the notion that they might reject the term 'Jew' itself. Hence the use of the Aramaic term 'Jews (*Yehūdā'ē*)' in the *Scroll of Fasting*, an entirely Jewish work approximately contemporary with the fourth Gospel. It follows that when another contemporary, Josephus, makes many declarations such as this: 'It is natural to all Jews right from their very birth to regard them [sc. the scriptures] as the decrees of God and abide by them and, if necessary, die willingly for them' (c. Ap. I, 43): we must note his vigorous and favourable use of the Greek term 'Jews (*Ioudaiois*)', and not suppose that it is used *merely* because Josephus was writing partly for Gentiles.[12]

With Jewish identity so regrettably misstated, Dunn approaches the Christian sources. When he gets to the fourth Gospel, he seeks to use the conflicts portrayed in it, especially themes of judgement and division, to divide Jewish people into two groups. 'All this seems to indicate something of a *contest* between the Johannine gospel and "the Jews" = the Jewish authorities, for the loyalty of "the Jews" = the people, with the gospel itself as the sifting, divisive factor' (Dunn 1991: 157). This makes nonsense of Johannine usage. As we have seen, the fourth Gospel has perfectly good words for the Jewish authorities. It could easily have portrayed a contest between authorities (*archontes*) and/or chief priests and/or Pharisees on the one hand, and the crowd (*ochlos*) or the people (*ethnos* or *laos*) on the other. The constant use of 'the Jews' for both sides of a severe conflict would be quite confused, and would cause confusion. Dunn then endeavours to be more precise.

> In these circumstances it is very likely that John's use of 'the Jews' (= the Jewish authorities) refers to a local Jewish leadership who identified with the objectives of the Yavnean rabbis, or possibly even to the Yavnean rabbis themselves. But it is also likely that John's usage reflects the claim beginning to be made at that time by the Yavnean authorities to be the only legitimate heirs to pre-70 Judaism, to be, in fact 'the Jews'.
>
> (Dunn 1991: 158)

Dunn cites no evidence for this claim, nor is there any. The leadership of the rabbis at Yabneh does make sense of some comments in the fourth Gospel. There is however nothing either in rabbinical sources or in this Gospel to suggest that rabbis at Yabneh disputed the Jewish identity of other Jews, nor that a group banned from Jewish meetings and virulently opposed to 'the Jews' could nonetheless consider themselves Jewish.

Finally, Dunn turns to 'the rhetoric of factional polemic' to explain the severity of Johannine polemic. He quotes the expression 'sons of Belial' from Jubilees 15.33 and 4Q174, notes Jesus' rebuke to Peter (Mk 8.33) and concludes, 'Even with John 8.44, therefore, we are still in the realm of intra-Jewish polemic' (Dunn 1991: 160). This does not follow. Jubilees 15.33 applies to apostasy from Judaism, and 4Q174, though less clear, is evidently dealing with enemies of Israel. Not one of these passages declares 'the Jews' as the alien group. Many passages of ancient literature do, however, all of them reflecting conflict between Jews and Gentiles, some of them dealing with apostasy, when some people do perceive a change of identity. For example, Josephus records a decision of Publius Servilius Galba, in which he notes that the council and people of Miletus have been attacking 'the Jews' and preventing them from observing the sabbath and other customs: his decision was that 'the Jews' should not be prevented from observing their own customs (A.J. XIV, 244–6). Here, as so often, 'the Jews' are so called to distinguish them from another group, in this case Milesians. Conversely, Josephus himself, dealing with precisely the same conflict as Jubilees 15.33, declares that some people who were born Jews 'concealed the circumcision of their genitals so that they might be Greeks even when undressed' (A.J. XII, 241). The Johannine use of 'the Jews' indicates a similar perception of identity. The Johannine community were not allowed to attend Jewish meetings. In the course of this dispute, they identified against 'the Jews', thereby displaying Gentile self-identification. Dunn's whole approach represents a basic failure of analysis. Instead of looking at this Gospel's attitude to such matters as circumcision and sabbath, and thereby analysing the Johannine community's hostility to 'the Jews', he has denied the basic evidence of the primary sources to fit them into a pattern more comfortable for modern Christians. Faced with new and more sophisticated analysis in my previous work, he has objected that it does not comport with the work of 'most scholars', who are mostly his fellow Christians making the same comfy mistakes. We should not proceed like this.

We must conclude that the Johannine *Ioudaioi* are 'the Jews'. It follows that this Gospel is genuinely anti-Jewish. We must consider next one of the historical features of the separation of Christianity from Judaism. It involved a profound change in covenantal nomism, one which is especially obvious in this Gospel's use of the purely Hellenistic concept of rebirth.

REBIRTH AND THE COVENANT COMMUNITY

At first sight, rebirth does not seem a likely concept for a monotheistic author to use, because it was associated with pagan religions. A whole Hermetic tractate (C.H. XIII) is devoted to it (cf. Dodd 1953: 44–53). The following example is from a Mithras liturgy (complete with some incomprehensible terms):

> This is the invocation of the word (*logos*): 'First origin (*genesis*) of my origin, aeēiouō first beginning of my beginning . . . if it seems good to you, meterta phōth ïerazath, to give me, held as I am by my existing nature, to immortal birth, in order that, after the present need which presses hard upon me, I may behold by immortal spirit the immortal Beginning, anchrephrenesouphiringch by immortal water, erounouï parakounēth by the most steadfast air, that I may be born again by thought, kraochrax oïm, I begin, that I may be initiated and that the sacred spirit may breathe in me . . . born mortal from a mortal womb, improved by mighty power and an incorruptible right hand. . . .' And gaze on the god, bellow long, and greet him thus: 'O Lord, hail, ruler of water, hail, founder of earth, hail, sovereign of wind/spirit. . . . Lord, born again I pass away; increasing and having been increased I come to an end; born of a life-giving birth I am set free for death and go on my way, as you ordained, as you enacted and made the mystery.'
>
> (Paris papyrus 574)

Early Christianity did not borrow much material of this kind. This borrowing can only be explained by a profound need for such a concept. To understand this need, we must recall that most Jews inherited their Jewish identity by birth. Although it was possible to be a proselyte, the majority of Jews had two Jewish parents, so much so that for most purposes Jews may fruitfully be described as an ethnic group. Entry to the covenant people was normally, therefore, by birth. It is this which is upset by John 3.3: 'Jesus answered and said to him, "Amen, amen I tell you, unless a person is born again/from above, he cannot see the kingdom of God."' The fourth Gospel has one Greek word, *anōthen*, which means both 'again' and 'from above', and we should understand both. When Nicodemus, described as a 'ruler of the Jews', has asked his not very bright question about going back into his mother's womb, Jesus reformulates the main point: 'Amen, amen I tell you, unless a person is born of water and spirit, he cannot enter the kingdom of God' (Jn 3.5). It is noteworthy that the fourth Gospel's only two uses of the term 'kingdom of God'[13] are precisely at the point where the standard Jewish version of covenantal nomism is rejected, and at the point where it introduces what is otherwise a pagan idea.

'Water' and 'spirit' were also traditional. Psalm 51 presents personal repentance with images including 'wash me' and 'do not take your holy spirit from me' (51.9, 13). Second Isaiah presents the salvation of Israel, declaring, 'I will pour water on a thirsty place. . . . I will pour my spirit on your seed' (Is 44.3). Ezekiel likewise looks for the restoration of Israel: 'I will throw water upon you. . . . And I will put my spirit within you' (Ezek 36.25, 27). The author of the Community Rule from Qumran declared that the stubborn of heart would 'not be cleansed by waters of purification, nor sanctified by seas and rivers' (1QS III, 4–5). Of the man who enters the covenant, on the other hand,

> And by the spirit of holiness in unity with his truth he shall be cleansed from all his sins . . . and in the submission of his soul to all the precepts of God, his flesh shall be cleansed by sprinkling with waters of purification and sanctified with waters of cleansing.
>
> (1QS III, 7–9)

John the Baptist took up this tradition. He baptised with water, to symbolise repentance and forgiveness of sins, and he predicted the coming of one who would baptise with holy spirit and with fire.[14]

This was taken up in early Christianity. Baptism in water is the means of entering the Christian community already in the early chapters of Acts, and the Holy Spirit may be received at the same time or separately. When Paul was faced with schism in Corinth, he wrote from Ephesus, seeking to play down the importance of the person by whom Christians were baptised (1 Cor 1.12–17). He did not however attempt to undermine the importance of baptism, surely because it was so widely accepted as the means of initiation into the Christian community. At Colossians 2.11–13 he interprets it vigorously as a replacement for circumcision. Replacing the ancient association between circumcision and death (Ex 4.24–6), he has Christians die and rise again with Christ in baptism. This is expounded in Romans 6, where there is an analogy between the believer's baptism and the atoning death of Christ, and the resulting life for the believer (cf. Jn 3.14ff.). When Paul preached in Ephesus, he met a dozen or so Christians who knew only the baptism of John, and not the Holy Spirit. They were clearly exceptional. Paul baptised them in the name of Jesus, laid his hands on them and the Holy Spirit came upon them (Acts 19.1–7).

It follows from this massive cultural background that the fourth evangelist and any Christian audience would necessarily have baptism in mind at John 3.5.[15] Why then is the term 'baptise' or 'baptism' not used at this point? There is a complex of cultural reasons for this too. One main point has just been made: it was culturally obvious that baptism was central to Christians being reborn by water and spirit. There was therefore no need to mention it until later in the chapter, when the main theological points had been made clear. Secondly, we know from the end of Chapter 6 that some Christians left the Johannine community after taking part in the eucharist, and the anti-Jewish way in which the eucharist is finally expounded to 'the Jews' entails that at least the majority of those who left self-identified as Jews.[16] A similar inference follows from the end of Chapter 12. Here we find that many of the rulers believed in Jesus, but they did not confess him, effectively because they would have been thrown out of the Jewish community.[17] It follows that baptised Christians had left the Johannine community, and remained in the Jewish community, and that some of them were prominent people. There was therefore little point in telling a leader of the Jews that Jews needed to be baptised! Moreover, the clear differentiation of flesh and Spirit at both 3.6 and 6.63 strongly suggests a perspective like that of 1QS III. Baptism is not mentioned at 3.5 because it is not enough: it could be gone through by people who were not reborn of the Spirit, as later experience appeared to show. Rebirth by water and the Spirit, which all Christians, and their Jewish opponents, knew was symbolised by the initiation rite of baptism, is therefore the centre of the opening exposition.

Further, rebirth, experienced by Christians entering the Christian community, is a simple opposite of birth, experienced by Jewish babies arriving in the Jewish community. This is the point of Nicodemus' apparently unintelligent question at 3.4: it bluntly mentions natural birth to clarify the frame of rebirth at 3.3 and 3.5, so that we can all see that rebirth is the spiritual equivalent of birth. Finally, the fourth evangelist found it difficult to write about Christian baptism within the framework of the historical ministry of Jesus. This is clear from 3.22–4.2. Here we are offered the quite unhistorical information that Jesus baptised (3.22), that everyone came to him (3.26), that the Pharisees heard that Jesus baptised more people than John (4.1), and then the true fact that Jesus did *not* baptise![18] The fourth evangelist was not all that good at dealing with the similar problem of expounding the eucharist before it had been instituted.[19] All this would be an additional deterrent to beginning this chapter with baptism. Hence his decision to deal with the theology of rebirth, followed by Jesus' atoning death and the need for faith leading to eternal life, before his final endeavour to put the baptism of John in its place.

We can now see what the opening of John 3 means and refers to. Its main point is the replacement of the Jewish community by the Christian community, the only one in which salvation is perceived to occur. It begins by contrasting entry into the two communities. Birth into the Jewish community is taken for granted. Rebirth by water and Spirit is contrasted with it, for everyone knew that this was the means of entry into the Christian community, largely by baptism. The contrast between flesh and Spirit, and the unknown origins and destination of those born of the Spirit (3.6–8), reflect the position of the Johannine community as baptised Christians, some of whose baptised fellow Christians had left to remain in the Jewish community. With this clear, we can follow the discourse through.

Nicodemus now asks a very general question, and receives the highly ironical reply, 'You are a/the teacher of Israel and you do not know these things?' (3.10). No indeed, no teacher of Israel did! That was a prerogative of the teacher from God (cf. 3.2). The point is reinforced as the discourse slips into the plural: 'Amen, amen I tell you [singular], we say what we know and we bear witness to what we have seen, and you [plural] do not receive our witness' (3.11). Of course 'the Jews' did not accept that witness! With that established, the discourse moves to the universal function of Jesus' death: 'And as Moses lifted up the serpent in the wilderness, so must the Son of man be lifted up, so that everyone who believes in him may have eternal life' (3.14–15).

'Everyone who believes in him' were now mostly Gentiles. To ensure their inclusion, the criteria of salvation have had to be shifted. Instead of birth, it is first rebirth and then faith in the central identity factor of the Christian community. The nature of salvation has been shifted too. Whereas in the Jewish community some people believed in eternal life but others did not, in the Christian community this belief has become necessary. Jesus' death has been seen as instrumental in the process. The comparison with Moses, like the use of the term 'kingdom of God' earlier in the discourse, serves to put the point more sharply. Whereas the people of Israel found deliverance under Moses, through Jesus salvation is open theoretically to everyone, and in practice the Jewish community are excluded.

The following verses make several related points. First of all, God is put in overall charge of these proceedings. The main function of the apparently 'subordinationist' statements of Johannine Christology is precisely this, for this is essentially what non-Christian Jews would deny. Then the role of faith is stressed, for this determines membership of the Christian rather than the Jewish community. The point is made both positively and negatively. The purpose of the Son's mission is 'so that everyone who believes should not perish but have eternal life' (3.16), whereas 'he who does not believe has already been judged, because he has not believed in the name of the only-begotten Son of God' (3.18). Like the need for rebirth, this removes non-Christian Jews from salvation. It also shows that the fading away of imminentist eschatology in the fourth Gospel is not only due to the passage of time: judgement and salvation have to be present realities, because people have to make up their minds whether they will remain in the Jewish community or leave it for the Christian community. To set up the alternatives clearly, the fourth Gospel uses its concept of the 'world': 'God did not send the Son into the world to judge the world, but so that the world might be saved through him' (3.17). The concept of the 'world' is not consistently used throughout the Gospel, because most Gentiles did not accept the Gospel. So we also have, for example, 'the world did not know him' (1.10), and 'I have overcome the world' (16.33). The situation is described neatly at 15.19: 'since you are not of the world, but I chose you out of the world, for this reason the world hates you'. We must again infer that the Johannine community at least contained people whose self-identification was 'Greek', 'Roman', 'Ephesian', 'Smyrnean', 'Lycian' or the like, as well as 'disciples': hence the apparently favourable use of 'world' at 3.17. The discourse continues by using 'their works' to contrast those who accept and those who reject the light (3.19–21).

Thus the nature of covenantal nomism has at one level changed little. Once in the community, members have to take quite drastic steps to get out: in effect, they have to reject the community. Membership can be characterised both by one's attitude to God, and by one's works. The community has other identity factors which are also so vital that they effectively determine membership or rejection. At another level, the change has been complete. The community is now the Christian community as opposed to 'the Jews', a religious rather than an ethnic group, largely composed of people who have joined it voluntarily in recent years, reborn rather than born into it.

With all these points clarified, the author puts John the Baptist's baptism in its place: he is to be completely eclipsed by Jesus, to whom he finally bears witness (3.22–36). At this point Jesus does baptise, and more successfully than John (3.22, 26; 4.1), and this is corrected to baptism by Jesus' disciples (4.2), two ways of making the point that Christian baptism is essential for salvation. John the Baptist concludes the discourse[20] by reiterating the main points of the basic shift in covenantal nomism, attributing the whole matter to the Father, having the Son at the centre, with faith in him vital for salvation, and the eschatology transmuted to express the need for immediate decision:

> The Father loves the Son and has given everything into his hand. He who believes in the Son has eternal life, but he who does not believe in the Son will not see life, but the wrath of God will remain on him.
>
> (3.35–6)

We can now see why the concept of rebirth was so useful to this author. It facilitated his first major exposition of the different view of the covenant community necessitated by the existence of the Christian community separate from the Jewish community. Seen in its new cultural context, it is not remotely like the Hermetic Corpus, nor the Mithras text quoted above.[21]

Given that it responds to a need visible in the exposition of baptism in earlier sources, including one in Ephesus some thirty years previously, it is possible that the concept of rebirth had been taken over years ago (cf. Tit. 3.5; 1 Pet. 1.23): it is certain that the fourth evangelist's exposition would not be perceived as pagan. The new view of covenantal nomism is pervasive in this Gospel. It is especially obvious in debates with 'the Jews', sometimes with the same complex of basic ideas as in Chapter 3. For example, Chapter 5 notes the intention of 'the Jews' to kill Jesus, on both legal and Christological grounds.[22] Jesus' reply immediately centres on the complete dependence of the Son on the Father. Having thus made clear that the God of 'the Jews' is responsible for his ministry, Jesus takes the next step of criticising non-Christian Jews: 'He who does not honour the Son does not honour the Father who sent him' (5.23). There follows the centrality of faith and the transmutation of eschatology: 'Amen, amen I tell you that he who hears my word and believes in him who sent me has eternal life and does not come to judgement, but has passed from death to life' (5.24). I have noted the similar view of the covenant community in the eucharistic discourse of Chapter 6, again in debate with 'the Jews'.[23] At 6.32, Jesus contrasts the manna in the wilderness with the true bread from heaven, given to them by his Father. By 6.47 it is the believer who has eternal life, and by making the Christian eucharist essential for life, 6.53 excludes non-Christian Jews from salvation.

Similar points are made in Chapter 8. Here too faith is essential. At 8.24, Jesus tells 'the Jews' (cf. 8.22): 'unless you believe that I am (He), you will die in your sins'. Setting the moment of recognition at his crucifixion, Jesus declares his dependence on the Father (8.28–9). In the following discussion, the Jews plead their descent from Abraham, another statement of the older view of covenantal nomism, in which people were born into the covenant community. They associate this with monotheism: 'We have one Father, God' (8.41). Stressing again that God sent him, Jesus declares that their Father is the devil (8.42–4). Works are mentioned intermittently throughout the discussion, transmuted from doing the Law into acceptance rather than murder of Jesus. The discourse ends with a ringing declaration of Jesus' superiority to Abraham, and the Jews' consequent attempt to stone him (8.58–9). Vigorous contrast with disciples of Moses (9.28–9) is presented in the next discourse, and leads to the allegory of the good shepherd (10.1ff.). Here the rejection of 'the Jews' is quite blatant, for Jesus tells them 'But you do not believe, because you do not belong to my sheep' (10.26, cf. 24).

Jesus' public ministry ends with several of these major points. The attempt of 'some Greeks' to see Jesus (12.20–1) is not successful, and is met with exposition of the significance of Jesus' death: 'And I, if I am lifted up from the earth, will draw all people to myself' (12.32). Jesus' atoning death let Gentiles into the covenant community. The evangelist explains the unbelief of the Jews from scripture (Is 53.1; 6.10), and criticises the partly ethnic life-stance of those who remained in the Jewish community when Christians were thrown out of it: 'For they loved the glory of men rather than the glory of God' (12.43). The remaining verses stress vigorously the need for faith in Jesus, the purpose of his mission being to save 'the world', and his absolute dependence on the Father.

In the final discourses, Jesus tells the disciples what to do in place of the Law. 'I give you a new commandment, to love each other. . . . If you love me, keep my commandments' (13.34 . . . 14.15, cf. 14.21–4; 15.10–17; 1 Jn 2.3ff.; 3.11–24; 4.21–5.3). This replaces the Old Testament commandments to love God and do the Law. Several main points are written in a passage which includes the *Shema*:

> Hear, Israel, the LORD your God, the LORD is one, and you shall love the LORD your God with all your heart. . . . And these words which I have commanded you to-day shall be upon your heart . . . you will surely keep the commandments of the LORD your God.
>
> (Deut 6.4–5, 17)

As for God, he is described in one of the ten commandments as 'showing loving kindness to thousands who love me and keep my commandments' (Ex 20.6; Deut 5.10). When the historical Jesus was asked which of the commandments is the most important, he isolated the *Shema* and Leviticus 19.18: 'You shall love your neighbour as yourself' (Mk 12.28–34). This is the cultural complex which has been rewritten in the Johannine community. Jesus occupies the place taken by God, and the disciples are to do his commandents rather than 'their Law' (15.25). Hence another crop of subordinationist statements, e.g. 'The words which I speak I do not speak of myself, but the Father who remains in me does his works' (14.10). For the same underlying reason, other comments associate Jesus and the Father together on equal terms: 'If anyone loves me he will keep my word, and my Father will love him and we will come to him and make our home with him' (14.23).

When we have been through all this material, we can see what a devastating shift in the covenant community is summarised in the prologue. 'He came to his own (place), and his own (people) did not receive him' (1.11). This is the rejection of 'the Jews', perceived as people who rejected Jesus. 'But as many as did receive him, to them he gave power to become children of God, even to those who believe on his name' (1.12). While 'the Jews' are not saved, the Johannine community is saved, and has replaced them as 'children of God', faith in Jesus being the central identity factor of the new community. This is then defined by birth, the birth of God which replaces birth into the Jewish community (1.13). This looks forward to the central presentation of rebirth in Chapter 3, and it is essentially the same as the description of the saved people as born of God in 1 John (cf. 1 Jn 3.9; 4.7; 5.1, 4, 18).

REPLACEMENT SYMBOLISM

This major shift in covenantal nomism is paralleled in this Gospel's replacement symbolism. At 2.13, Jesus went up to Jerusalem for 'the Passover of the Jews' (cf. 6.4; 11.55), but he was the Lamb of God (1.29, 36), and when he was slaughtered at the same time as the Jewish Passover victims (cf. 19.14), he fulfilled the scripture that 'a bone of it shall not be broken' (Jn 19.36, cf. Ex 12.46; Num 9.12). At a symbolic level we are being told that Jesus has replaced the Jewish Passover and indeed the whole sacrificial system, symbolised by the lambs which were sacrificed every day as the Tamid, the continual offering which symbolised God's presence with Israel.[24] As the Lamb of God, Jesus took away the sin, not of 'the Jews', but of 'the world' (1.29), a term which clearly includes Gentiles. Thus the replacement symbolism is organically associated with the change in the covenant community discussed in the previous section.

At the first Passover at the beginning of the public ministry, Jesus not only cleansed but also effectively replaced the Temple:

> Jesus answered and said to them, 'Destroy this Temple and in three days I will raise it up'. The Jews therefore said, 'This Temple took 46 years to build, and you will raise it up in three days?' But he was talking about the Temple of his body!
>
> (2.19–21)

This is said to have been understood by the disciples after the resurrection, when they remembered the words which he had spoken in debate with 'the Jews' (2.22). God dwells especially in Jesus' body while he is on earth, rather than in the Temple. It was the death and resurrection of his body which brought about the salvation of the Gentiles. Thus he has replaced the Temple of the Jews.[25] In Chapter 4, both Jerusalem and Gerizim are to be replaced as centres of worship (4.21): the true worshippers who worship the Father in spirit and truth (4.23) can only be the Christian community. Just before the second Passover, 'the feast of the Jews', Jesus fed some 5,000 people miraculously (Jn 6.4ff.). I have discussed the midrash in which he surpasses the manna in the wilderness: 'Amen, amen I say to you, Moses has not given you the bread from heaven, but my Father gives you the true bread from heaven. . . . I am the bread of life' (6.32, 35).[26] We have seen that, in the subsequent debate, participation in the Christian eucharist is essential for salvation. While 'the Jews' continue to eat the Passover, remembering the deliverance of their forefathers in the wilderness, they are excluded from the salvation now enjoyed by Gentiles.

Jesus also replaced 'the feast of the Jews, Tabernacles' (7.2). A significant aspect of the ceremonies was the water libation. The water was brought in a golden pitcher from the pool of Siloam, and the procession went through the Water Gate to the altar where the libation was poured out (M. Sukk. IV, 9).

But on the last great day of the feast Jesus stood and cried, saying, 'If anyone is thirsty, let him come to me and let him who believes in me drink. As the Scripture said, rivers of living water shall flow from his stomach'.

(Jn 7.37–8)

Light was another major aspect of the feast. When the golden candlesticks were lit in the court of the women, it is said that there was not a courtyard in Jerusalem that was not lit up by the light of the place of the water drawing (M. Sukk. V, 3). This is the cultural context in which Jesus declares, 'I am the light of the world' (Jn 8.12). Here again the fourth evangelist uses 'the world', the very broadest of terms which must include Gentiles, and he puts it in Jesus' mouth in a context where Jesus has acrimonious debate with 'the Jews'. At 9.5, Jesus repeats 'I am the light of the world', and at 9.7 the man born blind sent by him to wash in the pool of Siloam does so, and sees.

The shepherd is another significant symbol. The Old Testament portrays both God and accepted leaders of Israel, such as David, as shepherds, contrasting them with existing shepherds who do not look after the people (cf. Ezek 34; Zech 11.4–17; Ps 78.70–2). Jesus declares, 'I am the good shepherd' (Jn 10.11). This is part of a complex allegory setting off a discourse at the feast of Hanukkah, when Jews celebrated their deliverance from the persecution of Antiochus IV Epiphanes. Antiochus' full title was 'Antiochus God Manifest' (*Theos Epiphanes*), and statues of him were set up in the Temple during the persecution. For Jews, his claim to deity was blasphemous, and some people called him Antiochus *Epimanes*, 'Antiochus the Mad'. Some Jews also believed that the death of the righteous martyrs had enabled God to deliver Israel (cf. Dan 11.35; 2 Macc 7.37–8; 4 Macc 17.20–2). As soon as victory was won, the Temple, and especially a new altar, was once again made holy (1 Macc 4.36–59; 2 Macc 10.1–8). All these basic aspects of Hanukkah are reapplied to Jesus and the Jews. Jesus does not reject the accusation of 'the Jews' that he makes himself God (Jn 10.33), for he was God manifest. Many of 'the Jews' declare 'he is mad' (10.20). 'The Jews' make to stone him for blasphemy (10.31ff.), when they should have recognised the Son of God doing the works of the Father. The Father sanctified him (10.36). Jesus achieves more than the Maccabean martyrs, for it is not only Israel whom he delivers: 'I lay down my life for the sheep, and I have other sheep who do not belong to this fold. I must lead them too, and they will hear my voice, and they will become one flock with one shepherd. For this reason the Father loves me because I lay down my life to take it up again' (10.15–17). 'The Jews' ask him in a horrid pun, 'How long will you frustrate us?', literally, 'How long do you take our life?' (10.24). In his reply, Jesus tells them bluntly, 'But you do not believe, because you do not belong to my sheep' (10.26). This is another clear exclusion of 'the Jews' from salvation. Having thus excluded 'the Jews', Jesus continues, 'My sheep hear my voice and I know them and they follow me, and I give them eternal life' (10.27–8). Jesus is the good shepherd of a quite new flock.

The vine is another example of the fourth Gospel's replacement symbolism. It was a traditional symbol of Israel (cf. e.g. Isa 5.1–7; Ezek 19.10–14; Ps 80.9–20; Mk 12.1ff.//Mt 21.33ff.//Lk 20.9ff.). At John 15.1ff., Jesus is 'the true vine'. The disciples remain in him and bear much fruit, whereas anyone who does not remain in him is cast out. I have noted also the implication that Jewish purity laws are replaced by Christian purity, which results from baptism and from the words of Jesus (cf. 13.10; 15.3). The earthly life of Jesus ends with his death at the time of the sacrifice of the Passover victims, replacing the sacrificial system as the Lamb of God who takes away the sins of the world.[27]

All this material forms a coherent symbolic whole. The Johannine community perceived 'the Jews' as an alien group. The shift in the covenant community from Judaism to Christianity is reflected at the symbolic level by this extensive replacement symbolism.

A MIXED COMMUNITY IN EPHESUS

Where did this split between the Johannine community and 'the Jews' take place? According to later church tradition, the fourth Gospel was composed by the beloved disciple, John son of Zebedee, at Ephesus. We shall see that there are good reasons to doubt many aspects of this tradition.[28] Composition in Ephesus should however be regarded as the historical basis of the tradition, which was subsequently developed in accordance with the church's need for apostolic authorship of its writings. We shall see that careful study of the Johannine literature by Christians unaware of its origins would lead them to infer that it was written by the beloved disciple, John son of Zebedee, and that details of this process can be read in the church Fathers. A deduction that it was written in Ephesus would however be much more difficult to make, and its details have not been reported in the church Fathers.

Ephesus was also a very suitable place for the Johannine community to emerge.[29] It was the outstanding metropolis in the Roman province of Asia. Not only was it the largest city, but also politically, culturally and economically the most important. Here the Roman proconsul had his official residence. Greek was the normal language spoken there. Equally, the immigration of Aramaic-speaking Jews and the survival of native languages might help to explain the peculiarities of Johannine Greek.[30] There was a flourishing Jewish community. Josephus records several decrees in which Jewish citizens were to be allowed to observe their native customs, including sabbath and dietary laws, holding religious meetings and paying the Temple tax (A.J. XIV, 224–30, 234, 240, 262–4; XVI, 167–8, 172–3). Paul, Apollos, Priscilla and Aquila all worked there as Christian missionaries. Some Christians knew the baptism of John, but did not know of Christian baptism until Paul taught and baptised them (Acts 19.1–7). This is a good place for Jews who thought more highly of John the Baptist than of Jesus. Both Apollos and Paul preached vigorously to Jews. Paul's preaching met with such serious opposition that 'withdrawing from them he separated the disciples' (Acts 19.9), and taught them elsewhere. This is an excellent place for disciples who were so Jewish that they wanted to attend Jewish meetings, but who were prevented from doing so by Jewish opposition. There is no doubt that Gentile converts were made during the early period. With the disciples separated from the Jewish community to be taught, Jewish people joining the movement would encounter strong pressures to move out of the Jewish community when they became Christians. A Jewish community so hostile that Paul withdrew the disciples is just the sort of group to take great notice of Pharisees like Gamaliel II, and to exclude Christians from Jewish meetings.

At Ephesus, Paul and his fellow workers also encountered exceptional hostility from Gentiles. This included silversmiths who had enough influence to cause the assembly to go into virtually a state of riot and shout 'Great is Artemis of the Ephesians' for two hours (Acts 19.34)! Ephesus was the centre of the widespread worship of Artemis, a major centre of the imperial cult and a major centre for magic too (Arnold 1989: esp. 14–29). It was therefore an excellent place for the new Christian community to develop amid such vigorous opposition that it produced the Johannine concept of 'the world'. There is further evidence of conflict at 1 Timothy 1.3ff. (cf. 2 Tim 1.18). Serious conflict within the Christian community is also indicated by Ignatius (Eph 7–9). The same is true of the book of Revelation, which approves of the fact that Ephesian Christians had rejected both people who called themselves apostles, and Nicolaitans (Rev 2.2, 6). John the author of Revelation also indicates tension by his accusation that Ephesian Christians have fallen from their first love, and by his threatening call upon them to repent (2.4–5). Some persecution is also indicated (2.3). Severe conflict with Jewish communities in nearby Smyrna and Philadelphia is indicated by the references to Jews who are not real Jews (2.9; 3.9), which should probably be interpreted as John's rejection of ethnically Jewish people opposed to Christianity (Collins 1986). It also indicates circum-stances of severe persecution in Asia Minor, which is thus a suitable general area for the conflicts which lie behind this Gospel.

All these points together form a strong argument of cumulative weight. Two points are particularly important. Study of the secondary legitimating traditions of authorship implies that composition in Ephesus was the real bedrock of the tradition, and Acts displays conditions of such hostility as to account for the beleaguered nature of the community. With all the other points in support, and nothing against it, the tradition that this document was written in Ephesus should be accepted.

There have been attempts to reconstruct the background of this Gospel more precisely, or differently, or to locate it elsewhere. Most of these are not discussed here, for they make no significant difference to its truth. Arguments that it was written in Palestine might however be important if they could be established. We have seen that arguments based on the nature of Johannine Greek should not be accepted.[31] More precisely, Wengst has recently argued that the Johannine community and the Gospel were located in the territory of Trachonitis and Batanea ruled over by Agrippa II. His major reason is that Judaism was strong enough there to be the major threat indicated throughout this Gospel, powerful enough even for Jews to execute Christians (Wengst 1981: esp. 77–80, cf. Reim 1988). This overinterprets John 16.2 (cf. Wengst 1981: 49–53), which is satisfied by the execution of Jesus' brother Jacob and others, and by the ability of Jews anywhere to inform on Christians who would not worship the emperor. More generally, Wengst is quite wrong to argue, almost from silence, that Jews were not powerful enough to be such an opposing force in Ephesus and elsewhere. We have seen that Ephesus is a plausible place: neither Ephesus, nor many other places, are unsuitable merely because this degree of conflict is not supported by independent sources, when there are no independent sources describing the situation in any other way. This is a significant fault which recurs in scholarship, of trying to put the Gospel where one or more selected and overinterpreted detail would fit, when the details will fit elsewhere too. Nor is it entirely clear that Wengst has reconstructed accurately the situation in his chosen place (Hengel 1989: 114–17; 1993: 288–91).

All attempts to locate this document outside Ephesus suffer from serious defects, especially in using minor indications of origins, rather than major ones. Since the Ephesus tradition does not seem to be of secondary origin, and is consistent with all significant indicators of origins, it should be accepted.

CONCLUSIONS

We can now see the Johannine community more clearly. It was a group of people in Ephesus who had originally been of mixed ethnicity. Following the trauma of the Roman war of 66–70CE, the community was split. It was prevented from attending Jewish meetings, leaving at those meetings a number of Jews who had been sympathetic to the Christian message. These included people who had been baptised in the name of Jesus, who had apparently received the Holy Spirit, and who had taken part in eucharistic meals. Some of them were leading members of the Jewish community. The Johannine community, who were prevented from attending Jewish meetings, now had Gentile self-identification. They included people who had always been Gentile, and they completed the rewriting of covenantal nomism which had been gradually more important as the Christian communities split off from the Jewish. Salvation required not birth, but rebirth, symbolised in baptism. Faith in Jesus, the only-begotten Son of God, and participation in the eucharist were also held to be essential for salvation. The commandments of Jesus were to be observed, rather than the Law. The division between the Jewish and Christian communities was sufficiently sharp to be expressed in a transmuted eschatology, in which the crucial difference is whether you are in the saved community now.

All this is quite remote from the Jesus of history. We can at least begin to see why the Johannine Christ is so different from the synoptic Jesus. He is the reification of an anti-Jewish community, wholly different from the Galilean 'people of the land' among whom the historical Jesus exercised his ministry. This community spoke of the kingdom of God only to alter its message, dealing otherwise in discourses which expounded its replacement symbolism, and its need for salvation. But why has it attributed all this to Jesus? Why not read Luke's Gospel, and write theological discourses on the general lines of 1 John? To understand the secondary attribution of all this material to Jesus of Nazareth, we must go right back into Second Temple Judaism, and re-examine ancient Jewish assumptions about authorship, authority and tradition.

8

AUTHORSHIP AND
PSEUDEPIGRAPHY

AUTHORSHIP

A large proportion of ancient Jewish works are either anonymous or pseudepigraphical.[1] Anonymous works show that ancient Jews had not developed a concept of authorship as ownership. For example, the narrative accounts of Joshua, Judges, Ruth, Samuel and Kings are not attributed to any author. Occasionally, other works are cited by them. For example, towards the end of the account of the reign of Jehoshaphat, 'And the rest of the deeds of Jehoshaphat, and the might with which he acted and waged war, are they not written in the book of the deeds of the days of the kings of Judah?' (1 Kings 22.45). No doubt they were, but who wrote them? We are not told.[2] We should not assume that it was a single person: part of the reason why a concept of authorship as ownership was not developed may have been that several people were involved. This is particularly obvious with a book of chronicles of several kings, for this might well have been compiled over several generations, much too long to have a single author. The reference at 1 Kings 22.45 does however give something of an authority: we are hardly to imagine that the book of the chronicles of the kings of Judah got it wrong.

In the post-exilic period, part of Samuel-Kings was rewritten by the author(s) of 1 and 2 Chronicles.[3] This rewriting was evidently very important to some people. The resulting work cannot be described as the work of any single person, because it takes over verbatim so much from Samuel-Kings.[4] That may be another factor precluding a concept of authorship as ownership. The importance of the rewriting must be inferred from the changes made. The new authors believed that the Temple cultus was essential to the life of a good king, but it is frequently unmentioned in the account of Samuel-Kings. The author(s), knowing from inner conviction that good kings must have held appropriate feasts, inserted them, perhaps on the basis of earlier sources written in the same conviction. For example, Hezekiah was a very good king already in the view of the author(s) of 2 Kings 18–20. Among other things, he 'removed the high places' and 'kept

140

the commandments which Yahweh commanded Moses' (2 Kings 18.4, 6). There is however no mention of Passover. By the time Chronicles was written, the Law of Moses included the prescriptions for Passover now in our Pentateuch (Ex 12.1–27, 43–9). The author therefore proceeded to include a massive account of the celebration of the Passover by Hezekiah (2 Chron 30). It is not entirely orthodox, but Hezekiah himself, and the people of Judah, come out of it very well, whereas most of North Israel would not come, and those who did were unclean. Details are given down to the singing of the Levites and the provision of 2,000 bulls and 17,000 sheep for the sacrifices. Hence the need for the account of Samuel-Kings to be rewritten. It is duly referred to as 'the book of the kings of Judah and Israel' (2 Chron 32.32), no author being given. It has not therefore been rejected. The tradition took the same view as the author(s) of Chronicles. It kept both Samuel-Kings and the rewritten account of Chronicles, and we have both of them in our canon.

The books of Ezra, Esther and Job are also anonymous (albeit with Ezra 7.27–9.15 in the first person). When we add the works already considered, we find that a considerable slice of the Hebrew bible is anonymous, and this demonstrates the absence of our need to attribute works to the people who wrote them. Some works are however attributed to particular people. The first work of this kind in the English canon is the book of Nehemiah, which begins, 'The words of Nehemiah, son of Hacaliah' (Neh 1.1). It proceeds with a first-person narrative, and a perfectly plausible one at that. But by Chapter 8, all has changed. We get an account of Ezra, with references to Nehemiah in the third person (Neh 8.9; 10.1). Chapter 12 begins with neither, having rather a list of priests and Levites who came up with Zerubbabel and Joshua more than half a century previously. Before the book ends, the first-person narrative of Nehemiah is taken up again. What has happened? The work has been edited by someone for whom the maintenance of the first-person narrative of Nehemiah was not of any importance. It was originaliy a continuation of the book of Ezra, perhaps indeed the work of the anonymous Chronicler(s).[5] They incorporated sources written in the first person, supposedly by Ezra (Ezra 7.27–9.15) and Nehemiah (Neh 1.1–7.5; 13.6–31). These were put with generally associated material about the returns from Babylon and the attempts to reform Judaism which resulted. Believing that Nehemiah must have been associated with the reforms of Ezra, someone inserted him at Nehemiah 8.9 and 10.1. But the name of the author(s), or editor(s), was no more important than careful distinction between the parts written by Nehemiah and the rest, so none is given.

What then about the prophets? Surely their works are attributed to single people! They are indeed, so much so that the author(s) of Chronicles refers to one, informing us that the rest of the acts of Hezekiah are written 'in the vision of Isaiah son of Amos, the prophet', as well as in the 'book of the Kings of Judah and Israel' (2 Chron 32.32). But what happens when we turn to the book of Isaiah? We find some words of Isaiah the son of Amos, and a great deal else as well![6] The most striking piece is Isaiah 40–55, the work of a different prophet whose name we do not know. He preached during the exile in Babylon, assuming the exile because he lived in it, not prophesying it as an earlier prophet might have done. He genuinely prophesied deliverance. As edited, he does not give us any name for himself, and whoever the people responsible for the final editing of the book of Isaiah were, they were not concerned to remove the possible impression that his work was written by Isaiah of Jerusalem. They had collected together their traditions. In the opening of the book, they tell us the fountainhead of the tradition: 'The vision of Isaiah son of Amos, which he saw concerning Judah and Jerusalem in the days of Uzziah, Jotham, Ahaz, and Hezekiah, kings of Judah' (Is 1.1). For them, that was enough. Under that heading, we have the work of Second Isaiah (Is 40–55), some narrative about Isaiah of Jerusalem and Hezekiah (Is 36–9, cf. 2 Kings 18.13–20.19), some pieces from other post-exilic prophets perceived to be in the same tradition (Is 55–65), a later piece of proto-apocalyptic (Is 24–7), and a good deal of other secondary material. Thus the book of Isaiah is not the work of an author, as we understand that term. It is a collection of prophetic tradition, with a named fountainhead.

It is a well-known result of critical scholarship that other prophetic books also contain secondary material. This mode of authorship, collecting traditions round a named fountainhead, was so pervasive that it is frequently impossible for us to deduce with any sense of certainty which pieces are secondary, still less, when secondary pieces long since deprived of their context were originally produced.[7] The same happened to the psalms. We need not doubt that David wrote some of them. However, it is not probable that he wrote all the ones attributed to him, and the later tradition that he wrote the canonical psalms is not even consistent with the headings of some of them. The development of the tradition includes the attribution to him of 3,600 psalms and a further 450 songs (11QPsa. XXVII).[8]

Wisdom might similarly be attributed to Solomon (cf. Scott 1955; Meade 1986: Chapter 3). The book of Proverbs begins, 'The proverbs of Solomon, son of David, king of Israel' (Prov 1.1). This is not because Solomon personally wrote or dictated what follows: it is rather that he was the fountainhead of the tradition, to whom the work was therefore secondarily attributed. The attribution to him of the Wisdom of Solomon would be patently ludicrous, if it were to be taken literally, because it is written in Greek and includes Greek ideas such as the pre-existence of the soul (Wsd 8.19–20). Its language and culture had not even been invented at the time of the historical Solomon. But we do not know its real author(s), to the point where we cannot date it without a margin of error of a century. They were not concerned to tell us: they deliberately attributed the work to the fountainhead of their traditions, rather than to themselves.

The concept of authorship as ownership is essentially Greek. While the poems of Homer are as composite as some of the prophetic books, and Plato attributed his opinions to Socrates in obviously literary dialogues, major Greek authors wrote works under their own names. Neither Euripides nor anyone else would have attributed his plays to Aeschylus, nor would Thucydides have countenanced the attribution of his work to Herodotus. Moreover, this cultural habit corresponded to reality. Euripides really did write his plays, and they are very different from those of Aeschylus. Thucydides wrote his history himself; he was not one of a group of people re-editing Herodotus. Consequently, authorship as ownership was well established in the Greek world long before the date of the fourth Gospel. Its influence had also begun to be felt in Judaism. Philo's works were attributed to Philo himself, and the same is true of works which have survived only in fragments. Authors such as Aristobulus and Ezekiel the tragedian wrote under their own names, and their works were not attributed to others. Josephus takes credit for his own work at some length.[9] He was very proud of his priestly descent (*Life* 1–8), an important factor in his ability to interpret both dreams and the scriptures (B.J. III, 351–4). He considered himself sent as God's messenger to announce that Vespasian would be Roman emperor (B.J. III, 400–8), a striking contrast to false prophets and incorrect interpreters of signs and scripture (B.J. VI, 285–315). As an historian of the Roman war, he cites his position as a participant, his access to source material and praise from Vespasian, Titus and others, as testimony to his accuracy (c. Ap. I, 47–52). He was also learned in Greek historiography, being evidently familiar with Polybius, among others, and using the ideas and techniques of Greek historical criticism even when attacking Greek historians.

A Greek view of authorship did not however become universal. I have noted the Wisdom of Solomon, a thoroughly Hellenised example of Jewish literature whose author(s) are unknown because it is attributed to Solomon, in the traditional Jewish way. The first book of Maccabees has no attribution at all. It ends with an attribution in the manner of Samuel-Kings: 'The rest of the Acts of John. . . . look, they are written in the books of days of his high priesthood, from when he became high priest after his father' (1 Macc 16.23–4). This author was no more concerned with the authorship of those chronicles than with the transmission of his own name. The second book of Maccabees is written in Greek, and it is sufficiently Hellenised in its attitude to authorship to tell us that it has attempted to abridge a work which it attributes to Jason of Cyrene (2 Macc 2.23). It is not however interested in its own authorship. It is sent in the name of 'The Jews in Jerusalem and those in the land of Judaea' (2 Macc 1.1), a stunning piece of multiple authorship if one were to take it literally. Of course, it is not meant to be taken literally. The author(s) were not interested in their own authorship, and wrote in the name of their whole community. It is less surprising that purely Semitic works retained the ancient attitudes to authorship. Two striking examples contemporary with the fourth Gospel are 2 Baruch and 4 Ezra. Both are deliberately pseudepigraphical. What is so striking is that, written to try to come to terms with the fall of Jerusalem in 70CE, they are attributed to major sages from the period at and after the fall of Jerusalem in 587BCE. Ezra lived so long after the literary date of 557 (4 Ezra 3.1) as to be almost comical, if taken literally. But that is not the point. The tradition has been called up, and the writing is in its name. Who really wrote either work, we have no idea – they were not concerned to tell us.

PSEUDEPIGRAPHY

A number of Jewish works written in the Second Temple period are deliberately pseudepigraphical, that is to say, they are deliberately attributed to people other than their real authors. This habit arose naturally from the general attitudes to authorship already described. We have seen that both anonymous works and secondary editing regard the transmission of their contents as the important thing. Deliberate pseudepigraphy is only one stage further on, attributing all the material to the fountainhead of a tradition. In the cases we have so far considered, there is no great effort made to attribute the material to someone who did not write it. The book of Isaiah does not actually say that Isaiah of Jerusalem wrote Isaiah 40–55, it just leaves that impression to the unwary, and that became the later tradition. The Wisdom of Solomon assumes we will assume it was written by Solomon (cf. Wsd 9.7–8), but it makes no great fuss to ensure that we will take it literally in this matter.

Some books go further than this. I have noted 4 Ezra, deliberately given an incorrect date thirty years after the destruction of Jerusalem, intelligible only as the destruction of 587BCE, though it might represent a true date of 100CE. The book opens with this, and with the then traditional, though inaccurate, identification of Ezra with Salathiel. It ends with an elaborate pseudepigraphical device. In Chapter 14, Ezra is portrayed as obeying the command of God himself to go with five named men and write under divine inspiration. In this way, they are said to have written the twenty-four books of the author's canon, and seventy secret ones, which are to be given only to the wise. This explains the appearance among the people responsible for this work of 4 Ezra itself, and other apocalyptic works. In this respect, it typifies devices which look on the surface as if they are intended to deceive us about the authorship of the works. In fact, these devices perform the same function of the standard Jewish view of authorship – they sanctify the tradition, and ensure their membership of it. Ezra was selected as the central character because of his original role in providing the Torah after the exile in Babylon.

Other works consist of the rewriting of tradition, much in the way that 1 and 2 Chronicles rewrote Samuel-Kings. Two are outstanding, Jubilees and 11Q Temple. Both are in effect rewritten versions of part of the Pentateuch, and both claim the authority of God himself, or the angel of the presence, speaking to Moses on Mount Sinai. When in difficulties, because some Jews might not agree with it, Jubilees stresses with especial vigour that its version of the Law is written on the heavenly tablets. A number of its innovations are secondary legitimation of its own existence. We must look at its mode of authorship in more detail (cf. Endres 1987; Hall 1991: Chapter 2).

The work begins with its pseudepigraphical device:

> This is the history of the division of the days of the law and of the testimony, of the events of the years, of their weeks, of their jubilees throughout all the years of the world, as the Lord said to Moses on Mount Sinai when he went up to receive the tablets of the law and of the commandment, according to the voice of God as he said to him, 'Go up to the top of the mountain'.

After a substantial introduction, God commands the angel of the presence to write for Moses from the beginning of creation, and in Chapter 2 he does this. The result is an amplified version of the creation narrative in Genesis, partly in the first person. For example, at Jubilees 3.1, '*we*' brought all the beasts, cattle, birds and other creatures to Adam so that he could name them. The 'we' is part of the pseudepigraphical device, representing the angel of the presence speaking to Moses. In Chapter 15, there is a lengthy expanded account of the introduction of circumcision by Abraham. This was due to the Maccabean crisis, when some Jews did not circumcise their children (cf. 1 Macc 1.48, 52), a direct rejection of Jewish identity which was sufficiently widespread for Mattathias and his army to respond with forcible circumcision of all the uncircumcised boys whom they found within the borders of Israel (1 Macc 2.46). In Jubilees, the angel himself predicts that Jews will not circumcise their children, and declares that 'there will be great wrath from the Lord upon the children of Israel, because they have forsaken his covenant' (Jub 15.34). In addition to this pseudoprophecy, the pseudepigraphical device is heightened by the declaration that the law of circumcision is 'an eternal ordinance, ordained and written on the heavenly tablets' (Jub 15.25). Not content with this, the author then informs us that the two highest classes of angels were created circumcised (Jub 15.27). Circumcision was so important that it has been provided with a triple level of pseudepigraphy, running through Moses to the angel of the presence to the heavenly tablets, and that stream of revelation was expanded in rewriting the account of Abraham. The circumcision of the highest classes of angels is a further reinforcement of this tradition.

The angel has another surprise for us in his account of Abraham. At Jubilees 12.26, he says, in the first person, that he opened Abraham's mouth, and his ears and his lips, and began to speak with him in Hebrew, defined as the language of the creation. Then Abraham took the books of his Fathers, which were written in Hebrew, and transcribed and studied them, and the angel taught him what he could not understand. This is the sort of pseudepigraphic device commoner in apocalyptic works. It serves to stress the authority of the Hebrew language and the traditions of the sort of sages who wrote the book of Jubilees.

A similar attitude to authority, authorship and tradition pervades the rest of this work. For example, major feasts are celebrated by pre-Mosaic patriarchs. There is an especially vivid account of the celebration of the feast of Weeks, which has Isaac and Ishmael come from the Well of the Oath to Abraham (Jub 22). Since this is not in the fundamentalist canon, however, we do not have arguments that vivid details such as Rebecca making new cakes from the new grain, and giving them to Jacob to take to Abraham (Jub 22.4), must go back to an eyewitness. This is followed by Abraham's last speech, and his death, with many vivid details. For example, we are told that Jacob slept in Abraham's bosom, and when he awoke, 'Behold! Abraham was cold as ice' (Jub 23.3). Most of Chapter 23 looks forward to the Maccabean crisis, followed by a return to the observance of the Law and the triumph of the righteous. It ends with a direct address by the angel of the presence: 'And you, Moses, write these words, for thus they are written and recorded on the heavenly tablets for a testimony for the generations for ever' (Jub 23.32). At 25.14, Rebecca's lengthy non-biblical blessing of Jacob is preceded by the information that 'a spirit of truth descended upon her mouth'.

In Chapter 32, an angel descends during Jacob's dream (cf. Gen 28) with seven tablets. We are told that he gave them to Jacob, who 'read them and knew everything that was written in them which would happen to him and his sons throughout all the ages' (Jub 32.21). The angel tells him to write it all down, and in his quoted conversation with Jacob, reassures him that he will bring everything to his memory. We are told that Jacob did indeed remember everything he had read and seen, and wrote it all down, another legitimation of the authors' traditions, and one which is particularly close to the Johannine concept of remembering.

The use of this framework for the exposition of sectarian halakhah is most obvious with sabbath observance. It begins with the account of the creation in Chapter 2, where the angel quotes God himself:

> And all the angels of the presence, and all the angels of sanctification, these two great classes, he has ordered us to keep the sabbath with him in heaven and on earth. And he said to us, 'Look!, I will separate to myself a people from all the peoples and these shall keep the sabbath day . . . and I have chosen the seed of Jacob from among all that I have seen . . . and I will teach them the sabbath day, that they may keep sabbath on it from all work.'
>
> (Jub 2.18–20)

Twenty-two kinds of work are announced, and a longer list of prohibitions is given in Chapter 50. These include the prohibition of sexual intercourse, a view which was never widespread, and the prohibition of making war, a sectarian view first known from the Maccabean period and vigorously rejected by Israel as a whole (1 Macc 2.32–41). This is accompanied by vigorous reassertion of the death penalty for sabbath-breaking, a penalty which the author evidently believed should be enforced for violating any of the provisions mentioned by him.

A similar view of authorship, authority and tradition, expressed in a somewhat different way, is found in the Temple Scroll from cave 11 at Qumran. Like Jubilees, this is in effect a rewritten version of part of the Pentateuch, and it has the same basic legitimation, that of attribution to the will of God revealed to Moses on Mount Sinai. In extant parts, however, there is no mention of the angel of the Lord. In some cases, the mention of God in the third person is replaced, or added to, with the first person, to make clear that this is the unmediated revelation of God himself (cf. Callaway 1989; Stegemann 1989; Weinfeld 1991). After its general introduction, the work appears to have begun with the holiest places and then moved outwards. Its regulations are mostly biblical, but there are amplifications and some specifically sectarian halakhah. The following extract from column XLV illustrates several of these points.

> If a man has an emission of semen in the night, he shall not enter any of the sanctuary until he has [comp]leted three days. And he shall wash his clothes and bathe on the first day, and on the third day he shall wash his clothes and bathe, and after the sun has set, he shall come in to the sanctuary. And they shall not come in their sexual impurity into my sanctuary and make it unclean. If a man lies with his wife with emission of semen he shall not enter any of the city of the sanctuary, in which I cause my name to dwell, for three days. No blind man shall enter it all their days and shall not defile the city in whose midst I dwell, for I, YHWH, dwell among the sons of Israel for ever and ever.

Here purity regulations found in passages such as Deuteronomy 23.10–11 have been expanded. The results include the effective banning of sexual intercourse in Jerusalem, a sectarian view never held by the population of that city. The whole passage is legitimated by being attributed directly to God, mentioned here in the first person, and assumed to be speaking in person to Moses on Mount Sinai. In view of this treatment of authority and tradition, the real author, in our terms, if there were one rather than several, would not help matters by saying who he was, since this would interfere with the traditional and legitimating modes of his discourse. Rather the tradition requires its attribution of itself to its fountainhead, the revelation of God to Moses on Mount Sinai.

With the Pentateuch being rewritten like this, we might have imagined that it was being replaced. This was not however the case. Just as Chronicles has been transmitted in our canon with Samuel-Kings, so Jubilees and 11Q Temple were transmitted in addition to the Pentateuch by the Dead Sea Sect. The same rewriting of history is evident in works which survive only in fragments from Qumran.[10] We have a complete text of Jubilees only in an Ethiopic language, Ge'ez. We owe its transmission to Falashas and to Ethiopian Christians, who regarded both it and the Pentateuch as sacred texts. The reinforcement, recreation and expansion of the tradition does not entail the removal of its earlier version. The community may prefer to copy and venerate all its versions of its traditions.

This basic habit of pseudepigraphy was evidently widespread in the Judaism of our period. The majority of surviving works are either anonymous or pseudepigraphical, and the proportion that are pseudepigraphical is high. They contain all the important features noted in the above discussion. For example, the Testament of Levi contains a lengthy prediction of the future, attributed to Levi. It is by no means a random prediction, but rather one which contains the major features of Jewish life. Predicted offences include marrying Gentile wives, and a complex of such faults is given as the reason for the destruction of the Temple and the exile (T. Levi 14.4–15.1). Not content with attributing all this to Levi, the author cites the writings of Enoch as a source of Levi's knowledge of the future (T. Levi 14.1; 16.1). The pseudoprophecy ends with a prediction of the last times, when Israel will have eternal bliss under the eschatological high priest. There follows a conversation between Levi and his sons:

> 'And now, my children, you have heard everything. Choose therefore for yourselves either light or darkness, either the Law of the Lord or the works of Beliar.' And we answered our father, saying, 'Before the Lord we will walk according to his Law.'
>
> (T. Levi 19.1–3)

This author could have told us his name, and written a treatise on how necessary it is to observe the Law, quoting Deuteronomy on what will happen to Israel if she does, or does not, obey the Law. Instead of this, he has concealed his name with the traditional device of attributing his work to Levi. He has given us a rewritten traditional narrative, in which he has felt quite free to attribute both to Levi and his sons all the main points of concern to his community. These concerns include the need to obey the Law and the eventual deliverance of Israel. He has also cited recently written works of Enoch as a traditional authority. We must infer that he has the same views of authorship, tradition and authority as we have found in Jubilees and other works, and 'he' may have been several people rather than one. Extant Greek texts show that the process of rewriting the tradition continued when the document was copied by Christians.

Some works include basic stories, as well as legitimating conversations.

First Enoch includes the story of Enoch's rise into the presence of God (1 En 14), his heavenly and earthly travels (1 En 17ff.) and his translation (1 En 70–1). The story of his travels was copied several times at Qumran: there is no sign of anyone worrying about whether he really went. The earthly part includes appropriate topographical information which must refer to Petra and Wadi Musa (Milik 1976: 232–3; Black 1985: 174ff.). Since 1 Enoch is not in the evangelical canon, however, we do not have to endure scholarly arguments that this information entails that the story is literally true.[11] On the contrary, Black, who believes that the author must have visited the places concerned, reckons this part of 1 Enoch 'a combination of vision and legend, with an account of real scenes and places', and he notes that 'It is not always possible to distinguish the two strands in the author's narrative.' What we call 1 Enoch consists of several books: whoever was responsible for writing the Similitudes and editing the final result shows no signs of qualms about the historicity of the earlier part, let alone of that being relevant when concerned about its authority. Rather, his group has its traditions, which are authoritative because they express its identity. The final editor therefore collects and edits, and the more fruitfully he expresses the being of the community, the more true his work is perceived to be.

REWRITING HISTORY IN THE GRECO-ROMAN WORLD

I have considered Jewish cultural habits of authorship, authority and tradition first because traditions about Jesus originated in the Jewish community, and were first handed down in the Jewish community. Moreover, we have seen that the split between the Johannine community and 'the Jews' was a relatively recent event when this Gospel was being composed, towards the end of the first century, and that some of the rewriting dates from that period. It follows that this Gospel resulted from composition in Jewish mode, over a period of some fifty to seventy years, too long a period for a single person to have written the whole of it. Accordingly, Jewish cultural habits are the most important for understanding the ways in which this Gospel was composed. Nonetheless, it is written in Greek, and certain aspects of the ways in which the Greeks and Romans rewrote their traditions would naturally confirm the authorial habits which were inherited from Judaism. We must briefly consider these.

It is important to do so with the right presuppositions. The Johannine community did not inherit and alter modern historiography, our attempts to uncover what actually happened from behind biassed sources. Modern historiography is an unusual approach to historical traditions (cf. Breisach 1983; Momigliano 1990). In general, people do rewrite their traditions in accordance with their needs (cf. Samuel and Thompson 1990; Tonkin 1992). This was all the more so in the ancient period, when ideas of how to obtain historical truth were still being developed. Hence some historians were less than fully accurate. Their accounts of the earliest periods of history are especially at fault. Livy tells us of the ascension of Romulus. His story contains a highly convenient speech in which, during an appearance from heaven, Romulus foretells that Rome will be the capital of the world and her armed forces irresistible, in accordance with the will of heaven (I, XVI). For history so ancient, Livy enunciates a principle: 'in matters so ancient, I should be content if what be like truth be accepted as true' (V, XXI, 9). Moreover, some forms of creative inaccuracy were institutionalised. Nowhere is this more obvious than in speeches.

One of the classic discussions of this is by Thucydides, who was not merely read during our period, but imitated too. In many ways, he laid the foundations of modern historiography, detailing the care which he, unlike most people, had taken to establish true facts rather than repeat stories. Nonetheless, he comments,

> It was difficult to remember the precise words used in the speeches, both those which I listened to myself, and in the case of those reported to me from elsewhere. So my practice has been, while keeping as closely as possible to the general sense of the words that were actually used, to make the speakers say what, in my opinion, was called for by each situation.
>
> (*Peloponnesian War* I, 22)

This licence could be used in various ways (cf. Walbank 1965). Tacitus, with a speech of Claudius available to him in written record, nonetheless rewrote it, altering the style and reorganising the whole piece. He still kept the main arguments, but the result is a version which Tacitus himself could have created.[12] Historians were not always even that careful. We have seen this with Livy, reporting a speech from Romulus after he had been to heaven. Josephus behaved with a considerable amount of freedom too. For example, Joseph's speech at Genesis 45.3–13 has been quite rewritten at A.J. II, 161–5. One of Herod's speeches is given us in two quite different versions (cf. A.J. XV, 127–46 with B.J. I, 373–9).

What is more, what we think of as history was by no means the only way that people wrote about the past. Rhetoric apart, authors from Plato onwards wrote serious dialogues. These were not intended as accurate accounts of what was said on a given occasion, but they were intended to be precise accounts of what an author himself thought. Plato used the dialogue as his main vehicle for expounding the philosophy of Plato, and everyone knew this. Most of the philosophy was attributed to Socrates, and most of the contributions of the other characters were intended to provide a literary form which was held to be suitable for this exposition. In effect, this was an idealised version of the debates which Plato had attended with Socrates, and which he continued to hold. John 13.31–14.31 is quite similar to this in genre. It consists mostly of exposition by Jesus, helped along by questions from Simon Peter (13.36–7), Thomas (14.4), Philip (14.8) and Judas, not Iscariot (14.22). This means that when people familiar with Greek culture heard this discourse, they would expect to be hearing an exposition of Johannine thought, and they would not propose to distinguish this from the original words of Jesus and these disciples.

Hellenistic revelatory discourses, though extant only after the period when the fourth Gospel was written, are of similar significance. The Hermetic tractates have discourses by Hermes, which are helped along by questions from his disciple, Tat, some of which do not seem to us to be very bright. When people who knew this kind of tradition heard John 3.1–21, they would be expecting an exposition of Johannine thought. They would not conclude that Nicodemus was a numbskull, nor would they necessarily trouble themselves by considering whether this was an accurate record of an actual discourse between the historical Jesus and a 'ruler of the Jews' (Jn 3.1).

Another major literary form was that of the lives of important people. The fourth evangelist's contemporary Plutarch was famous for writing several of these. From the point of view of their literary genre, all four Gospels fall within the rather flexible limits of the Greek *Life* (Burridge 1992; Stibbe 1994a: Chapter 3). They have Jesus as their central character, and they select for mention those things about him which they consider to be most important.

The fourth Gospel is in effect rewritten history, within the broad parameters of a Greek *Life*. It is clearly marked off from fiction at times (19.35; 21.24), but in terms strongly reminiscent of Jewish legitimating devices. Unlike Greek history, it has the makings of a theory to legitimate its secondary and creative writing. This has been developed from the Jewish concept of the Holy Spirit, though it has some parallel in Greek Muses. For example, Homer does not rely on written inscriptions to give an account of the Greek fleet which set out for Troy. He introduces traditional information about it by informing us that he could not know of it 'unless the Muses of Olympia, daughters of aegis-bearing Zeus, remembered those who came beneath Ilion. I will tell the captains of the ships, and the ships' numbers' (Il 2.491–3). Veneration of Homer in the Greek world was unsurpassable, and the notion that the Muses remembered and revealed the past could be grafted imperceptibly onto Jewish traditions of the Holy Spirit. We must consider next the Paraclete.

THE PARACLETE [13]

At the beginning and end of Jesus' public ministry, there are two unusual references to remembering. The Cleansing of the Temple has been edited with a different scripture from that used by Jesus, Psalm 69.9, part of a psalm used to interpret his death (Jn 2.17).[14] This is followed by a brief debate between Jesus and 'the Jews', a sure sign of late redaction, and the account concludes, 'When therefore he had risen from the dead, his disciples remembered that he had said this, and they believed the scripture and the word which Jesus had spoken' (Jn 2.22). It is evident that the Johannine concept of 'remembering' includes the editing and interpreting of events, not merely exact recall of them. The account of the triumphal entry into Jerusalem, another real event much edited and interpreted, includes a similar comment: 'His disciples did not know this at first, but when Jesus had been glorified, then they remembered that these [sc. scriptures] were written about him, and that they had done this to him' (Jn 12.16). We have seen basically similar comments on 'remembering' material which is the recreation and development of tradition, in both Jewish and Greek sources (Jub 32; Il 2.491–3).

The Paraclete passages develop this almost to the point of a theory of authorship. The second one is quite explicit:

> I have said this to you while I remain with you, but the Paraclete, the Holy Spirit, whom the Father will send in my name, he will teach you everything and he will recall to your minds everything which I said to you.
>
> (Jn 14.25–6)

In practice, this must mean that words of Jesus can be supplied by people who claim inspiration by the Holy Spirit, rather than by written records from Israel c. 30CE. This is exactly what we find in the fourth Gospel. Some early material has been completely rewritten; other parts have been written in the first place by and for the Johannine community. The traditional concept of the Holy Spirit has been used to legitimate both procedures.

This is expanded at John 16.13–15. Here Jesus says that he will not tell the disciples everything, but when the Spirit of Truth comes, 'he will lead you in all truth; for he will not speak of his own accord, but he will speak what he will hear and will announce future events to you' (16.13). This also shows that authority for additional material has been attributed to the Holy Spirit. The inclusion of predictions is notable, especially in light of the quite anachronistic 16.2.[15] Equally important is the subordinationist comment. This is amplified:

> He will glorify me, because he will take from what is mine and announce it to you. Everything that the Father has is mine. That is why I said that he takes from what is mine and will announce it to you.

This legitimates new material via the Holy Spirit via Jesus to God himself, much as new material in the book of Jubilees is legitimated via Moses, the angel of the presence and the heavenly tablets to God himself. The Holy Spirit was traditionally God in action. This included prophecy and exegesis.

It is here further developed as the presence of God, and of Jesus, with the disciples, providing the new material which we now read in this Gospel.

Christological development is a particularly important point. At 16.14 Jesus says that the Spirit of Truth will glorify him, and similarly at 15.26, 'When the Paraclete comes, whom I will send to you from the Father, the Spirit of Truth who comes forth from the Father, he will bear witness about me.' We must infer deliberate legitimation of the creation of this Gospel's high Christology. We might have expected also some reference to prophecy, for early Christian prophets might have been expected to provide some of the new material. The community had however had trouble with Jewish prophets who denied Jesus (1 Jn 4.1–6), and the full Johannine confession of 'Jesus Christ come in the flesh' (1 Jn 4.2, cf. Jn 1.11, 14, 17) will have been made by Johannine Christians who did not prophesy. We should infer that prophets were not prominent in the composition of the fourth Gospel.

In teaching the Johannine community their developments of the tradition, the Paraclete is effectively the presence of Jesus with the disciples after his departure from the earth. This is explicit at the first mention of the Paraclete, which continues, 'I will not leave you as orphans, I am coming to you' (14.18). Similarly, the coming of the Paraclete is dependent on Jesus' departure: 'For if I do not go away, the Paraclete will not come to you, but if I go, I will send him to you' (16.7). Hence also the logic of Jesus saying that he has much to say to them, with the clear implication that the Spirit of Truth will say it (16.12–15). Hence also a certain degree of parallelism with Joshua, who succeeded Moses, 'full of the spirit of wisdom, for Moses laid his hands on him' (Deut 34.9, cf. Ass. Mos. 10–11); and with Elisha, who succeeded Elijah with a double share of his spirit (2 Kings 2.9–15). This is also underlined by the traditional description 'Spirit of Truth' (Jn 14.17, cf. 1QS III, 18–IV; T. Judah 20.1, 5; 1 Jn 4.6; 5.6), shortly after Jesus has described himself as 'the Truth' (Jn 14.6).

It follows that this material cannot be historically authentic, for it is so inconsistent with synoptic material, yet it contains elements which the synoptic Gospels could hardly have resisted if Jesus had produced them. During his ministry, Jesus predicted the coming of the kingdom in the very near future. The coming of the Paraclete can hardly be fitted into that picture. After Jesus' death, the early church developed this expectation, concentrating on the return of Jesus. The Johannine picture partly results from the passage of much more time. The preaching of the kingdom has been written out of the teaching of Jesus,[16] and the expectation of the parousia has only just been retained (21.22–3). More centrally, some of the language has been reapplied. Thus 'I am coming to you' (14.18); but this is no longer the Son of man coming on the clouds of heaven (Mk 13.26; 14.62; Mt 10.23, etc.), but the presence of the Paraclete in the church. Also, the appendix to the Gospel tells in story form of the death of all the first disciples, as if the expectation of the beloved disciple surviving until the parousia had been a misunderstanding. That is how the Johannine community saw it. They knew that Jesus had not come, and they restructured their religious experience and understood it as Jesus' renewed presence in the activity of the Holy Spirit.

This has been further developed to distinguish it from the experience of 'the Jews'. The most remarkable comment is at 7.39: 'Now he said this concerning the Spirit which those who believed in him were going to receive. For there was not yet any Spirit, because Jesus had not yet been glorified.' This is remarkable, for the Holy Spirit was normally seen as active in prophecy. The same understanding is however found in the resurrection story of Jesus imparting the Holy Spirit (Jn 20.19–23).[17] It is further extended with the term Paraclete, which is also absent from the synoptics. All this should have been particularly congenial to Luke, who had the same problem of the delay of the parousia to contend with. We must infer that the Paraclete is a purely Johannine development. This is further supported by the inability of scholars to find a suitable Aramaic and/or Hebrew word which might underly 'paraclete' – this term was first used in Greek. As the presence of Jesus with the disciples, it is a concept which also legitimated the production of other secondary material.

THE AUTHORSHIP OF THE FOURTH GOSPEL

We are now in a position to reconsider the authorship of the fourth Gospel in the light of its cultural background. It is clear from John 20.30–1 that this Gospel originally ended at the end of Chapter 20. It follows that John 1–20 was originally an anonymous work, as so many Jewish works were. This is not inconsistent with the authors' Gentile self-identification. The composition of this work effectively began during the historic ministry of Jesus, when all his followers were Jewish. The traditions were first handed down in a Jewish environment. As the Gospel spread to Gentiles, Christianity remained permeated with Jewish culture. We have seen moreover that the ferocious quarrel with 'the Jews' was a recent event, so much so that the fourth Gospel's hostile use of 'the Jews' is not found in the Johannine epistles, probably because some members of the Johannine community retained their Jewish self-identification.[18] Consequently, whoever was responsible for writing John 1–20 in its present form was able to follow the normal habit of Jewish culture, rewriting the tradition anonymously and attributing the most important teaching of his community to the fountainhead of the tradition, Jesus of Nazareth himself.

Like the authors of the Pentateuch, Jubilees and 11Q Temple, our anonymous author did not stop there. Just as they attributed Jewish traditions via Moses to God himself, so the Johannine community attributed its teaching via Jesus to God himself. At the end of his public ministry, Jesus comments on it:

For I did not speak of my own accord, but the Father who sent me has given me a commandment, what I am to speak and what I am to say, and I know that his commandment is eternal life. What therefore I say, as the Father has told me, so I say.

(12.49–50, cf. 8.26, 38)

This is only the most dramatic example of the functional nature of the subordinationist Christology of this Gospel – it sets the ultimate seal of authority on the teaching of the Johannine community. It is not only the teaching of Jesus – it is the teaching of God himself. This is also the force of the Jews' comment, 'We know that God has spoken to Moses, but we do not know where this fellow is from' (9.29). Jesus has said, 'I have come down from heaven' (6.38) and 'he who sent me is true, and what I heard from him, that I say to the world' (8.26, cf. 38).

This is the central reason for the complete rewriting of Jesus. As the fountainhead of the traditions of the Johannine community, he it is to whom all its teaching is appropriately attributed. He has not however been *more* rewritten than Moses, nor has he been distorted with *more* new teaching than Enoch. He has been altered in accordance with normal cultural patterns of authorship, authority and revelation. John the Baptist has been rewritten in accordance with these same patterns. He has been portrayed as a witness to Jesus because the Johannine community believed profoundly that this was his real significance. They no more had to keep to his original words than the author of the Testament of Levi had to check up on the verbatim comment of Levi's sons (T. Levi 19.2).[19]

When we look at the whole of the fourth Gospel as an example of the creative rewriting of the community's traditions, we find more and more basic points that can be paralleled in the Jewish community's rewriting of its traditions. Unwelcome tradition can be removed. Jesus' exorcisms are simply omitted, and the kingdom of God very nearly so.[20] Josephus, having undertaken to follow the scriptural records 'neither adding nor omitting anything' (A.J. I, 17), does both, by our standards of judgement. Omissions include the interpretation of Daniel's fourth kingdom, too desperately inconvenient because it was the Roman kingdom, to be destroyed by God in due course (cf. A.J. X, 210). Jubilees omits large parts of Genesis, having no reason to repeat all of it in its rewritten account.

The oldest traditions are nonetheless retained when they are functional, just as Chronicles retains much of Samuel-Kings and Jubilees retains large parts of Genesis. The tradition that Jesus performed miracles is retained because the stories impressed so many people (e.g. Mk 1.27//Lk 4.36; Mk 5.42//Mt 9.26//Lk 8.56). Already at John 2.23, 'many believed on his name, seeing his signs which he was doing'. Nicodemus put it in a nutshell: 'for no-one can do these signs which you do, unless God be with him' (Jn 3.2). The Christology of comments like this is characteristically low, because this is a

155

reaction possible for a faithful Jew (cf. 6.2, 14; 7.31; 9.16; 11.47–8; 12.18). So Jesus can argue that his works bear witness to him (5.36; 10.25), and he can even urge his disciples, 'Believe me that I am in the Father and the Father is in me. Otherwise, believe because of the works themselves' (14.11). In the same way, an authentic prophecy of John the Baptist is used at John 1.26–7, because it could be rewritten as evidence of John the Baptist's witness to Jesus.

These old traditions are not retained in a random or literal way, but to be interpreted in the Johannine manner. For example, the synoptic story of the feeding of the 5,000 is retained for the opening of John 6, but it leads to the quite unsynoptic discourse on Jesus as the bread of life.[21] John 5 opens with a healing on the sabbath. Though the healing itself is not a synoptic narrative, Jesus' sabbath healings themselves are a significant aspect of the synoptic tradition. In the fourth Gospel, however, the healing has been rewritten so that Jesus breaks the Law, and it leads to another quite unsynoptic discourse, in which we find that Jesus 'abrogated the sabbath' (Jn 5.18), which the synoptic Jesus never sought to do. The rewriting of John the Baptist's original prophecy (Jn 1.26–7) alters its meaning. Whereas John the Baptist prophesied the coming of an unknown figure, the rewriting and new context of John 1.26–7 turns it into a prophecy of the coming of the pre-existent Son as Jesus of Nazareth.[22] This rewriting leads to occasional problems. I have noted especially the eucharistic discourse of John 6, delivered before any institution of the eucharist.[23] This problem is however hardly more severe than the notion that Moses wrote the account of his own death. When the text of the Pentateuch was canonical, however, this could be interpreted as due to divine inspiration (Philo, *Life of Moses* II, 291). Its origin lies in the notion that Moses wrote the whole Pentateuch, a similar cause to the attribution of the discourse of John 6 to Jesus. Similar needs caused Levi to see a vision of himself as the future priest (T. Levi 8), and Enoch to see visions of himself as the eschatological judge (1 En 46ff.) (cf. Caquot 1972; Casey 1976). The application of later Law to the patriarchal period led to other inconcinnities. For example, the Law forbids polygamy, but David was known from the sacred text to have had several wives. The Damascus Rule explains that David had not read the sealed book of the Law, for it was not opened in Israel from the death of Eleazar and Joshua (CD V, 1ff.).

These irregularities in non-Christian Jewish documents are not the *same* as those of the fourth Gospel, nor should we expect them to be. They illustrate that the cultural habit of rewriting the tradition leads to obvious peculiarities, and that these may be ignored. This is the correct background for seeing the placing of John 6 before the institution of the eucharist, and the chaos caused by moving the Cleansing of the Temple to the beginning of the ministry and writing up the divisive effect of the raising of Lazarus. Eucharistic theology was too important to be left out: it is therefore simply expounded, in the knowledge that any audience would understand references to the Christian eucharist, as well as the arguments with 'the Jews' that it produced. The Cleansing of the Temple is such a good symbol of the replacement of Judaism by Jesus that it went at the beginning of the ministry, leaving out of account the fact that it should have led to more serious effects at the time.[24] The immediate effects of the raising of Lazarus were more important to the evangelist than carrying them through the rest of his Gospel.[25] The central point is the divisive effect of the most dramatic and most centrally symbolic of the signs. The resurrection of Jesus was at the centre of Johannine Christianity, and Jesus' portrayal of himself as the resurrection and the life (cf. Jn 11.25) is symbolised through his raising of Lazarus. The divisive effect of this miracle illustrates the community's dispute with 'the Jews'. On the one hand it leads many of the Jews to faith (cf. 11.45; 12.9–11, 17–18), yet it is the direct cause of the final action against him by the chief priests and Pharisees (11.47–8, 53, 57; 12.19), action which even includes a plot against the life of Lazarus (12.10–11).[26] The historical implausibility of this is quite overridden by its symbolic value.

As we read through the fourth Gospel, we can see other minor devices for carrying the narrative along and making the essential points clear, devices which we know from the rewriting of other documents in the Judaism of this period. Conversations can be added to the tradition when required. For example, at 1.19ff. the conversation between John the Baptist and the priests and Levites enables the author to clarify the status of John the Baptist. It is not just that the conversation is in some ways anachronistic.[27] It is that we should not necessarily expect it to be more historical than the conversation between Levi and his sons (T. Levi 19), or Rebecca's conversations with Jacob, Isaac and Esau (Jub 35). These are highly functional speeches written for the lives of traditional figures, and it is this pattern which the fourth Gospel has followed. The same applies to the witness borne by the crowd which saw Lazarus called out from the tomb (Jn 12.17), witness which is as symbolically essential as it is historically unlikely. These speeches may extend to whole discourses. We have seen that the Johannine discourses, and the comments which interrupt them and carry them forward, are generally the product of the Johannine community. They are written in the same mode as the discourse of Uriel, with numerous comments by Ezra, at 4 Ezra 4.1–5.13.

Incidents may be added as much as words. The linking of the call of Peter to the witness of John the Baptist can only be secondary, because the witness itself is secondary.[28] Some of the Chronicler's insertions of cultic events into the narrative of Samuel-Kings are equally secondary, due to the author(s)' profound conviction that good kings behaved properly by participating in the cultus in accordance with the Law. The same applies to the story of Ezra and his companions rewriting the Law, and writing other revelatory books under divine inspiration (4 Ezra 14.19–48). This supplied

the need to believe in the constancy and divine inspiration of the tradition –
any thought of historical verification is quite inappropriate. Pilate's attempt
to free Jesus (Jn 19.12) should be seen in a similar light – never mind that it
is historically implausible, it expresses the profound conviction that Jesus
was innocent.

We can now approach the eyewitness claims that are found in this
Gospel. The only one in Chapters 1–20 is at 19.35. This concerns the
emission of blood and water from Jesus' side when he was pierced with a
spear. The event is not recorded in any of the synoptic Gospels. By now this
should make us suspicious, and John 19.35 should make us more so: 'And
he who has seen has borne witness, and his witness is true, and he knows
that he speaks the truth, so that you too may believe.' The function of this
witness is the same as that of the whole of the secondary legitimating
tradition of this Gospel. The water and the blood were significant because of
baptism and the eucharist, and consequently the event was deemed
remarkable, even though it could occur naturally. Its importance for faith,
rather than verifiable evidence, will have caused people to believe that the
tradition which they knew as old, and which they needed so much, went
back ultimately to someone who was there at the time. In the same way, 1
Enoch 82.7 wants us to believe in the perfect correctness of its calendar
because it was revealed by Uriel to Enoch, who wrote it down in 1 Enoch
72ff. The stress on blood and water is similar to that at 1 John 5.6–8, where
the witness is the Spirit, an equally significant legitimating device.

The secondary nature of the tradition is further indicated by its being
treated as fulfilment of scripture.[29] The crucifixion of Jesus was exceptionally
short, so it might well occur to people familar with Jewish culture that Jews
had ensured that his legs were broken, as suggested at 19.31. As at 5.10,
however, what is culturally appropriate is anachronistically expressed by
means of the external use of 'the Jews', which indicates the final stages of the
redaction of this document. The scripture according to which his bones must
not be broken is associated with the incorrect dating of the crucifixion, so that
he dies at the same time as the Passover victims.[30] We must infer that the
scriptures were searched, and Zechariah 12.10, which was also used
midrashically at Revelation 1.7 and in an early church testimonium (Casey
1980: 142–4, 168–70, 177, 178, 197–8), led people to suppose that Jesus had
been pierced. It is possible that Numbers 20.11 was also used, since there was
a rabbinical tradition that when Moses struck the rock in the wilderness,
blood came out, and then water (e.g. Tg Ps-J Num. 20.11).

The importance, and the spurious nature, of this event is further
emphasised by the resurrection narrative of John 20.24–9, where Thomas is
told to put his hand into Jesus' side, and his faith when he has seen is
contrasted with the faith of those who believe even though they have not
seen. We shall see that there is no chance of this narrative being historically
accurate.[31] We must infer that the witness of 19.35 is quite secondary. The

community believed in this incident as a result of midrashic work on scripture fitted into its symbolism. They knew with internal conviction that it must have been seen at the time, and they wrote this out in the mode natural to them because their traditions always had been handed down in Jewish mode.

The anonymous disciple of 19.35 is often held to be the 'beloved disciple', because he is the only man specified at John 19.25-7 as present at the crucifixion. It is not probable that the evangelist thought this out and failed to say it at 19.35. This identification presupposes the literal truth of the Johannine narrative, and fails to explain why the disciple is anonymous. However, a vigorous claim for the authority of the tradition of the beloved disciple is made at 21.24: 'This is the disciple who bears witness concerning this and who wrote these things, and we know that his witness is true.' We must therefore discuss the identity and function of this figure. It is surprising that he is not recognisable in the synoptic Gospels, and quite alarming to see that even in the Fourth Gospel he is hardly mentioned during Jesus' ministry. He plays an important role only in the resurrection narratives. The traditional view is that he is John son of Zebedee, one of the twelve and the author of the Gospel. Numerous other suggestions include Lazarus, and an ideal figure.[32]

Close examination of the material about the beloved disciple does not inspire confidence in its historicity. Unmentioned during the public ministry, he turns up at 13.23 so that Jesus can tell him indirectly that he is to be betrayed by Judas. The description is hardly that of a particular person: 'One of Jesus' disciples was reclining in his bosom, one whom Jesus loved' (13.23). This is a necessary inference from his position, which is a necessary position if he is to receive this information without everyone knowing it. It introduces him as if he is not known to the Johannine community (contrast Mary at 11.2), and it does not tell us who he was. When he has 'leant back, on Jesus' breast' (13.25) and found out that the traitor is Judas (13.26), he is not mentioned again during the rest of the meal. Conversation with Jesus is left to Peter (first), Thomas, Philip, another Judas, fading out to 'some of his disciples' (16.17) and finally 'his disciples' (16.29). This is not the treatment of a central character – it is rather the chaos caused by making quite sure that we know that Jesus is completely in charge of the events leading up to the crucifixion. This disciple is not mentioned again until the crucifixion. Moreover, this is the *main* point. A disciple about whom we are told so little cannot be one of the twelve, nor a significant Jerusalem disciple, nor a disciple whom Jesus particularly loved at the time. The fourth Gospel's portrayal of him, with the words 'whom Jesus loved', and with only one mention of him before the crucifixion, is barely coherent. It is not however worse than Abraham celebrating the feast of Weeks, Enoch seeing a vision of himself, or Ezra debating with an angel in 557BCE. It is the decisive evidence that he is a secondary legitimating device, rather than a real character. Attempts to identify him are accordingly misplaced.

We can now see clearly two otherwise puzzling features of this narrative – this disciple does not seem to have told anyone else, not even Peter (cf. 13.28–9), and he does nothing to prevent the betrayal of Jesus taking place, even though it is presented as the work of Satan (13.27). Beloved disciples understand that Jesus died deliberately for our salvation. They would not do *anything* to prevent this from happening, not even tell Peter, who might. Hence a beloved disciple is a very suitable figure to let us know that Jesus was in charge of the final events, and was in control of Judas. This also explains the anonymity and description of this figure. Jesus loved all his disciples, as we are reminded at the beginning of this very narrative (13.1). The description 'whom Jesus loved' never could describe a particular disciple, and was never intended to.

It is in this light that we must consider the historicity of John 19.25–7, the only other incident during the ministry when the disciple whom Jesus loved is even mentioned. The events of 19.25–7 are again surprising. Here we find him with the mother of Jesus, his mother's sister, Clopas' Mary, and Mary Magdalene at the foot of the cross. This is in striking contrast to our earliest source, which has a Roman centurion in charge at the cross, and Galilean women, including Mary Magdalene, Mary the wife of Jacob the less and mother of Joses, and Salome, 'watching from afar off' (Mk 15.40–1). As always, historical probability is on Mark's side. Jesus was crucified as a sort of bandit, and hence crucified between two bandits. If leading disciples had been identified when he was executed, they would have been liable to the same fate, as Peter knew when he denied him, and all the disciples knew when they fled (Mk 14.50–2). The fourth Gospel has however followed Mark in interpreting 'the king of the Jews' anachronistically; it has eliminated the information that the two men crucified with Jesus were bandits; the flight of the disciples has been replaced with Jesus' order to let them go (Jn 18.8–9); Peter is admitted to the high priest's courtyard by a disciple who was known to the high priest (18.15); and Pilate is portrayed as wanting to release Jesus (18.38; 19.4, 6, 12).[33] Four women and a disciple whom Jesus loved at the cross remains improbable, but the Johannine story is coherent in that the large number of other changes have made it very much less improbable than it was when Jesus was really crucified. We must infer that the evangelist is telling a story for his own purposes.

What these purposes were has proved more difficult to tell. This is part of the Gospel where important things are said in story form.[34] It is true that, having honoured his Father throughout his ministry, Jesus honours his mother by making provision for her, thereby obeying the fifth commandment. This is likely to be one level of meaning. We must also ask ourselves who would normally have been responsible for caring for his mother after he died. The answer to that is not in doubt – her other children, the brothers of Jesus. They are mentioned at John 2.12, a separate group from his disciples, who believed in him (2.11), and at 7.2ff. they are portrayed at some length as not believing in him. The narrative of 7.2ff. is so careful and extensive that it can only be deliberate. Moreover, some of Jesus' real brothers, especially Jacob, the leader of the church in Jerusalem, were important in the early church. We must therefore infer that John 19.25–7 is telling us that it is disciples, whom Jesus loves, who inherit everything from him, rather than members of his natural family, who are nonetheless completely acceptable if they find their home among disciples whom Jesus loves. Mary cannot symbolise the whole church, because the central category of self-identification of the Johannine community in this Gospel is 'disciple'. Rather, it was obvious that Mary and other members of Jesus' family would become Jewish Christians if, like Jacob, they joined the disciples. The story is accordingly simpler than the massive symbolism which has been built on it. It portrays the determined union of potentially disparate elements in the churches (cf. e.g. 10.16; 17.20–4). It is another example of the real function of the disciple whom Jesus loved, of enabling the authors of the final part of the Gospel to present in story form points that were important for the Johannine community.

The resurrection narratives are notorious for the massive degree of inconsistency between them. The Johannine narratives in particular legitimate specific features of Johannine Christianity.[35] The major new point to be legitimated is the deity of Jesus, a recent and controversial development in the Johannine community, legitimated by doubting Thomas at 20.28. The layout of the clothes, the fact that Mary did not instantly recognise Jesus and the appearances through closed doors explain that Jesus' earthly body was transformed into a spiritual one. The addition in Chapter 21 reinforces this with another episode in which he is not at first recognised, and responds to the concerns aroused by the delay of the parousia. The narratives also legitimate the same points as the earlier narratives of the synoptics. It follows that the stories in which the beloved disciple is important belong to a long tradition of secondary legitimation.

Within this context, the first story[36] has been written round Mary Magdalene, who originally watched the crucifixion (Mk 15.40), Simon Peter, who originally had the first vision of Jesus after his death (1 Cor 15.5, the tradition rewritten at Lk 24.34), and the beloved disciple. We are told that when Mary found the stone removed from the tomb, she ran and came 'to Simon Peter and to the other disciple whom Jesus loved' (Jn 20.2). The central part of the story is well written at a narrative level, with 'the other disciple' winning the race to the tomb, Simon Peter going in first, and the other disciple following him in. Then there is the crucial point of the story. The beloved disciple, unlike Simon Peter, who played a leading role in both the historic ministry and in the early church, 'saw and believed'. That is what beloved disciples must do. They must have faith, when others have uncertainty or doubt. Even when they follow church leaders in a literal sense, it is the faith of the disciples whom Jesus loves which constitutes the

Christian community (cf. 20.30–1). With the essential point made, the author of John 20 saw no need to mention 'the disciple whom Jesus loved' again. Thus the original Gospel ended with this transparent legitimating device mentioned only three times. In each case, there was an important point to make, and this character was a narratively convenient way to make it.

Someone, however, felt that some more important points needed making. At this stage, they could be made by continuing the narrative form of the end of the Gospel. The stories are set in Galilee, so the two traditions of resurrection experiences in different places are reconciled narratively by having Galilee after Jerusalem (cf. Mt 28.9–10, 16–20). The disciples go fishing, a sound narrative setting because it was their original occupation and the occasion of Jesus' declaration that he would make them fishers of men (Mk 1.17//Mt 4.19, rewritten at Lk 5.10). From the point of view of the narrative symbolism, the context is the successful Christian mission. There are seven disciples, the number of perfection, with Simon Peter in the first place, the sons of Zebedee also from the original narrative, doubting Thomas from the previous story, Nathanael from the specifically Johannine story of the call of the disciples, and two anonymous disciples, one of whom must be the disciple whom Jesus loved. It follows that this author did not identify this disciple as one of the sons of Zebedee. He is mentioned only once, and his function is to identify Jesus, with the words 'It is the Lord' (Jn 21.7). He tells Simon Peter, with the result that the disciples know that it is the Lord (21.7, 12). Thus the function of beloved disciples is to ensure that the Christian community knows the Lord.

The next story is about Simon Peter. It stresses his love for Jesus, his leading task in caring for the church, properly reflecting his historical role in church leadership both in Jerusalem and as a missionary, and finally his martyrdom by crucifixion. This is expressed in indirect contrast to his denial of Jesus, when he did not follow Jesus to the cross, and ends appropriately with the injunction 'Follow me' (Jn 21.19). This leads neatly to 'the disciple whom Jesus loved', who is already following. This is again central to the function of beloved disciples, who always follow Jesus, both when church leaders deny Jesus and when they follow him. This is expanded, 'who also leant back on his breast at the supper'. This is a narrative reference by the author of the appendix back to the Gospel itself, to the scene at John 13.25. It should be accepted as such, not confused with a claim that the story is *literally* true. The beloved disciple is then used to deal with one of the serious crises faced by the early church, the delay of the parousia.

The historical Jesus predicted that the kingdom of God would come within a generation, and this prediction was falsified. What was worse, 'the Jews' knew this. We have already seen that this has caused Jesus' preaching of the kingdom of God to be written out of this Gospel.[37] One serious prediction was at Mark 9.1: 'There are some of those standing here who will not taste death until they see the kingdom of God come in power.' It was a prediction which Peter will have repeated, whether or not he was Mark's source for it. Mark could believe that this prediction was still to be fulfilled; Matthew could persuade himself to believe this more precisely, editing in the second coming so that they would see 'the Son of man coming in his kingdom' (Mt 16.28). Luke and John, however, had the serious problem that this generation had died out. One author had a go at this at John 3.3 and 3.5, where 'seeing' the kingdom of God is equated with 'entering' it, which may reasonably be thought to be something you can do in the here and now, or alternatively may be eschatological in the distant future. The passage then stresses rebirth by water and the spirit, so baptism, and all thought of the imminence of the kingdom has been removed.[38]

John 21.20–3 is another shot at the same problem. It had been consistently maintained throughout the earliest period of the church's history that some disciples would survive until the parousia. It is this which is presented at 21.23. Among other things, beloved disciples accepted the validity of the first generation of witnesses, who followed Jesus, whom he loved, and who had died. That generation were properly described as beloved disciples too, and properly portrayed in a narrative with the description 'the disciple whom Jesus loved'. The majority of beloved disciples, however, were not dead at all. Hence the narrative form of rewriting the prediction. Beloved disciples do not mind whether they survive until the second coming, and their continued survival, portrayed at length in the final discourses and in Jesus' final prayer, was obviously in accordance with the will of Jesus:

> I do not ask concerning these only, but also concerning those who believe in me because of their word, that all may be one, as you, Father, are in me and I in you, that they too may be one in us, so that the world may believe that you sent me.
>
> (Jn 17.20–1)

Peter is brought forward to ask about the survival of beloved disciples because he was central both in the Jesus movement and in the early church, he believed in Jesus' original predictions and he had tasted death before the kingdom came. When his death has been predicted and positively interpreted, he asks of the disciple following Jesus the most general of questions, 'What about him?' (21.21). Jesus' answer is highly functional in form: 'If I want him to remain until I come, what's that to you? You follow me!' (21.22). Everyone knew Peter had done just that. Moreover, this portrays the *correct* reaction of beloved disciples to the delay of the parousia. Beloved disciples follow Jesus, regardless. We are next told of a story which circulated among 'the brethren', otherwise an identity term for the community in 1 John and 3 John, but not in the fourth Gospel, except at John 20.17. In 1 John, 'we know that we have passed from death to life, because we love the brethren' (1 Jn 3.14), and 'beloveds' are urged, 'Let us love each other' (4.7). At the end of the Gospel, the incorrect story is that beloved disciples do not die, which they do, as everyone knew. So Jesus' prediction is rewritten to the perfectly correct, 'If I want him to remain until I come', which retains the old eschatological expectation without its timescale.

This leads to the completely true statement of John 21.24, completely true, that is, when we have grasped its genre as a narrative presentation of truth, not a literal statement. This Gospel was written by beloved disciples from beginning to end. Beloved disciples began transmitting the tradition when the followers of Jesus were as Jewish as Jacob his brother, beloved disciples transmitted and rewrote the tradition as the mission to the Gentiles got under way and flourished, beloved disciples wrote every detail of the final form of this Gospel as we have it. Beloved disciples certainly wrote both verses 23 and 24; the same beloved disciple may well have written both verses; and nothing is more obvious than that beloved disciples know that the witness of beloved disciples is true. They are presented as if single for narrative reasons. The whole Johannine community reclining in Jesus' bosom at the Last Supper, or standing at the foot of the cross, was too much even for an authorial tradition which expounded the eucharist before it was instituted. Moreover, the Greek definite article is more generic than the English definite article, which makes it that much easier to read 'the disciple whom Jesus loved' as a representative figure. The 'disciple whom Jesus loved' represents all disciples whom Jesus loved, in much the same way as Ezra in 4 Ezra represents Jews who remain in the covenant community.

Thus the presentation of a beloved disciple by these beloved disciples is natural, for it represents the centre of their lives. Their self-understanding has traditionally been concealed in two ways. One has been to identify the disciple whom Jesus loved with some or all of the anonymous characters in this Gospel. We should not do this, because it contradicts our text.[39] The second way of wrecking this document's description of its author(s) is to apply to it Greek assumptions about authorship. The traditions of its authorship in the early church did this, and we must consider them next.

THE LATER TRADITION OF AUTHORSHIP

We can now consider the traditional view of the authorship of this Gospel.[40] We have seen that its real authors had Gentile self-identification, and after their time the Gentile mission continued to be successful. In the Greco-Roman world, from which all the older traditions of authorship come, the split between Judaism and Christianity deepened. While Christians inherited the Jewish view of authorship as a means of declaring the authority of material derived from the fountainhead of a tradition, they also inherited the Greco-Roman view of authorship as ownership. They therefore had apostles as authors whenever possible, thereby guaranteeing the authenticity of their traditions on both counts. When the tradition of authorship was already strong, they seized on it, and gave the tradition additional authority by association. So Mark was indeed written by Mark, but he had heard the preaching of Peter: Luke-Acts was by Luke, and he was a companion of Paul: Revelation says it was by John, so he turns into the famous John, the son of Zebedee.

When this mode of handling authorship is applied to the fourth Gospel, the results are inevitable. The document itself tells us that the author was 'the disciple whom Jesus loved . . . who also reclined in his bosom at the supper and said, "Lord, who is the one who betrays you?"' (21.20, cf. 13.25 which is thus expanded, and 21.24). This must be an apostle if possible, and Matthew and Luke already have the tradition that only the twelve were at the final meal. Which apostle? It must be someone who is not generally named, but if he is so important, he must be called. At 1.35ff., two disciples are effectively converted from John the Baptist to Jesus, by means of the Baptist's witness, and one of them is unnamed. The other is Andrew. 'He first found his own brother Simon' (1.41), to tell him the good news, and Jesus hailed him as Cephas, i.e. Peter (1.42). Now at Matthew 4.18–22//Mark 1.16–20 (cf. Lk 5.1–11), four people are called, Andrew, Simon Peter, and Jacob and John, the sons of Zebedee. For the Christian tradition, all the Gospels must be right. It follows that when Andrew found his own brother Simon, Jacob found his own brother John, as John 1.41 could be thought to imply. The 'beloved disciple' of 21.20–4 must be one of these two. This is confirmed at 21.2ff., for he must be one of the group mentioned at 21.2, where the sons of Zebedee are mentioned. He could not be Jacob, because he was martyred by Herod Agrippa *c.* 43CE (Acts 12.1–2), whereas the 'beloved disciple' lived for a very long time (Jn 21.18–23). He was therefore John, son of Zebedee. And that was obviously right, since Peter and John are found together in the early chapters of Acts (e.g. Acts 3.1; 4.13; 8.14), like Peter and the beloved disciple in the fourth Gospel, and Paul knew that Peter, Jacob and John were the most important people in the Jerusalem church (Gal 2.9).

We have now got most of the main points of the later tradition. To get it, we have simply used the New Testament traditions in the way that the early church was bound to use them, if it began in ignorance. It was bound to begin in ignorance of a single author, because this Gospel was not written by a single author. It was written in Jewish mode, transmitted over a period of some sixty years and finally put together by beloved disciples. The second-century church was however bound to approach it with Greek assumptions of authorship, for these were now universal in the Greco-Roman world, where the vast majority of Christians were Gentiles. The tradition is first found in late-second-century sources. These sources are fragmentary, and some of them are legitimating traditions. The earliest relatively complete comment was written *c.* 180CE by Irenaeus: 'Then [sc.

after Matthew, Mark and Luke] John, the disciple of the Lord, who also leant back on his breast, he too published the Gospel, when staying at Ephesus in Asia' (Adv. Haer. III, 1, 1). Irenaeus also refers to John as an apostle (Adv. Haer. I, 9, 2, cf. e.g. II, 22, 5). It follows that, though he does not call him the son of Zebedee, Irenaeus believed that this Gospel was written by John, the son of Zebedee, the beloved disciple. He further specifies that he stayed in Ephesus until the time of Trajan (Adv. Haer. II, 22, 5; III, 3, 4).

The attribution of the Gospel to John, described as 'the disciple of the Lord', is evidently earlier, for it was the view of Ptolemy (Irenaeus, Adv. Haer. I, 8, 5). Epiphanius also quotes Ptolemy calling him 'the apostle' (*Panarion* 33, 3, 6), so Ptolemy too had either gone through the process of inferring the author from the document, or had inherited that result from earlier still. The description 'disciple of the Lord' is interesting because it fits the Gospel itself so well. The term 'disciple' is the nearest thing the Gospel has to a term which indicates the identity of people who come to faith in Jesus. It is used as purely positive description of them both narratively after the resurrection (20.26, cf. 30; 21.1, 14), and in looking forward to the Johannine community (16.29). It is used in opposition to 'the Jews', in similar circumstances (2.17–22; 12.16, cf. 9, 11; 20.19). It is also the only term for describing the 'disciple whom Jesus loved' (13.23; 19.26; 20.2; 21.7, 20). Moreover, this Gospel has 'the Lord' as a narrative description of Jesus, and accepted by him as a suitable term (Jn 13.13–14). It is commonest in the resurrection narratives (seven times), in which the 'beloved disciple' uses this term to identify Jesus (21.7), and to address him (21.20, referring to 13.25). We must infer that the early description of John as 'the disciple of the Lord' was based on this Gospel itself.

This tradition became widespread quite quickly, as it was bound to, given that it results directly from the application of Greek assumptions about authorship to this document. Theophilus of Antioch, *c.* 180CE, introduces a quotation from the prologue: '. . . the holy scriptures, and all those who bear the Spirit, of whom John says . . .' (Ad Aut. II, 22). We must infer that Theophilus knew the tradition well enough to expect this brief reference to call it up. A few years later, Polycrates, bishop of Ephesus, listed among the luminaries of Asia 'John, who leant back on the Lord's breast' (Eus. H.E. III, 31, 3; V, 24, 3), another brief reference which presupposes that the tradition was known. At the turn of the century P[66] was written with the superscription 'Gospel according to John', and the tradition was known to Clement of Alexandria and to Origen.

Apart from Marcion, who rejected too many scriptures to be taken into account at this point, serious Christian opposition to this Gospel is known only from Rome. The later church did not preserve the opposing arguments as well as we would like. It seems clear, however, that some Roman Christians were opposed to the Paraclete (Irenaeus, Adv. Haer. III, 11, 9), saw that this Gospel was not consistent with the synoptics, and attributed it to the gnostic Cerinthus (cf. Eus. H.E. II, 25, 6; III, 28, 1f.; 31, 4; Epiphanius, *Panarion* 51, 3–4). We can make excellent sense of these fragmentary data. Opposition to the Paraclete will have been due to opposition to Montanists, a movement which saw new prophecy as inspired by the Paraclete.[41] The attribution to Cerinthus reflects opposition to gnostics who made much use of this Gospel in the second century. Cerinthus himself appears as an opponent of John in an anecdote transmitted by Irenaeus (Adv. Haer. III, 3, 4), so he will have been chosen as an anti-legitimating device by Christians who knew the standard attribution to John the apostle. The differences between John and the synoptics are so glaring that opponents of the fourth Gospel with any sense of evidence would have used them. We must infer that by the end of the second century, the fourth Gospel was widely accepted in the churches, and attributed to John, the son of Zebedee, the 'beloved disciple', but that it had not quite reached unimpeachably canonical status.

Adherents of the normative tradition also sought to legitimate it by alleging contact with earlier people, so as to produce a chain of transmission which could be regarded as reliable. Some of the information in these reports is true. It is all the more important to perceive its frame of reference, an interpretative and legitimating tradition. It is within this framework that members of the standard tradition quote fragments of earlier sources which they always interpret, and sometimes, especially when Epiphanius is the tradent, they may be rewriting their 'quotations' as well. So Irenaeus claims to have seen Polycarp, and to remember the events of that time 'more clearly than those which happened recently'. His memories include 'the accounts which he [sc. Polycarp] gave of his meetings with John and with the others who had seen the Lord' (*Letter to Florinus*, at Eus. H.E. V, 20, 4–8). Similarly, Eusebius (H.E. III, 39, 3f.) quotes Papias, who claims to transmit 'whatever I have at any time learned well from the elders and remembered well, guaranteeing their truth'. When therefore he met a follower of the elders, he enquired into the sayings of the elders, what Andrew or Peter or others said. It should be clear that Eusebius quotes Papias telescoping a chain of transmission from the apostles through the elders through visitors.

Some of these traditions are certainly wrong. For example, Irenaeus, our earliest source for the tradition, describes Papias as the hearer of John (Adv. Haer. V, 33, 4), but this is contradicted by the work of Papias himself (Eus. H.E. III, 39, 1f.). This shows one standard mistake of legitimating traditions, that of shortening the chain of transmission. Polycrates says that John 'became a priest who wore the *petalon*' (Eus. H.E. III, 31, 3; V, 24, 3–4), which was part of the *high* priest's raiment. This is not plausible (Bauckham 1993a: 33–44). Irenaeus also says that the book of Revelation was written by John, 'the disciple of the Lord . . . who leant back on his [sc. the Word's] breast at the supper and asked who it was who was going to betray him', so the same John as the Gospel (Adv. Haer. IV, 20, 11; cf. V, 26, 1; 35, 2). On

167

stylistic grounds, however, this Gospel cannot be by the same author as Revelation, so Irenaeus is wrong again. Moreover, this tradition, which Irenaeus takes for granted rather than asserts, was also becoming widespread at this time. It seems to have been known already to Justin, who describes the author of Revelation as 'a man, by name John, one of the apostles of Christ' (*Dialogue* 81). Tertullian also describes the author of Revelation as 'John the apostle' (*Adv. Mc.* III, 14, 3; 24, 4). Clement of Alexandria has 'John the apostle' move from Patmos to Ephesus in terms which show that he could take his authorship of both the Gospel and Revelation for granted (*Quis Dives Salvetur* XLII), and Origen has John as the author of the Gospel, Revelation and at least one of the three epistles (*On the Gospel of John* V, III, at Eus. H.E. VI, 25, 9–10). In Rome, the opponents of the fourth Gospel rejected Revelation also (cf. Eus. H.E. III, 28, 1–2; Epiphanius, *Panarion* 51, 3), and Hippolytus defended them both. It follows that the legitimating tradition was vigorous and widespread when it was wrong, so we may not believe its other points merely because they too were part of a widespread and vigorous tradition by the end of the second century.

Irenaeus further claims that Polycarp was 'appointed by apostles in Asia bishop of the church of Smyrna' (Adv. Haer. III, 3, 4). According to the *Life of Polycarp* attributed to Pionius, however, he was ordained by Bucolus, and made bishop after Bucolus' death when the deacons enquired of the laity, the whole priesthood agreed, so Polycarp was made bishop by the bishops. The narrative is somewhat legendary and falling over itself to praise Polycarp: it is not probable that it would have failed to pick up a true and therefore old tradition of his ordination by apostles. Nor does Pionius mention any meetings between Polycarp and John.

Some traditions rewrite the story in terms of what happened in later times. Clement of Alexandria has 'John the Apostle' leave Patmos for Ephesus after the death of 'the tyrant', presumably Domitian, and go round the churches appointing bishops and the like (*Quis Dives Salvetur* XLII). Later sources get worse and worse. A piece prefixed to a ninth-century Vulgate manuscript tells us that Papias wrote down the Gospel at the dictation of John. Storytelling was a problem earlier than that. One source for John's residence in Ephesus is the Acts of John, a work of such fantastic stories that it is accepted as wildly legendary in nature.[42] A more obvious legitimating ploy is found in the Syriac Acts of John, 41b, where 'we' found John's arrival at Ephesus written in the archives of the wicked emperor Nero.

All this evidence is consistent. Even as early as Irenaeus, the tradition already has significant legitimating error. We must therefore see it for what it is – legitimating tradition based on central conviction, not the preservation of truth. By the early third century it contains the three ingredients of the later tradition: informed guesswork based on information supplied by the

New Testament, incorrect secondary legitimation, and legend. We should not look further.

The secondary and legitimating nature of church traditions has another consequence. We should not accept even the most learned and ingenious attempts to draw out of them a real author of the Gospel other than John son of Zebedee, especially not 'John the elder'. For example, Hengel notes the description of earlier people by Papias, as quoted by Eusebius, as 'Aristion and the elder John, the disciples of the Lord'; he combines this with the self-reference of the author of 2 and 3 John as 'the elder', and with other passages where Eusebius, in the name of Papias, refers to 'the elder John' (e.g. Eus. H.E. III, 39, 14); adds in Irenaeus' tradition that John the disciple of the Lord lived until the time of Trajan; and ends up with 'the authoritative *head of the school*', who worked in the Flavian period and early in the period of Trajan in Ephesus and founded a school there (Hengel 1989: esp. 24–32; 1993: esp. 96–119). To accept this result, we have to obey the legitimating traditions. Otherwise, the tradition that the author of the Gospel lived until the time of Trajan may be a legitimating inference from the description 'the elder', which has the function of enabling Irenaeus and his ilk to imagine the author of the fourth Gospel alive long enough to reduce the length of the chain of transmission and thereby make it seem more reliable. Likewise, only obedience to the legitimating tradition enables us to identify Papias' elder John with 'the elder' who wrote 2 and 3 John. Otherwise, Papias' description is intended to inflate the importance of John and Aristion, we have no reason to identify John the elder with the anonymous elder of 2 and 3 John and we have seen that one person did not write the fourth Gospel and all the Johannine epistles.

Hengel's argument also has an elitist assumption which was stated more clearly by Bauckham. Arguing for the identity of the beloved disciple, the author of the Gospel and John the elder, Bauckham suggests an advantage of his proposal: 'It avoids the supposition that the name of one of the greatest teachers of the early Church, author of one of its finest literary products, has inexplicably disappeared without any trace in the historical evidence' (Bauckham 1993a: 25). This presupposes, without evidence, that the work somehow *must* have had a single author, and ignores the fact that we have no such trace of an author of Deutero-Isaiah, 1–2 Chronicles, 11Q Temple, Jubilees and many other works. We have seen that this lack of a named author corresponded to the reality of the composition of Jewish works, which were written out of lengthy traditions by more than one person, so that final editors could hardly be regarded as authors in our sense. Accordingly, there was not a single great teacher whose name has inexplicably disappeared; there was a host of beloved disciples who have told us quite a lot about their community. Bauckham's view also presupposes a value judgement which is a great deal less than clear. Is this really great teaching? Is it a fine literary product? We have seen that it uses a reduced form of the Greek language with few particles, and that the course of the narrative is frequently unconvincing. We shall have to confront its anti-Jewish attitude.[43] Bauckham's judgement merely reflects the fact that he adheres to a tradition which holds this text sacred. That is not a satisfactory criterion for making historical judgements. It is characteristic of conservative scholarship, which we must now examine in detail.

AUTHORSHIP IN CONSERVATIVE SCHOLARSHIP

In recent years, the outstanding conservative attempt to establish the traditional view of the authorship of the fourth Gospel has been that of Leon Morris (Morris 1969). Before tackling the question of authorship directly, Morris has a massive chapter in which he argues that the testimony of an eyewitness underlies this Gospel. Most of his arguments are unconvincing in themselves, and when they do have force, they do not show that the supposed eyewitness of the actual event was anywhere near to the author. For example he suggests that the expression 'king of Israel', attributed to Nathanael (Jn 1.49), 'must go back to early days. This is the kind of touch which is natural enough in someone who remembered what took place, but which is difficult to explain in a late writer, composing freely without factual basis' (Morris 1969: 141). This judgement is quite arbitrary, and heedless of the context. Jesus has already hailed Nathanael as 'truly an Israelite in whom there is no guile' (1.47), some contrast with Jacob. Nathanael's confession accordingly does use some traditional Jewish material, with 'rabbi' as well as 'king of Israel'. It thereby gives a picture of a Jew being converted to Jesus, a functional picture for a community in conflict with 'the Jews'. Morris's account is misleading in putting up as the only alternative to eyewitness reminiscence 'a late writer, composing freely without factual basis'. This Gospel was composed on the basis of tradition and current conflict with 'the Jews'. We should not believe its account, because the Johannine accounts of the calls of the disciples have several secondary features, Nathanael does not occur in the synoptic Gospels, Jesus' knowledge of him is miraculous, Nathanael's use of the title 'Son of God' indicates later Johannine Christology and Jesus concludes with a midrash which was developed over a period of years in the early church.[44] Accordingly, this Gospel had a factual basis which was not the Jesus of history, but a combination of tradition with current concerns. This may not be regarded as an eyewitness account merely because it contains some tradition.

Morris continues with another ploy, citing other scholars who supported his view as if this were further evidence in its favour. In this case he has Dodd for the 'primitive title' which 'smacks of a messianism more Jewish than Christian', Plummer for its not being feasible after the destruction of Jerusalem, and Johnson for the detail coming from an eyewitness source, with Johnson especially important because he does not accept apostolic authorship 'yet cannot overlook the fact that some passages, at least, bear the stamp of an eyewitness' (Morris 1969: 141, quoting Plummer 1882: 87; Dodd 1963: 155, 216; Johnson 1966: 280). None of these arguments is stronger for having been suggested previously. They illustrate the drastic extent to which Morris's perceptions are controlled by the tradition to which he adheres.

Most of Morris's arguments are of this kind, and have no force at all. A few arguments are typified by his comments on John 10.22–3, where Jesus is portrayed as walking in the temple in Solomon's porch, at Hanukkah during the winter. He quotes Bernard, 'This vivid touch suggests that the writer is thoroughly familiar with the place and the conditions in which instruction was given there' (Morris 1969: 165–6, quoting Bernard 1928: II, 343). Somebody did know that Solomon's portico was in the Temple, that Hanukkah was celebrated during winter, and it is reasonable to suppose that Jesus has been deliberately put in Solomon's portico during winter because this was a better place to walk than out in the open. It does not however follow that the author himself knew this from being there. The Temple was very well known, and he may have been given accurate information by a source (cf. Acts 3.11; 5.12; Jos. B.J. V, 184f.; A.J. XV, 396–401; XX, 220f.). Nor does it follow that the discourse is authentic. It is possible that the author has deliberately given the discourse a plausible setting as a reality effect, and for all we know, he might have done so because he was very struck by the place when he saw it. The discourse has a number of secondary features,[45] so we must infer that the setting is secondary too, and refuse to imagine that we know whether the final author personally knew the place or not.

It follows that Morris's whole chapter does not show that the author was an eyewitness. His chapter on authorship follows the outline of the classic argument of Westcott (Morris 1969: Chapter 4, following Westcott 1908: I, ix–lxvii). As recently as 1991, Carson declared his first two points 'to-day rarely disputed', and his own comments on them are very brief, because 'they are so admirably handled by Morris' (Carson 1991: 71). Morris's first major section is devoted to showing that the author was a Jew (Morris 1969: 218–27, following Westcott 1908: I, x–xx). He notes for example that the author is familiar with Jewish messianic expectations, that he knows that the sabbath is observed and that circumcision overrides the sabbath. Morris believes that the linguistic argument, that John's Greek has an Aramaic cast of thought behind it, has been immeasurably strengthened since Westcott. He notes the importance of the Old Testament, that scripture cannot be broken (10.35) and that Moses wrote of Christ (5.46). Finally Morris notes 'the Jews', arguing that 'John does know the condition of the Jews at the time of Christ and he writes out of knowledge'. His examples include that they charge Jesus with sabbath violation (5.10ff.), that the Pharisees are always interested in religion (e.g. 1.24; 4.1) and that the chief priests take the direction of the final events into their own hands, plotting the murder of Lazarus (12.11), and saying 'we have no king but Caesar' (19.15).

This argument has two profound faults of method. Firstly, knowledge of Judaism does not show that a person is Jewish. The Johannine community inherited Jewish tradition. No Gentile Christian could be unaware of Jewish messianic expectations, for Christians believed that Jesus fulfilled them. Gentiles who joined the Christian community were, from a Gentile perspective, Judaising. They could hardly be unaware of sabbath observance, when a major question in the early church was whether Gentile Christians should become so Jewish as to observe it. Hence Morris's argument would make Jews of Westcott, Morris and most New Testament scholars, not to mention German scholars who were seriously *anti*-Jewish.[46] Details such as circumcision overriding the sabbath do not take Morris's argument further, because there is no limit to how detailed a knowledge a Gentile may have of Judaism, and it was not long since the Johannine community included Jews among its members. Nor do Westcott and Morris take proper account of evidence *against* the author being a Jew, such as his hostile use of 'the Jews', and his erroneous view that Jesus abrogated the sabbath (Jn 5.18). Nor could they do so, because their understanding of identity was so oversimplified.

The second major fault in Morris's argument is that it contains so many mistakes, and a number of circles. It is not true that the chief priests plotted the murder of Lazarus, nor that 'the Jews' (19.14) said 'We have no king but Caesar' (19.15).[47] Morris's argument is circular, because it is only his conservative convictions that have led him to believe in the historicity of the narrative in the first place. The only truth in his comments is that the narrative has a Jewish setting, because it was originally Jewish history which has been creatively rewritten. It is moreover misleading to cite the charge of 'the Jews' that Jesus violated the sabbath. In the synoptic Gospels, Jesus is accused by Pharisees of being responsible for sabbath violation (Mk 2.24; 3.2, 6), but they could not make the charge stick because he did not violate the written Law. The fourth evangelist has deliberately rewritten the situation so that Jesus is responsible for sabbath violation by telling a man to carry his pallet on the sabbath, and he attributes the charge to 'the Jews', which is culturally accurate but historically anachronistic. Moreover, the claim that Moses wrote of Christ (5.46) is made in a quite anti-Jewish context. Here the Jews are accused of not believing in Moses, a false and quite anti-Jewish charge. Accordingly, this may not be used as evidence that the author was Jewish.

The next section of Morris's argument is devoted to showing that the author was a Jew of Palestine (Morris 1969: 227–33, following Westcott 1908: I, xx–xxxix). This can hardly be successful when he has failed to show that the author was Jewish in the first place. He begins with a lengthy quotation from Westcott, who lists various matters, such as 'the real points at issue between true and false Judaism', which 'a Gentile, living at a distance from the scene of religious and political controversy which he paints', could not have realised. Once again, his list of what a Gentile could not have known is arbitrary. Moreover, it is not true that John lived at a distance from the scene of religious and political controversy which he paints, and nowhere is this clearer than in what Westcott called the real points at issue 'between true and false Judaism'. The authors of the fourth Gospel lived plum in the middle of points at issue between themselves and 'the Jews', which explains the vigour with which they present historically anachronistic controversies. Finally, Westcott's description of 'false Judaism' is wholly lacking in scholarly objectivity, owing to his committed membership of the tradition which Morris and Carson seek to continue.

Morris's second point is 'the Evangelist's topographical knowledge'. He follows Westcott in noting the inclusion of Cana of Galilee (2.1, 11; 4.46; 21.2) and Bethany beyond Jordan (1.28), which 'was forgotten by the time of Origen'. He finds the knowledge of Jerusalem even more conclusive, including the pool of Siloam (9.7) and 'the "winter torrent" Kedron (18.1)'. These are not mentioned in the synoptic Gospels. The synoptics do mention the praetorium and Golgotha, but Morris quotes Westcott for the view that John sees them 'with the vividness of an actual spectator' (Morris 1969: 228, following Westcott 1908: I, xxiii). He follows the investigation of R.D. Potter, who declares that 'time and again, it will be found that those who have lived long in palestine are struck by the impression that our author did so' (Morris 1969: 230, quoting Potter 1959: 335). He refers again to John's knowledge of the Old Testament, suggesting that evidence that he knew it in Hebrew 'favours a Palestinian origin'.

None of this is convincing. Accurate topographical knowledge, such as the inclusion of Cana of Galilee, may be due to an accurate source just as much as to the personal presence of the writer. Equally, the people responsible for Johannine tradition may have gone to Israel and included references to places such as the pool of Siloam because they were genuinely moved by going to places where they felt that Jesus had been. Accordingly, the evidence collected by Morris does not show that the author had been to Palestine; and if he had been to Palestine, it does nothing to show that he originally hailed from there. In either case, he could have used genuine topographical information as reality effects. The same applies to the complex evidence which suggests that somebody really did know the Old Testament in Hebrew. Learned people have read the Old Testament in Hebrew ever since, and some of us still do. There will not have been thousands of such people in Ephesus, but there may have been quite a few, particularly well equipped for arguing with 'the Jews'. They may have been responsible for the elaboration of secondary midrashim. Knowledge of Hebrew never guarantees residence in Israel, and midrashim constructed there are not characterised by historical accuracy.

Morris's use of Bethany beyond Jordan forms a circular argument. It may have been unknown rather than 'forgotten' by the time of Origen, for the reference to it may be mistaken. Morris's conviction that it shows accurate topographical knowledge is due to his prior conviction of the plenary inspiration of holy writ, and it typifies the quite spurious arguments which conservative scholars must use to defend their traditions. These are conspicuous in Morris's citations of Westcott and Potter. Westcott's view that John sees the praetorium 'with the vividness of an actual spectator' is quite arbitrary, and we have seen that some of the events recorded there are due to the secondary rewriting of tradition.[48] Potter's argument is already circular. Some people 'who have lived long in Palestine are struck by the impression that our author did so' because they are committed to the same traditions as Westcott, Potter and Morris, and this does nothing to increase the validity of arguments based on knowing that Cana was in Galilee, or on the vividness of secondary narratives set in the praetorium.

This concludes the two sections which Carson does not elaborate upon, because 'they are so admirably handled by Morris' (Carson 1991: 71). This further illustrates the way that this tradition feeds on itself.

Morris's third point is that the author of the fourth Gospel was an eyewitness of what he described (Morris 1969: 233–44, following Westcott 1908: I, xxxix–xliv). He begins with a quotation from Westcott, who notes 'minute details of persons, and time, and number, and place and manner, which cannot but have come from a direct experience'. Their large collection of examples includes the persons Nicodemus and Lazarus, the feast of Passover (2.13, 23; 6.4), the time 'by night' (3.2), the number 'two' of the disciples of the Baptist (1.35), the place 'Aenon' (3.23) and countless small traits such as John the Baptist standing (1.35) in patient expectation of the issue, and fixing his eyes on Jesus as he moves away (1.36). None of these examples demonstrates anything. In general, they merely indicate that the fourth Gospel is written as a story, for details are characteristic of primary and secondary material alike. Moreover, many details are associated with verifiably secondary material. When Nicodemus came to Jesus by night, he is described as a 'ruler of the Jews', the external usage of the term 'the Jews' which marks the fourth Gospel off from Judaism. He then receives a discourse which transmutes the meaning of 'see the kingdom of God', uses the Greek concept of rebirth, uses 'Son of man' in a manner characteristic of Johannine Christology and not possible in the original Aramaic, has a concept of Jesus as the only-begotten Son which is absent from the synoptics and a view of salvation which excludes non-Christian Jews.[49] We must infer that the discourse is secondary. The story of the raising of Lazarus is untrue, and causes narrative chaos.[50] Passover is mentioned at John 2.13 and 2.23, in moving the Cleansing of the Temple to the wrong place, an account which has the later and external use of 'the Jews' as a different group from 'the disciples', and 'signs' which are absent from the earliest account of the incident.[51]

Morris's fourth argument is that the author was an apostle. He takes this from Westcott, and suggests that it carries some weight, without being as strong as the other arguments (Morris 1969: 244–6, following Westcott 1908: I, xliv–xlv). He attaches particular weight to the evangelist's 'intimate acquaintance' with the feelings of the disciples, so that he knows their thoughts at critical moments (e.g. 2.11), and remembers words spoken among themselves (e.g. 16.17). Even more, he 'stood very near to the Lord', for he knew his emotions (e.g. 11.33), indeed he speaks as one to whom the mind of the Lord was laid open (e.g. 6.61; 13.1). This whole argument is circular – the evangelist knew these things only if his account is literally true from beginning to end, which is the main point at issue. Furthermore, some of these examples are particularly unconvincing. John 2.11 merely declares that the disciples had faith in Jesus, a widespread feature of Christianity not however characteristic of the synoptic Gospels, and following a Johannine miracle story with its distinctively external use of 'the Jews' (2.6). John 11.33 has the same usage of 'the Jews', and belongs to a deliberately written miracle story which is full of Johannine theology and which causes narrative chaos.[52] At John 6.61, Jesus' disciples 'murmur' like the wilderness generation because of a deliberately anti-Jewish rewrite of the eucharist before it was instituted, and Jesus, presented indeed as knowing this blindingly obvious response before he is told, responds with the purely Johannine belief in his pre-existence and a comment on the ineffectiveness of merely taking the eucharist which is dependent on the situation in the Johannine community, which some Jewish Christians had left.[53] At John 13.1, Jesus knows that his hour has come a day too soon.[54] It is quite remarkable that such a collection of secondary rewriting could be put forward as evidence that John was an apostle.

Morris's fifth point is that the author was the apostle John (Morris 1969: 246–53, following Westcott 1908: I, xlv–lii). The real basis of this view is the evidence of the Gospel, interpreted according to a Greek view of authorship and combined with harmonising use of other parts of the New Testament. We have seen that this does lead to Morris's result, but that it is secondary.[55] Morris seeks to support it with the fact that John the Baptist is never called 'Baptist' in the fourth Gospel, but only 'John' (likewise Westcott 1908: I, xlvii; Carson 1991: 72). This is quite odd. If the author were called John, and careful with names, he would surely be *more* careful to distinguish John the Baptist by calling him the Baptist. A more probable inference is that John is not called 'Baptist' because Jesus is presented, quite secondarily, as a more successful baptist than John (Jn 3.22–4.1).[56]

Morris also discusses the external evidence (Morris 1969: 256–64, following Westcott 1908: I, lix–lxvii). Many of his comments are true – we have seen that by the end of the second century, this Gospel was widely accepted in the churches as an authoritative work by John, and that while our earliest sources usually call him 'the disciple of the Lord', they did mean

John the apostle, son of Zebedee. Morris's discussion has however two faults. Firstly, he pushes the evidence in the direction of his tradition wherever he can. So the ascription of the Gospel to Cerinthus by the Alogi is dismissed as 'unimportant', without proper discussion of its rejection by a group of Christians in Rome in the late second century; and the evidence of sources such as Polycarp and Papias is treated as if cited tradents were extant, and without mention of legitimating mistakes in the tradition. Secondly, Morris writes as if his tradition were ultimately inviolable. He finds it significant that an alternative author was not known to the tradition, which presupposes that only single, known authors are possible, and he cannot explain its acceptance into the canon unless it was really written by an apostle. This is because he belongs to the same tradition. It is this tradition which produced apostolic authorship: this Gospel was written by several people when anonymous and pseudepigraphical compositions were normal.

We must therefore conclude that Morris's arguments are faulty from beginning to end. Consistent features are bias, circularity and error. It is significant that this is what is now required to defend the tradition. We must conclude that it is indefensible.

CONCLUSIONS

The following conclusions may therefore be drawn. The presence in the fourth Gospel of a large proportion of historically inaccurate material may be explained on the basis of the known habits of authors, and the needs of the Johannine community. It was normal for Jewish works to be anonymous or pseudepigraphical. It was normal for pseudepigraphical works to be attributed to fountainheads of traditions. It was also normal for them to be rewritten in accordance with the needs of the community. This is what has happened in the fourth Gospel. The teaching of Jesus was rewritten with Johannine theology, as was the witness of John the Baptist, and the whole was set in a narrative framework which was created and modified as required. In the first place, John 1–20 was not attributed to an author, because it was compiled over a period of years, and completed by more than one person. It was therefore left anonymous, as Jewish works often were, for the same reason. The author(s) of John 21 further developed the narratively convenient figure of the 'disciple whom Jesus loved', a representative of all the disciples whom Jesus loved. They then attributed its authorship to the disciple whom Jesus loved, because it was genuinely composed by and for beloved disciples.

The traditional attribution of the Gospel to John son of Zebedee is due to the continuing need to legitimate its authority. It was worked out from the evidence of New Testament documents. It presupposes the Greek model of authorship which was natural to the church, according to which documents were written by single people, and attributed to them. It is false. It includes, however, the true historical fact that the Gospel was written in its present form in Ephesus. It follows that the authorship of this work does not in any way stand against the arguments of the previous chapters of this book, that much of the material special to this Gospel is not historically accurate. On the contrary, it helps to explain how such an historically inaccurate work came to be composed.

9

CRUCIFIED UNDER PONTIUS PILATE, ON THE THIRD DAY HE ROSE AGAIN FROM THE DEAD

INTRODUCTION

The purpose of this chapter is to look at the fourth Gospel's account of the centre of the myth of Christian origins, the Passion and resurrection of Jesus. I work through John 13.21ff. and John 18–20, and point out aspects of the account which are secondary. Some account of Jesus' arrest, trial and death was one of the first parts of his story to be put together in continuous form. This was necessary, because he was crucified on the orders of the Roman prefect of Judaea, Pontius Pilatus, with two bandits (Mk 15.27). This was a shameful death reserved for serious criminals. A possible conclusion was that Jesus had been abandoned by God because he had done something seriously wrong. Accordingly, the earliest Christians needed to know, both for their own sakes and for the defence of the Gospel, the straightforward, practical reasons why he was executed. There are, however, serious discrepancies between the fourth Gospel's account and that of the synoptics. We have seen that the fourth Gospel has the crucifixion on the wrong day, and that consequently the Last Supper is not presented as a Passover meal.[1] We must now consider other aspects of this narrative which are plainly secondary.[2]

The resurrection was central to early Christianity. In some sense, the belief that God had raised Jesus from the dead to heaven was an early belief. It is however notorious that the Gospel accounts do not agree with each other. Here again we shall consider secondary aspects of the Johannine account.

A severe problem arises from the difficulty of determining what sort of account the fourth evangelist rewrote. It has been reasonably argued that some aspects of John's account which are not found in the synoptic Gospels may be due to independent tradition which he inherited (Dodd 1963: 21–151). These include features such as a Roman cohort and tribune involved in arresting Jesus (Jn 18.3, 12). The narrator attaches so little overt importance to this that it is not probable that he was inventing it. It has been further argued that John cannot have known the synoptic Gospels, because he

178

omits points in them which he would not have objected to. This is much more doubtful. It depends on the ingenuity of scholars in finding out why he omitted things, when we may simply fail to think of his reasons, and his need to select from too much information may have been overwhelming (cf. Jn 20.30; 21.25). For example, it has been suggested that he would not have omitted the rending of the veil of the Temple when Jesus died (Mk 15.38// Mt 27.51//Lk 23.45) (e.g. Dodd 1963: 129–30). But this story, which is not confirmed by independent Jewish sources, is a legendary development, and this may have been very well known in Ephesus, to the Johannine community and 'the Jews' alike. In view of the difficulties involved in assessing such matters, the aim of the following discussion is to determine points at which we have rewritten tradition before us. It will not necessarily be claimed that it was a synoptic Gospel which was rewritten, nor that all rewriting is due to the final redactor of the fourth Gospel.[3]

BETRAYAL AND ARREST

As in the synoptics, Jesus is betrayed by Judas Iscariot, following the Last Supper. We have seen that Jesus' last meal with his disciples was a Passover meal, and that the fourth evangelist has completely rewritten it to ensure that Jesus is crucified at the time when the Passover victims were slaughtered.[4] There is another significant difference. In the fourth Gospel, Jesus makes it clear to 'one of his disciples . . . whom Jesus loved' (13.23) that it is Judas who will betray him. This is the first mention of 'the beloved disciple', as he is usually called. The narrator is concerned that we should know that Jesus foresaw his betrayal, but the earlier tradition does not say explicitly that he knew who would betray him. If he is rewriting the tradition, which did not record that Jesus knew the identity of the traitor, he has to have the disciple who is told near enough to Jesus to be told privately. For this purpose, he must have him reclining next to him, and in that case he must be 'one of his disciples . . . whom Jesus loved' (13.23). This makes excellent sense of the otherwise extraordinary fact that this is the first description of this disciple, when the public ministry is already over. We have seen more extensive reasons for concluding that this disciple was not an historical figure in the ministry of Jesus, but a narratively convenient figure who behaves as the Johannine community felt that beloved disciples should behave.[5] His task done, he is not mentioned again during the rest of the meal, nor in the rest of the discourses. He does not even tell anyone else the identity of the traitor, for he is a means of telling *us* that *Jesus* knew the identity of the traitor, and a beloved disciple should not take measures to stop Jesus dying for the salvation of the world.

Jesus' extremely vigorous condemnation of the traitor (Mk 14.21//Mt 26.24) is omitted. In its place we have the theological declaration by the narrator, 'then Satan entered into him' (Jn 13.27), and the symbolic 'Now it was night' (13.30). This enables him to portray Jesus as in direct overall charge of the proceedings. After identifying Judas to the anonymous disciple 'whom Jesus loved', Jesus gives Judas his orders, 'Do what you are doing quickly' (13.27). If Jesus had been in this much control of events, the synoptic writers would surely have known. Where Mark's account makes sense only if it is historically accurate,[6] the Johannine account can be explained only if it is historically inaccurate.

The immediate sequel is distinctively Johannine, and it has two clearly secondary features. The first is the 'Son of man' statement at John 13.31: 'Now the Son of man was glorified, and God was glorified in him, and God will glorify him in himself, and he will glorify him immediately.' Mark's early and accurate account of the Last Supper has a double 'son of man' saying (Mk 14.21) which can be retroverted into convincing idiomatic Aramaic (Casey 1987: 40–2). This cannot be done with John 13.31, because the Aramaic term for 'son of man' is an ordinary term for 'man'. If genuine, therefore, John 13.31 would have to have a general level of meaning, but there is no convincing meaning available – people are not generally glorified by death, nor by making arrangements to die. Moreover, John 13.31 has an excellent *Sitz im Leben* in Johannine theology. Here the Greek term 'Son of man' is a Christological title which refers to Jesus alone; his death is his glorification and about to follow; and he has just set in motion the final events. We must therefore conclude that this part of the exposition is secondary.

An equally secondary feature is the use of the term 'the Jews' at 13.33. It is quite extraordinary that Jesus should refer to 'the Jews' as an alien group when all his disciples were Jewish. We have seen that this is due to the Gentile self-identification of the author(s) of this Gospel.[7] This usage in a saying of Jesus shows that we are dealing with the final level of the redaction of this document.

If it were not for these points, we might be tempted to believe that Jesus' teaching on love (13.34–5) was authentic. We might even swallow the conservative view that he gave more such teaching in private to the disciples than he did in public. However, it is absent from the synoptics, to whom it should have been congenial, and here it is associated with two clearly secondary features. We must infer that Jesus' injunctions that the disciples should love each other have their *Sitz im Leben* in the Johannine community. It lived under threat from both 'the Jews' and 'the world'. The injunctions to love one another are part of the internal dynamics of trying to keep together a rather beleaguered community.

The betrayal takes place after the final discourses (Jn 13.31–16) and Jesus' prayer (Jn 17). The first improbability is that Judas has a Roman cohort, normally some 600 men, to carry out the arrest. In Mark, he has 'a crowd with swords and clubs from the chief priests and scribes and elders' (Mk 14.43). Mark's account is entirely coherent, since it has the party sent from the people who were in charge and who still have to take Jesus to the

Roman governor. A Roman cohort at this stage would have been remarkable, and it would have necessitated a different course of events which Mark had no reason to alter. We should not try to harmonise the accounts by referring to the few passages of literature which use Roman terms for non-Roman troops (e.g. 2 Macc 8.23; Jos. A.J. XVII, 215). The narrator has the cohort led by a chiliarch, the normal Greek term for the tribunus militum who commanded a Roman cohort, and he distinguishes it from 'attendants from the chief priests and from the Pharisees' and 'the attendants of the Jews' (Jn 18.3, 12). He therefore meant a Roman cohort, and he was wrong.

This extraordinarily large number of people, perhaps read back from the scene of the mockery (cf. Mk 15.16), intensifies another secondary feature of the arrest. In the synoptics, Jesus is really *betrayed* by Judah, who addresses him as 'rabbi' and, following his prearranged plan, identifies him in the dark by kissing him (Mk 14.43–6). Luke transmits Jesus' actual protest to Judah, with its idiomatic use of the Aramaic term 'son of man': 'Judah, do you betray a/the (son of) man with a kiss?' (Lk 22.48). The synoptic account must surely be accurate, for the early church had no motive for inventing this, and Luke would hardly produce an Aramaic idiom by amplifying his Greek narrative (Casey 1987: 39). The fourth Gospel is significantly different. The kiss has been removed, and with it the act of betrayal. All Judah does is to take a cohort to the garden, where Jesus himself goes forward and says, 'Whom do you seek?' (Jn 18.4). In response to their reply 'Jesus the Nazarene', Jesus identifies himself with the divine revelatory expression, 'I am', which is also the equivalent of the English 'I am he'. 'When therefore he said to them, "I am", they retreated backwards and fell to the ground' (Jn 18.6). If this account were true, we would read of Jesus' mighty power, and total control of the proceedings, in Matthew, Mark and Luke. The fourth Gospel also omits the account of Jesus falling to the ground (Mk 14.35). We must infer that the fourth evangelist has rewritten history again.

Two other features of the Johannine account must also be regarded as secondary. In Mark, whose account is primitive and accurate up to this point because it is derived from disciples who were there at the time: 'And abandoning him, they all fled' (Mk 14.50). Peter apart, they do not reappear: only some women see the crucifixion from a distance (Mk 15.40–1), it being less likely that they would be arrested. The fourth Gospel does not record that the disciples fled. Instead, Jesus issues orders to the cohort arresting him: 'If therefore you seek me, let these (people) go' (Jn 18.8). The narrator makes this quite clear by explaining that it is in accordance with Jesus' statement and the Father's will (cf. Jn 6.39; 17.12). He retains the cutting off of the high priest's slave's ear (Mk 14.47//Mt 26.51//Lk 22.50), so that he can attribute it to Peter. This is historically unconvincing. If it were true, the early tradition would surely have known it and reported it. Moreover, it is hardly likely that the leader of the disciples would have had a sword, and launched an attack with it, without there being any other armed disciples who supported his action. Rather, a known event has been attributed to the leading disciple, so that Jesus was not thought to have been abandoned by his disciples. Apart from building into a tighter narrative of Peter, this also means that Jesus can make the declaration, 'The cup which the Father has given me, shall I not drink it?' (Jn 18.11). The historical Jesus tried something different: 'Take this cup away from me' (Mk 14.36). His ultimate submissiveness to the divine will, as he understood it, was not enough for the fourth evangelist, who has omitted Jesus' agony in the garden altogether (cf. Mk 14.32–42; Jn 12.27ff.). This picture of Jesus' control over the final events is as consistent as it is secondary.

CONDEMNATION

Jesus is taken next before Annas, who questions him, and then on to Caiaphas. The synoptic accounts are not repeated, but they are most unlikely to be accurate,[8] so this cannot be seriously held against the fourth Gospel. There are signs of confusion over the high priest. Caiaphas, high priest 18–36CE, is correctly described as high priest at 18.24, and Annas, high priest 6–15CE, is plausibly described as Caiaphas' father-in-law at 18.13, whether by sound independent tradition or by mistake. This makes it difficult to see why Jesus is taken first to Annas. Moreover, Annas is described as high priest by the narrator at 18.19, and by one of his servants at 18.22, which would explain why Jesus is taken to Annas and why his examination by Annas is the only Jewish examination reported before he is handed over to Pilate. We must infer that the narrator is confused, and that the description of Caiaphas as high priest 'that year' (11.49; 18.13) is due to the same confusion. The same trouble has arisen at Luke 3.2 and Acts 4.6, and it is not difficult to see why. Annas will have remained influential after his deposition in 15CE, which some observant Jews will not have regarded as satisfactory, and perhaps not as valid. Aramaic and Greek have the same word for high priest and chief priest, so Annas truly did remain *archiereus* (as at Jos. A.J. XVIII, 95, cf. B.J. II, 243) and *kōhen rab*.

Another remarkable feature of the Johannine narrative is that another disciple goes into the high priest's courtyard with Peter. This explains how Peter could get in, for 'that disciple was known to the high priest' (18.15). It looks very much like a secondary explanation, however, for the other disciple is not mentioned again. Later tradition identified him with the disciple whom Jesus loved, but the text does not do this. Moreover, the fourth evangelist has Peter challenged straight away. Taking over the true tradition that the challenge came from one of the high priest's female slaves (Mk 14.66–9), he makes her the gatekeeper, which is not very probable either. An especially Johannine point is Jesus' description of the Temple, 'where all the Jews congregate' (Jn 18.20). This has the external use of 'the

Jews' characteristic of this Gospel, and which indicates the Gentile self-identification of the author(s). Jesus also claims to have spoken to 'the world', another characteristically Johannine concept.

Finally, the account of Peter's denial has been watered down, yet made more precise. He no longer curses and swears (Mk 14.71//Mt 26.74). We could not expect the fourth evangelist to have Mark's bilingual mistake, 'throwing he wept' (i.e. throwing threats and curses, as one may in Aramaic but not in Greek); nor does he have the alternative ending to which Matthew and Luke could both turn, 'And going outside he wept bitterly' (Mt 26.75//Lk 22.62). Instead, the denials are given a more specific motivation: Peter drew his sword and was the person who cut off the high priest's slave's ear (18.10). He was therefore liable to be arrested even if the disciples as a whole were not, and the evangelist dramatises this by having the third denial in response to an accusation from that slave's kinsman, 'Did I not see you in the garden with him?' (18.26–7). We have seen that the story of Peter's action is secondary: this development must therefore be secondary too. Hence also its form 'I am not' (18.17, 25), the opposite of 'I am' (Jesus at 18.5, 6, 8), in response to the supposition that he might be one of 'his disciples', a precise use of the main identity term used in this Gospel for members of the Johannine community.

The trial before Pilate has a number of secondary features. Some of these are so central that we must infer that the whole account has been rewritten. The first is the refusal of Jesus' captors to enter the praetorium, 'so that they should not be polluted, but might eat the Passover' (Jn 18.28). This is dependent on the Johannine dating of these events. As we have seen, this is incorrect, and the Passover had already been eaten.[9] Nor is it probable that the Roman governor would come out of the praetorium merely because Jewish authorities both wanted to see him, and declared him and his house unclean. It follows that the fourth evangelist is rewriting history to conform to his secondary dating. He has done so in a deeply ironical manner. At one level, the Jews maintain their ritual purity as they prepare to kill an innocent person. At another, their ritual purity is only for eating an ordinary Passover victim, while they ensure the death of the replacement of Passover and of the whole sacrificial system, 'the Lamb of God who takes away the sin of the world' (1.29). This presentation is profoundly hostile to 'the Jews'.

Another remarkable feature of the trial before Pilate is the statement of 'the Jews', 'We are not allowed to kill anyone' (Jn 18.31). As a possible statement of fact, this is dubious.[10] Jewish Law provides for the death penalty for a variety of offences. The Romans had every reason to exercise the death penalty themselves, but rather less reason to take it away from the people who ran most of the country most of the time. This is the more probable in the synoptic account, where the trigger of the Passion is the Cleansing of the Temple, an offence in the one place where we know that Gentiles could be put to death if they violated Jewish Law by entering the inner courts. If however the Romans had removed the Jewish authorities' power to execute people, there was nothing to prevent Caiaphas and Pilate from coming to such agreements as they might wish: that if Caiaphas and his sanhedrin found Jesus guilty of an appropriate offence, Pilate would sentence him to whatever death penalty the pair of them found convenient. Consequently, the question is not only whether this statement is true, but whether there are circumstances in which 'the Jews' would need to say it to Pilate like this. Jesus has been arrested by a cohort with a tribune (Jn 18.3, 12), a piece of information not found in the synoptic Gospels, where Mark has 'a crowd with swords and clubs from the chief priests and scribes and elders' (Mk 14.43). If this were right, it could only be because Roman authorities were already concerned that Jesus was a potential revolutionary, a reasonable view if they had seen the Cleansing of the Temple in its synoptic position, a few days previously at most, and had one possible interpretation of 'kingdom of God' pushed at them by the chief priests. So the Johannine account cannot be completely right. Jesus could only be arrested by a Roman cohort if the synoptic version of the Cleansing of the Temple were true, and in that case Pilate would not need to be told by the anachronistically presented 'the Jews' that the death penalty was necessary, for he would know this already. He would more obviously not need telling that 'the Jews' could not administer the death penalty.

Furthermore, the fourth evangelist tells us his motivation for this part of his narrative, and we know it to be secondary: 'that the word of Jesus might be fulfilled, which he spoke, signifying by what kind of death he intended to die' (Jn 18.32). As we have seen,[11] the historical Jesus predicted his death, but not with this precision. He expected to pour out his blood for many (Mk 14.24), and that he would 'perish' (Lk 13.33). Only in the fourth Gospel does he predict that he would 'be lifted up' (Jn 3.14; 8.28; 12.32, 24), and this is due to further meditation after the event. This explains why Caiaphas and his associates do not make a specific accusation against him at 18.30, as the historical Caiaphas must surely have done. Indeed, the Johannine trial narrative has not given a reason why they sought the death penalty. The main narrative of the Gospel has given quite anachronistic reasons why 'the Jews sought to kill him' (5.18, cf. 7.19, 25, 32; 8.59; 10.31–3, cf. 11.8; 11.47–53; 19.7). On no such occasion has there been any indication that they were incapable of carrying out the death penalty. On the contrary, on two occasions they have taken up stones to throw at him (8.59; 10.31), stoning being the legally appointed penalty for blasphemy. Hence the other levels of meaning of 18.31. In the evangelist's view, Jesus is innocent according to Jewish Law; like Pilate, the Jews have no power to kill him except that given from above (cf. 19.11), and their desire to kill him is contrary to the Law (cf. Jn 5.45–7; 7.22–4, 51; 8.39–44, 56–9; 10.31–9).

One thing we know for certain is that Jesus was crucified. Moreover, Mark tells us that he was crucified as 'the king of the Jews' (Mk 15.26), and he relates a plausible story of him being mocked as such (Mk 15.16–20). This term 'king' was used of various minor figures who effectively functioned as bandits with armed followers. For example, Josephus records this man from the early years of the first century:

> Then a shepherd also dared to aspire to kingship. He was called Athrongaios and the only outstanding qualities, on which his hope was founded, were strength of body and a soul contemptuous of death and, in addition to these, four brothers like himself. He put each of them in charge of an armed band and used them as generals and satraps for his raids, but he himself, like a king, dealt with graver matters. So then he put on a diadem. . . .
>
> (B.J. II, 60–2; cf. 63–5, A.J. XVII, 278–85)

Jesus was crucified on the ground that he was that kind of figure, and for that reason he was crucified between two bandits (Mk 15.27//Mt 27.38). The 'Cleansing of the Temple' will have been important in his conviction.[12] Jesus' preaching of the kingdom of God must also have been significant. Some Jews envisaged that the coming of the kingdom of God would include the driving out of the heathen. Pilate was in Jerusalem for Passover, in case of disturbances founded on such hopes. Mark must be right in supposing that 'the chief priests accused him much' (Mk 15.3), even if Mark had to infer that information as we do. They will have used his preaching of the kingdom to present him to Pilate as a dangerous figure who should be executed in exemplary fashion.

All this will have been very well known to 'the Jews' in Ephesus, who could play up the political and/or military element no end if it suited them to do so. It is this to which Jesus replies at John 18.36:

> My kingdom is not of this world. If my kingdom were of this world, my attendants would have fought so that I should not be handed over to the Jews. But as it is, my kingdom is not from here.

There is nothing like this in the synoptic Gospels. It has both the specifically Johannine concept of 'the world' as the whole of humanity, a realm opposite to that of God, and it has the remarkable Johannine use of 'the Jews', when all Jesus' followers were Jewish. If a saying of this kind had reached the synoptic authors, they would surely have used it, because it answers an obvious problem so well. We must infer that, once again, this is rewritten history. We have noted already that Jesus' preaching of the kingdom has been written out of this Gospel, and we have seen the other awkward aspect of it, its imminence, deliberately transformed into rebirth in Chapter 3.[13] John 18.36 completes this picture.

Pilate's reply is an unlikely question, 'Are you not then a king?' In response, Jesus slithers into quite Johannine theology, with Jesus coming into 'the world' to 'bear witness' to 'the truth'. As we have seen, the specific theological vocabulary of this Gospel, shared with 1 John, is one of the general arguments against its historicity.[14] Pilate's response is to tell 'the Jews', 'I find no fault in him' (Jn 18.38). If this had been the view of the historical Pilate, Jesus would not have been crucified. Jesus' death as a condemned criminal was however a serious problem for the early Christians. It could not be denied, and it could be theologically interpreted. Here, history has been rewritten to put more blame on 'the Jews'.

The narrative continues with a brief summary of a story already strange in Mark, the release in place of Jesus of Barabbas, whose full name (Mt 27.16) may be translated, 'Jesus son of the Father'. Whether or not there is any truth in the original story, there should be no doubt about one aspect of John's rewriting. When 'the Jews' (18.38, 39) have cried for the release of 'Not him, but Barabbas' (18.40), the narrator gives the crucial information, 'Now Barabbas was a bandit'. This is the only use of the term 'bandit' in the Johannine Passion narrative. The term has been dropped as a description of the other two men crucified with Jesus. Elsewhere in the fourth Gospel, it is used only at 10.1 and 10.8, in an allegorical description of the leaders of Israel replaced by Jesus, the 'good shepherd'. The evangelist has portrayed 'the Jews' as quite consistent in demanding the release of the sort of leader to whom they were accustomed. He has seriously rewritten history in dropping the term 'bandit' as a description of the two men crucified with Jesus, and he has continued the synoptic rewriting of history by not making clear the charges on which Jesus was crucified.

Pilate then proceeds to have Jesus scourged. At an historical level, this is not a probable result of his public declaration that he found no fault in him (18.38). It has however a logic of its own. 'The king of the Jews' must be flogged, mocked and crucified to show that there must be no king but Caesar (cf. 19.15). 'The Jews' have just chosen the release of Barabbas the bandit, when they could have obtained the release of 'the king of the Jews'. Hence the tight connection at the beginning of 19.1, '*Then therefore* Pilate took Jesus and flogged him'. The declaration of Jesus' innocence is repeated after the mockery, and 'the Jews' make another quite anachronistic statement: 'We have a Law, and according to the Law he must die, because he made himself the Son of God' (Jn 19.7). In the ministry of Jesus, as in the rest of Judaism, all faithful Jews were sons of God. This accusation requires later Johannine Christology, according to which Jesus' position as Son of God is indicative of his deity, which is rejected by 'the Jews' as blasphemous.[15] Not only has the fourth evangelist failed to tell us the real reason why Jesus was crucified, he has replaced it with a central Johannine conviction which 'the Jews' are supposed to have been exceptionally wicked not to have accepted. At a different level, 'the Jews' are unknowingly right. Jesus' death was written in the Torah (cf. e.g. 5.45–7; Ex 12.46//Num 9.12 at Jn 19.36; Num 21.9 at Jn 3.14; and the midrash of Jn 6). This is another piece of profound Johannine irony.

Pilate's reaction also belongs in the realm of Johannine Christology. He is afraid, and goes back into the praetorium, as if the narrator has forgotten bringing Jesus outside (19.4f.), a secondary consequence of imagining that Jesus' accusers could not enter the praetorium for the spurious reason that they had yet to eat the Passover (18.28). Pilate asks Jesus, 'Where are you from?' His fear, and his question, stem from the Johannine belief that Jesus is fully divine and from heaven. The subsequent narrative hinges on the description of Jesus as 'king of the Jews'. This was the crime specified on his cross, but in the fourth Gospel it gradually changes in meaning out of hostility to 'the Jews'. At 19.12, we are told that Pilate sought to release Jesus, which the historical Pilate could certainly have done if he wished to. 'But the Jews shouted, asserting "If you release him, you are not a friend of Caesar. Everyone who makes himself a king opposes Caesar."' Thus 'the Jews', and not Jesus, fit in with the concept of kingship on the basis of which he was actually crucified, and they show the same concept as caused them to demand the release of Barabbas, the 'bandit'.

Then Pilate sat (or possibly sat Jesus) on the judgement seat, and we are given a time, about the sixth hour on the preparation of the Passover. We have seen that this is the wrong date and the wrong time, both to ensure that Jesus will be put to death when the Passover victims were slaughtered.[16] 'And he said to the Jews, "Look! Your king!"' (Jn 19.14). When they have called again for his crucifixion, the fourth evangelist represents the chief priests, the major representatives of Jewish power, as declaring 'We have no king but Caesar'. This is the climax to which this part of the narrative has led. Jewish people really believed that God was 'great king over all the earth' (Ps 47.2). The seventeenth Psalm of Solomon, which contains the longest extant plea to God to restore the only acceptable form of earthly kingship, that of the seed of David, begins, 'O Lord, you are our king for ever and ever'. The chief priests, on behalf of the Jewish people, have declared themselves traitors at every level. They have refused to recognise Jesus, who is really the king of Israel (Jn 12.13, 15, cf. 1.49), and in declaring that they have no king but Caesar, they have denied God. Once they have made their confession, Pilate hands Jesus over to be crucified. This is extensively rewritten history, in which the deity of Jesus and hostility to 'the Jews' have been major, related and formative features.

DEATH AND BURIAL

The account of Jesus' death is quite short. It has several unlikely features. The first is that Jesus carried the crossbeam himself (Jn 19.17). This is what should have happened at a Roman crucifixion, but the tradition that the Romans impressed Simon of Cyrene, father of Alexander and Rufus, into carrying it (Mk 15.21) is incomprehensible unless it is true. We must infer that Jesus was too weak to carry the crossbeam. In saying that Jesus carried his cross, the narrator puts in the unnecessary word 'himself (*heatō*)', so we must infer that he was deliberately contradicting true tradition. The Johannine Jesus must be literally as well as theologically in control of events.

The fourth Gospel omits the important information that the two men between whom Jesus was crucified were bandits, and proceeds with a significantly rewritten account of the charge on which Jesus was crucified. The expression 'the king of the Jews' in our oldest source (Mk 15.26) is expanded to 'Jesus the Nazarene, the king of the Jews'. This picks up the specifically Johannine 'Jesus the Nazarene' whom 'they' (the whole cohort?) said they wanted to arrest when Jesus identified himself, controlling his arrest by using the divine revelatory formula 'I am'.[17] Since it was secondary there, it is not likely to be primary here. If we read the fourth Gospel on its own, without the synoptic Gospels or Christian tradition in mind, it is most natural to suppose that Pilate wrote the inscription and put it on the cross personally at the scene of the crucifixion, where he argued with 'the chief priests of the Jews', another clear piece of Johannine editing. This is not plausible. The fourth Gospel has the inscription in three languages, which is what one would expect of the inscription of a great king rather than a common criminal. 'The chief priests of the Jews' are on hand to tell Pilate to alter his inscription, and what they propose is hardly plausible. Pilate responds by rebuffing them: since they have no king but Caesar (19.15), Caesar's representative can ignore them, in a way that he did not ignore them before.

Another unlikely feature is the group of people beside the cross.[18] Mark has a group of women watching from a long way off (Mk 15.40-1), which is highly plausible. The fourth Gospel's group of people beside the cross includes Jesus' mother and the beloved disciple. It is most unlikely that these people would be allowed this close to a Roman crucifixion. If they had been, and they included people central to Jesus' life and ministry, it is most unlikely that Mark would merely have women watching from a distance. If a major male disciple had approached this close, it is likely that he would have been arrested. The beloved disciple is a mysterious figure, because he represents beloved disciples when, and only when, the fourth evangelist finds such a figure narratively convenient.[19] Accordingly, we should not believe that he took Jesus' mother to his own home, and since this story is our only reason for believing that she was involved in the ministry, we should not believe in her presence either. We must infer that John 19.25-7 is a very late legendary development. It portrays the position of Jesus' natural family, and of Jewish Christians in general, in story form – they are acceptable in the Christian community if, and only if, they find their home among disciples whom Jesus loves, rather than with 'the Jews' (cf. 7.1-13).

The incident of the sour wine given to Jesus to drink has also been rewritten. At Mark 15.36, Jesus is given a sponge full of sour wine lifted up on a reed while he is mocked. He has quoted Psalm 22.1, which implies belief that God has forsaken him, and when the text has been misunderstood as a reference to Elijah, his expectation is also mocked. The fourth evangelist omits Psalm 22.1 and Elijah (like Luke before him), nor does he have Jesus mocked at this point. He informs the reader that Jesus knew that everything was done, and said 'I thirst' so that scripture might be fulfilled (Jn 19.28). This has Jesus in complete charge of the proceedings, even while being crucified. The sour wine is thus given him in fulfilment of Psalm 69.21, the same psalm quoted at the Cleansing of the Temple and used elsewhere in the New Testament with reference to Jesus' death.[20] The fourth evangelist also has the sponge of sour wine put round hyssop, instead of on a reed. If taken too literally, this is impractical, and we must attribute the change to the importance of hyssop in the narrative of Passover. The bunch of hyssop was dipped in the blood of the Passover victim, and it was the smeared blood on the door which enabled the Lord to pass over the door (Ex 12.21–7). The evangelist has therefore written a midrash to include it. He probably assumed that a reed was used as well (Beetham and Beetham 1993). Straight afterwards, Jesus declares 'It is finished', 'and reclining his head he gave up the spirit' (19.30), fully in charge even of his death (cf. 10.17–18).

A uniquely Johannine event follows. 'The Jews', again a sign of late redaction, ask Pilate to break the legs of the crucified men, so that their bodies should not remain on the cross on the sabbath (19.31). This has a logic of its own, for dead men should not be left hanging on a tree overnight (Deut 21.22–3). The biblical text says nothing about what should be done to live men hanging on trees, but obviously they might die before dark on Saturday night, and they should not be taken for burial on the sabbath because no one should carry a burden on the sabbath (Jer 17.21–2).

In Mark, Joseph of Arimathaea asked Pilate for Jesus' body when 'it was already late, since it was the Preparation, which is the day before the sabbath' (Mk 15.42). Mark describes Joseph of Arimathaea as 'an honorable councillor, who was also expecting the kingdom of God' (Mk 15.43). It follows that Joseph was not a disciple of Jesus, but a pious Jew performing the religious duty of burying a criminal who would not otherwise be buried, and that he was probably acting in accordance with arrangements made on the orders of the high priest (cf. Acts 13.29). This explains why he had no contact with the women (cf. Mk 15.40–1, 47). He risked violating the sabbath if he were too slow, out of zeal to observe the written Torah, and an observant Jew who could not know laws written down much later might argue that fulfilling Deuteronomy 21.22–3 justified this. He would try to finish before the sabbath started all the same.

Most of this has gone from the fourth Gospel, and the new material is pointed directly to the fulfilment of scripture. The breaking of the other two victims' legs highlights the fulfilment of scripture in the case of Jesus. Like the Passover victim, a bone of him shall not be broken (Ex 12.46; Num 9.12), so the fulfilment of these scriptures is part of the replacement theology of this Gospel and part of the reason for the incorrect dating of the Passion.[21] We must infer that the incident is secondary.

The piercing of Jesus' side is likely to be secondary too, since it results from a soldier who hasn't broken his legs making sure he was dead, and is consequently not mentioned by the synoptic Gospels. The synoptic accounts do not have room for it, and it was obviously not known to Luke, who could hardly have omitted it from the identification scene at Luke 24.39. At one level, it was created from Zechariah 12.10, quoted at John 19.37. It is possible that Numbers 20.11 was also used, since there was a rabbinical tradition that when Moses struck the rock in the wilderness, blood came out, and then water (e.g. Tg Ps-J Num. 20.11). It was of much greater symbolic importance than this, but it has been difficult for scholars to work out what the symbolism of water and blood is. Its importance to the Johannine community is underlined by the equally emphatic and difficult language about water, blood and spirit at 1 John 5.6– 8. The most probable symbolism is of baptism and the eucharist (cf. Jn 3.5; 6.53–63; 7.37–9).[22]

Despite rather obvious arguments for the secondary nature of this incident, many critical scholars have hesitated because of the apparently vigorous eyewitness claim at 19.35 (e.g. Dodd 1963: 133–6). We should not however understand John 19.35 as based on an eyewitness tradition as we would understand it. The central point is the strong convictions which it involves, convictions confirmed by 1 John 5.6–8 and found in scripture. We have an author who knows from the strength of his convictions that, since this happened, it must have been observed, and who has inferred that the tradition which he received *must* go back to an eyewitness. In the same way, the author of Jubilees knew that when it was written a second time that a man must not lie with his father's wife, all the holy ones of the Lord said 'Amen, amen' (Jub 33.12). Rewritten history *must be true*, and the strength of that conviction has led the Johannine community to imagine that the event was seen. The modern historian should not follow that kind of evidence. Indeed, by this stage we should have realised that such a strong protestation is suspicious rather than irrefragable. An eyewitness claim is in any case not the whole of the evangelist's meaning. He has used perfect tenses where he could have used aorists – he who has seen still does, he has borne witness and still does, and he knows rather than merely knew that he speaks the truth. This must at least include 'seeing' as perceiving through scripture, and the purpose is given 'so that you too may believe'. The eyewitness claim generally seen here is only just consistent with the rewriting of history which characterises this document, whereas perception, witness, faith and scripture are central to it. The form of the quotation confirms other evidence that Zechariah 12.10 was part of an early Christian testimonium, and the people who will look are more likely to be faithful

Christians contemplating the crucifixion than people who were there at the time (Casey 1980: 142–4, 168–70, 177, 178, 197–8; Menken 1993c).

The account of Jesus' burial has been rewritten to prepare the way for the resurrection. The synoptic accounts already show signs of this, and the fourth evangelist carries them further. Mark's description of Joseph of Arimathea would not do for Matthew, who turned him into a disciple of Jesus (Mt 27.57), a view evidently unknown to Luke. The fourth evangelist explains all. Joseph was 'a disciple of Jesus, but secretly for fear of the Jews' (Jn 19.38)! This explains how the earlier tradition had not realised that Joseph was a disciple. Its secondary nature is clear from comparison with Mark.[23] The original reason that he was burying a criminal has been replaced with the description of him as a secret disciple, and the Johannine use of 'the Jews' also indicates secondary editing. This also makes him a suitable associate for Nicodemus who brings enough spices to bury a king, a tribute to 'the king of the Jews'. Nicodemus was unknown to the synoptic writers, none of whom records the bringing of spices. If Jesus had received a decent burial, Mark would surely have recorded this, instead of having an outsider who had to buy some linen and who had certainly no time, and perhaps no inclination, to wash, anoint and/or spice the corpse. Nicodemus functions in this Gospel as a sort of Jewish foil. The burial is thus carried out by people who are more favourable than 'the Jews', but who nonetheless belong to them. There will have been such people in Ephesus. This account can only just be taken literally, and certainly should not be believed.

The fourth Gospel further records that Jesus was buried in a 'new tomb, in which no one had yet been laid' (19.41–2). There is none of that in Mark. Matthew, however, has the tomb be new (Mt 27.60), and Luke tells us, not that it was new, but rather that no one had yet been laid in it (Lk 23.53). The fourth Gospel has further development of the tradition, which functions to exclude the possibility that Jesus' dead and decaying body had been confused with another one. Nicodemus' spices further exclude that possibility. We must infer that the Johannine developments are entirely secondary.

RISEN FROM THE DEAD

The resurrection of Jesus is central to the myth of Christian origins. Less than thirty years after Jesus' death, Paul declared, 'But if Christ has not been raised, then our preaching is empty, and your faith is empty' (1 Cor 15.14). What Paul meant by 'resurrection' is quite another matter. He repeats an early formula which does not mention an empty tomb, and his own language about resurrection is so figurative that we cannot infer whether he must, or need not, have believed that Jesus' tomb was empty. The empty tomb is also conspicuously absent from the speeches in the early part of Acts. It is equally important that it is unmentioned in the narrative. If Jesus were raised from the dead, leaving empty a decent rock-hewn tomb in which no one had been laid, the disciples would surely have gone to it and pointed it out to each other and to some of the myriads of sceptical Jews who were in Jerusalem at that time and over the following years. Acts has ample narrative space: if the Johannine resurrection narratives were true, Acts would surely have reported the importance of the empty tomb over the succeeding years. We must infer that Jesus was buried by Joseph of Arimathea in a common tomb for criminals (cf. Acts 13.29).

The synoptic narratives, however, show massive secondary development, which is partly evident in the lack of agreement between them. Moreover, the narratives attribute to Jesus teaching which he did not give during his earthly life, and which has an excellent *Sitz im Leben* in the early church. This teaching legitimates significant aspects of the Christian community's existence (cf. Graß 1956; Evans 1970; Fuller 1971; Perkins 1984; Craig 1989; Casey 1991a: 98–105; Lüdemann 1994). Thus rewriting of the resurrection traditions had been going on for years before the fourth Gospel was written. Its resurrection narratives are remarkable for their independence of the synoptic narratives. In Chapter 20, they take place entirely in Jerusalem, as in Luke. The appendix to this Gospel follows the other tradition, and has an appearance in Galilee. Both versions have resulted from further secondary development. In the first one, Mary Magdalene goes to the tomb alone and finds the stone rolled away. She runs to Simon Peter and 'the other disciple whom Jesus loved', and says, 'They have taken the Lord from the tomb and *we* do not know where they put him' (Jn 20.2, my italics). There are two new things wrong already. Mary Magdalene's 'we' shows that the fourth evangelist is rewriting the earlier tradition, for in all the synoptic Gospels she goes with other women (different women, for the synoptic stories are not true either). The fourth evangelist is preparing for the uniquely Johannine story of Jesus' appearance to Mary Magdalene, and, as so often, his rewriting is less than 100 per cent efficient. We should also note her description of Jesus as 'the Lord'. This term is generally absent from early sources, but it was an important Christological title to the early church, and it has penetrated the narrative usage of both Luke (sixteen times) and the fourth Gospel (4.1; 6.23; 11.2; 20.20; 21.12), which also has Jesus accept it (Jn 13.13–14).

The second major problem in this narrative is 'the other disciple whom Jesus loved'. We have already seen that he is a narratively convenient figure, rather than an historical character.[24] The narrator makes no effort to discount the obvious interpretation that Simon Peter was also a disciple whom Jesus loved, for he certainly was. The central part of the story is well written at a narrative level, with 'the other disciple' winning the race to the tomb, Simon Peter going in first and the other disciple following him in. Then there is the crucial point of the story. The beloved disciple, unlike Simon Peter, who played a leading role in both the historic ministry and in the early church, 'saw and believed'. That is what beloved disciples must do. They must have faith, when others have uncertainty or doubt. Even when they follow church leaders in a literal sense, it is the faith of the disciples whom Jesus loves which constitutes the Christian community (cf. 20.30–1). This faith is achieved without scripture (20.9), appearances or angels. In that respect, it mirrors the situation of beloved disciples who are not learned in the scriptures and do not have visions, real people in the Johannine community. They would however know the story of Lazarus. This disciple believed when he saw the graveclothes, and realised that Jesus had raised himself permanently and emerged from the graveclothes, a contrast with his mighty demonstration of power when he raised Lazarus, who came forth still bound up (11.44). With the essential point made, the author of John 20 saw no need to mention 'the other disciple whom Jesus loved' again. When all these points have been taken into account, we must infer that the author knew perfectly well that he was creating a story. We cannot treat the result as if it might be literally true.

The next narrative is of the appearance to Mary Magdalene. Now that two men, the witnesses required by the Law, have seen that Jesus has been raised from the dead, there is no reason for there to be more than one woman to see the angels in the tomb, nor is there any reason why she should not be the first to see Jesus. Mary Magdalene is the only one of the women to figure in all three synoptic stories of their visit to the tomb, a fact which probably reflects her real importance during the historic ministry (cf. Lk 8.2–3; Mk 15.40, 47). Hence the selection of her here. She sees two angels, a clearer description than Mark's 'young man' (Mk 16.5) or Luke's 'two men' (Lk 24.4), sitting 'one at the head and one at the feet, where the body of Jesus had lain' (Jn 20.12). This description, more careful than the synoptics, intensifies the impression that the author knows clear evidence that the body was in a particular place. Mary again witnesses that it was not in its original place, and angels mark that place. In imagining that it had been taken away, she fits perfectly into the evangelist's refutation of any notion that the disciples had taken away the body. Such a view was already known to Matthew, who testifies that it was current among Jews known to him and previously (Mt 27.62–6; 28.11–15). It cannot have failed to occur to 'the Jews' in Ephesus. We may note also Mary's description of Jesus as 'my Lord' (Jn 20.13), which is again a sign of late narrative composition.

The legitimating effect of this narrative is reinforced by Jesus' appearance to Mary. This has another major Johannine theme, Jesus' return to the Father (7.33; 13.1, 3; 14.4, 28; 16.5, 17, 28; 17.13). This Johannine theme is absent from the synoptics. It is surely secondary. If the historical Jesus had really expounded his return to the Father, the synoptic Gospels could hardly have omitted it. It has positive religious value in its understanding of Jesus' death, and it adds significant material for resolving the potentially dangerous problem posed by his execution as a criminal. The exposition of it here, with the term 'ascend', recalls particularly John 3.13 and 6.62, both of which were formed by midrashic exegesis of scripture.[25] This is carried further in Jesus' plea, 'do not cling to me' (Jn 20.17). Just as Jesus is more effective for salvation than the serpent lifted up by Moses (3.13–15) and the manna in the wilderness (Jn 6), so his presence with the church is to be more profound than a lover's embrace. The contrast is with another passage of scripture: 'Scarcely had I passed from them when I found him whom my soul loves. I will grasp him and I will not let him go until I have brought him to the house of my mother . . .' (S.S. 3.4) (Hanson 1991: 227–30; Stibbe 1993a: 205). Mary must not behave like this!

The underlying point is the presence of Jesus with the Johannine community. They were in conflict with 'the Jews', who knew enough, indeed rather too much, about the Jesus of history.[26] They were bound to take Paul's view, 'So from now onwards we know no-one according to the flesh. Even if we knew Christ according to the flesh, yet now we no longer know [sc. him like this]' (2 Cor 5.16). Regular visions of the risen Jesus had stopped long ago, and those who saw him in dreams and visions could not continue a relationship with him as one continues with a lover or friend whose *bodily* presence is important. Moreover, those who did see him in dreams and visions would find that they might be uncertain whether it was really him (cf. 20.14–16), and that in the end he disappeared. Jesus could be present with the disciples when he had returned to the Father (14.18ff., 28; 16.16ff.), an experience which could be interpreted as the presence of the Holy Spirit, or Paraclete (14.16ff., 26; 15.26; 16.13ff.). Jesus' gift of the Holy Spirit is expounded in story mode in the next resurrection appearance (20.19–23). His return to the Father was a precondition for this experience (7.39; 16.7). Events must happen one after the other because story mode has been chosen for the whole exposition of the Gospel. Mary must not cling to Jesus, must let him go, must not even take him to a house, not even to meet the disciples. Rather, Jesus must return to the Father, and Mary must tell the disciples so that they may be prepared for him to return, and give them the abiding presence of the Holy Spirit. The message given by Mary to the disciples, that Jesus said 'I am ascending to my Father . . .' (Jn 20.17–18), is an especially striking contrast to the earlier tradition, in which the women failed to transmit the angelic message, 'He is going before you to Galilee. There you will see him, as he told you' (Mk 16.7). There are no Galilean appearances in John 20 either!

We must infer that the evangelist was not concerned about two problems which have worried commentators. He was not telling us that Mary could not touch Jesus before he went to the Father, whereas Thomas could touch him later (20.27). Mary was holding Jesus tight already – hence the present imperative *haptou* (20.17), to be interpreted strictly, 'do not keep hold of me' (cf. Mt 28.9). She, who faithfully loved Jesus, was to let go narratively so that Jesus could go to the Father, and existentially because Christians cannot relate to the risen Lord by clinging to his body. Thomas, who did not at first believe, did not touch Jesus physically when he came to faith. Narratively, the faith of a doubting disciple completes the Gospel story, and existentially it means that Christians relate to Jesus by faith. Secondly, the evangelist is not saying that Jesus literally ascended to the Father and was glorified between John 20.17 and 20.19. He uses expressions like 'go to the Father' because Jesus was patently absent, and had been absent since his death, and this was the only symbolic language readily available to the community. He used 'ascend' specifically because it was used in the midrashic work on scripture which he inherited, and it fitted in with traditional symbolism.

It follows that this narrative is not literally true. It is a story with a message, created partly by means of a midrash on scripture which was still being developed in the Johannine community. Hence the secondary expressions 'my Father' (20.17) and 'the Lord' (20.18). Now that the disciples know that Jesus has ascended to the Father, everything is prepared for them to receive the Holy Spirit, the Paraclete sent by God, or by Jesus, as their presence with the believers.

The next appearance takes place behind closed doors, 'where the disciples were for fear of the Jews' (Jn 20.19). This again has the external use of 'the Jews' characteristic of this document, especially as contrasted with 'the disciples'. We must infer that the introduction is secondary, and the narrative requires it. Jesus appears, as heavenly figures do in visions: this also tells us that he cannot have merely survived his exceptionally short crucifixion. We are next told that 'Jesus showed them his hands[27] and his side' (Jn 20.20). The reference to 'his side' is distinctively Johannine. It is not consistent with Luke 24.39, where he identifies himself by nail marks in hands and feet. The function of this reference is to assert, in story mode, that the risen Jesus was really the same being as the earthly Jesus. The identity of earthly and risen bodies has always been a conundrum for people who believe in bodily resurrection. One of the fourth evangelist's contemporaries dealt with it explicitly, describing the time of the final resurrection itself:

> For the earth will surely give back the dead at that time; it receives them now in order to keep them, not changing anything in their form. But as it has received them, so it will give them back. And as I have delivered them to it, so also it will raise them. For then it is necessary to show those who live that the dead are alive, and that those who went away have come back. And it will come to pass that when those who know each other now have recognized each other, then the judgement will prevail, and those things which have been spoken of before will come. And it will come to pass, when this day which he appointed is over, that both the form of those who are found guilty as also the glory of those who have been found righteous will be changed.
>
> (2 Bar 50.2–51.1)

While this is a prediction rather than a narrative set in the past, it deals with the same problem as Luke 24.39 and John 20.20, and does so in a similar story mode. It has successive events, and a recognition scene, deliberately created by an author to present some of his most cherished convictions. He attributes it to Baruch, a fountainhead of tradition, supposedly repeating a speech by God. We must infer that Luke 24.39 and John 20.20 are separate attempts to assert that the risen Jesus was identical to the historical Jesus, and that they are not more literally accurate than 2 Baruch.

Jesus next gives the disciples the Holy Spirit, and the power to forgive or retain sins. There is an obvious intertextual echo of Genesis 2.7. The gift of the Holy Spirit is neither partial nor preliminary. The story is accordingly not consistent with Matthew, whose resurrection narrative in Galilee is an alternative commissioning of the disciples: nor with Luke-Acts, which has the Holy Spirit come down at the following Pentecost instead. We must infer that we have three different legitimating narratives. Further signs of late redaction are the description of Jesus as 'the Lord', and the distinctively developed Johannine theme of 'sending'.

This Gospel ends with the distinctively Johannine story of doubting Thomas. He refused to believe a story of Jesus appearing to the disciples, and thereby represents the majority reaction of the time. He is represented as saying, 'Unless I see the mark of the nails in his hands, and put my finger into the mark of the nails and put my hand into his side, I will not believe' (Jn 20.25). This appears to be directed against a possible view of the resurrection experiences, that they were the appearance of a mere spirit, who was not more real than any other spirit which one might see, and not correctly identified with the risen Jesus. This is especially probable after the previous narrative, in which Jesus evidently passed through closed doors, as a spirit might do, and as human beings cannot. There is then a repeat performance of Jesus appearing when the doors are shut, and Jesus urges Thomas to do as he had declared. Thomas does not however do so, but reacts in the approved manner, 'My Lord and my God' (Jn 20.28). Like Mary, he has realised that touch is an inappropriate way to communicate with the risen Lord. The sight of Jesus is enough to bring him to faith.

The confession of Jesus' deity is also central. No such confession is found in any of the other Gospels, nor do the disciples go quite so far elsewhere in this one. It is the final piece of evidence of what Johannine resurrection narratives are about. They are to reaffirm the faith of the community. Here, the full deity of Jesus forms a conclusion in harmony with the opening of the prologue. The prologue declared the full deity of the Word, his incarnation as 'Jesus Christ', and 'only-begotten God' as the revealer of the otherwise unseen deity (Jn 1.1, 14, 17, 18). Thomas now declares the deity of Jesus, the central confession denied by 'the Jews'. This confession was intertwined with the separation of the Johannine community from the Jewish community (Casey 1994a). Like John 6.53, it violates the Jewish identity of

Jesus of Nazareth, and marks out the rewriting of history in this Gospel as the large-scale preaching of falsehood.

The Johannine community's basic need, presented throughout this chapter, is made crystal clear in the final saying of Jesus. 'Have you believed because you have seen me? Blessed are those who do not see and come to faith!' The average Christian could not see Jesus, as Thomas is incorrectly reported to have done. This is the evangelist in story mode, urging Christians to have faith in their own origins myth. It is as false as possible, and reinforced by the evangelist's own conclusion. In their own way, Thomas's confession and the summons to faith are as devastating as the condemnation which concludes the public ministry in Chapter 12. It is not just that the stories are inaccurate. It is also that the rejection of the Jews, including the demand for rebirth and drinking blood, ends with confession of Jesus' deity and the repeated claim that only through him can eternal life be obtained. This contradicts the Jewish identity of Jesus of Nazareth. Hence this is much more important than, say, Jesus not going to Tabernacles (Jn 7.8), and then actually going (7.14). It is not probable that these little bits of information are historically accurate, but they do no harm either. Jesus was a faithful Jew. He must surely have gone to Tabernacles, and he might have hesitated before going, changed his mind and actually gone. The confession of his deity is not mundane fiction which could have been true. It is not the kind of distortion inevitable in historical narrative. It contradicts the Judaism which Jesus did so much to recreate, and is thereby seriously false.

CONCLUSIONS

There should be no doubt as to what has happened in the fourth Gospel's account of Jesus' death and resurrection. It has been substantially rewritten in accordance with the needs of the Johannine community. It is not trivially inaccurate, but has been rewritten to avoid serious problems and to affirm serious falsehoods. The crucifixion has been put on the wrong day, with the result that the Last Supper is no longer a celebration of the Jewish Passover. The account is hostile to 'the Jews' from beginning to end. They demand Jesus' crucifixion, but they give no plausible reason for demanding that he undergo this horrific punishment. The charge that Jesus was king of the Jews has been reinterpreted, with the removal of the information that he was crucified with bandits and the effective omission of his preaching of the kingdom of God, replaced with the assertion that he declared his kingdom not of this world. Pilate has been rewritten as an unconvincing figure who tries to have Jesus released. Jesus is presented as in control of events from beginning to end. The resurrection narratives have been rewritten to demonstrate in a quite spurious manner that Jesus rose bodily from an empty tomb, and to put forward a view of Jesus as present with the Johannine community through the Holy Spirit. The whole account has a very high Christology, including the full deity of Jesus, which was alien to the Jesus of history. The resulting stories are untrue from beginning to end. Thus the fourth evangelist has quite rewritten the central part of the myth of Christian origins. We must conclude that his work is a presentation of falsehood.

10

THE 'PRIORITY' OF JOHN

INTRODUCTION: ROBINSON AND COAKLEY

One approach undertaken by conservative scholars who need to defend the accuracy of the fourth Gospel has been to concentrate on comparison with the synoptic Gospels. The most recent book of this kind is the posthumous work of an Anglican bishop (Robinson 1985). Robinson's main point was already made in an earlier article, 'The New Look on the Fourth Gospel' (Robinson 1959b). This title evinces the doublespeak characteristic of commitment. Robinson's work is not a 'new look', but the restatement of older tradition over against modern scholarship. I have criticised a number of his arguments already.[1] One purpose of this chapter is to expose the basic flaws of method which characterise his whole treatment of the historicity of John.

In a subsequent article, Robinson's evangelical pupil and editor J.F. Coakley interpreted him to mean that the quality of historical tradition embodied in John's Gospel 'is in many respects higher than that of the Synoptics'. It follows that, for those who find this view persuasive, 'it is clear that much commentary on the Gospel will need to be rewritten' (Coakley 1988: 241). Coakley's detailed examination of John 12.1–8//Mark 14.3–9// Matthew 26.6–13 is a good example of where some evangelical scholarship is liable to go next. Accordingly, I examine his treatment of this passage, and of related issues, as an example of how detailed examination of parallel passages in the fourth Gospel and Mark should, and should not, be carried out.

Coakley begins with the brief summary of Robinson's work from which I have quoted. It asserts the superior quality of Johannine over Marcan narratives, where the two coincide, and hence the 'priority' of John. This justifies Coakley's selection of John 12.1–8//Mark 14.3–9//Matthew 26.6–13 for detailed examination, for here the 'strong, even exceptionally strong, consensus of scholarly opinion . . . needs to be challenged'. But one of Robinson's most serious faults has already been repeated. The proof that the fourth evangelist was not writing an historically accurate account emerges primarily and most easily from his *non*-Marcan material. Those passages in which his account overlaps with Mark are the most reliable parts of his work, because they are the oldest traditions that he used. This is why they figure so largely in Robinson's book, and this is how Robinson manages to leave so many main points out.

ROBINSON'S 'NEW LOOK' AT THE 'PRIORITY' OF JOHN

Robinson begins his book with a discussion of 'presuppositions' or 'presumptions', as if he merely wants to challenge a widely-held view. This is an improvement on his earlier article, where 'presuppositions' appear to be what they usually are, views unquestioningly held by people before they have properly studied the evidence (Robinson 1959b: 339–40, cf. 348). Nonetheless, he still has the basic fault of giving too much weight to those parts of the fourth Gospel which are paralleled in the synoptics, and this means that he never takes the force of the fact that he is dealing with two sources, one of which, the fourth Gospel, contains a lot of verifiably secondary material. This has, and should have, influenced scholars in their assessment of passages which are found in both Mark and John, but Robinson treats this as unacceptable prejudice.

This frame of reference leads to a number of errors of method. These errors have in common that the evidence of the fourth Gospel is valued too highly, merely because Robinson has opened with a commitment in its favour. It is convenient to look at these judgements under four headings: topography, authorship, chronology and counting.

Robinson correctly notes that this Gospel contains a number of geographical and topographical references, and that some of them are not found in the synoptics. Almost at once, however, he begins to exaggerate. He claims that 'recent archaeological studies have tended to reinforce the belief that in Johannine topography we are in touch with a tradition which knew Palestine intimately'. He quotes the uncritical work of Schein, to the effect that 'the author of the material must have known the land like the back of his hand' (Robinson 1985: 53, citing Schein 1980). Schein *assumes* the literal truth of the fourth Gospel, and infers from his examination of Israel the places where everything *must* have taken place. This is not sufficient to show that anything took place, nor even that the author(s) of this Gospel knew Israel half as well as Schein does. After Schein, Robinson quotes Westcott to similar effect, thereby demonstrating that this is not a 'new look' (Robinson 1985: 53, n. 85, quoting Westcott 1908: I, xxi). One major point is the concentration on Jerusalem and its environs (Robinson 1985: 59, cf. Westcott 1908: I, xxiii–xxvi). For major festivals every year, pilgrims went to Jerusalem, not to Capernaum. When Paul was in Jerusalem after leaving Ephesus for the last time, he was accused by Jews from Asia

Minor, and Luke suggests that this was due to the presence with him of a Gentile, Trophimus of Ephesus (Acts 21.27–9). Some Jews will have gone to Jerusalem from Ephesus each year for some thirty-five years between Jesus' death and its fall, and we have seen how recent was the final breach between the Johannine community and 'the Jews'. It is not probable that Trophimus was the only Gentile Christian to visit this major centre. It follows that details of 'Jerusalem and its environs' might have accrued secondarily over the years.

Robinson notes, for example, that Jesus is said to have been walking in Solomon's portico, in the Temple, in winter (Jn 10.22ff.). He regards it as in general an advantage of John over against the synoptics that he gives more precise details about Jesus' movements, and proposes to believe vivid details (Robinson 1985: 216–17). But the vividness and detail of these references tells us nothing at all about the historicity of Johannine discourses. Solomon's portico was famous enough (Robinson quotes Acts 3.11; 5.12; Jos. B.J. V, 18f.; A.J. XV, 396–401; XX, 220f.). We have seen ample reason to regard the discourse set there as secondary.[2] We must infer that the setting is secondary too, though it is likely enough that Jesus walked in Solomon's portico from time to time. Robinson further quotes Dodd to the effect that 'there is no reason to suppose that a fictitious topography would in any way assist the appeal of the gospel to an Ephesian public' (Robinson 1985: 50, quoting Dodd 1953: 452–3). The central point is, however, that the topography is *not* fictitious, any more than it is all symbolic: it is a perfectly sound reality effect. John 10.22f. demonstrates this as well as any example. Given the overwhelming reasons for regarding the discourse as secondary, we must infer that correct topographical information has been inserted to give the impression of reality. Comparing this with the narrative outlines in the synoptic Gospels is of no help at all.

Robinson proposes to believe the tradition that the author of the Gospel was the beloved disciple, John son of Zebedee. Once again, this is not a new look, but the resurgence of ancient ecclesiastical tradition (e.g. Eus. H.E. III, 39; Sanday 1872: 286–97; Lightfoot 1893; Westcott 1908: I, ix–lxvii; Morris 1969: Chapter 4; pp. 154–64 of this book). Robinson's discussion completely ignores authorship customs in the Jewish and Greek worlds at the time when the fourth Gospel was written. This has three drastic consequences. Firstly, Robinson suggests that 'it is unscientific to invent unknown characters such as the author of this major contribution to New Testament literature and theology who have left no other trace behind them' (Robinson 1985: 117). We have however seen that the authors of such works as Deutero-Isaiah, Jubilees and 1 Enoch are unknown, because anonymity, pseudepigraphy, plagiarism and multiple authorship were perfectly normal.[3] Like them, the authors of the fourth Gospel left behind them a visible piece of literature, and a vigorous community which has left no other permanent trace, beyond the Johannine epistles and the much broader community for whom these documents have become a sacred text. In requiring that the author be known to us, Robinson does no more than signify his membership of church tradition.

Secondly, Robinson starts with the pseudepigraphical device as if it must represent literal historical truth. He notes that John 21.24 claims authorship for the beloved disciple, and takes 19.35 to be an eyewitness claim for a single event. In the following discussion, the only possibilities that he contemplates are that this is literally true, or a false claim to be literally true (Robinson 1985: 95–6), and he does not take the second possibility seriously, because he has not taken into account pseudepigraphical customs of legitimating traditions. Thirdly, Robinson interprets later church tradition in an equally simple way. So, for example, in assessing Irenaeus' claim that the Gospel was written by John, the disciple of the Lord, he takes into account the story that John had met Polycarp, but he does not take into account the way that all the canonical psalms were attributed to David, even contrary to some of their headings (Robinson 1985: 100–4). Accordingly, in dealing with external as well as internal evidence, Robinson has simply followed the legitimating traditions of his own social subgroup.

Robinson's handling of the chronology is equally naïve. His basic argument is that the Johannine framework should be accepted as historically accurate, and that the synoptic material should be fitted into it. This argument displays one of his major faults of method, that of finding John to be right whenever comparison with the synoptics shows that they are inadequate. This is a case where all are wrong. The Johannine chronological outline is self-consistent, the synoptic one barely exists before the final events, and most of the overlaps are in the same order. Accordingly, the fact that the synoptic material can be incorporated into the Johannine outline demonstrates nothing. Robinson has not got far before he meets the Cleansing of the Temple, and we have already seen that this is in quite the wrong place.[4] Robinson then places the ministry of John the Baptist before that first Passover, but this merely reflects the relative coherence of the Johannine narrative, it does nothing to make all of it true. Robinson then simply follows the Johannine narrative, and when this gets Jesus back to Galilee, Robinson comments truthfully,

> The Synoptists here provide far the fuller record. From the point of view of plotting the course of the ministry, however, the difficulty is that it is impossible with confidence to place their material in chronological sequence, since the connections are for the most part topical rather than temporal.
>
> (Robinson 1985: 137)

This is a major fault of method: on its account, Robinson can put synoptic material into the Johannine framework as he pleases.

Accordingly, Robinson tries to find details which are striking. He first suggests that the Johannine account takes Jesus back to Galilee in May. This is basically because the barley harvest was in May, and the harvest of John 4.35 would be that of barley if Jesus' comments were to be edited to produce an iambic trimeter which would be part of an otherwise unknown Greek version of a quite differently worded calendar from Gezer. Robinson has this synchronise with John the Baptist's move to Aenon near Salim (3.23), if this were a place where Samaritans would go to avoid the unbearable heat of the Jordan in summer. He then identifies this, as being before John's imprisonment (Jn 3.24), with Mark's report that 'the incarceration of John is the turning-point that marks Jesus' move from Judaea to Galilee (1.14)' (Robinson 1985: 136). Robinson then identifies the plucking of grain on the sabbath (Mk 2.23–8//Mt 12.1–8//Lk 6.1–5) with 'the Galilean wheat-harvest in June'. This is immediately preceded by comments on 'the fasting-disciplines of the followers of John and of Jesus' (Mk 2.18–22//Lk 5.33–9//Mt 9.14–17). 'This suggests a period when the two movements were still actively operating in parallel' (Robinson 1985: 138). It follows that the feast of John 5.1 is Tabernacles, and Jesus returns to Galilee where he still is at the beginning of John 6, some six months later. Then Mark 4.2–41 has three parables about seeds, followed by a violent squall on the lake, and it has been suggested that these would fit well in December, the time of sowing and of storms. Robinson's comment befits the desperate nature of his case: 'Obviously nothing can be based on that, but it would fit well' (Robinson 1985: 139).

In the course of carrying this through, Robinson twice makes a major error of method in assessing previous scholarship. In dealing with the Cleansing of the Temple, he cannot believe that Jesus' view of John the Baptist was so positive, and his importance to the people so great, and to the chief priests so negative, that he could have asked about John's authority when questioned about his own (Mark 11.28–30). Consequently, he would like to set this question early in the ministry. He comments,

> If the question about the Baptist's activity had occurred in John and the Johannine chronology in the Synoptists instead of the other way round, no one I think would have doubted that the cleansing of the temple belonged most naturally to the period when the people were still 'all wondering about John, whether perhaps he was the Messiah' (Luke 3.15).
>
> (Robinson 1985: 129–30)

This is a fantasy based on no evidence at all. Scholars prefer the synoptic accounts because they are usually more accurate, for the kinds of reasons given in this book. These form a large-scale inference. If the evidence were different, we would draw different conclusions. To imagine the evidence generally the same, but the opposite on an occasional issue, is to have a fantasy which is not even internally coherent. Robinson does the same with the Johannine dating of the crucifixion, and we have seen that there is more to this problem than scholarly prejudice.[5]

These comments illustrate Robinson's faulty method. In the first place, everything depends on the assumption, rather than demonstration, of the accuracy of the Johannine framework. Secondly, much of the argument about the Johannine framework is circular, for its self-consistency is taken as a reason for supposing it is right. Thirdly, Robinson knows the synoptic material is for the most part not chronologically marked: accordingly, that it can be made to fit the Johannine outline demonstrates nothing. Fourthly, the reasons for detailed coincidences being striking are pathetically inadequate. Some are large unknowns: the location of Aenon near Salim, the existence, wording and Greek translation of the calendar known centuries earlier from Gezer. Others are simply creative: the harvest of John 4.35 is barley in May, that of Mark 2.23–8 is wheat in June. Finally, Robinson has not taken the force of the arguments against the Johannine position of the Cleansing of the Temple. One of the major events he uses is in quite the wrong place. All Robinson has shown is the desperate measures necessary to defend the Johannine outline.

Robinson's reluctance to count can be equally misleading. Two points are outstanding, the Sonship of Jesus and the hostile use of the term 'the Jews'. We have seen his extraordinary attempt to downplay the evidence of John's high Christology:

> Equally, 'Son of God' as a title occurs but once on the lips of Jesus during the ministry, in 11.4, where the purpose of Lazarus' illness is seen as being not death but the glorification, i.e. the manifest vindication, of the Son of God.[12]
>
> 12. 3.18 must be regarded as evangelist's comment and 5.25 refers to the Son of God's activity at the last day. In 1.49; 10.36; 11.27; and 19.7 the title is addressed or attributed to Jesus by others; and in 1.34; 6.69; and 9.35 other readings are to be preferred on textual grounds.
>
> (Robinson 1985: 348)

This is a stunning effort to remove a major piece of evidence. The opening statement results partly from Robinson's decision to refer only to the full form 'Son of God'. If we include references to 'the Son', the correct figure is twenty-three. We must include them, because 'the Son' is consistently used by the fourth evangelist to denote Jesus as Son of God, sometimes in contexts which imply his deity (cf. 5.18–26; 10.30–9). The decision to regard 3.18 as evangelist's comment is arbitrary,[6] and if 5.25 referred only to the last day, it would still refer to Jesus as the Son of God. At 10.36 Jesus is quoting himself, and 19.7 represents the Johannine Christ perfectly accurately. Robinson has not laid out the evidence, but removed it.[7]

Robinson's failure to count examples of the Johannine use of 'the Jews' is equally striking. His comments (Robinson 1985: 81–91, cf. 271–5) are largely directed towards minimising the difference between John and other sources. He tries to remove 19.7 as 'a bad example, since "the Jews" are clearly here being distinguished from Pilate and the Romans not from Jesus and Christians' (Robinson 1985: 82). But the verse is secondary. 'The Jews' are portrayed as completely hostile, for they want Jesus killed, on the ground that he made himself Son of God. Since all Jesus' first disciples were Jewish, this description is highly anti-Jewish. Moreover, every faithful Jew was a son of God: as an offence carrying the death penalty, this requires the Johannine concept of Sonship.

Robinson also equates Matthean and Pauline usage with that of John. He inserts 'the' into Matthew 28.15, which merely reports that a story was in circulation 'among Jews': this will have been true, and is difficult to express in any other way. Robinson adds Matthew 10.17 and 23.34, but neither passage mentions 'the Jews'. Robinson then has Johannine usage 'fundamentally no different' from Matthew 28.15 and 1 Thessalonians 2.14–16. Yet 1 Thessalonians 2.14 is unique in the Pauline corpus. One external use of 'the Jews' is not the same as permanent and repeated hostility (it is no help to make it two examples, as Robinson's translation does). At one level, Robinson's argument has the same fault as his discussion of Sonship: he will not count.

BEGINNING, MIDDLE AND END

Chapters 4–6 of Robinson's book work through the ministry of Jesus. The account is however highly selective, and suffers seriously from concentrating on comparison with the synoptic Gospels. We must exemplify errors of method.

Robinson looks for several indications of eyewitness testimony or the like in the opening section of the Gospel. Many of these are absent from the synoptics, but they are not realistic indications of early tradition either, so they do not establish a case for the priority of John. For example, Robinson fastens on two of the fourteen uses of the Greek word *houtōs* which are difficult to translate into English, for they are not covered by the semantic areas of the English 'so', 'thus', 'like this', as most examples of this word are. At John 4.6 and 13.25, assuming that it must fall within this range of meaning, he declares, 'I find it difficult to account for this vivid touch . . . except on the basis of some personal reminiscence recalled in the telling . . .' (Robinson 1985: 160–1; cf. Westcott 1908: II, 155–6). This imaginative leap is quite spurious, for two reasons. In the first place, there are other passages in which the Greek word *houtōs* is used similarly (e.g. S. *Ant* 315; Pl. *Symp* 176E). The second point is almost given by Robinson himself: 'though of course traces of oral communication are not the same as signs of first-hand witness' (Robinson 1985: 161). Indeed they are not! Both settings might be due to imaginative storytellers telling and retelling stories of Jesus in the sixty-odd years since his death. Nothing is true merely because there are signs that it was transmitted orally before it was written down.

Robinson finds further evidence in the words 'This is the man of whom I spoke when I said' (Jn 1.15, 30), which to him 'suggests that it comes from a circle privy to a previous announcement or conversation which has not, now at any rate, been included in the evangelist's narrative'. This argument presupposes its result. It must come 'from a circle privy to a previous announcement or conversation' only if it is a literally accurate record of an actual saying, and we have seen good reason to suppose that it has been produced to introduce a drastically rewritten version of John the Baptist.[8] Nor should we slide over the tense of 1.15, where John the Baptist says 'This was he of whom I said . . .', thereby revealing the perspective of the early church.

Robinson turns to the chronological indicators at John 1.29, 35, 39, 43 and 2.1. His major concern is to juxtapose two alternatives, that 'they were remembered to have happened like that', and the theory that John opens with a symbolic week. He then comments that he 'would wish to rest no great weight on the eyewitness character of the narrative' (Robinson 1985: 161–8). Indeed we should not, for Robinson's alternatives are too constrained. We might be dealing with reality effects by the author, or with somewhat earlier tradition which has accrued secondarily over a period of years. No conclusions about the historicity of this narrative can be drawn from the difficulties of supposing that these indicators are symbolic, and there are reasons to consider much of the narrative secondary.[9] Robinson's quotations from Sanday and Scott Holland remind us that his argument is in no way new (Robinson 1985: 167, n. 30, quoting Sanday 1872: 46, and Scott Holland 1920: 171f.).

Robinson's account of John the Baptist has further errors of method. He points out that the synoptics do not account for the relationship between John the Baptist and Jesus. He suggests that the fourth Gospel provides the necessary explanation, both giving us an account of Jesus at an earlier time, and enabling us 'to glimpse a new Jesus, a Jesus who was for some time the disciple and protégé of the Baptist' (Robinson 1985: 170). This last point is not a reasonable description of the dominant figure of Jesus, witnessed to by John in the fourth Gospel. More fundamentally, Robinson's view that what explains is genuine is methodologically faulty. When a late source explains what is missing from earlier sources, this may be due either to an unknown early source, or to secondary development. Robinson always assumes the first possibility, and this fault runs right through his book. In this case, we have seen good reason to suppose that the fourth Gospel's account of the early ministry of Jesus, overlapping with that of John, is secondary.[10]

Robinson proposes to defend the fourth Gospel's account of John denying that he was the Christ, Elijah or the prophet. For this purpose, he makes a quite faulty comparison with the synoptic accounts. In addition to the genuinely old tradition of Mark 1.7//Matthew 3.11//Luke 3.16, he uses Acts 13.25, dubiously translated 'I am not what you think I am', suggests that this refers to the speculation 'whether perhaps he was the Messiah' at Luke 3.15, and regards this as evidence 'that the denials are not just created by the fourth evangelist but are reflected in the Synoptic tradition' (Robinson 1985: 171). There are several things wrong with this. Luke 3.15 is a piece of Lucan editing, incorporating a Christological title which is absent from the earliest tradition, and which would not make proper sense in Aramaic.[11] Acts 13.25 is not in the synoptic tradition at all. These texts are not *reflecting* the Johannine denials – they are part of the developing tradition which the fourth evangelist eventually used when he wrote his account. It is a repeated fault of Robinson's work that he compares the fourth Gospel with *anything* in a synoptic Gospel: as here, however, what he selects for comparison may itself be secondary tradition.[12] Finally, Robinson does not at any point face the problem of envisaging the Johannine denials in Aramaic.[13]

In the middle of the ministry, Robinson offers a defence of the historicity of John 6.14–15. Here, Robinson would have us believe that Jesus withdrew because he knew that people were coming to seize him to make him king (Jn 6.15). He argues that this explains the 'manic excitement of the mob' at Mark 6.32–44. He suggests that their being 'like sheep without a shepherd' has a political background in the Old Testament, that the companies of hundreds and fifties may perhaps have quasi-military overtones, and even uses the fact that they are numbered as 'males' as evidence of a nationalist setting in the desert (Robinson 1985: 203–4, cf. Sanday 1872: 123–5).

There are two faults of method here. If information in an independent Johannine account appears to explain a Marcan setting, there are always two possible reasons for this: the fourth Gospel may be right, or the Marcan problem may have been solved secondarily. There is good reason to prefer the second view here: if a whole crowd wanted to make Jesus king, if this was a plausible reaction to his ministry, if Jesus did nothing more drastic than send the disciples away and follow, the problem would have recurred, and we would have other reports of it. The supporting arguments for a political background are exceptionally feeble: Robinson pushes small points because there are no big ones. Most of his points are not, however, new.[14]

Robinson proceeds to defend more than this. The whole of John 6 is to be taken seriously as history, a defence which characteristically leaves out a number of main points. These are dismissed with reference to the secondary literature (Robinson 1985: 209, quoting Brown 1966a: 248). Robinson's selective quotation from Brown refers only to the part of John paralleled in Mark. Brown also notes that that John 6.51–8 could not have been understood by the crowd or even by the disciples, and was added to 35–50 at a late stage in the editing of this Gospel (Brown 1966a: 287). The main points are that the synoptics do not have Jesus pre-existent as the bread from heaven, they do not have the theology of the unmentioned eucharist, they do not have the new form of covenantal nomism in which faithful Jews are excluded from salvation, they do not have a discourse which has no reasonable *Sitz im Leben* in the ministry of Jesus. This is what Robinson left out, and in that light, his conclusion that John was not 'developing the theology at the expense of the history' is completely hollow.

Robinson begins his discussion of the end of the ministry by noting correctly that the synoptic topography and chronology is not nearly as clear as the Johannine (Robinson 1985: 212ff.). The problem here, as always, is that the clear account is liable to be secondary. This is particularly evident as we move into the raising of Lazarus and the anointing at Bethany.

JOHN 12.9–19 AND THE RAISING OF LAZARUS

The Lazarus story is a Johannine composition from beginning to end.[15] The narrator tells us that many of 'the Jews' believed in Jesus because of this miracle (11.45). The reaction of the chief priests and the Pharisees is remarkable. They convened a sanhedrin and said, 'What are we doing? – for this man is doing many signs. If we let him go on like this, everyone will believe in him, and the Romans will come and destroy our place and people' (11.47–8). Widespread faith in Jesus would not have given the Romans cause to do this. This is an extraordinary perception, formed by the Neronian persecution, which showed genuine Roman hostility to Christianity, and by the destruction of Jerusalem after the Roman war of 66–70ce. Some Jews attributed this to failure to observe the Torah, and Christians did not observe it. From this perspective, everyone having faith in Jesus could indeed lead to the destruction of the place and the people. This perspective has however no place in the Judaism of 30ce. It leads through the prophecy of Caiaphas to the decision to have Jesus put to death. This is also profoundly ironical. Jesus has been presented as the Resurrection and the Life, and the source of life to those who believe in him. His gift of life to Lazarus is now presented as the reason why the chief priests and Pharisees seek to have him put to death.

After the anointing story, things get worse and worse. At 12.9–11, many were leaving 'the Jews' and believing in Jesus, and consequently the chief priests took counsel to kill Lazarus. This begins a set of statements according to which Lazarus was exceptionally important. If this were true, we would not be able to explain the omission of Lazarus from the synoptic Gospels. Secondly, the plot is incredible. Killing someone raised from the dead is not a feasible Jewish reaction to such a miracle, and the plot is never mentioned again. It either worked or it did not. It is difficult to see how the plot against Lazarus could fail, when that against Jesus succeeded. Nonetheless, it is not acted upon, yet Lazarus does not reappear in the early chapters of Acts. Nor does he appear again in the fourth Gospel, surviving an unsuccessful plot. Finally, in the Judaism of Jesus' time, having faith in Jesus did not mean 'leaving' in any reasonable sense. The fourth evangelist has imposed on the Judaism of Jesus' time the situation of his own, when Jews converted to Jesus did indeed leave the Jewish community.

But the narrator has not yet finished. Verse 12.12 slides into the old tradition of 12.13–15. More trouble begins at verse 16, where the disciples are to 'remember' what they had not previously known.[16] It becomes serious in verses 17–19, where the crowd bear witness that Jesus had raised Lazarus, so the Pharisees declare, 'the world has gone after him'. Lazarus, however, is heard of no more. The Johannine narrative is thus internally incoherent, as well as inconsistent with the synoptics. The decisive incoherence is that the story of Lazarus just stops. With so many Jews 'leaving' because of the raising of Lazarus, with the crowd who saw this miracle bearing witness to it, with a crowd meeting because they have heard of this sign, with a plot against Lazarus' life, Lazarus was such an important figure that his further presence, and his fate, were bound to have been recorded. But they are not recorded. Why not? The only possible explanation emerges from the absence of Lazarus from the synoptic Gospels. His fate is not recorded because he never was an important figure. He does not turn up in Acts, and he neither wrote nor figures in any epistle, for the same reason. This also tells us something about the way in which this Gospel has been written. The profound and real feeling that Jesus brought life and 'the Jews' brought death (cf. 16.2) to the Johannine community is presented in story mode. Hence the stress on the love of Jesus for Lazarus, as even 'the Jews' notice (11.36), and for Martha and Mary (11.5), for Jesus loves his disciples. Hence also the narrative precedents for Jesus' own resurrection, especially the difference in the graveclothes, for Lazarus came forth bound (11.44), whereas Jesus left the graveclothes behind and vanished, a difference great enough for a disciple whom Jesus loved to come to faith (20.7–8).[17] Such factors have quite overridden the historical inconcinnities which we can see.

We can now see what Coakley avoided by confining himself to detailed comparison of John 12.1–8 with its synoptic parallels. All the latest theological development and all the historical incoherences have been set on one side. Robinson is worse (Robinson 1985: 217–29). Against the view that the Lazarus story is a Johannine construction, he sets up a partially parallel account from the 'Secret Gospel of Mark', commenting, 'By any standard this is a much inferior tradition, being largely a pastiche of Markan phrases and clearly influenced by Gnostic motifs' (Robinson 1985: 221). Nonetheless, he builds Ossa on Pelion. Firstly, it is independent of John; then John did not simply create it; then resurrections are part of the synoptic tradition; then Dodd says the Lazarus story 'is not in principle different in form or content' from the synoptic stories.

This argument has several ingredients essential to the Robinson/Coakley approach. Firstly, two judgements are very uncertain, and incompletely stated. The narrative may be independent of the fourth Gospel, but it may not. The Secret Gospel of Mark is a late source, and the Lazarus story may have been an input at some stage. That 'John' did not create the Lazarus story is equally uncertain, and not quite the point, whoever 'John' may be thought to be. If the final redactor did not create the story, it may be merely an earlier legend, and the use made of it in this document might be secondary and extensive. Maybe, might, perhaps and possibly. Such pure conjecture is little better than making up a story. What we can actually demonstrate is that the story in its present form is not literally true, and that it has been extensively used to present Johannine theology.

A second unsatisfactory feature of Robinson's argument is his use of the synoptic tradition. That it contains some evidence of incidents in which Jesus raised the dead is not sufficient to make the Johannine narrative true, in the light of the objections to it noted above. At the crucial point, Robinson makes his third mistake, in citing Dodd. Whatever Dodd said, the Lazarus story is very different from synoptic stories of raising the dead, because it contains a large amount of secondary Johannine theology. Unlike them, it also declares that Lazarus had been dead for more than three days, well known as the length of time required to ensure that he was really dead (cf. Mk 5.39; Jn 11.11–14, 39; bT Sem. 8, 1). Robinson then relies on earlier scholarship to turn natural language into 'quasi-technical terms', supposing for example that at 11.57 *didonai entolās*, which means 'give orders', describes the issue of a writ, and *mēnuein*, which means 'reveal, inform, report', is a technical term for the activity of an informer (Robinson 1985: 224–5). There are two things wrong with this. Some Johannine expressions could be used in a legal situation, but could be used elsewhere too. People did not confine giving orders to the issue of writs. Herod's orders to have Mariamne and Alexandra murdered were not a legally valid writ (Jos. A.J. XV, 186, cf. 204). Secondly, legal terminology is no guarantee of historicity. A technical word for 'inform' could have been used by someone writing an inaccurate narrative.

Robinson proceeds to bT San. 43a, and proposes to believe in its forty-day interval between Jesus' incrimination and his execution. His reason is that it 'would scarcely have been invented in order to be explained away' (Robinson 1985: 225–6, cf. 228). But the Talmud is a fifth-century document, and its anonymous *baraithas* are generally much later in date than New Testament documents. It is therefore most unlikely to turn up correct new information. The contents of Robinson's *baraitha* do not inspire confidence. The announcement that Jesus would be stoned is barely consistent with his crucifixion, and if there had been a heraldic accouncement of the forthcoming 'stoning' for forty days before Jesus' crucifixion, the synoptic Passion narratives would surely relate it. And what sort of reason is 'would scarcely have been invented in order to be explained away'? This merely means that Robinson cannot detect reasons for secondary growth. This factor runs right through his book and Coakley's article. It is a serious fault of method, because we often need explicit empirical data to see quite why a secondary tradition has arisen, and this is rarely available. In this case, however, an inference is not unduly difficult. 'The Jews' were already being vigorously accused of causing Jesus' death in the fourth Gospel. BT San. 43a has him properly condemned, and that is the reason for the story's origin. Like the fourth Gospel, it is rewritten history, only it has been rewritten for the Jewish rather than the Johannine community.

Robinson never deals properly with the end of the Lazarus story. He does have another circular argument. He follows the fourth Gospel, and is inclined to follow the Talmud, in having Jesus withdraw for a considerable period. John tells us where, 'information which could only have been known to the inner circle' (Robinson 1985: 228). It could have been known only if it were true. Robinson's addition of another late source, a Jew reported by Celsus, does not help. He thought Jesus was 'escaping most disgracefully'. Robinson does not believe this, but in support of John, almost anything counts. This time some of Robinson's arguments have been new: but his convictions are those of his tradition (e.g. Robinson 1908: 39–51). This is hardly a 'new look'.

THE ANOINTING AT BETHANY[18]

We can now consider Coakley's detailed arguments. These are dominated by his commitment to follow Robinson, his thinking shifting 'toward the view that the Johannine account depends more or less directly on eyewitness memory', as he tries to 'understand John's story of the anointing at Bethany on this more thoroughgoing hypothesis of his priority' (Coakley 1988: 242).

Coakley begins with Jesus coming to Bethany six days before Passover (Jn 12.1). Noting the Johannine picture of Jesus convicted in his absence (11.47–53), lying low and re-emerging in public in Bethany, he comments, 'Taken by itself this is a coherent and circumstantial picture that does not appear artificial. It only needs to be tested against the different information in Mark and Luke' (Coakley 1988: 242–3). These criteria are quite inadequate. Firstly, 'a coherent and circumstantial picture that does not appear artificial' may be produced either by simple truth or by adequately written secondary editing. Secondly, the supposed absence of artificiality has been produced by selective description. Artificial elements include the Johannine use of 'the Jews' (11.54, 55; 12.9, 11) and several aspects of the Lazarus story and its aftermath. Thirdly, testing only against Mark and Luke may make the fourth Gospel seem right when the synoptic account merely appears improbable. We have seen that this is a major fault in Robinson's work. A fourth problem is inherent in the assessment of the other three: subjective and/or merely plausible judgements are liable to be made.

Coakley mentions an alternative to his first criterion, citing Robinson's discussion against it: 'Unless it be insisted that *all* such pictures are redactional, on the grounds that the Gospel tradition only preserves single pericopes and not the connections between them' (Coakley 1988: 243, n. 8). This view is an extremely dogmatic form of radical criticism, and no recent proponents of it are cited. It enables Coakley to give the impression that the only alternative to his view is dogmatic and wrong. Both Robinson and Coakley misuse the history of scholarship in this way (e.g. Coakley 1988: 244; Robinson 1985: 165–7).

Coakley passes to Mark's dating of the anointing in Bethany *two* days before Passover. He prefers John's setting to Mark's on two grounds: traditional scholarship has not found an adequate reason why John should alter Mark's two days to six, and Mark's dating is due to a redactional connecting link to a date really concerned with the priests' plot to kill Jesus, not with the anointing. This is barely consistent. Coakley believes that John did not know Mark's Gospel. If he knew only the traditions of the anointing and the triumphal entry, it is not likely that he knew Mark's redactional links, so he had nothing to alter. More fundamentally, Coakley's criteria are wrong. We cannot expect to know the reasons for such detailed redactional changes, without our author's source and some account from him of the reasons for his changes. It has been right for critical scholars to try to work them out: that they cannot always find them, and have made mistakes, does not show that the Johannine chronology is correct.

Nonetheless, we can do better than Coakley's targets, on the assumption that the fourth evangelist knew the Marcan tradition that we know. He had to alter Mark's date because he dated Jesus' crucifixion at the time of the sacrifice of the Passover victims, Friday afternoon, 14 Nisan, the day before Passover (Friday evening and Saturday, 15 Nisan). If he left the anointing two days before Passover, that would put it at the Last Supper, which takes place on Thursday, 13 Nisan in the fourth Gospel, before night at John 13.30 (Thursday night, 14 Nisan). He knew that was wrong. He took the date of Mark 14.3 literally: 'While he was in Bethany' need not tell us on which day. The fourth evangelist therefore had a free choice of date for the anointing, provided it was during Jesus' stay there. Thus his *strong* motivation was merely to move it, so his reasons for placing it *exactly* where he does might have been arbitrary. However, he read Mark 11.20–14.2, 10–11 as a single day, (Wednesday evening and) Thursday, 13 Nisan. Mark took him back two further days to the triumphal entry (cf. Mark 11.11–12, 20), which he therefore placed on Tuesday, 11 Nisan. He thus put the anointing on Monday, 10 Nisan (rather than Sunday evening, 10 Nisan, since there is no indication that the meal took place after dark). This is six days before Passover (Jn 12.1), counting inclusively. In this way, the fourth evangelist could weave Lazarus into the story. Jesus is anointed and looks forward to the day of his burial (Jn 12.7) on 10 Nisan, the biblical date for choosing the Passover victim (Ex 12.3). His royal entry into Jerusalem (Jn 12.12–15) becomes also his final entry.

It may be replied that this is conjectural and uncertain. Some of it is, and that is one of the main points. Once we leave major differences between Mark and the fourth Gospel and focus on such details, all we can do is make inferences from our texts. Sometimes, we can make plausible conjectures of different kinds, and this demonstrates nothing. In this case, however, the cumulative weight of arguments for the Johannine setting being secondary is overwhelming.

Coakley proceeds to Mary, Martha and Lazarus, 'friends of Jesus in Bethany, who naturally appear in any scenes in which Jesus comes to their village' (Coakley 1988: 246). He begins by attacking 'the "form-critical axiom" that names are an indication of lateness in a tradition' (Coakley 1988: 244). Names can be genuine. The important fact, obscured by making other scholars sound like adherents of an arbitrary dogma, is that they may also be secondary. At Numbers 21.32, for example, Pseudo-Jonathan identifies the anonymous spies of the Hebrew text as Phinehas and Caleb. At Mark 7.17, anonymous 'disciples' ask Jesus about what he has just said: Matthew 15.15 alters this so that the question is asked by Peter. At Mark 14.12–13, Jesus sends two anonymous disciples to prepare the Passover. Luke 22.8 identifies them as Peter and John. Mark 15.39, followed by Matthew 27.54//Luke 23.47, has an anonymous centurion in charge of the crucifixion. In the Gospel of Peter 8, he is Petronius; in the Acts of Pilate 16.4, Longinus.

Coakley goes on to suggest that if John 'were composing freely, he might be expected to have made Martha the central character in the anointing scene', and Lazarus the host (Coakley 1988: 244–5). There is no satisfactory basis for these expectations. All Coakley has done is to invent an alternative version of aspects of the Johannine narrative, and draw conclusions from the fact that the evangelist has not followed him. It is difficult to see how to invent a weaker argument. Two further arguments are not much stronger. John 11.2 suggests to Coakley that the anointing was already linked with Mary's name in traditions known to the Gospel's first readers. But it could equally well be designed to convey that information, and traditions known to this Gospel's first readers are not necessarily genuine. Finally, Mark 14.9 makes best sense if the woman's name was at an earlier time well known. Of course, if the incident is genuine, the woman's name was once known. But Mark did not know it, so it is not very probable that it was one of Jesus' friends in Bethany.

Coakley then begins to approach a main point: 'Beyond this, a verdict on the accuracy of the proper names depends on the view taken of John 11.1–44' (Coakley 1988: 245). This is indeed significant, for it shows that Lazarus is secondary: we have seen him inserted between pieces of old tradition, with historically chaotic and theologically significant results; and if Lazarus is secondary, the probability of Mary being genuine decreases significantly. We thus have a strong argument of cumulative weight against the accuracy of these names.

Coakley proceeds to another argument which is faulty in method. Noting that scholars have been reluctant to accept the historicity of John 11.1–44, he comments, 'But hypotheses that seek instead to explain its development and connections with 12.1–8 in terms of heavy Johannine redaction also have to work hard'. This means that Coakley will believe in John 11.1–44, unless previous scholarship has given a precise and verifiable account of its secondary generation. This standard of judgement is quite inappropriate, because we have none of the fourth evangelist's sources, unless they are the synoptic Gospels, we have no direct information about his method of working, and even his purposes have to be inferred from the single surviving text. Coakley's example typifies this:

> According to one representative hypothesis, John has borrowed the three names throughout from traditions more originally preserved in Luke, where Martha served and Mary sat at the Lord's feet (Luke 10:38– 42) and Lazarus is a character in a parable who *might* rise from the dead (Luke 16:19–31). Such raw material, along with a resurrection miracle and a Mark-like story of anointing in Bethany, would then lie behind the Johannine finished product. A theory like this is probably beyond disproof, involving so many hypothetical components.
>
> (Coakley 1988: 245)

Even so, but this merely reflects the absence of sufficient evidence. Such theories are created from what evidence we have, and their level of probability is sometimes quite low. Coakley counts it an objection that such a theory 'would remove Lazarus, Mary, and Martha of Bethany to a shadowy or fictional status. But it has already been argued above that the anointing was ascribed to Mary in early tradition' (Coakley 1988: 246). We have seen how strong the arguments against Lazarus are, and how weak is that for the originality of Mary.

Coakley continues, 'and in the case of Lazarus it is at least easier to see how a real person might become a character in a parable than the reverse'. This is the wrong question again. Neither movement is easy to see, and neither hypothesis should be regarded as more than plausible. Coakley concludes, 'Detaching the names of Mary, Martha and Lazarus from 12:1–8 thus seems to create more problems than it solves.' This is true only if we make an unmentioned assumption. It presupposes that, if only we believe the Johannine account, what we have got is knowledge: if however we do not believe it, we have only inadequate theories to explain its secondary generation: therefore the Johannine account is true. If we do not proceed with an assumption of this kind, detaching the names of Mary, Martha and

Lazarus from 12.1–8 creates no problems at all. We are left with a perfectly coherent Marcan version, and some gaps in our knowledge. We particularly do not know where Lazarus came from, whether from something like Luke 7.36–50 or not, and even our most plausible guesses are not to be compared with an historical account known to be true. But that is no argument for the historicity of anything. It merely reflects the fact that, when we cease to believe an untrue account, we may end up in relative uncertainty or even complete ignorance.

Coakley passes to the anointing of Jesus' feet (Jn 12.3). Most of his argument is devoted to showing that the Johannine account is not incredible, and that scholarly assertions that aspects of it are absurd are to be denied. For the last time, let us recall the main points. The fourth Gospel contains a massive amount of secondary tradition, in sections which do not overlap with Mark. Where the fourth Gospel does overlap with Mark, we can sometimes show that its traditions are secondary. For example, it dates the Cleansing of the Temple at the wrong time, and omits Jesus' prohibition of carrying through (Mk 11.16): in the Passion narrative, the evangelist inserts a spurious speech which he attributes to 'the Jews', even though Jesus' disciples were Jewish (19.7). If, therefore, in another passage, Mark's account is intelligible and coherent, and the fourth Gospel is different, Mark is more likely to be right. Consequently, to show that the Johannine account is possible does not show that it is true, and to enter unconventional judgements about what is probable, or what is not quite beyond belief, does not make the Johannine account right either. Consequently, all Coakley's arguments are of the wrong kind. To show that the woman's anointing of Jesus' feet would have been exceptional rather than impossible, does nothing to make Mark wrong: to find that Jesus' saying (Mk 14.6, cf. Jn 12.7) 'would have been more naturally evoked by a rubbing of ointment on the feet' (Coakley 1988: 248) is to make a subjective judgement of a quite arbitrary kind. That does not make the fourth Gospel wrong: but it does nothing to make the fourth Gospel right or Mark wrong, because verifiable fact has been left far behind in favour of plausible and implausible judgement.

We must conclude that Coakley's methods could not establish anything. This is because he accepted from Robinson his teacher an intellectually arbitrary commitment which fitted his frame of reference, and consequently adopted criteria which are too weak. We should not proceed like this.

OMISSIONS

Unlike Coakley, Robinson had ample space in his book to deal with all the important points relevant to the historicity of the fourth Gospel. It is remarkable that he failed to come to terms with so many points of significance. Jesus' pre-existence is hardly mentioned. Robinson does note, for example, the view that his divine nature is based partly on his knowledge of his pre-existence (Robinson 1985: 353). He does not however face the fact that the absence of Jesus' pre-existence from the synoptic Gospels, combined with evidence of its development in passages such as Philippians 2.6–7 seen against the background of similar developments in the Judaism of the period, means that this item is secondary, and significant evidence that the Johannine portrait of Jesus is inaccurate.[19] We have noted his attempt to play down the Johannine concept of the Sonship of Jesus, another massive piece of secondary development.[20] He also attempts to downplay Thomas's full confession of Jesus' deity (Jn 20.28), declaring that this is language 'not of ontological identity', and 'He is not a divine being who came to earth . . .' (Robinson 1985: 393–4). Yet the fact remains that Jesus is not presented as God in the synoptics, and in the fourth Gospel the exposition of his deity is accompanied by accusations of blasphemy from 'the Jews'.[21] Robinson never faces the implications of these points.

The Johannine use of 'the Jews' is another case in point. This hostility has no *Sitz im Leben* at the time of Jesus. We have seen that it reflects the Gentile self-identification of the Johannine community, and we have noted that Robinson never counts the occurrences, but tries to align Johannine use with other sources.[22] The net result is that he never comes to terms with this major argument against the historicity of the fourth Gospel. The nature of covenantal nomism is another major point which Robinson does not discuss. Neither in treating the term 'the Jews', nor in a whole chapter on 'The Person of Christ', does Robinson ever observe the effect of excluding non-Christian Jews from salvation. Nor can he cope with replacement theology. While he argues vigorously that Jesus must have preached in Solomon's portico in winter because this is a vivid detail, he does not relate the contents of the discourse, which imply that Jesus has replaced Hanukkah and is fully God, to the position of the Johannine community far from the historical Jesus. Neither the chapter on the beginning of the ministry, nor the later attempt to identify Nicodemus (Robinson 1985: 184–5, 282–7), discusses the nature of the Hellenistic concept of rebirth and its effect on concepts of salvation.

Aramaic is another omission. We have seen that some of Jesus' sayings in the fourth Gospel cannot be reconstructed in the language which Jesus spoke.[23] Like many New Testament scholars, Robinson could not assess this because he could not read Aramaic. This is part of the effect of devotion to a sacred text which is written in Greek. Even in Greek, Robinson has no statistics of important Johannine words, such as 'love' and 'world', which provide an objective measure of secondary Johannine theology.[24] Nor does he explain the writing out from the fourth Gospel of major synoptic themes, such as the kingdom of God.[25] While favouring John son of Zebedee as the beloved disciple and author of the fourth Gospel (Robinson 1985: 105–22), he does not explain why he left out exorcisms (cf. esp. Mk 1.21–34; 3.14–17; 6.7, 13; cf. Lk 10.18).

The omission of all these main points is a serious defect in Robinson's method. It is not however a random defect. Robinson omitted main points which cannot be reconciled with a specific tradition to which he uncritically adhered.

SCRIPTURE AND TRADITION

Robinson's view of the fourth Gospel is not a result of critical scholarship. Its source is the treatment of John's Gospel as holy scripture. What Robinson called a 'new look' is ecclesiastical tradition. As his uncle wrote, in a book edited by Robinson's father for Anglican clergy, 'it makes its abiding appeal to the Christian consciousness as an inspired record of eternal truth which can brook no imputation of a falsified origin' (Robinson 1902: 131). Several of Robinson's arguments are to be found in the published work of his father and his uncle. Many of the rest are to be found in the work of scholars such as Sanday and Westcott. Some are as old as the church Fathers. Robinson's book revives the Robinson family's version of the old Cambridge version of church tradition. The unusual feature here is only the way that published material runs in the family. Otherwise, Robinson's behaviour is normal. He adhered to the traditions in which he was brought up, in which he spent his career, and which made his life meaningful. He passed them on to Coakley, and to such other pupils as would believe him. This is the way that large communities carry false belief. We should not follow them.

11

WHAT IS TRUTH?

INTRODUCTION

'Pilate said to him, "What is Truth?"' (Jn 19.38). The question Pilate never asked has reverberated down the centuries. For most of this time, the Gospel attributed to John has held an honoured place in Christian scripture. This position must now be questioned, for two related reasons. One is that much of it is not historically true. The second reason is the more devastating. This Gospel is profoundly anti-Jewish. What is worse, these two points are closely related. The historically inaccurate information contained in this document is a product of the serious quarrel between the Johannine community and the Jewish community. Consequently, it gives an un-Jewish picture of Jesus, and a hostile picture of 'the Jews'.

It follows that this document embodies a basic rejection of the Jewish identity of Jesus and his earliest followers. Consequently, its high Christology cannot be regarded as genuine insight into his real significance. Moreover, this document's rejection of 'the Jews' is not just an abstract error. Present in a sacred text, it is liable to fuel prejudice, and to be acted on. The history of Christian anti-Semitism shows how serious is the prejudice which it can fuel. The fourth Gospel's presentation of Jesus' ministry is therefore not merely inaccurate, but also morally dubious.

HISTORICITY AND TRUTH

We have seen in earlier chapters that, as an historical document, the fourth Gospel is seriously inaccurate. In Chapter 2, we saw that its chronology is seriously awry. The Cleansing of the Temple has been moved from the end of the ministry to the beginning. This is not one simple mistake, but the use of profound conviction in such a way that it causes narrative chaos. The reason for the move was, in the first place, replacement symbolism. The narrative embodies the replacement of the Temple with Jesus (Jn 2.23), and it is at the beginning for this reason. The result is that the narrative does not have sufficient consequence. When we compare it with the account of

Mark, we can see that specifically Jewish features of the original narrative have also been lost. More drastically, its historical function as the trigger of the Passion has been removed. In this respect, it is replaced by the raising of Lazarus. The use of that narrative has also caused narrative chaos, the result being highly improbable Jewish opponents, and the figure of Lazarus being so important that his disappearance from the face of history cannot be explained. The chronology of the Passion was altered for similar reasons. Passover, presented as a feast of 'the Jews', has been replaced by the Lamb of God who takes away the sin of the world. Jesus' last meal with his disciples was therefore not a Passover meal: rather, he died at the same time as the Passover victims, and, in fulfilment of a scripture referring to the Passover lamb, no bone of him was broken. This chronology was therefore associated with the change in covenantal nomism which permeates the Gospel. The covenant community is no longer 'the Jews', but the Johannine community, which has Gentile self-identification.

The picture of Jesus himself is quite distorted. In Chapter 3, we saw that the unhistorical material includes a massive amount of Christological development. Here Jesus is presented as incarnate and divine, a view of him offensive to the Jewish identity of both himself and of the first apostles, and essential to the Christian doctrine of the Trinity. The charge of blasphemy, necessarily incurred by the Johannine community, is put in the mouths of Jewish people arguing with Jesus during the historic ministry. These people are labelled 'the Jews', as if Jesus and the disciples were not Jewish, and as if these charges were made by the Jewish people as a whole. The main Christological term used by Jesus is 'the Son (of God)'. Whereas the Jesus of history did not use this term of himself in a special sense, the Johannine Christ uses it to expound his relationship with the Father in a way that makes it clear that he is himself divine. His pre-existence, again absent from the synoptics, is treated by Johannine Jews, as well as by Jesus himself, as an indication of deity. There are a number of dramatic 'I am' sayings, some of which are associated with the shift of covenantal nomism characteristic of this Gospel. What is so damaging about 'I am the way and the truth and the life' is the continuation, 'No-one comes to the Father except through me' (Jn 14.6). This excludes non-Christian Jews from salvation, a view as alien to Jesus of Nazareth as his deity.

Equally remarkable is Jesus' exposition of the eucharist before it was even instituted, in a discussion which would have been unintelligible at the time. This too involves a shift in covenantal nomism, for the eucharist is presented as essential for salvation, and non-Christian Jews did not share in it. This write-up is centrally anti-Jewish. The crowd turn into 'the Jews', who complain because Jesus expresses belief in his pre-existence, a belief which the historical Jesus did not hold, and which in this document indicates his deity. Their identity as 'the Jews' is reinforced at John 6.52 for the quintessentially anti-Jewish moment of 6.53: 'Amen, amen I say to you, unless you eat the flesh of the Son of man and drink his blood, you do not have life in yourselves.' This has two *ipsissima verba* of the historical Jesus, Amen and Son of man, and two features as remote from him as possible – the demand for drinking his blood, and the declaration that taking the Christian eucharist is necessary for salvation. This builds into the picture of disciples leaving him, which no one in the historic ministry had such reasons for doing. The write-up of his 'signs' is equally anti-Jewish. The exorcisms have been removed, and two healing narratives have been written up to make Jesus abrogate the sabbath and reveal his deity, both anti-Jewish features which mispresent him and, consequently, the opposition to him. Some signs have been written up to ensure that they are impossible events, which his opponents nonetheless should have believed in. Nowhere is this more true than in the raising of Lazarus, which looks forward to the rewritten accounts of Jesus' resurrection. It has been written to be an impossible event, full of Johannine theology, and it replaces the Cleansing of the Temple as the trigger of the Passion. The result is narrative chaos and theological coherence, a theological coherence which portrays Jesus' opponents as impossibly wicked.

Jesus' disciples, however, at various points confess him as messiah, which was not the case during the historic ministry. None of the Johannine Son of man sayings are authentic either. With all this new material, Jesus' preaching of the kingdom of God has almost been removed. We had to conclude that Jesus has been completely rewritten, in accordance with the needs of the Johannine community. This rewriting is deeply interwoven with the community's anti-Jewish outlook.

The same is true of John the Baptist, as we saw in Chapter 4. The historical John the Baptist was an eschatological prophet of judgement who was not sure whether Jesus was the coming one. Jesus underwent baptism by him, and hailed him as more than a prophet, even as Elijah. All that has been removed from the fourth Gospel. In its place, we have a John who gives clear and unambiguous witness that Jesus is the central salvation figure, to the point where John is not even labelled 'the Baptist', for Jesus is presented as a more successful baptist than he. John is represented as portraying Jesus as pre-existent, and he clearly implies that Jesus is the messiah. His comments include the same shift in covenantal nomism that we have noted elsewhere. The picture of him has been distorted beyond recognition for set purpose, and some of the changes reflect the quarrel with the Jewish community which controlled so many aspects of the rewriting of history in this document.

The main shift in covenantal nomism permeates the teaching of Jesus throughout the Gospel. It is most remarkably presented in John 3, using the Hellenistic concept of rebirth. Here Jesus expounds to an uncomprehending Jewish teacher rebirth by water and the spirit, entry into the Christian community, which replaces birth into the Jewish community. This refers to

Christian baptism, which was not known to the historical Jesus, any more than the eucharist. Nicodemus is also not alone in having speeches attributed to him which he did not make (if, indeed, there was a Nicodemus present in the historic ministry at all). This happens to all significant characters in the Gospel, who are given plausible things to say to carry the narrative along. They include the Pharisees of John 9, who examine a miraculously healed man in the context of the declaration that 'The Jews had agreed that if anyone confessed him [sc. Jesus] as Christ, he would be made *aposunagōgos*.' As we saw in Chapter 6, this is as anachronistic as possible. An agreement by 'the Jews' was not possible when Jesus and his followers were Jewish. It reflects the Gentile self-identification of the Johannine community many years later. The confession of Jesus as Christ is a feature of the early church, not of the historic ministry. Nobody came to an agreement to ban Jesus' followers from Jewish meetings during the historic ministry. Thus the whole of John 9, from the impossibly written-up and technically unlawful healing of the blind man to the blindness of the sinful Pharisees, is a dramatisation of what the Johannine community wanted to believe, not a record of events in the ministry of the historical Jesus.

Accordingly, we can infer quite a lot about the Johannine community which produced this Gospel. In this, we are helped considerably by the Johannine epistles. We saw in Chapter 5 that listing major words gives an objective measure of the vast extent to which the concepts and style of the fourth Gospel differ from those of the synoptic Gospels and overlap with 1 John, which adds to our reasons for seeing the theology of the fourth Gospel as the product of the Johannine community. This was a Christian community in Ephesus towards the end of the first century. It may well have been multilingual and multiethnic, but its members understood Greek and, when this document was finally completed, they had been involved in the massive quarrel with the Jewish community as part of which they were banned from Jewish meetings. This dispute was a formative factor in the production of secondary material in this Gospel. There was a complex identity situation. As we saw in Chapter 7, the Johannine community had contained Jews, as well as Gentiles who were, from a normal Gentile perspective, Judaising. When the Gospel was finally edited, however, the community had firmly taken on Gentile self-identification, as the authors of the Johannine epistles had apparently not done. Equally, 'the Jews', as the authors of the Gospel called them, included people who had been baptised and had participated in the Christian eucharist.

This is the social context for the production of the fourth Gospel. It was effectively written over a long period of time by a lot of people. The authors of 1 John addressed them as 'beloveds', and the people finally responsible for the Gospel produced a representative figure, a/the 'disciple whom Jesus loved'. Like the authors of Jubilees and 4 Ezra, they rewrote history out of tradition in accordance with current need. They attributed their major beliefs to Jesus, the fountainhead of their traditions, and through him to God himself. The author(s) of Chapter 21, an appendix to the Gospel as a whole, added another level of pseudonymity by attributing the Gospel to the representative figure, 'the disciple whom Jesus loved', a presentation of their own identity.

There should therefore be no doubt that, at a purely historical level, the fourth Gospel is seriously untrue. We may not however end the argument at that point. A serious defence of this Gospel can be mounted, not from a fundamentalist perspective, but from a Christian perspective which takes its culture seriously. Clement already declared that the fourth Gospel is the most spiritual of the four Gospels (Eus. H.E. VI, 14, 7). We could continue to argue that it shows great spiritual insight into Christianity as it ought to develop, and we could explain that it was never intended to be historically accurate. Explicitly or implicitly, this seems to have been the position of critical commentators who come in from a Christian perspective:

> This is a Gospel designed to root the believer deeper in his faith.

> The gospel itself ensures that those who take it seriously shall direct their attention to the Word made flesh, and to the Holy Spirit, by whom the presence of the Word continues to be effected; by this they are related, not to a bygone past or to a particular kind of religious experience, but to God.
> (Brown 1966a: lxxviii; Barrett 1978: 144; cf. Lindars 1981: 63–6)

Further support for such a view might be sought by analogy with sacred texts in other cultures. Cantwell Smith has recently surveyed them, and noted the wide variety of modes in which texts may be held sacred (Cantwell Smith 1993). He calls above all for the development of understanding rather than continued commitment to traditional positions, which are often held in ignorance and/or condemnation of others. Among the possibilities opened up by his discussion is that of understanding scripture as a record of the Christian community, to be held as precious and as fallible as we are. The additional material surveyed in Chapter 8 could be used to develop further an historical understanding of the fourth Gospel. We have seen that it was quite normal for Jewish works to be anonymous or pseudepigraphical. These works attributed the community's views to the fountainhead of the tradition. The fourth Gospel therefore fits a normal cultural pattern. We might argue that it is a necessary consequence of the incarnation that the Gospel be preached in the only ways that culturally conditioned human beings can preach it. The fourth Gospel was bound to be culturally conditioned. We should absorb the profundity of its theology, and discard the culturally normal mode in which it is cloaked.

There are two reasons why arguments on these lines should be regarded as dubious. Firstly, the form of the fourth Gospel is comprehensible in our culture, and a conservative use of the concept of honesty is natural to us. If we read that 'Jesus said' something, we assume that, in the author's view, Jesus did indeed say it. As long as this Gospel is in a canon of sacred scripture, most people in the pew are likely to continue believing that much of it is historically true. Since it is not, the presence of the fourth Gospel in scripture is liable to mislead people.

It is not only individuals in the pew who read the fourth Gospel as true because it is scriptural. Whole communities believe every word of it because it is scripture, and in many cases this is reinforced rather than undermined by critical scholarship, because they reject critical scholarship as hostile to God's Word. Consequently, many millions of people have a wholly misleading picture of the life and teaching of Jesus. That is bad enough. It is much worse that they have a wholly misleading picture of 'the Jews', and this is the second reason why the theological truth of this document is difficult to defend.

ANTI-SEMITISM, IDENTITY AND THE TEACHING OF JESUS

We have seen throughout this book that the fourth Gospel is seriously anti-Jewish. In the first place, the universalism which commends it so warmly to Gentile Christians has an unhappy obverse side: Jews are not saved. We have considered one of the central texts of the sacrificial love of the Son of God: 'For God so loved the world, that he gave his only-begotten Son, so that everyone who believes in him should not perish but should have eternal life' (3.16). When this was written, everyone knew that most Jews did not believe in him. So, 'he who does not believe has already been judged, because he has not believed in the name of the only-begotten Son of God' (3.18). Hence the need for rebirth into the Christian community, replacing birth into the Jewish community.[1] We have seen that this shift in covenantal nomism is pervasive throughout this Gospel. Another striking example is the eucharistic discourse of Chapter 6: 'Amen, amen I tell you, unless you eat the flesh of the Son of man and drink his blood, you do not have life in yourselves' (6.53). This is as anti-Jewish as possible.

This rejection of Jewish people is not confined to abstract theology. There is more vigorous criticism on two further levels. Firstly, the rejection of the whole Jewish community is openly declared. At 10.26, Jesus says to 'the Jews', 'But you do not believe, because you do not belong to my sheep' (cf. 10.24; 1.11). In fact, all the earliest disciples were Jews, but this has been lost sight of, and the whole Jewish people are now placed outside the covenant community. The detailed discussion is worse. At 5.45–7, the Jews are accused of not believing in Moses, a charge which is patently false. At 8.44, Jesus tells them that their father is not God, but the devil. This condemnation of 'the Jews' is intensified by the presentation of 'the disciples' as a separate group. For example, in the aftermath of the Cleansing of the Temple, the immediate questions of 'the Jews' are contrasted with the later memories of 'the disciples' (2.17ff.).[2]

As well as this inaccurate condemnation of 'the Jews', the fourth Gospel provides an inaccurate presentation of their words and deeds. For example, at 8.48, 'The Jews answered and said to him, "Are we not right to say that you are a Samaritan and have a demon?"' In the historic ministry, 'the Jews' said no such thing. On the contrary, when Jesus' ministry of preaching and exorcism was being very well received by Jews in Galilee, the accusation that he cast out demons by Beelzebub was made by 'scribes who came down from Jerusalem' (Mark 3.22). The accusation has not merely been altered: the attribution to 'the Jews' is desperately anti-Jewish, a complete misrepresentation of a situation when many Jews were on Jesus' side. Some comments are simply more remote from reality, but they contribute to a picture of Jewish rejection of Jesus. For example, at 6.52, 'The Jews disputed vigorously with each other, saying, "How can this man give us his flesh to eat?"' This portrays the whole Jewish people as culpably ignorant of the Christian eucharist, at a stage when it had not even been instituted. They act on some of their words. At the end of the discourse of Chapter 8, 'They therefore picked up stones to throw at him' (8.59). This threat to kill him is repeated (cf. 5.18; 10.31), and it does not correspond to the situation in the historic ministry. At 10.33, 'the Jews' give an explanation: 'We are not stoning you for a good work but for blasphemy, and because you, being a man, make yourself (a) God' (cf. 10.31). Given that this presentation of 'the Jews' is incorrect, it is most profoundly misleading. The baleful charge of deicide has begun.

We have seen that all this polemic reflects a later conflict situation, when the Johannine community was banned from Jewish meetings.[3] This *explains* the fourth Gospel's inaccurate picture of 'the Jews', but it does nothing to justify its continued presence in scripture which is held to be true. A fundamental difference would be made if the expression generally rendered 'the Jews' meant something else. In Chapter 7, I considered in detail the two major suggestions in the standard secondary literature, that *Ioudaioi* really means 'Judaeans', or 'Jewish authorities' or the like. We saw that both suggestions are verifiably false.[4] It follows that scholars should not mislead people by adopting other translations of *Ioudaioi*, or by tampering with the text in any other way.

Stibbe has recently proposed 'an ethical reading of Johannine polemic', offering a detailed discussion of John 8.31–59 'because it is the text which is most often cited by Jewish authors as the *locus classicus* of New Testament anti-Semitism' (Stibbe 1994a: 109). This is a phenomenally inaccurate passage which encourages prejudice, so much so that Stibbe's attempt at an 'ethical reading' should not be accepted. He begins by setting the passage in its overall context in the Gospel, but he does not engage with the unhistorical nature of the whole presentation, and underplays its anti-Jewish stance, arguing for example that 'conflict is absent from the plot in John 2–4' (Stibbe 1994a: 111). The *plot* is not all that matters. As we have seen, the prologue presents the quite un-Jewish belief in Jesus' deity, with the inaccurate information 'his own did not receive him' (1.11), inaccurate because all the first disciples were Jewish. John the Baptist is misrepresented as expounding Jesus' pre-existence, a mark of deity in this document, and presenting him as 'the Lamb of God who takes away the sin of the world' (1.29). Replacement theology permeates Chapters 1–4, and in Chapters 2–3 'the disciples' and 'the Jews' are separate groups. Christian baptism replaces birth into the Jewish community, and people who do not believe in the only-begotten Son of God are condemned, so that Jewish people are not saved.[5] It is no help to this absolute and pervasive rejection of the Jews that conflict has not yet entered the *plot*, understood as event rather than discussion.

Stibbe locates John 8.31–59 as the seventh dialogue of John 7–8, within the major conflict of John 5–10. He regards its genre as central to its interpretation, and describes its genre as 'informal satire'. This is not merely dubious, it is surely much less important than Stibbe thinks. It is dubious because it is not clear that 'informal satire' was a recognisable genre at the time – what was recognisable was that it was customary to write fiercer polemic than we might find acceptable (Johnson 1989). What this does, however, is to explain why Johannine polemic is so vitriolic; it does not render it accurate or acceptable. Finally, Stibbe makes another attempt to have *Ioudaioi* not quite be 'the Jews', a concern which we have seen to be widespread in scholarship. He summarises, '*Jesus is not attacking the Jewish people in general. Far from it. He is satirizing apostasy in 8.31–59. He is satirizing those who start on the road of discipleship, but who give up when the going gets tough*' (Stibbe 1994a: 124, original italics).

There is some truth in this claim, but not enough to rescue this document. Some of the attacks in this document are launched at people who have left the Johannine community. John 8.31 suggests they are partly in view here. More generally, we have seen that people who remained in the Jewish community when the split came included baptised Christians who had taken the eucharist. There are however three problems with Stibbe's approach. Firstly, there is an underlying assumption that apostasy is so wicked that these attacks would be somehow less wicked if their objects were apostates, in practice, Jewish apostates from Christianity. This assumption should not be accepted. Secondly, the description of these people as apostate is not a satisfactory description because it misrepresents the centre of their life-stance. These people saw themselves as Jews. We have no reason to suppose that most of them ever wavered in their commitment to Judaism. They had been members of the Johannine community when this was consistent with being Jewish, just as all Jesus' first disciples had been his disciples when they were also Jewish. They did not give up when the going got tough, they continued with their Jewish commitment however tough the going got. They will always have believed 'We have one Father, God' (Jn 8.41). Holding to that belief from a Jewish perspective, most of them will never have accepted the deity of Jesus, or the Johannine interpretation of his pre-existence, nor will they have believed that baptism and the eucharist were essential to salvation. They will have believed that Jesus revealed the truest form of Judaism, and that the Gentile mission presented it in such a form that Gentiles could be saved: they will have maintained their traditional assumption that other Jews were in the covenant community anyway.

Consequently, the fourth Gospel is culturally correct to subsume these people under the description 'the Jews'. Most of them will not suddenly have believed that Jesus was a Samaritan and had a demon (cf. Jn 8.48), but their decision was to remain in a community of people some of whom made such polemical statements when warding off a perceived threat from the Johannine community. It is the Jewish community which is replaced by the Johannine community throughout the fourth Gospel, from the declaration of the deity and incarnation of the Word violating Jewish monotheism at the beginning, to the need for faith that Jesus is the Christ the Son of God, which violates it just as securely at the end. Moreover, it is 'the Jews' who were for centuries major victims of Christian persecution. Indeed, the use of this Gospel in subsequent attacks on 'the Jews' shows how dangerous a work it can be, when it is treated as a sacred text which must be wholly true. Some comments appear at first sight to be merely exegetical, but the use of the Johannine term 'the Jews' lends itself to actualisation of the text. For example, St Cyril of Alexandria comments on John 19.13–14, 'By saying this the evangelist puts as it were the whole charge of murdering Christ on the heads of the Jews above all' (*Commentary on the Gospel According to S. John*). When this is attributed to the whole Jewish people, as if Jesus and the disciples were not Jewish, it is but a short step to attributing later Jewish misfortunes to these incidents. Commenting on John 19.15, St Cyril declares that Israel abandoned God for Caesar, and thereby deserved the calamities they had suffered, including war and expulsion from their land.

More direct attacks on 'the Jews' were made by St John Chrysostom, who was confronted with the possibility that people might worship God in the synagogue. He comments,

> But they [sc. the Jews] will assuredly say that they, too, worship God. But that should certainly not be said. No Jew worships God! Who says this? The Son of God. 'If you were to know my Father', he says, 'you would also know me. But you neither know me nor do you know my Father' [Jn 8.19, in a variant text]. What more trustworthy witness than this could I produce? If, then, they do not know the Father, they

crucified the Son, they reject the help of the Spirit, who should not boldly and plainly declare that the place [i.e. the synagogue] is a dwelling of demons? God is not worshipped there. Certainly not! But it is, furthermore, a place of idolatry.

(Discourses against the Jews I, 3)

Here John 8.19 is the crucial piece of authoritative witness in a quite bigoted piece of polemic. It is precisely this use of the fourth Gospel which is possible because it is literally untrue, and unsafe as too sacred a text.

A number of passages focus on the identity factors of Judaism. For example, Chrysostom comments on John 12.35,

'He who walks in the darkness does not know where he is going.' How many things, indeed, the Jews do now, and do not know what they are doing, but as it were walk in darkness. They think they are going the right way, but they are walking in the opposite direction – keeping the Sabbath, and maintaining the Law, and observing the dietary laws. And they do not know where they are walking.

(Homilies on St John LXVIII)

Jesus of Nazareth kept the sabbath, maintained the Law, and observed the scriptural dietary laws. But in the fourth Gospel the sabbath is abrogated, 'their Law' (Jn 15.25) is not maintained and the dietary laws are not mentioned. The fourth Gospel is again the crucial witness in this anti-Jewish outburst.

As Christians became more powerful, anti-Jewish writing was accompanied by specific practical measures against the Jewish community, and especially against Jews who sought to maintain their identity. In the Reformation period, Luther was able to draw on centuries of Christian persecution of Jews in a work of baleful influence (Luther 1543; cf. Hillerbrand 1990, with bibliography). Unable to convert them, he compared his efforts with preaching the Gospel to a pig, referring to the veil over Moses' face which still prevented them from understanding God's commandment (cf. 2 Cor 3). He referred to John 8.39 and 8.44 to characterise them as children of the devil, commenting that they could not bear to hear that they were the devil's children either then or in Luther's own time. This indicates actualisation of Johannine polemic, fired at 'the Jews', not at Judaeans, Jewish authorities or apostates. Luther also used John 5.23 and 15.23 for the rejection of those who reject the Son, actualising this too by referring explicitly to Jews contemporary with him. He also used Matthew 27.42 and John 7.31, 41 and 11.47 for Jesus' appearance as the expected messiah during his ministry being obvious, with 1,500 years of successful preaching of the Gospel making it more obvious still. The fourth Gospel is not the only scriptural work used by Luther, but it is the dominant one. The reason for its dominance in this kind of context is quite straightforward – it is the most profoundly anti-Jewish, and its anti-Jewish life-stance is organically related to its secondary theology. The rejection of those who reject the Son functions easily as a means of rejecting 'the Jews', and the accusation that their father is the devil is the kind of blanket polemic which lends itself to anything, however wicked. Luther's recommendations included burning down the synagogues or schools of 'the Jews', destroying their houses, confiscating all copies of their prayer books and Talmud, and forbidding their rabbis to teach on pain of death (Luther 1543: 170–1, 141, 278, 281–4, 289–91, 268–70). At this level the Reformation changed nothing, and it could change nothing because its return to scripture sent it to such a profoundly anti-Jewish document.

It is in this area that inaccuracy moves from being regrettable in its own right to being morally wrong. The history of Christian anti-Semitism shows us that untrue stories, complete with the attribution to 'the Jews' of words which they did not say, have been a standing invitation to attack a whole ethnic group. The fourth Gospel was used, even hundreds of years after it was written, to legitimate action against Jewish people who could not possibly have been responsible for the words and actions described in it, even had the stories been true. It was used like this not least because it was so sacred that Christians 'knew' it was true.

Nothing could be more clearly contrary to the teaching of Jesus, and this at two levels. In the first place, he and the first apostles were Jewish. These attacks therefore were in a profound sense an attack upon him, because they were essentially an attack upon his Jewish identity. Anti-Semitic outbreaks are also contrary to the explicit teaching of Jesus on how we should treat other people. Asked to specify the greatest commandment of all, he gave two: 'This is the second: "You shall love your neighbour as yourself" (Lev 19.18). There is no other commandment greater than these' (Mk 12.31). He then vigorously approved of the agreement expressed by the scribe who had questioned him (Mk 12.32–4). Similar teaching is further developed elsewhere. 'Love your enemies, do good to those who hate you, bless those who curse you, pray for those who maltreat you' (Lk 6.27–8, cf. Mt 5.44ff.). This teaching was part of a vigorous ministry to Jews who were encouraged to return to the Lord. Jesus did condemn scribes and Pharisees who resisted this ministry, but he did not seek to make the love of God and our neighbours dependent on belief that salvation was only through him, let alone that he was divine. Thus the history of Christian anti-Semitism is not only horrifyingly wicked: it is centrally deceitful. The fourth Gospel is at the centre of this deceit. Here Jesus is wrongly represented as condemning 'the Jews'. Here grounds such as his deity are put forward which were never put forward by him, and which safely ensured that Jews who maintained their identity, the same identity as that of Jesus and the first apostles, would turn down the Gospel and therefore suffer persecution.

JOHN'S GOSPEL IS PROFOUNDLY UNTRUE

Our major conclusion follows ineluctably. The fourth Gospel is profoundly untrue. It consists to a large extent of inaccurate stories and words wrongly attributed to people. It is anti-Jewish, and as holy scripture it has been used to legitimate outbreaks of Christian anti-Semitism. A cultural defence is therefore inadequate.

This is a serious problem for Christian churches which have it among their most sacred texts. Equally important, the doctrine of the Trinity has been central to Christian history and theology. It includes the deity of Jesus. What we have seen in this document, however, is that the deity of Jesus infringes Jewish monotheism. Even as this Gospel's discussions of Jesus' deity are historically inaccurate, they are culturally correct. Exposition of the deity of Jesus entails charges of blasphemy, and rejection of Jesus by 'the Jews'.

What the churches do about this is a matter for them. On past form, most of them will do precious little, and false belief will continue to flourish among them. In this book, I have tried to make what contribution an independent academic can make. I have demonstrated what critical scholars have said quietly for years, that this Gospel is not literally true. I have also laid bare the organic connections between this Gospel's secondary theology and its anti-Jewish outlook. Consequently, I have been able to offer for the first time a complete explanation of how such an inaccurate document came to be written by otherwise decent people. It follows that this Gospel is a standing contradiction of the Jewish identity of Jesus and the first apostles. It is not a source of truth.

229

NOTES

1 INTRODUCTION

1 For the meaning of this term, see pp. 111–16.

2 FROM BEGINNING TO END

1 The following comments are partly based on a reconstruction of the Aramaic source of Mark 11.15–17, and it is this source which is translated here.

2 I cannot discuss here the chaos caused by discussion of the English article (and the French and German articles) as a translation of the Greek article as a translation of the Aramaic definite state. The Aramaic definite state was not an article, and in Mark's source here it will have meant nothing more than that we may reasonably have been expected to know already that there were chief priests and scribes and elders, if indeed it meant anything much at all. There is no satisfactory treatment of this in the secondary literature. Cf. Casey 1987: 27–36; 1991b: 40–1.

3 There are also problems with the trial before Pilate. We should infer that no one present at the sanhedrin or the trial before Pilate joined the Christian movement and/or passed on true information about it: the accounts read well as conjectures made by the early church. For discussion, with comprehensive bibliography, Brown 1994: I, 315–560, 665–877.

4 For detailed discussion of the term 'the Jews', Gentile self-identification and the Johannine community, see Chapter 7.

5 Never in Mark; in Q, only in the 'thunderbolt from the Johannine sky', the entirely secondary Mt 11.27//Lk 10.22. Otherwise, Mt 7.21, not Lk 6.46; Mt 10.32–3, not Lk 12.8–9; Mt 12.50, secondary editing of Mk 3.35; Mt 15.13, inserted into Mk 7; Mt 16.17, an addition to Peter's confession at Mk 8.29; Mt 18.10, 19, 35; 20.23, added to Mk 10.40; Mt 25.34; Mt 26.29, editing Mk 14.25; Mt 26.39, editing Mk 14.36; Mt 26.42, added to Mk 14.39; Mt 26.53; Lk 2.49; 22.29; 24.49.

6 See further Chapter 3.

7 Cf. pp. 151–2.

8 Cf. p. 230, n. 3.

9 For careful discussion of the alternatives, Ogg 1940: 162–7.

10 For detailed discussion see pp. 140–51.

11 I cannot reconstruct the Aramaic source here. I have done so in a seminar paper which is being prepared for publication in a book on the Aramaic sources of the Gospel of Mark. This also includes critical discussion of modern scholarship on the Marcan account.

12 The Greek definite articles, conventionally rendered with English definite articles, as before 'son', or omitted, as before 'man', represent the Aramaic definite state, in an idiom by which a speaker used a general statement referring especially to himself. For detailed discussion, Casey 1987: esp. 27–34.

13 See pp. 208–9.

14 Cf. p. 230, n. 3.

15 See pp. 183–7.

16 On this term see pp. 111–16.

17 See Chapter 6.

18 Cf. pp. 10, 134–6.

19 Cf. pp. 136–7; Trebilco 1991; Collins 1986.

20 He is not alone in this. For recent discussion, with information on previous work, Hanson 1991: 218–22.

21 In addition to Hanson and the commentators, see Freed 1965; Reim 1974.

22 The classic survey of the evidence, including the main theories in the ancient church, as well as modern scholarship, is still Ogg 1940.

23 Cf. pp. 15–16.

24 See pp. 4–14.

25 See pp. 42–51.

26 See pp. 10, 20, 134–6.

27 See pp. 11–13.

28 For further criticism of Robinson, see pp. 202-4.

3 CHRISTOLOGY

1 Cf. Davey 1958; Sidebottom 1961; Käsemann 1966; Borgen 1968; Du Toit 1968; Sevenster 1970; Meeks 1972; Mastin 1975; Müller 1975; Bühner 1977; Smith 1977; Mealand 1978; Dunn 1980: Chapter 7; Matsunaga 1981b; Fennema 1985; Hartin 1985; Sproston 1985; Hultgren 1987: Chapter 8; Schnelle 1987; Watson 1987; Boismard 1988; De Jonge 1977a, 1988: Chapter 9; Neyrey 1988; Thompson 1988; Loader 1989; Morris 1989; Meeks 1990; Ashton 1991: esp. Chapters 7–9, 12–13; Painter 1991; Scott 1992; Schnackenburg 1992; Evans 1993; Menken 1993b.

2 For a convincing defence of this reading, Mastin 1975; cf. also Fennema 1985.

3 For the statistics, see p. 84.

4 See pp. 208–9.

5 Robinson's argument is not new: cf. Robinson 1902: 156. On the secondary nature of these examples, cf. e.g. Barrett 1967: 24–8.

6 Cf. Casey 1991a: 44–6, 148–9. Robinson's fault is an old one: cf. Robinson 1924: 59.

7 See pp. 42–51.

8 See Chapter 4.

9 See pp. 57–9.

10 See pp. 42–51.

11 See pp. 55–6, 208–9.

12 On the narrative of the arrest, see pp. 180–2.

13 In addition to the commentators, see the careful discussion of Painter 1991: 217–27.

14 *Eucharistēsas* Jn 6.11//Mk 8.6//Mt 15.36, cf. *eulogēsen* Mk 6.41//Mt 14.19//Lk 9.16//Mk 8.7.

15 In addition to the commentators, cf. Menken 1988; Hanson 1991: 83–7; Schuchard 1992: 33–46.

16 On 6.63 and its interpretation within the framework of Jn 6, cf. esp. Matsunaga 1981a; Rensberger 1988: 70–81.

17 Hence another massive bibliography! In addition to the commentators, cf. especially Bornkamm 1956; Borgen 1965; Dunn 1970–1; Matsunaga 1981a; Roberge 1982 (with bibliography); Rensberger 1988: 70–81; Cosgrove 1989; Koester 1990 (with history of exegesis); Menken 1993a (with bibliography); Perry 1993.

18 See Chapter 8.

19 For further discussion of Robinson, see pp. 207–8.

20 This material is so distinctive that many scholars have believed in a special 'signs source'. I do not accept this, because the criteria used to isolate it are not strong enough. For presentation of this source, see esp. Bultmann 1941; Fortna 1970. Cf. further, in addition to the commentators, Ruckstuhl 1951, 1977; Smith 1965, 1976a, 1976b; Nicol 1972; Freed and Hunt 1975; De Jonge 1977a: 117–40; Richter 1977: 281–7; Heekerens 1984; Fortna 1988; Von Wahlde 1989; Ruckstuhl and Dschulnigg 1991; Ashton 1994: 90–113; Johns and Miller 1994; Van Belle 1994.

21 In addition to the commentators, see esp. Manns 1991: 93–110.

22 See pp. 8–10 and Chapter 7.

23 See p. 10.

24 See p. 32.

25 See pp. 42–51.

26 See pp. 57–9.

27 On Jn 9, cf. esp. Martyn 1968: 24–62; Rensberger 1988: 41–9; Painter 1991: Chapter 8; Lee 1994: 161–87 (with bibliography).

28 See pp. 41–2, 134–6.

29 See Chapter 6.

30 On these, see further pp. 208–9.

31 See pp. 57–9.

32 Cf. p. 52.

33 See pp. 41–2.

34 Cf. pp. 85–6.

35 Attempts to separate Johannine redaction from an earlier source are uniformly dubious. In addition to the commentators, cf. e.g. Fortna 1970: 74–87; Kremer 1985; Marchadour 1988; Wagner 1988; Fortna 1988: 94–109; Hanson 1991: 150–62; Painter 1991: 313–20; Lindars 1992; Lee 1994: Chapter 7; Burkett 1994; Stibbe 1994b.

36 See Chapter 9.

37 See Chapter 6.

38 Cf. pp. 41–2.

39 See pp. 98–110.

40 Casey 1980, 1985, 1987, 1991a: 46–56, 1991b, 1994b, 1995.

41 On the Johannine material, cf. esp. Freed 1967; Maddox 1974; Moloney 1976 (with Forschungsberichte); Lindars 1983: Chapter 9; Müller 1984: 142–6, 205–18; Hare 1990: Chapter 4; Rhea 1990; Ashton 1991: Chapter 9; Burkett 1991 (with bibliography); Pazdan 1991; Müller 1991; Davies 1992: Chapter 8; Painter 1992; Walker 1994.

42 Cf. pp. 41–2.

4 JOHN THE BAPTIST

1 In addition to the scholarship on the fourth Gospel, there is specialised secondary literature on John the Baptist. The major monographs have bibliographies: see esp. Scobie 1964; Wink 1968; Ernst 1989; Backhaus 1991; Webb 1991; Stowasser 1992.

2 Mark is usually interpreted to mean 'the one who is stronger than me'. This is not enough to conjure up any particular figure, and no feasible Aramaic version of it has been proposed. I assume אתה חסיני כ תרי: detailed discussion of reasonable possibilities must be offered elsewhere.

3 There is no straightforward Aramaic word for 'lesser' or 'least'. I assume z'īrā, which could give rise to Q's *mikroteros*.

4 See pp. 98–127.

5 See pp. 41–2; Casey 1991a: 42–4, 149.

6 See pp. 81–3.

7 See pp. 10, 134–6.

8 See pp. 18–25.

9 Beasley-Murray 1962: 51–2; 1987: 24–5. The latter discussion also supposes that T. Jos. 19.8 is a Jewish text. This has been taken up by Sandy 1991: 453–5. Both rely on O'Neill 1979. This use of Christian recensions of Jewish texts is methodologically unsatisfactory, but the text of the Testaments of the Twelve Patriarchs is too complex and technical to deal with here.

10 When this chapter had been written, an attempt to reconstruct an Aramaic 'Song of the Lamb' was published: De Moor and Van Staalduine-Sulman 1993; Van Staalduine-Sulman 1993. Convincing evidence of early material has not however been provided: in particular, Ps-Philo, *Bib Ant* LXI should not be used to argue for an early date of relevant material when it contains neither a messiah nor a lamb. If an early date for this material could be demonstrated, it would add to the background material noted above, on all of which the author(s) of this passage could draw: it could not validate the arguments of Dodd and Sandy.

11 See pp. 98–139.

12 See p. 64.

13 For defence of the reading 'chosen', and discussion, see in addition to the commentators, Hanson 1991: 34–6.

14 See pp. 57–9.

15 See p. 68.

16 See pp. 127–32.

17 See pp. 51–7.

5 WORDS: CONTENT AND STYLE

1 This matter cannot be pursued here. The secondary literature suffers from an inappropriate model of authorship, on which see Chapter 8. For discussion, cf. esp. Dodd 1937; Brown 1982: 14–30; Ruckstuhl and Dschulnigg 1991: 44–54.

2 See pp. 77–8.

3 CIL XIII, 1668, readily available in Smallwood 1967: 97–9, rewritten at Tac. Ann. XI, 24. For brief discussion and bibliography, Huzar 1984: 627–32; Suerbaum 1990: 1368–73; Bérard 1991: 3015–17.

4 These figures have been selected from standard sources and checked with texts and concordances. For a more complete list, Abbott 1905: 160–87.

5 See pp. 135–6.

6 Cf. pp. 98–100.

7 For a more extensive list, Abbott 1905: 195–239.

8 Detailed discussion of stylistic differences between John and 1 John lies beyond the scope of this book.

9 See pp. 33–6.

10 Cf. pp. 57–9.

11 Cf. pp. 151–4.

12 See pp. 61, 71–2.

13 See pp. 127–32.

14 On baptism, see pp. 128–32.

15 See pp. 111–27.

16 See pp. 111–39.

17 Schweizer 1939; Ruckstuhl 1951, 1977; Ruckstuhl and Dschulnigg 1991. Source-critical theories are not generally dealt with in this book, since I am not convinced that the criteria used lead anywhere, and other criteria are in any case necessary to decide the question of historicity, even when sources are found. Cf. Hengel 1989: 88–93.

18 Cf. pp. 93–4; Schnelle 1987: Chapter 2.

19 For critical discussion, Horsley 1989. Horsley does not however discuss Jewish languages in general. Cf. pp. 93–4.

20 See p. 75.

21 For problems encountered in counting asyndeton, and claims about usage in Epictetus and the papyri, Colwell 1931: 10–17.

22 See p. 63.

23 See pp. 73–4.

24 See pp. 42–51.

25 See pp. 127–33.

26 Cf. pp. 59–61.

27 See p. 88.

28 Proper discussion cannot be offered here, and is planned for a book on Aramaic sources of Mark's Gospel. For recent introductions, with bibliographies, Baker 1992; Edwards 1994; and on interference, Schmidt 1989.

29 For the emergence of a reduced form of Greek in the modern world, see Tamis 1990.

30 See pp. 43, 69, 82.

31 See pp. 57–9.

32 Cf. pp. 59–61.

33 See pp. 42–51, esp. 44–5.

34 For detailed discussion of the meaning and usage of *aposunagōgos*, see Chapter 6; and on the Paraclete, see pp. 151–4.

35 See further pp. 33–6.

36 For more detailed discussion, see pp. 44–5, 96.

6 BANNED FROM JEWISH MEETINGS

1 See esp. Hengel 1971; Kraabel 1979; Cohen 1987; Levine 1987; Kee 1990; Sanders 1992: 198ff.; Noy 1992; Oster 1993; Kee 1994; McKay 1994; Kee 1995.

2 On Sardis, Hanfmann 1983: esp. 168–90; Trebilco 1991: 37–54.

3 For the Second Temple period, Oster 1993: 186; Kee 1995: 486; later, Levine 1987: 13; Wexler 1981b.

4 Such usage may lie behind the fact that the fourth Gospel does not use the related term *proseuchomai*, the ordinary verb for 'to pray': see pp. 82,84.

5 Cf. pp. 136–8, with bibliography.

6 See pp. 57–9.

7 Cf. Casey 1991a: 41–4; and above pp. 57–9.

8 Similar remarks apply if we follow the reading 'Son of God', which is less well attested in early manuscripts.

9 Cf. pp. 59–61.

10 See pp. 57–9.

11 See pp. 111-27.

12 For full discussion, Horbury 1982. For the text, Evans 1995: 277–83.

13 Forkman 1972; Schäfer 1978; Townsend 1979; Finkel 1981; Kimelman 1981; Horbury 1982; Katz 1984; Schiffman 1985: Chapter 5; Horbury 1985; Robinson 1985: 72–81; Thornton 1987; Manns 1991: 470–509; Davies 1992: 294–301; Joubert 1993; Van der Horst 1994.

14 See pp. 111–27.

7 THE JOHANNINE COMMUNITY

1 See pp. 182–7.

2 Cf. further pp. 127–32.

3 Dunn's comments on this are uncomprehending, and made without reference to the primary sources and secondary literature to Jewish identity: 'At what point an "assimilating Jew" becomes a "former Jew" (= a Gentile?) is not clear. How can an ethnic Jew become a "former Jew"?' (Dunn 1994: 443). There is no 'point', because perceptions vary. For example, people with a racialist view of identity believe that ethnicity is purely a matter of descent, so do not believe that people can cease to be Jewish. If however people who are not observant self-identify as 'Roman', 'British' or whatever, and not as Jewish, they may pass as Gentile in everyone's eyes, however Jewish they once were in ethnicity and behaviour. There is a perception, widespread and vigorously contested, that Jews who become Christians cease to be Jewish. Personally, I accept people's self-identification whenever this is reasonable. As analysts, we should catalogue perceptions and explain them, a process which requires proper familiarity with primary sources and secondary literature. Cf. Sklare 1971: 40:

> Assimilation is sociological death in the sense that the individual is lost to the group. However, sociological death is much more ambiguous than physical death; it is difficult to determine the point at which an individual has assimilated. Thus it is easier to count births, deaths and migration than it is to measure and evaluate intermarriage, conversion, apostasy and assimilation.

4 Cf. esp. Meeks 1975; Lowe 1976; Townsend 1979; Von Wahlde 1982; Culpepper 1983: 125–32; Leibig 1983; Ashton 1985; Freyne 1985; Tomson 1986; Smith 1990; Dunn 1991: Chapter 8, esp. 143–6, 156–60; Culpepper 1992; Dunn 1992: esp. 195–203; De Jonge 1993; Ashton 1994: 36–70.

5 For discussion of the discourse, see pp. 42–51.

6 Lowe shows some awareness of this at p. 108, n. 22.

7 Lowe effectively does not face this problem, cf. Lowe 1976: 120–1; 122, n. 67. On John 6, see pp. 42–51.

8 Lowe offers no proper discussion of this. Cf. Lowe 1976: 117–18, n. 54; 129.

9 Cf. pp. 44–5; and on the eucharistic discourse in general, pp. 00–00.

10 See pp. 54–5. Cf. Lieu 1988; Painter 1991: Chapter 8; Lee 1994: Chapter 6.

11 Von Wahlde 1982: 43–4; see pp. 43–5.

12 Since there is not a single ancient Jewish source in which the term 'Jew' is rejected, the source of the notion that Jews rejected the term 'Jew' is to be sought in the environment of K.G. Kuhn, who was working for the *Reichsinstitut für Geschichte des neuen Deutschlands* set up by the Nazis when his article (Kuhn 1938) was originally published. This illustrates how careful New Testament scholars should be with some of their standard reference works. This matter must be pursued further elsewhere.

13 Cf. pp. 81–3.
14 See Chapter 4, esp. pp. 63–4.
15 On this, and on the unity of the whole of Jn 3, Rensberger 1988: 52–70. Cf. Lee 1994: Chapter 2.
16 Cf. pp. 43–6.
17 Cf. pp. 98, 101–2.
18 On the historicity of Jn 3.22–4.2, see pp. 75–8.
19 See pp. 42–51.
20 On the structural problems of the end of this discourse, see pp. 77–8.
21 See p. 127.
22 Cf. pp. 32, 53.
23 See pp. 42–51.
24 See pp. 20, 71.
25 On the Cleansing of the Temple, see pp. 4–14.
26 See pp. 42–5.
27 See pp. 71, 134.
28 See pp. 154–77.
29 Cf. Miltner 1958; Johnson 1975; Oster 1976; Knibbe and Alzinger 1980; Trudinger 1988; Mussies 1990; Oster 1990; Rogers 1991; Schnackenburg 1991; Horsley 1992.
30 See pp. 87–97.
31 See pp. 87–97.

8 AUTHORSHIP AND PSEUDEPIGRAPHY

1 In general, cf. Hengel 1972; Metzger 1972; Smith 1972; Childs 1979; Gruenwald 1979; Van Seters 1983; Meade 1986; Hall 1991.
2 For recent theories of the composition of this part of the bible, cf. Nelson 1981; Van Seters 1983: Chapters 8–10; Cohn 1985; Halpern 1988; Van Seters 1990; McKenzie 1991.
3 Cf. Willi 1972; Welten 1973; Japhet 1985; McKenzie 1985; Duke 1990; Sugimoto 1990, 1992.
4 Cf. e.g. Myers 1965: xlix–lxiii.
5 In addition to the commentators, cf. Newsome 1975; Williamson 1977; Braun 1979; Throntveit 1982; Talshir 1988; Japhet 1991.
6 Cf. Jones 1955; Eaton 1959; Hanson 1975: 32–208; Vermeylen 1977–8; Rendtorff 1984; Clements 1985; Meade 1986: Chapter 2; Seitz 1991; Gosse 1992; Carr 1993; Clifford 1993; Konkel 1993.
7 Cf. e.g. Thiel 1981; Tov 1985; Peckham 1986; Holt 1989; Redditt 1989; Seitz 1989; Snyman 1989; Pohlmann 1991; Prinsloo 1992; Watts 1992; Nogalski 1993a, b; Schaefer 1993; Williams 1993; Coggins 1994.
8 Cf. Preuß 1959; Holm-Nielsen 1960; Childs 1979: 504–25; Slomovic 1979; Wilson 1985a, b; Wachholder 1988; Brueggemann 1991; Smith 1991.
9 Cf. Blenkinsopp 1974; Van Unnik 1978; Rajak 1983; Varneda 1986; Cohen 1988; Eckstein 1990; Hall 1991: 24–30.
10 These cannot be discussed in a book of this kind.
11 Cf. pp. 146, 171, 173.
12 See pp. 232, n. 3.
13 Brown 1970: App. 5 is an especially helpful display of the main points of the evidence. Cf. further Brown 1966b; Johnston 1970; De la Potterie 1977: 329–466; Boring 1978; Grayston 1981; Franck 1985; Burge 1987; Hall 1991: Chapter 13; Manns 1991: 339–81; Painter 1991: Chapter 12; Draper 1992.
14 See pp. 9–10.

15 See p. 107.
16 See pp. 81–3.
17 Cf. further pp. 194–6.
18 Cf. pp. 86, 115–16.
19 See p. 148.
20 Cf. pp. 81–4.
21 See pp. 42–51.
22 See pp. 63–7, 69–70.
23 See pp. 42–51.
24 Cf. pp. 8–14.
25 See pp. 208–9.
26 On the problems of this narrative, see pp. 55–6, 208–9.
27 See pp. 68–70.
28 Cf. pp. 74–5.
29 In addition to the commentators, cf. Hanson 1991: 213–34; Schuchard 1992: 133–40.
30 See pp. 20, 24–5, 134.
31 See pp. 196–7.
32 Cf. Johnson 1966; Lorenzen 1971; Minear 1977; De Jonge 1979; Gunther 1981; Eller 1987; Bonsack 1988; Kügler 1988; Ruckstuhl 1988: 355–95; Quast 1989; Davies 1992: 340f.; Goulder 1992; Bauckham 1993b; Culpepper 1994: Chapter 3.
33 For detailed discussion of these inaccuracies, see pp. 181–7.
34 For discussion of Chapters 19–20, see Chapter 9.
35 See pp. 191–7.
36 For discussion of the main aspects of this story, see pp. 192–3.
37 See pp. 81–3.
38 See pp. 127–30.
39 Cf. further pp. 182, 190–1.
40 Cf. Morris 1969: 139–292; Gunther 1980; Robinson 1985: 93–122; Hengel 1989; Davies 1992: 242–55; Hengel 1993; Bauckham 1993a, b; Culpepper 1994: Chapters 5–7.
41 The sources are collected and translated by Heine 1989, with bibliography. Cf. further Heine 1987; Trevett 1989; Williams 1989; Culpepper 1994: 120–2.
42 The early date often given for this work is dubious, and partly surviving texts are hardly stable. For a sober account, Culpepper 1994: 187–205.
43 See pp. 88–94, 217–28.
44 See pp. 74–5, 33-9, 60.
45 See pp. 31–2, 38, 55, 135–6.
46 Cf. pp. 107, 235.
47 See pp. 185–7, 208–9.
48 See pp. 18–19, 21–4, 183–7.
49 Cf. pp. 33–9, 59–61, 81–3, 111–39.
50 See pp. 55–6, 208–10.
51 Cf. pp. 18–25, 27, 52, 111–27.
52 See pp. 55–6, 208–10.
53 See pp. 42–51.
54 See pp. 18–21.
55 See pp. 164–70.
56 Cf. pp. 75–7.

9 CRUCIFIED UNDER PONTIUS PILATE, ON THE THIRD DAY HE ROSE AGAIN FROM THE DEAD

1 See pp. 18–25.
2 In addition to the commentators, Brown 1994, with comprehensive bibliography.
3 For attempts to determine the relationship of this account to synoptic material, using similar methods to obtain different results, cf. e.g. Dauer 1972; Sabbe 1977. For a recent attempt to separate John's source from his redactional work, Fortna 1988: esp. 149ff. For a Forschungsberichte of the relationship between the fourth Gospel and the synoptics, Smith 1992.
4 See pp. 14–25.
5 See pp. 159–64.
6 See pp. 14–18.
7 See pp. 111–27.
8 This opinion cannot be justified here. Cf. pp. 8, 12, 229.
9 See pp. 14–25.
10 In addition to the commentators, cf. Sherwin-White 1963: 1–47; Burkill 1970; Bammel 1974; Lémenon 1981; Millar 1990; Brown 1994: I, esp. 363–72.
11 See pp. 16–18, 59.
12 See pp. 4–8; Casey (forthcoming).
13 See pp. 81–3, 127–30.
14 See pp. 84–7.
15 For more detailed discussion, see pp. 33–6.
16 See pp. 14–25.
17 See pp. 41–2.
18 For further discussion, summarised here, see p. 160.
19 See pp. 159–64.
20 See pp. 9–10. Cf. Hanson 1991: 211–14; Brawley 1993.
21 Cf. pp. 20, 24–5, 134, 186.
22 Cf. pp. 42–51, 75–7, 128–32, 158.
23 See pp. 189.
24 See pp. 159–64.
25 See pp. 60–1.
26 Cf. pp. 73–4, 82–4.
27 The word 'hands' includes the wrists, through which the nails would be driven if used. On such details, Brown 1994: II, 885–7, 945–52, with bibliography.

10 THE 'PRIORITY' OF JOHN

1 See pp. 24–5, 28, 36–9, 51, 66–7, 109–10, 112–13.
2 See pp. 31–2, 38, 41–2, 55, 78, 83–4, 135–6.
3 See Chapter 8.
4 See pp. 18–25.
5 See pp. 18–25. Cf. further Robinson 1985: 89, end of n. 233, 148, and much earlier Brooke 1909: 302.
6 Not new! Brown 1966a: 149 cites Westcott in 1880, among others.
7 For further discussion of Robinson's treatment of Jesus' Sonship, see pp. 36–9.
8 See pp. 39–40, 67–8, 73.
9 See pp. 71–5.
10 Cf. pp. 66, 71–8.
11 Cf. pp. 57–9.

12 Cf. pp. 36–9, 210.
13 Cf. pp. 68–9, 95.
14 Cf. e.g. Lightfoot 1893: 24–6, 151–3, catalogued by Robinson 1985: 203 with n. 33, as 'earlier, as one discovers so often': true, and consequently not a 'new look'.
15 See pp. 55–7.
16 Cf. pp. 151–2.
17 Cf. pp. 192–3.
18 For detailed discussion, cf. recently Sabbe 1992.
19 See pp. 39–40.
20 See pp. 36–9.
21 See pp. 31–2, 135.
22 See pp. 111–27, 205.
23 See pp. 94–7.
24 See pp. 84–7.
25 Cf. pp. 81–4.

11 WHAT IS TRUTH?

1 See pp. 34–5, 127–31.
2 Cf. pp. 8, 111–27.
3 See pp. 98–110.
4 See pp. 116–27.
5 See pp. 34–6, 127–36.

BIBLIOGRAPHY

Abbott, E.A. (1905) *Johannine Vocabulary*, London: Black.

Arnold, C.E. (1989) *Ephesians: Power and Magic* (MSSNTS 63), Cambridge: Cambridge University Press.

Ashton, J. (1985) 'The Identity and Function of the 'Ιουδαῖοι in the Fourth Gospel', *NT* 27: 40–75.

—— (1991) *Understanding the Fourth Gospel*, Oxford: Clarendon.

—— (1994) *Studying John: Approaches to the Fourth Gospel*, Oxford: Clarendon.

Askwith, E.H. (1910) *The Historical Value of the Fourth Gospel*, London: Hodder & Stoughton.

Backhaus, K. (1991) *Die 'Jüngerkreise' des Taüfers Johannes: Eine Studie zu den religionsgeschichtlichen Ursprüngen des Christentums*, Paderborn/Munich: Schöningh.

Baker, M. (1992) *In Other Words: A Coursebook on Translation*, London: Routledge.

Bammel, E. (1974) 'Die Blutsgerichtsbarkeit in der römischen Provinz Judäa vor dem ersten jüdischen Aufstand', *JJS* 25: 35–49.

Barr, J. (1988) '"Abba isn't "Daddy"'', *JThS NS* 39: 28–47.

Barrett, C.K. (1967) *Jesus and the Gospel Tradition*, London: SPCK.

—— (1978) *The Gospel According to St. John: An Introduction with Commentary and Notes on the Greek Text* (2nd edn), London: SPCK.

—— (1982) *Essays on John*, London: SPCK.

Bauckham, R. (1993a) 'Papias and Polycrates on the Origin of the Fourth Gospel', *JThS NS* 44: 24–69.

—— (1993b) 'The Beloved Disciple as Ideal Author', *JSNT* 49: 21–44.

Beasley-Murray, G.R. (1962) *Baptism in the New Testament*, London: Macmillan.

—— (1987) *John* (WBC 36), Milton Keynes: Word (UK).

Becker, J. (1982) 'Aus der Literatur zum Johannesevangelium (1978–1980)', *ThR NF* 47: 279–301, 305–47.

—— (1986) 'Das Johannesevangelium im Streit der Methoden (1980–1984)', *ThR NF* 51: 1–78.

Beetham, F.G. and Beetham, P.A. (1993) 'A Note on John 19:29', *JThS NS* 44: 163–9.

Bérard, F. (1991) 'Tacite et les Inscriptions', *ANRW* II.33.4: 3007–50.

Bernard, J.H. (1928) *A Critical and Exegetical Commentary on the Gospel According to St. John* (ICC, 2 vols), Edinburgh: T. & T. Clark.

Black, M. (1967) *An Aramaic Approach to the Gospels and Acts* (3rd edn), Oxford: Clarendon.

—— (1985) *The Book of Enoch or 1 Enoch* (SVTP 7), Leiden: Brill.

Blenkinsopp, J. (1974) 'Prophecy and Priesthood in Josephus', *JJS* 25: 239–62.

Blomberg, C.L. (1987) *The Historical Reliability of the Gospels*, Leicester: IVP.

Boismard, M.E. (1988) *Moses or Jesus: An Essay in Johannine Christology* (ET 1993), Minneapolis/Leuven: Fortress/Peeters.

Bonsack, B. (1988) 'Der Presbyteros des dritten Briefs und der geliebte Jünger des Evangeliums nach Johannes', *ZNW* 79: 45–62.

Bonsirven, J. (1949) 'Les aramaïsmes de S. Jean l'Evangéliste', *Bib* 30: 405–32.

Borgen, P. (1965) *Bread from Heaven* (NT.S 10), Leiden: Brill.

—— (1968) 'God's Agent in the Fourth Gospel', in J. Neusner (ed.), *Religions in Antiquity: Essays in Memory of E.R. Goodenough* (SHR 14), Leiden: Brill: 137–48.

—— (1977) 'Some Jewish Exegetical Traditions as Background for Son of Man Sayings in John's Gospel (Jn 3.13–14 and Context)', in De Jonge 1977b: 243–58.

Boring, M.E. (1978) 'The Influence of Christian Prophecy on the Johannine Portrayal of the Paraclete and Jesus', *NTS* 25: 113–23.

Bornkamm, G. (1956) 'Die eucharistische Rede im Johannes-Evangelium', *ZNW* 47: 161–9.

Braun, R.L. (1979) 'Chronicles, Ezra and Nehemiah: Theology and Literary History', in J.A. Emerton (ed.), *Studies in the Historical Books of the Old Testament, VT.S* 30: 52–64.

Brawley, R.L. (1993) 'An Absent Complement and Intertextuality in John 19:28–29', *JBL* 112: 427–43.

Breisach, E. (1983) *Historiography: Ancient, Medieval and Modern*, Chicago: University of Chicago Press.

Brixhe, N. (forthcoming) 'Panorama linguistique de l'Asie Mineure au début de notre ère: Le grec et les quelques langues indigènes documentées', *ANRW* II.29.3.

Brodie, T.L. (1993a) *The Gospel According to John: A Literary and Theological Commentary*, Oxford: Oxford University Press.

—— (1993b) *The Quest for the Origin of John's Gospel: A Source-oriented Approach*, New York/Oxford: Oxford University Press.

Brooke, A.E. (1909) 'The Historical Value of the Fourth Gospel', in H.B. Swete (ed.), *Essays on Some Biblical Questions of the Day, by Members of the University of Cambridge*, London: Macmillan: 289–328.

Brooke, G.J. (ed.) (1989) *Temple Scroll Studies* (JSP.SS 7), Sheffield: JSOT Press.

Brown, R.E. (1966a) *The Gospel According to John*, vol. 1 (AB 29), London/New York: Chapman/Doubleday.

—— (1966b) 'The Paraclete in the Fourth Gospel', *NTS* 13: 113–32.

—— (1970) *The Gospel According to John*, vol. 2 (AB 29), London/New York: Chapman/Doubleday.

—— (1979) *The Community of the Beloved Disciple: The Life, Loves and Hates of an Individual Church in New Testament Times*, New York/Toronto: Paulist.

—— (1982) *The Epistles of John* (AB 30), London: Chapman.

—— (1994) *The Death of the Messiah: From Gethsemane to the Grave: A Commentary on the Passion Narratives in the Gospels* (ABRL, 2 vols), London/New York: Chapman/Doubleday.

Brueggemann, W. (1991) 'Bounded by Obedience and Praise: The Psalms as Canon', *JSOT* 50: 63–92.

Bubenik, V. (1989) *Hellenistic and Roman Greece as a Sociolinguistic Area*, Amsterdam: Benjamins.

Bühner, J.-A. (1977) *Der Gesandte und sein Weg im 4 Evangelium: Die kultur- und religionsgeschichtlichen Grundlagen der johanneischen Sendungschristologie sowie ihre traditionsgeschichtliche Entwicklung* (WUNT 2; 2), Tübingen: Mohr (Siebeck).

Bultmann, R. (1941) *The Gospel of John: A Commentary* (ET 1971), Oxford: Blackwell.

Burge, G.M. (1987) *The Anointed Community: The Holy Spirit in the Johannine Tradition*, Grand Rapids: Eerdmans.

241

Burkett, D. (1991) *The Son of the Man in the Gospel of John* (JSNT.SS 56), Sheffield: JSOT Press.

—— (1994) 'Two Accounts of Lazarus' Resurrection in John 11', *NT* 36: 209–32.

Burkill, T.A. (1970) 'The Condemnation of Jesus: A Critique of Sherwin-White's Thesis', *NT* 12: 321–42.

Burney, C.F. (1922) *The Aramaic Origin of the Fourth Gospel*, Oxford: Clarendon.

—— (1925) *The Poetry of Our Lord*, Oxford: Clarendon.

Burridge, R.A. (1992) *What are the Gospels? A Comparison with Graeco-Roman Biography* (MSSNTS 70), Cambridge: Cambridge University Press.

Callaway, P.R. (1989) 'Extending Divine Revelation: Micro-compositional Strategies in the Temple Scroll', in Brooke 1989: 149–62.

Cantwell Smith, W. (1993) *What Is Scripture? A Comparative Approach*, London: SCM.

Caquot, A. (1972) 'La Double Investiture de Lévi (Brèves remarques sur Testament de Lévi, VIII)', *SHR* 21: 156–61.

Carr, D. (1993) 'Reaching for Unity in Isaiah', *JSOT* 57: 61–80.

Carson, D.A. (1991) *The Gospel According to John*, Leicester/Grand Rapids: IVP/Eerdmans.

Casey, P.M. (1976) 'The Use of the Term "Son of Man" in the Similitudes of Enoch', *JSJ* 7: 11–29.

—— (1980) *Son of Man: The Interpretation and Influence of Daniel 7*, London: SPCK.

—— (1985) 'The Jackals and the Son of Man (Matt. 8.20//Luke 9.58)', *JSNT* 23: 3–22.

—— (1987) 'General, Generic and Indefinite: the Use of the Term "Son of Man" in Aramaic Sources and in the Teaching of Jesus', *JSNT* 29: 21–56.

—— (1991a) *From Jewish Prophet to Gentile God: The Origins and Development of New Testament Christology* (The Cadbury Lectures at the University of Birmingham, 1985–6), Cambridge/Louisville: James Clarke/Westminster/John Knox.

—— (1991b) 'Method in our Madness, and Madness in their Methods: Some Approaches to the Son of Man Problem in Recent Scholarship', *JSNT* 42: 17–43.

—— (1994a) 'The Deification of Jesus', in E.H. Lovering, Jr (ed.), *Society of Biblical Literature 1994 Seminar Papers*, Atlanta: Scholars: 697–714.

—— (1994b) 'The Use of the Term *bar (ᵉ)nash(ā)* in the Aramaic Translations of the Hebrew Bible', *JSNT* 54: 87–118.

—— (1995) 'Idiom and Translation: Some Aspects of the Son of Man Problem', *NTS* 41: 164–82.

—— (forthcoming) 'Culture and Historicity: the Cleansing of the Temple', *CBQ*.

Charlesworth, J.H. (ed.) (1990) *Jews and Christians: Exploring the Past, Present and Future*, New York: Crossroad.

Childs, B.S. (1979) *Introduction to the Old Testament as Scripture*, London: SCM.

Clements, R.E. (1985) 'Beyond Tradition-History: Deutero-Isaianic Development of First Isaiah's Themes', *JSOT* 31: 95–113.

Clifford, R.J. (1993) 'The Unity of the Book of Isaiah and its Cosmogonic Language', *CBQ* 55: 1–17.

Coakley, J.F. (1988) 'The Anointing at Bethany and the Priority of John', *JBL* 107: 241–56.

Coggins, R.J. (1994) 'The Minor Prophets – One Book or Twelve?', in S.E. Porter, P. Joyce and D.E. Orton (eds), *Crossing the Boundaries: Essays in Biblical Interpretation in Honour of Michael D. Goulder*, Leiden: Brill: 57–68.

Cohen, S.J.D. (1984) 'The Significance of Yavneh: Pharisees, Rabbis and the End of Jewish Sectarianism', *HUCA* 55: 27–53.

—— (1987) 'Pagan and Christian Evidence on the Ancient Synagogue', in Levine 1987: 159–81.

—— (1988) 'History and Historiography in the Against Apion of Josephus', in A. Rapaport-Albert (ed.), *Essays in Jewish Historiography* (*History and Theory* Beiheft 27): 1–11.

Cohn, R.L. (1985) 'Literary Technique in the Jeroboam Narrative', *ZAW* 97: 23–35.

Collins, A.Y. (1986) 'Vilification and Self-definition in the Book of Revelation', *HThR* 79: 308–20.

Colwell, E.C. (1931) *The Greek of the Fourth Gospel: A Study of its Aramaisms in the Light of Hellenistic Greek*, Chicago: University of Chicago Press.

Cosgrove, C.H. (1989) 'The Place where Jesus is: Allusions to Baptism and the Eucharist in the Fourth Gospel', *NTS* 35: 522–39.

Craig, W.L. (1989) *Assessing the New Testament Evidence for the Historicity of the Resurrection of Jesus*, Lampeter/New York: Mellen.

Crossan, J.D. (1991) *The Historical Jesus: The Life of a Mediterranean Jewish Peasant*, Edinburgh: T. & T. Clark.

Culpepper, R.A. (1983) *Anatomy of the Fourth Gospel: A Study in Literary Design*, Philadelphia: Fortress.

—— (1992) 'The Gospel of John as a Threat to Jewish–Christian Relations', in J.H. Charlesworth (ed.), *Overcoming Fear Between Jews and Christians*, New York: Crossroad: 21–43.

—— (1994) *John, the Son of Zebedee: The Life of a Legend*, Columbia: University of South Carolina Press.

D'Angelo, M.R. (1992), '*Abba* and "Father": Imperial Theology and the Jesus Traditions', *JBL* 111: 611–30.

Dauer, A. (1972) *Die Passionsgeschichte im Johannesevangelium: Eine traditions-geschichtliche und theologische Untersuchung zu Joh 18, 1–19, 30* (StANT 30), Munich: Kosel.

Davey, J.E. (1958) *The Jesus of St. John*, London: Lutterworth.

Davies, M. (1992) *Rhetoric and Reference in the Fourth Gospel* (JSNT.SS 69), Sheffield: JSOT Press.

De Jonge, M. (1966) 'The Use of the Word "Anointed" in the Time of Jesus', *NT* 8: 132–48.

—— (1977a) *Jesus: Stranger from Heaven and Son of God: Jesus Christ and the Christians in Johannine Perspective*, Missoula: Scholars.

—— (ed.) (1977b) *L'Evangile de Jean: Sources, rédaction, théologie* (BEThL 44), Gembloux/Leuven: Duculot/Leuven University Press.

—— (1979) 'The Beloved Disciple and the Date of the Gospel of John', in E. Best and R.McL. Wilson (eds), *Text and Interpretation: Studies in the New Testament Presented to Matthew Black*, Cambridge: Cambridge University Press: 99–114.

—— (1986) 'The Earliest Christian Use of *Christos*: Some Suggestions', *NTS* 32: 321–43.

—— (1988) *Christology in Context: The Earliest Christian Response to Jesus*, Philadelphia: Westminster.

—— (1993) 'The Conflict between Jesus and the Jews and the Radical Christology of the Fourth Gospel', *Perspectives in Religious Studies* 20: 341–55.

De la Potterie, I. (1977) *La Vérité dans Saint Jean* I (Anbib 73), Rome: Pontifical Biblical Institute.

De Moor, J.C. and Van Staalduine-Sulman, E. (1993) 'The Aramaic Song of the Lamb', *JSJ* 24: 266–79.

Denniston, J.D. (1954) *The Greek Particles* (2nd edn), Oxford: Clarendon.

Derrett, J.D.M. (1982) *The Anastasis: The Resurrection of Jesus as an Historical Event*, Shipston-on-Stour: Drinkwater.

Dodd, C.H. (1937) 'The First Epistle of John and the Fourth Gospel' *BJRL* 21: 129–56.

—— (1953) *The Interpretation of the Fourth Gospel*, Cambridge: Cambridge University Press.

—— (1963) *Historical Tradition in the Fourth Gospel*, Cambridge: Cambridge University Press.

Dowell, T.M. (1990), 'Jews and Christians in Conflict: Why the Fourth Gospel Changed the Synoptic Tradition', *Louvain Studies* 15: 19–37.

Draper, J.A. (1992) 'The Sociological Function of the Spirit/Paraclete in the Farewell Discourses in the Fourth Gospel', *Neotestamentica* 26: 13–29.

Duke, P.D. (1985) *Irony in the Fourth Gospel*, Atlanta: Knox.

Duke, R.K. (1990) *The Persuasive Appeal of the Chronicler* (JSOT.SS 88), Sheffield: JSOT Press.

Dunn, J.D.G. (1970–1) 'John vi – A Eucharistic Discourse?', *NTS* 17: 328–38.

—— (1980) *Christology in the Making*, London: SCM.

—— (1983) 'Let John be John', in P. Stuhlmacher (ed.), *Das Evangelium und die Evangelien* (WUNT 28), Tübingen: Mohr (Siebeck): 309–39.

—— (1991) *The Partings of the Ways Between Christianity and Judaism and their Significance for the Character of Christianity*, London: SCM.

—— (1992) 'The Question of Anti-Semitism in the New Testament Writings of the Period', in J.D.G. Dunn (ed.), *Jews and Christians: The Parting of the Ways A.D. 70 to 135* (WUNT 66), Tübingen: Mohr (Siebeck): 177–211.

—— (1994) 'The Making of Christology – Evolution or Unfolding?', in Green and Turner 1994: 437–52.

Du Toit, A.B. (ed.) (1968) *The Christ of John: Essays on the Christology of the Fourth Gospel* (*Neotestamentica 2*).

Eaton, J.H. (1959) 'The Origin of the Book of Isaiah', *VT* 9: 138–57.

Eckstein, A.M. (1990) 'Josephus and Polybius: A Reconsideration', *Classical Antiquity* 9: 175–208.

Edwards, J. (1994) *Multilingualism*, London/New York: Routledge.

Edwards, R.B. (1988), 'Χάριν ἀντὶ χάριτος (John 1.16): Grace and Law in the Johannine Prologue', *JSNT* 32: 3–15.

—— (1994) 'The Christological Basis of the Johannine Footwashing', in Green and Turner 1994: 367–83.

Eller, V. (1987) *The Beloved Disciple*, Grand Rapids: Eerdmans.

Endres, J.C. (1987) *Biblical Interpretation in the Book of Jubilees* (CBQ.MS 18), Washington, DC: Catholic Biblical Association of America.

Ernst, J. (1989) *Johannes der Taüfer: Interpretation-Geschichte-Wirkungsgeschichte* (BZNW 53), Berlin: De Gruyter.

Evans, C.A. (1993) *Word and Glory: On the Exegetical and Theological Background of John's Prologue* (JSNT.SS 89), Sheffield: JSOT Press.

—— (1995) *Jesus and His Contemporaries*, Leiden: Brill.

Evans, C.F. (1970) *Resurrection and the New Testament* (SBT 2nd Ser. 12), London: SCM.

Fennema, D.A. (1985) 'John 1.18: "God the Only Son"', *NTS* 31: 124–35.

Finkel, A. (1981) 'Yavneh's Liturgy and Early Christianity', *JES* 18: 231–50.

Fishman, J.A. (ed.) (1981) *The Sociology of Jewish Languages* (*IJSL* 30).

—— (ed.) (1985) *Readings in the Sociology of Jewish Languages*, Leiden: Brill.

—— (ed.) (1987) *The Sociology of Jewish Languages* (*IJSL* 67).

Forkman, G. (1972) *The Limits of the Religious Community: Expulsion from the Religious Community within the Qumran Sect, within Rabbinic Judaism, and within Primitive Christianity* (CB.NT 5), Lund: Gleerup.

Fortna, R.T. (1970) *The Gospel of Signs: A Reconstruction of the Narrative Source Underlying the Fourth Gospel* (MSSNTS 11), Cambridge: Cambridge University Press.

—— (1988) *The Fourth Gospel and its Predecessor*, Edinburgh: T. & T. Clark.

Fortna, R.T. and Gaventa, B.R. (eds) (1990) *The Conversation Continues: Studies in Paul and John in Honor of J. Louis Martyn*, Nashville: Abingdon.

France, R.T. (1994), 'Jesus the Baptist?', in Green and Turner 1994: 94–111.

Franck, E. (1985) *Revelation Taught: The Paraclete in the Gospel of John* (CB.NT 14), Lund: Gleerup.

Freed, E.D. (1965) *Old Testament Quotations in the Gospel of John* (NT.S XI), Leiden: Brill.

—— (1967) 'The Son of Man in the Fourth Gospel', *JBL* 86: 402–9.

Freed, E.D. and Hunt, R.B. (1975) 'Fortna's Signs-source in John', *JBL* 94: 563–79.

Freyne, S. (1985), 'Vilifying the Other and Defining the Self: Matthew's and John's Anti-Jewish Polemic in Focus', in J. Neusner and E.S. Frerichs (eds), *'To See Ourselves as Others See Us': Christians, Jews, 'Others' in Late Antiquity*, Chico: Scholars: 117–43.

Fuller, R.H. (1971) *The Formation of the Resurrection Narratives*, New York: Macmillan (British publication: London: SPCK, 1972).

Geldenhuys, N. (1951) *Commentary on the Gospel of Luke* (NIC), Grand Rapids: Eerdmans.

Gosse, B. (1992) 'Isaïe 1 dans la rédaction du livre d'Isaïe', *ZAW* 104: 52–66.

Goulder, M.D. (1992) 'An Old Friend Incognito', *SJTh* 45: 487–513.

Graß, H. (1956) *Ostergeschehen und Osterberichte* (4th edn 1970), Göttingen: Vandenhoeck & Ruprecht.

Grayston, K. (1981) 'The Meaning of PARAKLETOS', *JSNT* 13: 67–82.

Green, J.B. and Turner, M. (eds) (1994) *Jesus of Nazareth: Lord and Christ, in Honour of Prof. I.H. Marshall*, Grand Rapids/Exeter: Eerdmans/Paternoster.

Gruenwald, I. (1979) 'Jewish Apocalyptic Literature', *ANRW* II.19.1: 89–118.

Gunther, J.J. (1980) 'Early Identifications of Authorship of the Johannine Writings', *JEH* 31: 407–27.

—— (1981) 'The Relation of the Beloved Disciple to the Twelve', *ThZ* 37: 129–48.

Hall, R.G. (1991) *Revealed Histories: Techniques for Ancient Jewish and Christian Historiography* (JSP.SS 6), Sheffield: JSOT Press.

Halpern, B. (1988) *The First Historians: The Hebrew Bible and History*, San Francisco: Harper & Row.

Hanfmann, G.M.A., *et al.* (1983) *SARDIS from Prehistoric to Roman Times*, Cambridge, Mass.: Harvard University Press.

Hanson, A.T. (1991) *The Prophetic Gospel: A Study of John and the Old Testament*, Edinburgh: T. & T. Clark.

Hanson, P.D. (1975) *The Dawn of Apocalyptic*, Philadelphia: Fortress.

Hare, D.R.A. (1990) *The Son of Man Tradition*, Minneapolis: Fortress.

Hartin, P.J. (1985) 'A Community in Crisis: The Christology of the Johannine Community as the Point at Issue', *Neotestamentica* 19: 37–49.

Hartman, L. (1987) 'Johannine Jesus-belief and Monotheism', in L. Hartman and B. Olsson (eds), *Aspects on the Johannine Literature* (CB.NT 18), Uppsala: Almquist & Wiksell.

Headlam, A.C. (1948) *The Fourth Gospel as History*, Oxford: Blackwell.

Heekerens, H.-P. (1984) *Die Zeichen-Quelle der johanneischen Redaktion: Ein Beitrag zur Entstehungsgeschichte des vierten Evangeliums* (SBS 113), Stuttgart: Katholisches Bibelwerk.

Heine, R.E. (1987) 'The Role of the Gospel of John in the Montanist Controversy', *Second Century* 6: 1–19.

—— (1989) *The Montanist Oracles and Testimonia*, Macon: Mercer University Press.

Hengel, M. (1971) 'Proseuche und Synagoge: Jüdische Gemeinde, Gotteshaus und Gottesdienst in der Diaspora und in Palästina', in G. Jeremias, H.-W. Kuhn and H. Stegemann (eds), *Tradition und Glaube: Festgabe für K.G. Kuhn*, Göttingen: Vandenhoeck & Ruprecht: 157–84.

—— (1972) 'Anonymität, Pseudepigraphie und "Literarische Fälschung" in der jüdisch-hellenistischen Literatur', in Von Fritz 1972: 229–308, with discussion 309–29.

—— (1989) *The Johannine Question*, London/Philadelphia: SCM/Trinity.

—— (1993) *Die johanneische Frage* (WUNT 67), Tübingen: Mohr (Siebeck).

Higgins, A.J.B. (1960) *The Historicity of the Fourth Gospel*, London: Lutterworth.

Hillerbrand, H.J., *et al.* (1990) 'Martin Luther and the Jews', in Charlesworth 1990: 127–50.

Hollenbach, P.W. (1982) 'The Conversion of Jesus: From Jesus the Baptizer to Jesus the Healer', *ANRW* II.25.1: 196–219.

Hollis, H. (1989) 'The Root of the Johannine Pun – ΥΨΩΘΗΝΑΙ', *NTS* 35: 475–8.

Holm-Nielsen, S. (1960) 'The Importance of Late Jewish Psalmody for the Understanding of Old Testament Psalmodic Tradition', *StTh* 14: 1–53.

Holt, E.K. (1989) 'The Chicken and the Egg – Or: Was Jeremiah a Member of the Deuteronomist Party?', *JSOT* 44: 109–22.

Horbury, W. (1982) 'The Benediction of the *Minim* and Early Jewish–Christian Controversy', *JThS NS* 33: 19–61.

—— (1985) 'Extirpation and Excommunication', *VT* 35: 13–38.

Horsley, G.H.R. (1989) 'The Fiction of "Jewish Greek"', in G.H.R. Horsley, *New Documents Illustrating Early Christianity*, vol. 5: *Linguistic Essays*, Marrickville: Southwood: 5–40.

—— (1992) 'The Inscriptions of Ephesos and the New Testament', *NT* 34: 105–68.

Horsley, R.A. (1987) *Jesus and the Spiral of Violence: Popular Jewish Resistance in Roman Palestine*, Minneapolis: Fortress.

Horsley, R.A. and Hanson, J.S. (1985) *Bandits, Prophets and Messiahs: Popular Movements in the Time of Jesus*, Minneapolis: Winston.

Howard, W.F. (1955), *The Fourth Gospel in Recent Criticism and Interpretation* (4th edn, rev. C.K. Barrett), London: Epworth.

Hultgren, A.J. (1987) *Christ and His Benefits: Christology and Redemption in the New Testament*, Philadelphia: Fortress.

Hunter, A.M. (1968) *According to John*, London: SCM.

Huzar, E. (1984) 'Claudius – the Erudite Emperor', *ANRW* II.32.1: 611–50.

Japhet, S. (1985) 'The Historical Reliability of Chronicles', *JSOT* 33: 83–107.

—— (1991) 'The Relationship between Chronicles and Ezra-Nehemiah', in J.A. Emerton (ed.), *Congress Volume Leuven 1989* (VT.S 43): 298–313.

Jeremias, J. (1966) *The Eucharistic Words of Jesus* (2nd ET), London: SCM.

Johns, L.L. and Miller, D.B. (1994) 'The Signs as Witnesses in the Fourth Gospel: Reexamining the Evidence', *CBQ* 56: 519–35.

Johnson, L.T. (1989) 'The New Testament's Anti-Jewish Slander and the Conventions of Ancient Polemic', *JBL* 108: 419–41.

Johnson, N.E. (1966) 'The Beloved Disciple and the Fourth Gospel', *CQR* 167: 278–91.

Johnson, S.E. (1975) 'Asia Minor and Early Christianity', in Neusner 1975: pt 2, 77–145.

Johnston, G. (1970) *The Spirit-Paraclete in the Gospel of John* (MSSNTS 12), Cambridge: Cambridge University Press.

Jones, D.R. (1955) 'The Tradition of the Oracles of Isaiah of Jerusalem', *ZAW* 67: 226–46.

Joubert, J. (1993) 'A Bone of Contention in Recent Scholarship: The "Birkat ha-Minim" and the Separation of Church and Synagogue in the First Century A.D.', *Neotestamentica* 27: 351–63.

Kanter, S. (1980) *Rabban Gamaliel II: The Legal Traditions* (Brown Judaic Studies 8), Chico: Scholars.

Käsemann, E. (1966) *The Testament of Jesus: A Study of the Gospel of John in the Light of Chapter 17* (ET 1968), London: SCM.

Katz, S.T. (1984) 'Issues in the Separation of Judaism and Christianity after 70 C.E.: A Reconsideration', *JBL* 103: 43–76.

Kee, H.C. (1990) 'The Transformation of the Synagogue after 70 C.E.: Its Import for Early Christianity', *NTS* 36: 1–24.

—— (1994) 'The Changing Meaning of Synagogue: A Response to Richard Oster', *NTS* 40: 281–3.

—— (1995) 'Defining the First-Century C.E. Synagogue: Problems and Progress', *NTS* 41: 481–500.

Kieffer, R. (1985) 'L'Espace et le temps dans l'évangile de Jean', *NTS* 31: 393–409.

Kimelman, R. (1981) '*Birkat Ha-Minim* and the Lack of Evidence for an Anti-Christian Jewish Prayer in Late Antiquity', in E.P. Sanders (ed.), *Jewish and Christian Self-Definition*, vol. 2, London: SCM: 226–44.

Knibbe, D. and Alzinger, W. (1980) 'Ephesos vom Beginn der römischen Herrschaft in Kleinasien bis zum Ende der Principatszeit', *ANRW* II.7.2: 748–830.

Koester, C.R. (1990) 'John Six and the Lord's Supper', *Lutheran Quarterly* 4: 419–37.

Konkel, A.H. (1993) 'The Sources of the Story of Hezekiah in the Book of Isaiah', *VT* 43: 462–82.

Kraabel, A.T. (1979) 'The Diaspora Synagogue: Archaeological and Epigraphic Evidence since Sukenik', *ANRW* II.19.1: 477–510.

Kremer, J. (1985) *Lazarus: Die Geschichte einer Auferstehung: Text, Wirkungsgeschichte und Botschaft von Joh 11, 1–46*, Stuttgart: Katholisches Bibelwerk.

Kügler, J. (1988) *Der Jünger, den Jesus liebte: Literarische, theologische und historische Untersuchungen zu einer Schlüsselgestalt johanneischer Theologie und Geschichte* (SBB 13), Stuttgart: Katholisches Bibelwerk.

Kuhn, K.G. (1938) '*Israel, Ioudaios, Hebraios* in Jewish Literature after the Old Testament', *TDNT* 3: 359–69.

Kysar, R. (1975) *The Fourth Evangelist and his Gospel: An Examination of Contemporary Scholarship*, Minneapolis: Augsburg.

—— (1985) 'The Fourth Gospel: A Report on Recent Research', *ANRW* II.25.3: 2389–480.

Lee, D.A. (1994) *The Symbolic Narratives of the Fourth Gospel: The Interplay of Form and Meaning* (JSNT.SS 95), Sheffield: JSOT Press.

Leibig, J.E. (1983) 'John and "the Jews": Theological Antisemitism in the Fourth Gospel', *JES* 20: 209–34.

Lémenon, J.-P. (1981) *Pilate et le gouvernement de la Judée* (EB), Paris: Gabalda.

Levine, L.I. (1987), 'The Second Temple Synagogue: The Formative Years', in L.I. Levine (ed.), *The Synagogue in Late Antiquity*, Philadelphia: ASOR: 7–31.

Lieu, J.M. (1988) 'Blindness in the Johannine Tradition', *NTS* 34: 83–95.

Lightfoot, J.B. (1893) *Biblical Essays*, London: Macmillan: 1–198.

Lindars, B. (1981) *The Gospel of John* (NCB), London: Marshall, Morgan & Scott.

—— (1983) *Jesus Son of Man*, London: SPCK.

—— (1992) 'Rebuking the Spirit: A New Analysis of the Lazarus Story of John 11', *NTS* 38: 89–104.

Loader, W.R.G. (1989) *The Christology of the Fourth Gospel: Structure and Issues* (BET 23), Frankfurt am Main: Lang.

Lorenzen, T. (1971) *Der Lieblingsjünger im Johannesevangelium: Eine redaktionsgeschichtlicher Studie* (SBS 55), Stuttgart: Katholisches Bibelwerk.

Lowe, M. (1976) 'Who were the ΙΟΥΔΑΙΟΙ?', *NT* 18: 101–30.

Lüdemann, G. (1994) *The Resurrection of Jesus* (ET), London: SCM.

Luther, M. (1543) 'Von den Juden und ihren Lügen', in *D. Martin Luther's Werke: Kritische Gesamtausgabe* (1883–), vol. 53: 417–552; ET 'On the Jews and Their Lies', tr. M.H. Bertram, ed. F. Sherman, in *Luther's Works*, vol. 47, ed. J. Pelikan and H.T. Lehman, Philadelphia: Fortress, 1971: 123–306.

McDonald, J.I.H. (1989), *The Resurrection: Narrative and Belief*, London: SPCK.

McHugh, J. (1992) '"In Him was Life": John's Gospel and the Parting of the Ways', in J.D.G. Dunn (ed.), *Jews and Christians: The Parting of the Ways A.D. 70 to 135* (WUNT 66), Tübingen: Mohr (Siebeck): 123–58.

McKay, H.A. (1994) *Sabbath and Synagogue*, Leiden: Brill.

McKenzie, S.L. (1985) *The Chronicler's Use of the Deuteronomistic History* (HSM 33), Atlanta: Scholars.

—— (1991) *The Trouble with Kings: The Composition of the Book of Kings in the Deuteronomic History* (VT.S 42), Leiden: Brill.

Maddox, R. (1974) 'The Function of the Son of Man in the Gospel of John', in R. Banks (ed.), *Reconciliation and Hope: Festschrift for L. Morris*, Exeter: Paternoster: 186–204.

Mahoney, R. (1974) *Two Disciples at the Tomb: The Background and Message of John 20.1–10* (Theologie und Wirklichkeit 6), Berne/Frankfurt am Main: Lang.

Malatesta, E. (1967) *St. John's Gospel 1920–65: A Cumulative and Classified Bibliography of Books and Periodical Literature on the Fourth Gospel* (AnBib 32), Rome: Pontifical Biblical Institute.

Manns, F. (1991) *L'Evangile de Jean à la lumière du Judaïsme* (SBF Analecta 33), Jerusalem: Franciscan.

Marchadour, A. (1988) *Lazare: Histoire d'un récit, récits d'une histoire* (LeDiv 132), Paris: Cerf.

Martin, R.A. (1989) *Syntax Criticism of Johannine Literature, the Catholic Epistles, and the Gospel Passion Accounts*, New York: Mellen.

Martyn, J.L. (1968), *History and Theology in the Fourth Gospel*, New York: Harper & Row.

—— (1978) *The Gospel of John in Christian History*, New York/Toronto: Paulist.

Mastin, B.L. (1975) 'A Neglected Feature of the Christology of the Fourth Gospel', *NTS* 22: 32–51.

Matsunaga, K. (1981a) 'Is John's Gospel Anti-Sacramental? A New Solution in the Light of the Evangelist's Milieu', *NTS* 27: 516–24.

—— (1981b) 'The "Theos" Christology as the Ultimate Confession of the Fourth Gospel', *AJBI* 7: 124–45.

Meade, D.G. (1986) *Pseudonymity and Canon: An Investigation into the Relationship of Authorship and Authority in Jewish and Earliest Christian Tradition* (WUNT 39), Tübingen: Mohr (Siebeck).

Mealand, D.L. (1978) 'The Christology of the Fourth Gospel', *SJTh* 31: 449–67.

Meeks, W.A. (1972) 'The Man from Heaven in Johannine Sectarianism', *JBL* 91: 44–72.

—— (1975), 'Am I a Jew? Johannine Christianity and Judaism', in Neusner 1975: pt 1, 163–86.

—— (1990) 'Equal to God', in Fortna and Gaventa 1990: 309–21.

Menken, M.J.J. (1985) 'The Quotation from Isa 40, 3 in Jn 1, 23', *Bib* 66: 190–205.

—— (1988) 'The Provenance and Meaning of the Old Testament Quotation in John 6.31', *NT* 30: 39–56.

—— (1993a) 'John 6, 51c–58: Eucharist or Christology?', *Bib* 74: 1–26.

—— (1993b) 'The Christology of the Fourth Gospel: A Survey of Recent Research', in M.C. de Boer (ed.), *From Jesus to John: Essays on Jesus and New Testament Christology in Honour of Marinus de Jonge* (JSNT.SS 84), Sheffield: JSOT Press: 292–320.

—— (1993c) 'The Textual Form and the Meaning of the Quotation from Zechariah 12:10 in John 19:37', *CBQ* 55: 494–511.

Metzger, B.M. (1972) 'Literary Forgeries and Canonical Pseudepigrapha', *JBL* 91: 3–24.

Milik, J.T. (1976) *The Books of Enoch: Aramaic Fragments of Qumrân Cave 4*, Oxford: Clarendon.

Millar, F. (1990) 'Reflections on the Trial of Jesus', in P.R. Davies and R.T. White (eds), *A Tribute to Geza Vermes: Essays on Jewish and Christian Literature and History* (JSOT.SS 100), Sheffield: JSOT Press: 355–81.

Miltner, F. (1958) *Ephesos: Stadt der Artemis und des Johannes*, Wien: Deuticke.

Minear, P.S. (1977) 'The Beloved Disciple in the Gospel of John: Some Clues and Conjectures', *NT* 19: 105–23.

Moloney, F.J. (1976) *The Johannine Son of Man* (BSRel 14, 2nd edn 1978), Rome: LAS.

Momigliano, A. (1990) *The Classical Foundations of Modern Historiography*, Berkeley: University of California Press.

Morris, L. (1969) *Studies in the Fourth Gospel*, Exeter: Paternoster.

—— (1971) *The Gospel According to John: The English Text with Introduction, Exposition and Notes*, Grand Rapids: Eerdmans.

—— (1989) *Jesus is the Christ: Studies in the Theology of John*, Leicester/Grand Rapids: IVP/Eerdmans.

Moulton, J.H. and Howard, W.F. (1920) *A Grammar of New Testament Greek*, vol. 2, Edinburgh: T. & T. Clark.

Müller, M. (1984) *Der Ausdruck 'Menschensohn' in den Evangelien: Voraussetzen und Bedeutung* (ATD 17), Leiden: Brill.

—— (1991) '"Have you Faith in the Son of Man?" (John 9.35)', *NTS* 37: 291–4.

Müller, U.B. (1975) *Die Geschichte der Christologie in der johanneischen Gemeinde* (SBS 77), Stuttgart: Katholisches Bibelwerk.

Murphy O'Connor, J. (1990) 'John the Baptist and Jesus: History and Hypotheses', *NTS* 36: 359–74.

Mussies, G. (1990) 'Pagans, Jews and Christians at Ephesus', in P.W. van der Horst and G. Mussies (eds), *Studies on the Hellenistic Background of the New Testament*, Utrecht: Faculteita der Godgeleerdheid, Rijksuniversiteit Utrecht: 177–94.

Mussner, F. (1965) *The Historical Jesus in the Gospel of St. John* (ET 1967), London: Burns & Oates.

Myers, J.M. (1965) *I Chronicles* (AB 12), New York: Doubleday.

Nelson, R.D. (1981) *The Double Redaction of the Deuteronomistic History* (JSOT.SS 18), Sheffield: JSOT Press.

Neumann, G. (1980) 'Kleinasien', in G. Neumann and J. Untermann (eds), *Die Sprachen im römischen Reich der Kaiserzeit: Kolloquium vom 8. bis 10. April 1974* (Bonner Jährbücher, Beihefte 40), Cologne: Rheinland: 167–85.

Neusner, J. (1970) *A Life of Yohanan ben Zakkai Ca.1–80 C.E.* (2nd edn StPB 16), Leiden: Brill.

—— (ed.) (1975) *Christianity, Judaism and Other Greco-Roman Cults: Studies for Morton Smith at Sixty* (SJLA 12, 4 vols), Leiden: Brill.

Newsome, J.D. (1975) 'Toward a New Understanding of the Chronicler and his Purposes', *JBL* 94: 201–17.

Neyrey, J.H. (1988) *An Ideology of Revolt: John's Christology in Social-science Perspective*, Philadelphia: Fortress.

Nicol, W. (1972) *The Sēmeia in the Fourth Gospel: Tradition and Redaction* (NT.S 32), Leiden: Brill.

Nogalski, J. (1993a) *Literary Precursors to the Book of the Twelve* (BZAW 217), Berlin: De Gruyter.

—— (1993b) *Redactional Processes in the Book of the Twelve* (BZAW 218), Berlin: De Gruyter.

Noy, D.A. (1992) 'A Jewish Place of Prayer in Roman Egypt', *JThS NS* 43: 118–22.

Ogg, G. (1940) *The Chronology of the Public Ministry of Jesus*, Cambridge: Cambridge University Press.

O'Neill, J.C. (1979) 'The Lamb of God in the Testaments of the Twelve Patriarchs', *JSNT* 2: 2–30.

Oster, R.E. (1976) 'The Ephesian Artemis as an Opponent of Early Christianity', *JAC* 19: 24–44.

—— (1990) 'Ephesus as a Religious Center under the Principate, I: Paganism before Constantine', *ANRW* II.18.3: 1661–728.

—— (1993) 'Supposed Anachronism in Luke-Acts' Use of συναγωγή: A Rejoinder to H.C. Kee', *NTS* 39: 178–208.

Painter, J. (1991) *The Quest for the Messiah: The History, Literature and Theology of the Johannine Community*, Edinburgh: T. & T. Clark.

—— (1992) 'The Enigmatic Johannine Son of Man', in Van Segbroeck *et al.* 1992: III, 1869–87.

Pazdan, M.M. (1991) *The Son of Man: A Metaphor for Jesus in the Fourth Gospel*, Collegeville: Liturgical.

Peckham, B. (1986) 'The Vision of Habakkuk', *CBQ* 48: 617–36.

Perkins, P. (1984) *Resurrection: New Testament Witness and Contemporary Reflection*, London: Chapman.

Perry, J.M. (1993) 'The Evolution of the Johannine Eucharist', *NTS* 39: 22–35.

Pesch, R. (1978) *Das Abendmahl und Jesu Todesverständnis* (QD 80), Freiburg/Basel/Vienna: Herder.

Plummer, A. (1882) *The Gospel According to S. John* (CGTC), Cambridge: Cambridge University Press.

Pohlmann, K.-F. (1991) *Ezechielstudien: Zur Redaktionsgeschichte des Buches und zur Frage nach den ältesten Texten* (BZAW 202), Berlin: De Gruyter.

Potter, R.D. (1959) 'Topography and Archaeology in the Fourth Gospel', in *Studia Evangelica*, vol. 1, ed. K. Aland *et al.* (TU 73), Berlin: Akademie: 329–37.

Preuß, H.D. (1959) 'Die Psalmenüberschriften in Targum und Midrasch', *ZAW* 71: 44–54.

Prinsloo, W.S. (1992) 'The Unity of the Book of Joel', *ZAW* 104: 66–81.

Quast, K. (1989) *Peter and the Beloved Disciple: Figures for a Community in Crisis* (JSNT.SS 32), Sheffield: JSOT Press.

Rajak, T. (1983) *Josephus: The Historian and his Society*, London: Duckworth.

Redditt, P.L. (1989) 'Israel's Shepherds: Hope and Pessimism in Zechariah 9–14', *CBQ* 51: 631–42.

Reim, G. (1974) *Studien zum alttestamentlichen Hintergrund des Johannesevangeliums* (MSSNTS 22), Cambridge: Cambridge University Press.

—— (1988) 'Zur Lokalisierung der johanneischen Gemeinde', *BZ* 32: 72–86.

Rendtorff, R. (1984) 'Zur Komposition des Buches Jesaja', *VT* 34: 295–320.

Rensberger, D.K. (1988) *Johannine Faith and Liberating Community*, Philadelphia: Westminster (English edn, *Overcoming the World: Politics and Community in the Gospel of John*, London: SPCK, 1989).

Rhea, R. (1990) *The Johannine Son of Man* (AThANT 76), Zurich: Theologischer.

Richter, G. (1977) *Studien zum Johannesevangelium* (BU 13), Regensburg: Pustet.

Roberge, M. (1982) 'Le Discours sur le Pain de Vie, Jean 6, 22–59', *LTP* 38: 265–99.

Robinson, A.W. (1924) *The Christ of the Gospels*, London: SCM.

Robinson, J. Armitage (1902) *The Study of the Gospels* (Handbooks for the Clergy, ed. A.W. Robinson), London: Longmans.

—— (1908) *The Historical Character of St. John's Gospel* (2nd edn 1929), London: Longmans.

Robinson, J.A.T. (1959a) 'The Destination and Purpose of St John's Gospel', *NTS* 6: 117–31 (also in Robinson 1962: 107–25).

—— (1959b) 'The New Look on the Fourth Gospel', in K. Aland *et al.* (eds), *Studia Evangelica* I (TU 73), Berlin: Akademie: 338–50 (also in Robinson 1962: 94–106).

—— (1962) *Twelve New Testament Studies* (SBT 34), London: SCM.

—— (1985) *The Priority of John*, London: SCM.

Rogers, G.M. (1991) *The Sacred Identity of Ephesos: Foundation Myths of a Roman City*, London: Routledge.

Ruckstuhl, E. (1951) *Die literarische Einheit des Johannesevangeliums* (NTOA 5, 2nd edn 1987), Fribourg/Göttingen: Universitätsverlag/Vandenhoeck & Ruprecht.

—— (1977) 'Johannine Language and Style: The Question of their Unity', in De Jonge 1977b: 125–47.

—— (1988) *Jesus im Horizont der Evangelien* (Stuttgarter Biblische Aufsatsbände 3), Stuttgart: Katholisches Bibelwerk.

Ruckstuhl, E. and Dschulnigg, P. (1991) *Stilkritik und Verfasserfrage im Johannesevangelium: Die johanneischen Sprachmerkmale auf dem Hintergrund des Neuen Testaments und des zeitgenössischen hellenistischen Schrifttums* (NTOA 17), Fribourg/Göttingen: Universitätsverlag/Vandenhoeck & Ruprecht.

Sabbe, M. (1977) 'The Arrest of Jesus in Jn 18, 1–11 and its Relation to the Synoptic Gospels: A Critical Evaluation of A. Dauer's Hypothesis', in De Jonge 1977b: 203–34.

—— (1992) 'The Anointing of Jesus in Jn 12, 1–8 and its Synoptic Parallels', in Van Segbroeck 1992: III, 2051–82.

Samuel, R. and Thompson, P. (eds) (1990) *The Myths We Live By*, London: Routledge.

Sanday, W. (1872) *The Authorship and Historical Character of the Fourth Gospel*, London: Macmillan.

Sanders, E.P. (1992) *Judaism: Practice and Belief 63 BCE – 66 CE*, London/Philadelphia: SCM/Trinity.

Sanders, J.N. and Mastin, B.A. (1968) *The Gospel According to St. John* (Black's New Testament Commentaries), London: Black.

Sandy, D.B. (1991) 'John the Baptist's "Lamb of God" Affirmation in its Canonical and Apocalyptic Milieu', *JETS* 34: 447–60.

Schaefer, K.R. (1993) 'Zechariah 14 and the Composition of the Book of Zechariah', *RB* 100: 368–98.

Schäfer, P. (1978) 'Die sogennante Synode von Jabne', *Studien zur Geschichte und Theologie des rabbinischen Judentums*, Leiden: Brill: 45–55.

Schein, B.E. (1980) *Following the Way: The Setting of John's Gospel*, Minneapolis: Augsburg.

Schiffman, L.H. (1985) *Who Was a Jew? Rabbinic and Halakhic Perspectives on the Jewish Christian Schism*, Hoboken: Ktav.

Schmidt, H. (ed.) (1989) *Interferenz in der Translation* (Ubersetzungswissenschaftliche Beiträge 12), Leipzig: Enzyklopädie.

Schmithals, W. (1992) *Johannesevangelium und Johannesbriefe: Forschungsgeschichte und Analyse* (BZNW 64), Berlin: De Gruyter.

Schnackenburg, R. (1965–84) *The Gospel According to St. John* (4 vols: ET vols 1–3, 1968–82), London/New York: Burns & Oates/Herder & Herder.

—— (1991) 'Ephesus: Entwicklung einer Gemeinde von Paulus zu Johannes', *BZ NF* 35: 41–64.

—— (1992) 'Synoptische und johanneische Christologie – ein Vergleich', in Van Segbroeck 1992: III, 1723–50.

Schnelle, U. (1987) *Antidocetic Christology in the Gospel of John* (ET 1992), Minneapolis: Augsburg Fortress.

—— (1990) 'Perspektiven der Johannesexegese', *SNTU* 15: 59–72.

Schuchard, B.G. (1992) *Scripture Within Scripture: The Interrelationship of Form and Function in the Explicit Old Testament Citations in the Gospel of John* (SBL.DS 133), Atlanta: Scholars.

Schuyler Brown (1964) 'From Burney to Black: The Fourth Gospel and the Aramaic Question', *CBQ* 26: 323–39.

Schweizer, E. (1939) *Ego Eimi* (FRLANT NF 38), Göttingen: Vandenhoeck & Ruprecht.

Scobie, C.H.H. (1964) *John the Baptist*, London: SCM.

Scott, M. (1992) *Sophia and the Johannine Jesus* (JSNT.SS 71), Sheffield: JSOT Press.

Scott, R.B.Y. (1955) 'Solomon and the Beginnings of Wisdom in Israel', in M. Noth and D. Winton Thomas (eds), *Wisdom in Israel and in the Ancient Near East: Presented to Professor H.H. Rowley* (VT.S 3): 262–79 (also in J.L. Crenshaw (ed.), *Studies in Ancient Israelite Wisdom*, New York: Ktav, 1976: 84–101).

Scott Holland, H. (1920) *The Philosophy of Faith and The Fourth Gospel*, London: Murray.

Seitz, C.R. (1989) 'The Prophet Moses and the Canonical Shape of Jeremiah', *ZAW* 101: 3–27.

—— (1991) *Zion's Final Destiny: The Development of the Book of Isaiah*, Minneapolis: Fortress.

Sevenster, G. (1970) 'Remarks on the Humanity of Jesus in the Gospel and Letters of John', in *Studies in John: Presented to Professor Dr. J.N. Sevenster* (NT.S 24), Leiden: Brill: 185–93.

Sherwin-White, A.N. (1963) *Roman Society and Roman Law in the New Testament* (Sarum Lectures 1960–1), Oxford: Clarendon.

Sidebottom, E.M. (1961) *The Christ of the Fourth Gospel*, London: SPCK.

Sklare, M. (1971) *America's Jews*, New York/Toronto: Random House.

Slomovic, E. (1979) 'Toward an Understanding of the Formation of Historical Titles in the Book of Psalms', *ZAW* 91: 350–80.

Smalley, S.S. (1978) *John: Evangelist and Interpreter*, Exeter: Paternoster.

Smallwood, E.M. (1967) *Documents Illustrating the Principates of Gaius Claudius and Nero*, Cambridge: Cambridge University Press.

Smiga, G.M. (1992) *Pain and Polemic: Anti-Judaism in the Gospels*, New York: Paulist.

Smith, D.M. (1965) *The Composition and Order of the Fourth Gospel: Bultmann's Literary Theory* (YPR 10), London/New Haven: Yale University Press.

—— (1976a) 'The Milieu of the Johannine Miracle Source: A Proposal', in R. Hamerton-Kelly and R. Scroggs (eds), *Jews, Greeks and Christians: Essays in Honor of W.D. Davies* (SJLA 21), Leiden: Brill: 164–80 (also in Smith 1984: 62–79).

—— (1976b) 'The Setting and Shape of a Johannine Narrative Source', *JBL* 95: 231–41 (also in Smith 1984: 80–93).

—— (1977) 'The Presentation of Jesus in the Fourth Gospel', *Interp* 31: 367–78.

—— (1984) *Johannine Christianity: Essays on its Setting, Sources and Theology*, Columbia: University of South Carolina Press.

—— (1990) 'Judaism and the Gospel of John', in Charlesworth 1990: 76–99.

—— (1992) *John Among the Gospels: The Relationship in Twentieth-Century Research*, Minneapolis: Fortress.

Smith, M. (1972) 'Pseudepigraphy in the Israelite Literary Tradition', in Von Fritz 1972: 189–227.

Smith, M.S. (1991) 'The Levitical Compilation of the Psalter', *ZAW* 103: 258–63.

Snyman, S.D. (1989) 'Cohesion in the Book of Obadiah', *ZAW* 101: 59–71.

Sproston, W. (1985) '"Is not this Jesus, the son of Joseph? . . . " (John 6.42): Johannine Christology as a Challenge to Faith', *JSNT* 24: 77–97.

Stanton, V.H. (1920) *The Gospels as Historical Documents*, Part III: *The Fourth Gospel*, Cambridge: Cambridge University Press.

Stegemann, H. (1989) 'The Literary Composition of the Temple Scroll and its Status at Qumran', in Brooke 1989: 123–48.

Stibbe, M.W.G. (1992) *John as Storyteller: Narrative Criticism and the Fourth Gospel* (MSSNTS 73), Cambridge: Cambridge University Press.

—— (1993a) *John* (Readings: A New Biblical Commentary), Sheffield: JSOT Press.

—— (1993b) (ed.) *The Gospel of John as Literature: An Anthology of Twentieth-century Perspectives*, Leiden: Brill.

—— (1994a) *John's Gospel* (New Testament Readings), London: Routledge.

—— (1994b) 'A Tomb with a View: John 11.1–44 in Narrative-critical Perspective', *NTS* 40: 38–54.

Story, C.I.K. (1989) 'The Bearing of Old Testament Terminology on the Johannine Chronology of the Final Passover of Jesus', *NT* 31: 316–24.

Stowasser, M. (1992) *Johannes der Taüfer im Vierten Evangelium: Eine Untersuchung zu seiner Bedeutung für die johanneische Gemeinde*, Klosterneuburg: Osterreichisches Katholisches Bibelwerk.

Suerbaum, W. (1990) 'Zweiundvierzig Jahre Tacitus-Forschung: Systematische Gesamtbibliographie zu Tacitus' Annalen 1939–1980', *ANRW* II.33.2: 1032–476.

Sugimoto, T. (1990) 'The Chronicler's Techniques in Quoting Samuel-Kings', *AJBI* 16: 30–70.

—— (1992) 'Chronicles as Independent Literature', *JSOT* 55: 61–74.

Talshir, D. (1988) 'A Reinvestigation of the Linguistic Relationship between Chronicles and Ezra-Nehemiah', *VT* 38: 165–93.

Tamis, A.M. (1990) 'Language Change, Language Maintenance and Ethnic Identity: the Case of Greek in Australia', *Journal of Multilingual and Multicultural Development* 11: 481–500.

Tcherikover, V.A. and Fuks, A. (eds) (1957) *Corpus Papyrorum Judaicarum*, vol. 1, Cambridge, Mass.: Harvard University Press.

Thiel, W. (1981) *Die deuteronomistische Redaktion von Jeremia 26–45; mit einer Gesamtbeurteilung der deuteronomistischen Redaktion des Buches Jeremia* (WMANT 52), Neukirchen-Vluyn: Neukirchener.

Thomas, J.C. (1991) *Footwashing in John 13 and the Johannine Community* (JSNT.SS 61), Sheffield: JSOT Press.

Thompson, M.M. (1988) *The Humanity of Jesus in the Fourth Gospel*, Philadelphia: Fortress.

Thornton, T.C.G. (1987) 'Christian Understandings of the *Birkath Ha-Minim* in the Eastern Roman Empire', *JThS NS* 38: 419–31.

Throntveit, M.A. (1982) 'Linguistic analysis and the question of authorship in Chronicles, Ezra and Nehemiah', *VT* 32: 201–16.

Thyen, H. (1974, 1977, 1978, 1979) 'Aus der Literatur zum Johannesevangelium', *ThR NF* 39: 1–69, 222–52, 289–330; 42: 211–70; 43: 328–59; 44: 97–134.

Titus, E.L. (1968) 'The Fourth Gospel and the Historical Jesus', in F.T. Trotter (ed.), *Jesus and the Historian: Written in Honor of E.C. Colwell*, Philadelphia: Westminster: 98–113.

Tomson, P.J. (1986) 'The Names Israel and Jew in Ancient Judaism and the New Testament', *Bijdragen* 47: 120–40, 266–89.

Tonkin, E. (ed.) (1992) *Narrating our Pasts: The Social Construction of Oral History*, Cambridge: Cambridge University Press.

Torrey, C.C. (1923) 'The Aramaic Origin of the Gospel of John', *HThR* 16: 305–44.

—— (1931) 'The Date of the Crucifixion according to the Fourth Gospel', *JBL* 50: 227–41.

—— (1937) *Our Translated Gospels*, London: Hodder & Stoughton.

—— (1951–2) 'In the Fourth Gospel the Last Supper was the Paschal Meal', *JQR* 42: 237–50.

Tov, E. (1985) 'The Literary History of the Book of Jeremiah in the Light of its Textual History', in J.H. Tigay (ed.), *Empirical Models for Biblical Criticism*, Philadelphia: University of Pennsylvania Press: 211–37.

Townsend, J.T. (1979) 'The Gospel of John and the Jews: The Story of a Religious

Divorce', in A.T. Davies (ed.), *Anti-Semitism and the Foundations of Christianity*, New York/Toronto: Paulist: 72–97.

Trebilco, P.R. (1991), *Jewish Communities in Asia Minor* (MSSNTS 69), Cambridge: Cambridge University Press.

Trevett, C. (1989) 'Apocalypse, Ignatius, Montanism: Seeking the Seeds', *VC* 43: 1–19.

Trudinger, P. (1988) 'The Ephesus Milieu', *DR* 106: 286–96.

Van Belle, G. (1988) *Johannine Bibliography 1966–1985: A Cumulative Bibliography on the Fourth Gospel* (BEThL 82), Leuven: Leuven University Press/Peeters.

—— (1994) *The Signs Source in the Fourth Gospel Historical Survey and Critical Evaluation of the Semeia Hypothesis* (BEThL 116), Leuven: Leuven University Press/Peeters.

Van der Horst, P.W. (1994) 'The Birkat ha-minim in Recent Research', *ExpT* 105: 363–8.

Van Segbroeck, F., Tuckett, C.M., Van Belle, G. and Verheyden, J. (eds) (1992) *The Four Gospels 1992: Festschrift Frans Neirynck* (BEThL C), Leuven: Leuven University Press/Peeters: 1723–2221.

Van Seters, J. (1983) *In Search of History: Historiography in the Ancient World and the Origins of Biblical History*, New Haven: Yale University Press.

—— (1990) 'Joshua's Campaign of Canaan and Near Eastern Historiography', *SJOT* 2: 1–12.

Van Staalduine-Sulman, E. (1993), 'The Aramaic Song of the Lamb', in J.C. de Moor and W.G.E. Watson (eds), *Verse in Ancient Near Eastern Prose*, Neukirchen-Vluyn: Neukirchener: 265–92.

Van Tilborg, S. (1993) *Imaginative Love in John*, Leiden: Brill.

Van Unnik, W.C. (1978) *Flavius Josephus als historischer Schriftsteller*, Heidelberg: Schneider.

Varneda, P.V.I. (1986) *The Historical Method of Flavius Josephus* (ALGHJ XIX), Leiden: Brill.

Vermeylen, J. (1977–8) *Du Prophète Isaïe à l'Apocalyptique: Isaïe I–XXXV, miroir d'un demi-millénaire d'expérience réligieuse en Israel* (2 vols), Paris: Gabalda.

Von Fritz, K. (ed.) (1972) *Pseudepigrapha I: Entretiens sur l'antiquité classique* XVIII, Geneva: Fondation Hardt.

Von Wahlde, U.C. (1982) 'The Johannine "Jews": A Critical Survey', *NTS* 28: 33–60.

—— (1989) *The Earliest Version of John's Gospel: Recovering the Gospel of Signs*, Wilmington: Glazier.

Wachholder, B.Z. (1988) 'David's Eschatological Psalter 11Q Psalms[a]', *HUCA* 59: 23–72.

Wagner, J. (1988) *Auferstehung und Leben: John 11, 1–12, 19 als Spiegel johanneischer Redaktions- und Theologiegeschichte* (BU 19), Regensburg: Pustet.

Walbank, F.W. (1965) 'Speeches in Greek Historians', Myres Memorial Lecture 1965, in F.W. Walbank, *Selected Papers*, Cambridge: Cambridge University Press, 1985: 242–61.

Walker, W.O. (1994) 'John 1.43–51 and "The Son of Man" in the Fourth Gospel', *JSNT* 56: 31–42.

Watson, F. (1987) 'Is John's Christology Adoptionist?', in L.D. Hurst and N.T. Wright (eds), *The Glory of Christ in the New Testament: Studies in Christology in Memory of G.B. Caird*, Oxford: Clarendon: 113–24.

Watts, J.W. (1992) 'Text and Redaction in Jeremiah's Oracles Against the Nations', *CBQ* 54: 432–47.

Webb, R.L. (1991) *John the Baptizer and Prophet* (JSNT.SS 62), Sheffield: JSOT Press.

Weinfeld, M. (1991) 'God Versus Moses in the Temple Scroll – "I do not Speak on my Own Authority but on God's Authority" (Sifrei Deut. sec. 5; John 12.48f)', *RQ* 15: 175–80.

Weiss, H. (1979) 'Foot Washing in the Johannine Community', *NT* 21: 298–325.

Welten, P. (1973) *Geschichte und Geschichtsdarstellung in den Chronikbüchern* (WMANT 42), Neukirchen-Vluyn: Neukirchener.

Wengst, K. (1981) *Bedrängte Gemeinde und verherrlichter Christus: Der historische Ort des Johannesevangeliums als Schlüssel zu seiner Interpretation*, Neukirchen-Vluyn: Neukirchener.

Westcott, B.F. (1908) *The Gospel According to St. John* (2 vols), London: Murray.

Wexler, P. (1981a) 'Jewish Interlinguistics: Facts and Conceptual Framework', *Language* 57: 99–149.

—— (1981b) 'Terms for "Synagogue" in Hebrew and Jewish Languages: Explorations in Historical Jewish Interlinguistics', *REJ* 140: 101–38.

—— (1985) 'Recovering the Dialects and Sociology of Judeo-Greek in Non-Hellenic Europe', in Fishman 1985: 227–40.

Whitacre, R.A. (1982) *Johannine Polemic: The Role of Tradition and Theology*, (SBL.DS 67), Chico: Scholars.

Willi, T. (1972) *Die Chronik als Auslegung* (FRLANT 106), Göttingen: Vandenhoeck & Ruprecht.

Williams, D.H. (1989) 'The Origins of the Montanist Movement: A Sociological Analysis', *Religion* 19: 331–51.

Williams, M.J. (1993) 'An Investigation of the Legitimacy of Source Distinctions for the Prose Material in Jeremiah', *JBL* 112: 193–210.

Williamson, H.G.M. (1977) *Israel in the Book of Chronicles*, Cambridge: Cambridge University Press.

Wilson, G.H. (1985a) *The Editing of the Hebrew Psalter* (SBL.DS 76), Chico: Scholars.

—— (1985b) 'The Qumran Psalms Scroll Reconsidered: Analysis of the Debate', *CBQ* 47: 624–42.

Wilson, J. (1981) 'The Integrity of John 3:22–36', *JSNT* 10: 34–41.

Wink, W. (1968) *John the Baptist in the Gospel Tradition* (MSSNTS 7), Cambridge: Cambridge University Press.

Wright, B.G. (1985) 'A Note on the Statistical Analysis of Septuagintal Syntax', *JBL* 104: 111–14.

Zeitlin, S. (1932) 'The Date of the Crucifixion according to the Fourth Gospel', *JBL* 51: 268–70.

—— (1951–2) 'The Last Supper as an Ordinary Meal in the Fourth Gospel', *JQR* 42: 251–60.

Zimmermann, F. (1979) *The Aramaic Origin of the Four Gospels*, New York: Ktav.

INDEX OF REFERENCES

256

Other Christian Sources

INDEX OF SCHOLARS

INDEX OF NAMES AND SUBJECTS

267